FUNDAMENTALS OF
ENGLISH
GRAMMAR

Second Edition

Betty Schrampfer Azar

PRENTICE HALL REGENTS
Englewood Cliffs, New Jersey 07632

Library of Congress Cataloging-in-Publication Data

Azar, Betty Schrampfer, 1941–
  Fundamentals of English grammar / Betty Schrampfer Azar.—2nd
ed.
    p. cm.
  Includes index.
  ISBN 0–13–338278–8
  1. English language—Textbooks for foreign speakers. 2. English
language—Grammar—1950– I. Title.
PE1128.A965 1992b   92-7657
428.2′4—dc20   CIP

Publisher: *Tina B. Carver*
Managing editor, production: *Sylvia Moore*
Editorial/production supervision: *Janet Johnston*
Prepress buyer: *Ray Keating*
Manufacturing buyer: *Lori Bulwin*
Scheduler: *Leslie Coward*
Illustrations: *Don Martinetti*
Cover supervisor: *Karen Salzbach*
Cover designer: *Joel Mitnick Design*
Interior designer: *Ros Herion Freese*
Page makeup: *Mary Fitzgerald*

© 1992 by Prentice Hall Regents
Prentice-Hall, Inc.
A Paramount Communications Company
Englewood Cliffs, New Jersey 07632

Printed in the United States of America

20 19 18 17 16 15 14 13

ISBN 0-13-338278-8
ISBN 0-13-327552-3 {VOL.A}
ISBN 0-13-347139-X {VOL.B}

Prentice-Hall International (UK) Limited, *London*
Prentice-Hall of Australia Pty. Limited, *Sydney*
Prentice-Hall Canada Inc., *Toronto*
Prentice-Hall Hispanoamericana, S.A., *Mexico*
Prentice-Hall of India Private Limited, *New Delhi*
Prentice-Hall of Japan, Inc., *Tokyo*
Simon & Schuster Asia Pte. Ltd., *Singapore*
Editora Prentice-Hall do Brasil, Ltda., *Rio de Janeiro*

FUNDAMENTALS OF
ENGLISH
GRAMMAR
Second Edition

To my sister,
JO

Contents

PREFACE TO THE SECOND EDITION . . . .**xv**

ACKNOWLEDGMENTS . . . .**xvi**

Chapter 1 PRESENT TIME **1**

    1-1   THE SIMPLE PRESENT AND THE PRESENT PROGRESSIVE 3
    1-2   FORMS OF THE SIMPLE PRESENT AND THE PRESENT
            PROGRESSIVE 3
    1-3   SPELLING: FINAL *-S* vs. *-ES* 8
    1-4   NONPROGRESSIVE VERBS 9
    1-5   SIMPLE PRESENT AND PRESENT PROGRESSIVE: SHORT
            ANSWERS TO QUESTIONS 12

Chapter 2 PAST TIME **18**

    2-1   EXPRESSING PAST TIME: THE SIMPLE PAST 18
    2-2   FORMS OF THE SIMPLE PAST 19
    2-3   THE PRINCIPAL PARTS OF A VERB 21
    2-4   IRREGULAR VERBS: A REFERENCE LIST 22
    2-5   SPELLING OF *-ING* AND *-ED* FORMS 29
    2-6   THE SIMPLE PAST AND THE PAST PROGRESSIVE 32
    2-7   FORMS OF THE PAST PROGRESSIVE 32
    2-8   EXPRESSING PAST TIME: USING TIME CLAUSES 37
    2-9   EXPRESSING PAST HABIT: *USED TO* 42
    2-10   PREPOSITIONS OF TIME: *IN, AT,* AND *ON* 45

Chapter 3   FUTURE TIME **47**

3-1   EXPRESSING FUTURE TIME: ***BE GOING TO*** AND ***WILL*** 47
3-2   FORMS WITH ***WILL***. 49
3-3   USING ***PROBABLY*** WITH ***WILL*** 50
3-4   ***BE GOING TO*** vs. ***WILL*** 51
3-5   EXPRESSING FUTURE TIME IN TIME CLAUSES AND ***IF***-CLAUSES 53
3-6   PARALLEL VERBS 58
3-7   USING THE PRESENT PROGRESSIVE TO EXPRESS FUTURE TIME 61
3-8   USING THE SIMPLE PRESENT TO EXPRESS FUTURE TIME 63
3-9   PRESENT PLANS FOR FUTURE ACTIVITIES: USING ***INTEND, PLAN, HOPE*** 64
3-10   IMMEDIATE FUTURE: USING ***BE ABOUT TO*** 65

Chapter 4   NOUNS AND PRONOUNS **67**

4-1   PLURAL FORMS OF NOUNS. 68
4-2   SUBJECTS, VERBS, AND OBJECTS 70
4-3   OBJECTS OF PREPOSITIONS 71
4-4   USING ADJECTIVES TO DESCRIBE NOUNS 72
4-5   USING NOUNS AS ADJECTIVES 73
4-6   PERSONAL PRONOUNS: SUBJECTS AND OBJECTS. 76
4-7   POSSESSIVE NOUNS 77
4-8   POSSESSIVE PRONOUNS AND ADJECTIVES 79
4-9   ***A FRIEND OF*** + POSSESSIVE 80
4-10   REFLEXIVE PRONOUNS 81
4-11   SINGULAR FORMS OF ***OTHER: ANOTHER*** vs. ***THE OTHER*** 84
4-12   PLURAL FORMS OF ***OTHER: OTHER(S)*** vs. ***THE OTHER(S)***. 86
4-13   SUMMARY OF FORMS OF ***OTHER*** 88
4-14   CAPITALIZATION 91

Chapter 5 MODAL AUXILIARIES **94**

5-1 THE FORM OF MODAL AUXILIARIES 94
5-2 EXPRESSING ABILITY: *CAN* AND *COULD* 95
5-3 EXPRESSING POSSIBILITY: *MAY* AND *MIGHT*
     EXPRESSING PERMISSION: *MAY* AND *CAN* 98
5-4 USING *COULD* TO EXPRESS POSSIBILITY 100
5-5 ASKING FOR PERMISSION: *MAY I, COULD I, CAN I* 100
5-6 ASKING FOR ASSISTANCE: *WOULD YOU, COULD YOU,
     WILL YOU, CAN YOU* 102
5-7 EXPRESSING ADVICE: *SHOULD, OUGHT TO, HAD BETTER* . .105
5-8 EXPRESSING NECESSITY: *HAVE TO, HAVE GOT TO, MUST* . . .108
5-9 EXPRESSING LACK OF NECESSITY: *DO NOT HAVE TO*
     EXPRESSING PROHIBITION: *MUST NOT* 109
5-10 MAKING LOGICAL CONCLUSIONS: *MUST* 112
5-11 GIVING INSTRUCTIONS: IMPERATIVE SENTENCES 114
5-12 MAKING SUGGESTIONS: *LET'S* AND *WHY DON'T* 116
5-13 STATING PREFERENCES: *PREFER, LIKE . . . BETTER,
     WOULD RATHER* 119

Chapter 6 ASKING QUESTIONS **124**

6-1 YES/NO QUESTIONS AND SHORT ANSWERS 124
6-2 YES/NO QUESTIONS AND INFORMATION QUESTIONS 128
6-3 USING *WHO, WHO(M),* AND *WHAT* 132
6-4 USING *WHAT* + A FORM OF *DO* 135
6-5 USING *WHAT KIND OF* 137
6-6 USING *WHICH* 139
6-7 USING *WHOSE* 141
6-8 USING *HOW* 144
6-9 USING *HOW OFTEN* 145
6-10 USING *HOW FAR* 146
6-11 EXPRESSING LENGTH OF TIME: *IT* + *TAKE* 147
6-12 USING *HOW LONG* 148
6-13 MORE QUESTIONS WITH *HOW* 152
6-14 USING *HOW ABOUT* AND *WHAT ABOUT* 154
6-15 TAG QUESTIONS 156

Chapter 7   THE PRESENT PERFECT AND THE PAST PERFECT 160

  7-1   THE PAST PARTICIPLE 160
  7-2   FORMS OF THE PRESENT PERFECT 161
  7-3   MEANINGS OF THE PRESENT PERFECT 162
  7-4   USING THE SIMPLE PAST vs. THE PRESENT PERFECT. 164
  7-5   USING *SINCE* AND *FOR* 171
  7-6   THE PRESENT PERFECT PROGRESSIVE 176
  7-7   THE PRESENT PERFECT vs. THE PRESENT PERFECT
         PROGRESSIVE. 177
  7-8   MIDSENTENCE ADVERBS 181
  7-9   USING *ALREADY, YET, STILL,* AND *ANYMORE* 184
  7-10   USING THE PAST PERFECT 189

Chapter 8   COUNT / NONCOUNT NOUNS AND ARTICLES. **193**

  8-1   COUNT AND NONCOUNT NOUNS. 193
  8-2   NONCOUNT NOUNS 194
  8-3   MORE NONCOUNT NOUNS 198
  8-4   NOUNS THAT CAN BE COUNT OR NONCOUNT 202
  8-5   USING UNITS OF MEASURE WITH NONCOUNT NOUNS 204
  8-6   GUIDELINES FOR ARTICLE USAGE 206
  8-7   USING EXPRESSIONS OF QUANTITY AS PRONOUNS 216
  8-8   NONSPECIFIC OBJECT PRONOUNS: *SOME, ANY,* AND *ONE* . . .217

Chapter 9   CONNECTING IDEAS **221**

  9-1   CONNECTING IDEAS WITH *AND*. 222
  9-2   CONNECTING IDEAS WITH *BUT* AND *OR* 224
  9-3   CONNECTING IDEAS WITH *SO*. 226
  9-4   USING AUXILIARY VERBS AFTER *BUT* AND *AND* 228
  9-5   USING *AND* + *TOO, SO, EITHER, NEITHER* 230
  9-6   CONNECTING IDEAS WITH *BECAUSE*. .234
  9-7   CONNECTING IDEAS WITH *EVEN THOUGH/ALTHOUGH* 237
  9-8   PHRASAL VERBS (SEPARABLE) 241
  9-9   PHRASAL VERBS (NONSEPARABLE) 243

Chapter 10   GERUNDS AND INFINITIVES **246**

    10-1   GERUNDS AND INFINITIVES: INTRODUCTION 246

    10-2   VERB + GERUND 247

    10-3   *GO* + *-ING* 250

    10-4   VERB + INFINITIVE 251

    10-5   VERB + GERUND OR INFINITIVE 253

    10-6   UNCOMPLETED INFINITIVES 259

    10-7   PREPOSITION + GERUND 260

    10-8   USING *BY* AND *WITH* TO EXPRESS HOW SOMETHING
           IS DONE 262

    10-9   USING GERUNDS AS SUBJECTS: USING *IT* + INFINITIVE 264

    10-10   *IT* + INFINITIVE: USING *FOR* (*SOMEONE*) 266

    10-11   INFINITIVE OF PURPOSE: USING *IN ORDER TO* 267

    10-12   USING INFINITIVES WITH *TOO* AND *ENOUGH* 270

    10-13   MORE PHRASAL VERBS (SEPARABLE) 273

Chapter 11   PASSIVE SENTENCES **276**

    11-1   ACTIVE SENTENCES AND PASSIVE SENTENCES 276

    11-2   TENSE FORMS OF PASSIVE VERBS 277

    11-3   TRANSITIVE AND INTRANSITIVE VERBS 282

    11-4   USING THE "*BY*-PHRASE" 283

    11-5   THE PASSIVE FORMS OF THE PRESENT AND
           PAST PROGRESSIVE 288

    11-6   PASSIVE MODAL AUXILIARIES 289

    11-7   SUMMARY: PASSIVE VERB FORMS 290

    11-8   USING PAST PARTICIPLES AS ADJECTIVES
           (STATIVE PASSIVE) 294

    11-9   PARTICIPIAL ADJECTIVES: *-ED* vs. *-ING* 298

    11-10   *GET* + ADJECTIVE; *GET* + PAST PARTICIPLE 301

    11-11   USING *BE USED/ACCUSTOMED TO* AND *GET USED/
           ACCUSTOMED TO* 305

    11-12   USING *BE SUPPOSED TO* 307

Chapter 12   ADJECTIVE CLAUSES 309

    12-1   ADJECTIVE CLAUSES: INTRODUCTION 309
    12-2   USING *WHO* AND *WHOM* IN ADJECTIVE CLAUSES 310
    12-3   USING *WHO, WHOM,* AND *THAT* IN ADJECTIVE CLAUSES 312
    12-4   USING *WHICH* AND *THAT* IN ADJECTIVE CLAUSES 313
    12-5   SINGULAR AND PLURAL VERBS IN ADJECTIVE CLAUSES 315
    12-6   USING PREPOSITIONS IN ADJECTIVE CLAUSES 316
    12-7   USING *WHOSE* IN ADJECTIVE CLAUSES 318
    12-8   MORE PHRASAL VERBS (SEPARABLE) 323
    12-9   MORE PHRASAL VERBS (NONSEPARABLE) 325

Chapter 13   COMPARISONS 327

    13-1   MAKING COMPARISONS WITH *AS . . . AS* 328
    13-2   COMPARATIVE AND SUPERLATIVE 331
    13-3   COMPARATIVE AND SUPERLATIVE FORMS OF
           ADJECTIVES AND ADVERBS 332
    13-4   USING COMPARATIVES 334
    13-5   USING *MORE* WITH NOUNS 336
    13-6   REPEATING A COMPARATIVE 337
    13-7   USING DOUBLE COMPARATIVES 338
    13-8   USING SUPERLATIVES 339
    13-9   USING *THE SAME, SIMILAR, DIFFERENT, LIKE, ALIKE* 342

Chapter 14   NOUN CLAUSES 346

    14-1   NOUN CLAUSES: INTRODUCTION 346
    14-2   NOUN CLAUSES THAT BEGIN WITH A QUESTION WORD 347
    14-3   NOUN CLAUSES WITH *WHO, WHAT, WHOSE* + *BE* 348
    14-4   NOUN CLAUSES WHICH BEGIN WITH *IF* OR *WHETHER* 352
    14-5   NOUN CLAUSES WHICH BEGIN WITH *THAT* 357
    14-6   SUBSTITUTING *SO* FOR A ''*THAT*-CLAUSE'' IN
           CONVERSATIONAL RESPONSES 359
    14-7   OTHER USES OF ''*THAT*-CLAUSES'' 361

Chapter 15   QUOTED SPEECH AND REPORTED SPEECH **364**

    15-1   QUOTED SPEECH 364

    15-2   QUOTED SPEECH vs. REPORTED SPEECH..........................366

    15-3   VERB FORM USAGE IN REPORTED SPEECH: FORMAL
            SEQUENCE OF TENSES 367

    15-4   USING *SAY* vs. *TELL* 368

    15-5   USING *ASK IF*...369

    15-6   USING VERB + INFINITIVE TO REPORT SPEECH 375

    15-7   SOME TROUBLESOME VERBS: *ADVISE, SUGGEST,* AND
            RECOMMEND 378

Chapter 16   USING *WISH*; USING *IF* **381**

    16-1   EXPRESSING WISHES ABOUT THE PRESENT/FUTURE..........381

    16-2   EXPRESSING WISHES ABOUT THE PAST 384

    16-3   USING *IF*: CONTRARY-TO-FACT IN THE PRESENT/FUTURE ...389

    16-4   USING *IF:* TRUE vs. CONTRARY-TO-FACT IN THE
            PRESENT/FUTURE 392

    16-5   USING *IF*: CONTRARY-TO-FACT IN THE PAST...............394

    16-6   SUMMARY: VERB FORMS IN SENTENCES WITH *IF*
            (CONDITIONAL SENTENCES)...............................395

Appendix 1   PREPOSITION COMBINATIONS.............................**A1**

Appendix 2   PHRASAL VERBS **A4**

Appendix 3   GUIDE FOR CORRECTING WRITING ERRORS **A6**

Appendix 4   BASIC VOCABULARY LIST **A8**

**Appendix 5   DIFFERENCES BETWEEN AMERICAN ENGLISH AND
                 BRITISH ENGLISH** **A15**

INDEX **A17**

Preface to the Second Edition

Fundamentals of English Grammar remains a developmental skills text for mid-level students of English as a second or foreign language. It focuses on key structures and provides ample opportunities for practice through extensive and varied exercises. While focusing on grammar, it promotes the development of all language skills.

The chief difference in the second edition of *Fundamentals of English Grammar* is the inclusion of additional grammar areas that are important at the intermediate level. The principal additions deal with personal pronouns; forms of *other*; connecting ideas with coordinating and subordinating conjunctions, including the use of commas and periods; and comparisons. Other short units have also been included: for example, the use of *must* to make logical conclusions; expressing immediate future with *be about to*; nonspecific vs. specific pronouns (e.g., *May I have one* vs. *May I have it*); uncompleted infinitives; and using a gerund after a preposition. This edition seeks to fill in gaps in an intermediate grammar syllabus. Not every class will cover every unit, but the second edition makes a broad table of contents available. Other changes in the second edition are directed toward clarifying the structure presentations in the charts and improving the exercises.

Another significant difference in the second edition lies in the support material: a workbook and a teacher's guide.

The workbook provides independent study opportunities in the form of Selfstudy Practices (with the answers given). It also provides Guided Study Practices (no answers given) for additional classwork, homework, and individualized instruction as the teacher sees the need.

The teacher's guide contains presentation suggestions; specific techniques for handling the varied types of exercises; background grammar notes; item notes on cultural content, vocabulary, and structure usage; problems to anticipate; suggestions for oral and written student-centered activities; and answers to the exercises.

Acknowledgments

Many people have parts in the work I do as a writer. They make my work possible and enjoyable.

I wish especially to thank Donald Azar, Tina Carver, Barbara Matthies, and Janet Johnston.

In addition, I wish to thank Joy Edwards, R. T. Steltz, Susan Abbott, Jonni Reed, Ralph Hastings, Gordon Adams, Frank Sullivan, Sylvia Moore, Andy Martin, Efrain Rojas, Gil Muller, Noel Carter, Dennis Hogan, Anne Riddick, Mary Vaughn, Don Martinetti, Gordon Johnson, Rick Spencer, Eric Bredenberg, Ed Stanford, Rick Essig, Jack Ross, David Haines, Sally Howard, Ray Keating, Ed Perez, Roger Olsen, Judy Winn-Bell Olsen, Martin Tenney, Wayne Spohr, Norman Harris, Terry Jennings, Jerry Smith, Bruce Kennan, Connie Hernandez, Amelia Azar, and Chelsea Parker.

Special appreciation is due the seven reviewers who marked up copies of the first edition to guide the revisions: Gari Browning, Arline Burgmeier, Linda Misja, Larry Robinson, Luis Sanchez, Grace Tanaka, and Cheryl Youtsey. Their insights were invaluable.

Last, I want to thank my amazing parents. Both are retired educators in their late 80s. My father wrote reams of ideas for exercise entries, for this revision and for the workbook. My mother input the entire text of the first edition so that I had it available for revision on disk. How can I thank them enough? Maybe by saying it in print—Thanks, Mom and Dad. Thank you very, very much.

CHAPTER *1*
Present Time

☐ **EXERCISE 1—ORAL:** Pair up with another student in the class. Interview each other. Then introduce each other to the rest of the class. In your conversation with the other person, find out this person's *name, native country, residence, field of study or place of work, and free-time activities or hobbies.* Take notes during the interview.

1. Below is an example of a possible conversation.

 A: Hi. My name is Kunio.

 B: Hi. My name is Maria. I'm glad to meet you.

 KUNIO: I'm glad to meet you, too. Where are you from?

 MARIA: I'm from Mexico. Where are you from?

 KUNIO: I'm from Japan.

 MARIA: Where are you living now?

 KUNIO: On Fifth Avenue in an apartment. And you?

 MARIA: I'm living in a dorm.

 KUNIO: What is your field of study?

 MARIA: Business. After I study English, I'm going to attend the School of Business Administration. How about you? What's your major?

 KUNIO: Chemistry.

 MARIA: What do you like to do in your free time? Do you have any hobbies?

 KUNIO: I like to swim. How about you?

 MARIA: I read a lot, and I collect stamps from all over the world.

 KUNIO: Really? Would you like some stamps from Japan?

 MARIA: Sure! That would be great. Thanks.

KUNIO: I have to write your full name on the board when I introduce you to the class. How do you spell your name?

MARIA: My first name is Maria: M-A-R-I-A. My last name is Lopez.

KUNIO: My first name is Kunio: K-U-N-I-O. My family name is Akiwa.

MARIA: Kunio Akiwa. Is that right?

KUNIO: Yes, it is. It's been nice talking with you.

MARIA: I enjoyed it, too.

2. Later Kunio stands up, writes Maria's full name on the board, and says:

I would like to introduce you to Maria Lopez. Maria, would you please stand up? Thank you. Maria is from Mexico. She's living in a dorm. Her field of study is business administration. She likes to read a lot, and her hobby is collecting stamps from all over the world.

3. Next, Maria introduces Kunio to the class. What is Maria going to say?

_____

_____

_____

_____

_____

4. Write the names of your classmates in your book as they are introduced in class.

_____	_____
_____	_____
_____	_____
_____	_____
_____	_____
_____	_____
_____	_____
_____	_____

1-1 THE SIMPLE PRESENT AND THE PRESENT PROGRESSIVE

THE SIMPLE PRESENT	(a) Ann *takes* a shower every day. (b) I usually *eat* lunch at the cafeteria. (c) Babies *cry*. (d) The earth *revolves* around the sun. (e) A square *has* four equal sides. (f) The sky *is* blue.	The simple present expresses *daily habits* or *usual activities*, as in (a) and (b). The simple present expresses *general statements of fact*, as in (c) and (d). In sum, the simple present is used for events or situations that exist always, usually, or habitually in the past, present, and future.
THE PRESENT PROGRESSIVE	(g) Ann can't come to the phone right now because she *is taking* a shower. (h) It's noon. I *am eating* lunch at the cafeteria right now. (i) Jimmy and Susie are babies. They *are crying*. I can hear them right now. Maybe they are hungry.	The present progressive expresses *an activity that is in progress (is occurring, is happening) right now*. The event is in progress at the time the speaker is saying the sentence. The event began in the past, is in progress now, and will probably continue into the future. FORM: *am, is, are* + *-ing*.

1-2 FORMS OF THE SIMPLE PRESENT AND PRESENT PROGRESSIVE

		SIMPLE PRESENT	PRESENT PROGRESSIVE
STATEMENT:		{I-You-We-They} *work.* {He-She-It} *works.*	I *am working.* * {You-We-They} *are working.* {He-She-It} *is working.*
NEGATIVE:		{I-You-We-They} *do not work.* ** {He-She-It} *does not work.*	I *am not working.* {You-We-They} *are not working.* ** {He-She-It} *is not working.*
QUESTION:		*Do* {I-you-we-they} *work?* *Does* {he-she-it} *work?*	*Am* I *working?* *Are* {you-we-they} *working?* *Is* {he-she-it} *working?*

* Contractions of pronouns with *be*: *I'm, you're, we're, they're, he's, she's, it's.*

** Contractions of verbs with *not*: *don't, doesn't, aren't, isn't.* (Note: *am* and *not* are not contracted.)

□ **EXERCISE 2:** Complete the sentences by using the words in parentheses. Use the SIMPLE PRESENT or the PRESENT PROGRESSIVE.

1. Shhh. The baby (*sleep*) _____**is sleeping**_____ . The baby

   (*sleep*) _____**sleeps**_____ for ten hours every night.

2. Right now I'm in class. I (*sit*) _____ at my desk. I

   usually (*sit*) _____ at the same desk in class every day.

3. Ali (*speak*) _____ Arabic. Arabic is his native

   language, but right now he (*speak*) _____ English.

4. Our teacher (*stand, not*) _____ up right now. She

   (*sit*) _____ on the corner of her desk.

5. It's 6:00 P.M. Mary is at home. She (*eat*) _____

   dinner. She always (*eat*) _____ dinner with her

   family around six o'clock.

6. It (*rain, not*) _____ right now. The sun (*shine*)

   _____, and the sky (*be*) _____ blue.

7. (*Rain, it*) _____ a lot in southern California?

8. Look out the window. (*Rain, it*) _____?

   Should I take my umbrella?

9. It's 7:30 A.M. and the Wilsons are in their kitchen. Mrs. Wilson (*sit*) ____

   _____ at the breakfast table. She (*read*) _____

the morning paper. She (*read*) _____ the newspaper every morning. Mr. Wilson (*pour*) _____ a cup of coffee. He (*drink*) _____ two cups of coffee every morning before he (*go*) _____ to work. There is a cartoon on TV, but the children (*watch, not*) _____ it. They (*play*) _____ with their toys instead. They usually (*watch*) _____ cartoons in the morning, but this morning they (*pay, not*) _____ any attention to the TV. Mr. and Mrs. Wilson (*watch, not*) _____ the TV either. They (*like, not*) _____ to watch cartoons.

10. Alice (*take, not*) _____ the bus to school every day. She usually (*walk*) _____ instead. (*Take, you*) _____ the bus to get to school every day, or (*walk, you*) _____?

☐ **EXERCISE 3—ORAL (BOOKS CLOSED):** STUDENT A: Perform an action. STUDENT B: Describe the action, using STUDENT A's name and the present progressive.

> *Example:* stand next to your desk
> STUDENT A: (Student A stands up.)
> TEACHER: Who is standing next to her desk? OR: What is (Maria) doing?
> STUDENT B: (Maria) is standing next to her desk.

1. stand up
2. smile
3. whistle
4. open or close the door
5. hum
6. bite your fingernails
7. read your grammar book
8. erase the board
9. look at the ceiling
10. hold your pen in your left hand
11. rub your palms together
12. kick your desk (softly)
13. knock on the door
14. sit on the floor
15. shake hands with someone
16. look at your watch
17. count aloud the number of people in the room
18. shake your head "no"
19. scratch your head
20. Perform any action you choose. Use objects in the classroom if you wish.

□ **EXERCISE 4—ORAL:** Describe *your* daily activities by making sentences with frequency adverbs and the SIMPLE PRESENT. Put the frequency adverb between the subject and the simple present verb.

FREQUENCY ADVERBS: (From 100% of the time to 0% of the time.)*

100% always
usually
often
sometimes
seldom
rarely
0% never

Example: eat breakfast
Response: STUDENT A: I usually eat breakfast.
STUDENT B: I never eat breakfast.
STUDENT C: (Student A) usually eats breakfast. (Student B) never eats breakfast.

1. drink coffee in the morning
2. put sugar in my coffee
3. drink more than two cups of coffee in the morning
4. drink tea in the morning
5. drink orange juice in the morning
6. drink tomato juice in the morning
7. drink milk two times a day
8. have a sandwich for lunch
9. eat dinner around six o'clock
10. come to class
11. get to class on time
12. walk to school
13. take a bus to school
14. take a taxi to school
15. drive to school
16. ride a bike to school
17. watch TV in the evening
18. study in the library
19. do my homework

□ **EXERCISE 5—ORAL (BOOKS CLOSED):** Practice using the SIMPLE PRESENT. Beginning with the time you get up until the time you go to bed, discuss your daily activities. Your teacher will develop and complete a brief conversation with STUDENT A, and then ask STUDENT B to tell the class about STUDENT A. STUDENT B should say each final *-s* loudly and clearly.

Example: from 6:00 A.M. to 9:00 A.M.
TEACHER (to STUDENT A): Tell us about your daily activities from the time you get up until 9:00 A.M. What are some of the things you usually do?

---

* See Chart 7-8, MIDSENTENCE ADVERBS, for more information about frequency adverbs.

STUDENT A: I get up at seven.
      T: Always?
      A: Usually. I put on my clothes. I eat breakfast.
      T: Do you always eat breakfast?
      A: Yes.
      T: What do you usually have for breakfast?
      A: Bread and cheese and coffee. Sometimes I have an egg.
      T: Do you ever have cereal for breakfast?
      A: No, I don't.
TEACHER (to STUDENT B): Can you tell us about (. . .)? What does he/she usually do in the morning?
STUDENT B: He/She usually gets up at seven. He/She eats breakfast.
      T: Always?
      B: Yes. He/She always eats breakfast. He/She usually has bread and cheese and coffee for breakfast, but sometimes he/she has an egg. He/She never has cereal for breakfast.

1. from 6:00 A.M. to 9:00 A.M.
2. from 9:00 A.M. to noon
3. from noon to 3:00 P.M.
4. from 3:00 P.M. to 6:00 P.M.
5. from 6:00 P.M. until you go to bed

☐ EXERCISE 6—ORAL (BOOKS CLOSED): Answer the questions. Use frequency adverbs.

Example: take a bus to school
How often do you take a bus to school?

Response: I usually take the bus. OR: I never take the bus. OR: I always take the bus. (etc.)

PART I: How often do you . . . ?
1. sleep past noon
2. wear a hat to school
3. wash dishes after dinner
4. eat fish for dinner
5. go to (*a particular place in this city*) on weekends
6. drink (*a particular beverage*)
7. speak (*your native language*) instead of English when you're with your friends
8. go swimming before you come to class in the morning
9. watch TV before you come to school in the morning
10. listen to the radio in the evening

PART II: What are some things you always/usually/often/sometimes/seldom/ rarely/never do . . . ?

1. when you eat dinner
2. when you get ready to go to bed at night
3. when you travel abroad
4. when you meet a new person
5. when you're on vacation
6. in this classroom

PART III: What are some things people in your country always/usually/often/ sometimes/seldom/rarely/never do . . . ?

1. at the dinner table
2. at a wedding
3. when a child misbehaves
4. when they have a cold
5. to celebrate their birthdays
6. when they want to have fun

1-3 SPELLING: FINAL -*S* vs. -*ES*

(a) visit → visits answer → answers speak → speaks happen → happens	Final -*s*, not -*es*, is added to most verbs. (INCORRECT: *visites, speakes, answeres, happenes*)
(b) hope → hopes write → writes	Many verbs end in -*e*. Final -*s* is simply added.
(c) catch → catches fix → fixes wash → washes buzz → buzzes pass → passes	Final -*es* is added if the verb ends in -*ch*, -*sh*, -*s*, -*x*, or -*z*.
(d) do → does go → goes	Final -*es* is added to ***do*** and ***go***.
(e) study → studies try → tries	If a verb ends in a consonant + -*y*, change the -*y* to -*i* and add -*es*. (INCORRECT: *studys*)
(f) pay → pays buy → buys	If a verb ends in a vowel* + -*y*, simply add -*s* (INCORRECT: *paies* or *payes*)

* Vowels = *a, e, i, o, u*. Consonants = all the other letters in the alphabet.

☐ **EXERCISE 7:** Underline the VERB in each sentence. Add final -*s*/-*es* to the verb if necessary. Do not change any other words.

1. A bird sing. → *A bird sings.*

2. Birds sing. → *(no change)*

3. Wood float on water.

4. Rivers flow toward the sea.

5. My mother worry about me.

6. A student buy a lot of books at the beginning of each term.

7. Airplanes fly all around the world.

8. Mr. Wong teach Chinese at the university.

9. The teacher ask us a lot of questions in class every day.

10. Mr. Smith watch game shows on TV every evening.

11. Music consist of pleasant sounds.

12. Pesticides destroy insects.

13. Dust travel through the air.

14. The front page of a newspaper contain the most important news of the day.

15. Water freeze at 32°F (0°C) and boil at 212°F (100°C).

16. Ms. Taylor never cross the street in the middle of a block. She always walk to the corner and use the pedestrian walkway.

17. Many parts of the world enjoy four seasons: spring, summer, autumn, and winter. Each season last three months and bring changes in the weather.

1-4 NONPROGRESSIVE VERBS

(a) I *hear* a bird. It is singing. (b) I'm hungry. I *want* a sandwich. (c) This book *belongs* to Mikhail.	Some verbs are not used in progressive tenses. CORRECT: *I hear a bird (right now).* INCORRECT: *I am hearing a bird (right now).*

NONPROGRESSIVE VERBS

hear	*believe*	*be*	*own*	*need*	*like*	*forget*
see	*think**	*exist*	*have**	*want*	*love*	*remember*
	understand		*possess*	*prefer*	*hate*	
	know		*belong*			

* Sometimes *think* and *have* are used in progressive tenses.
  COMPARE:
    I think that grammar is easy. → When *think* means *believe*, it is nonprogressive.
    I am thinking about grammar right now. → When *think* expresses thoughts that are going through a person's mind, it can be progressive.
    Tom has a car. → When *have* expresses possession, it is not used in the present progressive.
    I'm having a good time. → In certain idiomatic expressions (e.g., *have a good time*), *have* can be used in the present progressive.

□ **EXERCISE 8:** Complete the sentences with the words in parentheses. Use the SIMPLE PRESENT or the PRESENT PROGRESSIVE.

1. Right now Yoko (*read*) ____**is reading**____ an article in the newspaper, but she (*understand, not*) ____**doesn't understand**____ it. Some of the vocabulary (*be*) ____**is**____ too difficult for her.

2. Right now I (*look*) _____ at the board. I (*see*) _____ some words on the board.

3. I (*need*) _____ to call my parents today and tell them about my new apartment. They can't call me because they (*know, not*) _____ my new telephone number.

4. This tea is good. I (*like*) _____ it. What kind is it? I (*prefer*) _____ tea to coffee. How about you?

5. Right now the children (*be*) _____ at the beach. They (*have*) _____ a good time. They (*have*) _____ a beach ball, and they (*play*) _____ catch with it. They (*like*) _____ to play catch. Their parents (*sunbathe*) _____. They (*try*) _____ to get a tan. They (*listen*) _____ to some music on a transistor radio. They also (*hear*) _____ the sound of sea gulls and the sound of the waves.

6. Right now I (*think*) _____ about sea gulls and waves.

7. I (*think*) _____ that sea gulls are beautiful birds.

8. A: Who is that man? I (*think*) _____ that I (*know*) _____ him, but I (*forget*) _____ his name right now.

   B: That's Mr. Martin.

   A: That's right! I (*remember*) _____ him now.

9. Sam is at the library. He (*sit*) _____ at a table. He (*write*) _____ a composition. He (*use*) _____ a dictionary to look up the spelling of some words. The dictionary (*belong, not*) _____ to him. It (*belong*) _____ to his roommate. Sam (*look*) _____ up words in the dictionary because he (*want*) _____ to make sure that he doesn't have any misspelled words in his paper.

10. A: (*Believe, you*) _____ in flying saucers?

    B: What (*talk, you*) _____ about?

    A: You know, spaceships from outer space with alien creatures aboard.

    B: In my opinion, flying saucers (*exist*) _____ only in people's imaginations.

11. A: Which color (*prefer, you*) _____, red or blue?

    B: I (*like*) _____ blue better than red. Why?

    A: According to this magazine article I (*read*) _____ right now, people who (*prefer*) _____ blue to red (*be*) _____ calm and (*value*) _____ honesty and loyalty in their friends. A preference for the color red (*mean*) _____ that a person (*be*) _____ aggressive and (*love*) _____ excitement.

    B: Oh? That (*sound*) _____ like a bunch of nonsense to me.

1-5 SIMPLE PRESENT AND PRESENT PROGRESSIVE: SHORT ANSWERS TO QUESTIONS

	QUESTION	SHORT ANSWER	LONG ANSWER
SIMPLE PRESENT	*Does* Bob *like* tea?	Yes, he **does**. No, he **doesn't**.	Yes, he *likes* tea. No, he *doesn't like* tea.
	Do you *like* tea?	Yes, I **do**. No, I **don't**.	Yes, I *like* tea. No, I *don't like* tea.
PRESENT PRO-GRESSIVE	*Are* you *studying*?	Yes, I **am**.* No, I**'m not**.	Yes, I *am studying*. No, I *'m not studying*.
	Is Yoko *studying*?	Yes, she **is**.* No, she**'s not**. OR: No, she **isn't**.	Yes, she *is studying*. No, she *'s not studying*. OR: No, she *isn't studying*.
	Are they *studying*?	Yes, they **are**.* No, they**'re not**. OR: No, they **aren't**.	Yes, they *'re studying*. No, they *'re not* studying. OR: No, they *aren't studying*.

* *Am, is,* and *are* are not contracted with pronouns in short answers.
INCORRECT SHORT ANSWERS: *Yes, I'm. Yes, she's. Yes, they're.*

☐ **EXERCISE 9:** Complete the following dialogues by using the words in parentheses. Also give short answers to the questions as necessary. Use the SIMPLE PRESENT and the PRESENT PROGRESSIVE.

1. A: (*Mary, have*) _____**Does Mary have**_____ a bicycle?

   B: Yes, _____**she does**_____ . She (*have*) _____**has**_____ a
   ten-speed bike.

2. A: (*It, rain*) _____ right now?

   B: No, _____. At least, I (*think, not*) _____
   _____ so.

3. A: (*You, like*) _____ sour oranges?

   B: No, _____. I (*like*) _____ sweet ones.

4. A: (*Your friends, write*) _____ a lot of letters?

   B: Yes, _____. I (*get*) _____ lots of
   letters all the time.

5. A: (*The students, take*) _____ a test in class right now?

   B: No, _____. They (*do*) _____ an
   exercise.

6. A: (*You, know*) _____ Tom Adams?

   B: No, _____. I've never met him.

7. A: (*Your desk, have*) _____ any drawers?

   B: Yes, _____. It (*have*) _____ six
   drawers.

8. A: (*Jean, study*) _____ at the library this
   evening?

   B: No, _____. She (*be*) _____ at the
   student union. She (*play*) _____ pool with her
   friend.

   A: (*Jean, play*) _____ pool every evening?

   B: No, _____. She usually (*study*) _____
   at the library.

   A: (*She, be*) _____ a good pool player?

   B: Yes, _____. She (*play*) _____ pool three
   or four times a week.

   A: (*You, know*) _____ how to play pool?

   B: Yes, _____. But I (*be, not*) _____
   very good.

   A: Let's play sometime.

   B: Okay. That sounds like fun.

□ **EXERCISE 10:** Complete the sentences by using the words in parentheses. Use the SIMPLE PRESENT or the PRESENT PROGRESSIVE. Some of the sentences are negative. Some of the sentences are questions. Supply the short answer to a question if necessary.

1. A: Where are the children?

   B: In the living room

   A: What are they doing? (*They, watch*) _____ TV?

   B: No, _____. They (*play*) _____ a game.

2. A: Shhh. I (*hear*) _____ a noise. (*You, hear*) _____

   _____ it, too?

   B: Yes, _____. I wonder what it is.

3. A: My sister (*have*) _____ a new car. She bought it last

   month.

   B: (*You, have*) _____ a car?

   A: No, _____. Do you?

   B: No, but I have a ten-speed bike.

4. A: Shhh.

   B: Why? (*The baby, sleep*) _____?

   A: Uh-huh. She (*take*) _____ her afternoon nap.

   B: Okay, I'll talk softly. I (*want, not*) _____ to

   wake her up.

5. A: Ron, (*be*) _____ this your hat?

   B: No, _____. It (*belong, not*) _____

   to me. Maybe it (*belong*) _____ to Kevin. Why don't

   you ask him about it?

   A: Okay.

6. A: Johnny, (*you, listen*) _____ to me?

   B: Of course I am, Mom. You (*want*) _____ me to take

   out the garbage. Right?

   A: Right! And right now!

7. A: What (*you, think*) _____ about every night
   before you fall asleep?

   B: I (*think*) _____ about all of the pleasant things that
   happened during the day. I (*think, not*) _____
   about my problems.

8. A: A penny for your thoughts.

   B: Huh?

   A: What (*you, think*) _____ about right now?

   B: I (*think*) _____ about English grammar. I (*think,
   not*) _____ about anything else right now.

   A: I (*believe, not*) _____ you!

   B: But it's true.

9. A: (*You, see*) _____ that man over there?

   B: Which man? The man in the brown jacket?

   A: No, I (*talk*) _____ about the man who (*wear*)
   _____ the blue shirt.

   B: Oh, that man.

   A: (*You, know*) _____ him?

   B: No, I (*think, not*) _____ so.

   A: I (*know, not*) _____ him either.

10. A: (*You, know*) _____ any tongue-twisters?

    B: Yes, _____. Here's one: *She sells seashells down by the
    sea shore.*

    A: That (*be*) _____ hard to say! Can you say this: *Sharon
    wears Sue's shoes to zoos to look at cheap sheep?*

    B: That (*make, not*) _____ any sense.

    A: I (*know*) _____.

☐ **EXERCISE 11—ORAL/WRITTEN:** To discuss your classmates' immediate activities, divide into two groups, I and II.

GROUP I: Do anything you each feel like doing (stand up, talk, look out the window, etc.). You may wish to do some interesting or slightly unusual things. All perform these activities at the same time.

GROUP II: Describe the immediate activities of the students in GROUP I (e.g., *Ali is talking to Ricardo. Yoko is scratching her chin. Spyros is leaning against the wall.*). Be sure to use your classmates' names.

Later, GROUP I and GROUP II should reverse roles, with GROUP II acting and GROUP I describing.

☐ **EXERCISE 12—PREPOSITIONS:** Use the following prepositional expressions of place in sentences. Talk about things and people in the classroom. Perform actions to demonstrate the meaning of the expressions if necessary.★

Example: on
Responses: My book is on my desk.
My pen is on my book.
My hand is on my head.

1. on
2. above
3. under/below
4. next to/beside
5. against
6. in front of
7. in back of/behind
8. between
9. among
10. in
11. on (the) top of

12. around
13. across from
14. near/close to
15. (far) away from
16. in the front of
17. in the middle of
18. in the back of
19. at the top of
20. at the bottom of
21. in the corner of
22. on the corner of

☐ **EXERCISE 13—PREPOSITIONS:** Complete the sentences with prepositions. This exercise contains prepositions that follow adjectives. (See Appendix 1 for a list of preposition combinations.)

1. Mr. Porter is nice ___***to***___ everyone.

2. Kathy was absent _____ class yesterday.

★ See Chart 4-3 for more information about prepositional phrases.

3. Are you ready _____ the test?

4. I'm angry _____ Greg.

5. I'm mad _____ Greg.

6. Are you afraid _____ dogs?

7. Sometimes people aren't kind _____ animals.

8. One inch is equal _____ 2.54 centimeters.

9. I'm thirsty _____ a big glass of ice water.

10. Joe has good manners. He's always polite _____ everyone.

11. I'm not familiar _____ that book. Who wrote it?

12. Jack's thermos bottle is full _____ coffee.

CHAPTER 2
Past Time

☐ **EXERCISE 1—ORAL (BOOKS CLOSED):** Answer the questions. Use the SIMPLE
    PRESENT or the SIMPLE PAST.

1. What are some things you usually do every morning?
   What are some things you did yesterday (OR: this) morning?
2. What do you usually do in the evening?
   What did you do last night?
3. What do we usually do in this class?
   What did we do in this class yesterday?
4. What do you usually do after this class?
   What did you do after class yesterday?
5. What did you do two days ago? Last week? Last month? Last year?
6. Take out a piece of paper. Write what you did (your activities) yesterday.
   Write as fast as you can.

2-1 EXPRESSING PAST TIME: THE SIMPLE PAST

(a) Mary **walked** downtown yesterday. (b) I **slept** for eight hours last night.	The simple past is used to talk about activities or situations that began and ended in the past (e.g., *yesterday, last night, two days ago, in 1990*).
(c) Bob **stayed** home yesterday morning. (d) Our plane **arrived** on time.	Most simple past verbs are formed by adding **-ed** to a verb, as in (a), (c), and (d).
(e) I **ate** breakfast this morning. (f) Sue **took** a taxi to the airport.	Some verbs have irregular past forms, as in (b), (e), and (f). See Chart 2-4.

2-2 FORMS OF THE SIMPLE PAST

STATEMENT	$\left\{$ I - You - She - He - It - We - They $\right\}$	***worked*** yesterday. ***ate*** breakfast.
NEGATIVE*	$\left\{$ I - You - She - He - It - We - They $\right\}$	***did not*** (***didn't***) ***work*** yesterday. ***did not*** (***didn't***) ***eat*** breakfast.
QUESTION*	***Did*** $\left\{$ I - you - she - he - it - we - they $\right\}$	***work*** yesterday? ***eat*** breakfast?
SHORT ANSWER	Yes, $\left\{$ I - you - she - he - it - we - they $\right\}$ No,	***did***. ***didn't***.

* NOTE: *Did* is NOT used with *was* and *were*.

NEGATIVE: {I - She - He - It} ***was not*** (***wasn't***) busy.
　　　　　 {We - You - They} ***were not*** (***weren't***) busy.

QUESTION: ***Was*** {I - she - he - it} right?
　　　　　 Were {we - you - they} right?

☐ **EXERCISE 2:** All of the following sentences have inaccurate information. Correct them by:

(a) writing a negative sentence; and
(b) writing an affirmative statement with accurate information.

1. Thomas Edison invented the telephone.

(a) ___***Thomas Edison didn't invent the telephone.***___

(b) ___***Alexander Graham Bell invented the telephone.***___

2. Rocks float.

(a) ___***Rocks don't float.***___

(b) ___***They sink.***___

3. Wood sinks.

(a) _____

(b) _____

4. You took a taxi to school today.

(a) _____

(b) _____

5. You're sitting on a soft, comfortable sofa.

(a) _____

(b) _____

6. You stayed home all day yesterday.

   (a) _____

   (b) _____

7. Spiders have six legs.

   (a) _____

   (b) _____

8. The population of the world is getting smaller.

   (a) _____

   (b) _____

9. Our teacher wrote *Romeo and Juliet.*

   (a) _____

   (b) _____

☐ **EXERCISE 3—ORAL (BOOKS CLOSED):** Correct the inaccurate statements by using negative then affirmative sentences. Some verbs are past and some are present.

Example: You drank two cups of tea this morning.

Response: No, that's not true. I didn't drink two cups of tea this morning. I had coffee with my breakfast.

Example: (. . .) took a subway to school today. Right?

Response: That's not possible! I know that (. . .) didn't take a subway to school because there aren't any subways in (*this city*).

1. You got up at 4:30 this morning.
2. (. . .) is standing in the corner of the classroom.
3. (. . .) stands in a corner of the classroom during class each day.
4. (. . .) stood in a corner during class yesterday.
5. This book has 354 pages.

6. Shakespeare wrote novels.
7. A river flows from the bottom of a valley to the top of a mountain.
8. We cook food in a refrigerator.
9. (...) taught this class yesterday.
10. Butterflies have ten legs.
11. This morning, you drove to school in a (*name of a kind of car*).
12. (...) takes a helicopter to get to school every day.
13. You speak (French and Arabic).
14. This room has (*supply an incorrect number*) windows.
15. (...) and you studied together at the library last night.
16. (...) went to (*an impossible place*) yesterday.

2-3 THE PRINCIPAL PARTS OF A VERB

	SIMPLE FORM	SIMPLE PAST	PAST PARTICIPLE	PRESENT PARTICIPLE
REGULAR VERBS	finish stop hope wait play try	finished stopped hoped waited played tried	finished stopped hoped waited played tried	finishing stopping hoping waiting playing trying
IRREGULAR VERBS	see make sing eat put go	saw made sang ate put went	seen made sung eaten put gone	seeing making singing eating putting going
PRINCIPAL PARTS OF A VERB: (1) the simple form	English verbs have four principal forms or "parts." **The simple form** is the form that is found in a dictionary. It is the base form with no endings on it (no final -s, -ed, or -ing).			
(2) the simple past	**The simple past** form ends in -ed for regular verbs. Most verbs are regular, but many common verbs have irregular past forms. See the reference list of irregular verbs that follows in Chart 2-4.			
(3) the past participle	**The past participle** also ends in -ed for regular verbs. Some verbs are irregular. It is used in perfect tenses (Chapter 7) and the passive (Chapter 12).			
(4) the present participle	**The present participle** ends in -ing (for both regular and irregular verbs). It is used in progressive tenses (e.g., the present progressive and the past progressive).			

2-4 IRREGULAR VERBS: A REFERENCE LIST

SIMPLE FORM	SIMPLE PAST	PAST PARTICIPLE	SIMPLE FORM	SIMPLE PAST	PAST PARTICIPLE
be	was, were	been	lie	lay	lain
become	became	become	light	lit (lighted)	lit (lighted)
begin	began	begun	lose	lost	lost
bend	bent	bent	make	made	made
bite	bit	bitten	mean	meant	meant
blow	blew	blown	meet	met	met
break	broke	broken	pay	paid	paid
bring	brought	brought	put	put	put
broadcast	broadcast	broadcast	quit	quit	quit
build	built	built	read	read	read
buy	bought	bought	ride	rode	ridden
catch	caught	caught	ring	rang	rung
choose	chose	chosen	rise	rose	risen
come	came	come	run	ran	run
cost	cost	cost	say	said	said
cut	cut	cut	see	saw	seen
dig	dug	dug	sell	sold	sold
do	did	done	send	sent	sent
draw	drew	drawn	set	set	set
drink	drank	drunk	shake	shook	shaken
drive	drove	driven	shoot	shot	shot
eat	ate	eaten	shut	shut	shut
fall	fell	fallen	sing	sang	sung
feed	fed	fed	sit	sat	sat
feel	felt	felt	sleep	slept	slept
fight	fought	fought	slide	slid	slid
find	found	found	speak	spoke	spoken
fit	fit	fit	spend	spent	spent
fly	flew	flown	spread	spread	spread
forget	forgot	forgotten	stand	stood	stood
forgive	forgave	forgiven	steal	stole	stolen
freeze	froze	frozen	stick	stuck	stuck
get	got	gotten (got)	strike	struck	struck
give	gave	given	swear	swore	sworn
go	went	gone	sweep	swept	swept
grow	grew	grown	swim	swam	swum
hang	hung	hung	take	took	taken
have	had	had	teach	taught	taught
hear	heard	heard	tear	tore	torn
hide	hid	hidden	tell	told	told
hit	hit	hit	think	thought	thought
hold	held	held	throw	threw	thrown
hurt	hurt	hurt	understand	understood	understood
keep	kept	kept	upset	upset	upset
know	knew	known	wake	woke	waked (woken)
lay	laid	laid	wear	wore	worn
lead	led	led	win	won	won
leave	left	left	withdraw	withdrew	withdrawn
lend	lent	lent	write	wrote	written
let	let	let			

☐ EXERCISE 4—IRREGULAR VERBS: Complete the sentences by using the SIMPLE PAST of the given verbs. *Use each verb only one time.* All of the verbs have irregular past forms.

begin	go	read
cut	hold	shake
✓ drink	keep	shut
eat	lose	speak
find	meet	spend

1. Sue _____**drank**_____ a cup of coffee before class this morning.

2. We _____ a delicious dinner at a Mexican restaurant last night.

3. When it _____ to rain yesterday afternoon, I _____ all of the windows in the apartment.

4. Chris hurt his finger when he was fixing his dinner last night. He accidentally _____ it with a sharp knife.

5. I don't have any money in my pocket. I _____ my last dime yesterday. I'm flat broke.

6. Jessica didn't throw her old shoes away. She _____ them because they were comfortable.

7. I _____ an interesting article in the newspaper yesterday.

8. Jack _____ his pocketknife at the park yesterday. This morning he _____ back to the park to look for it. Finally he _____ it in the grass. He was glad to have it back.

9. Peter was nervous when he _____ his baby in his arms for the first time.

10. I _____ Jennifer's parents when they visited her. She introduced me to them.

11. Yesterday I called Jason on the phone. He wasn't home, so I _____ to his sister.

12. When I introduced Tom to Ryan, they _____ hands and smiled at each other.

☐ **EXERCISE 5—IRREGULAR VERBS:** Complete the sentences by using the SIMPLE PAST of the given verbs. *Use each verb only one time.* All of the verbs have irregular past forms.

bite	feel	leave
draw	forget	lend
✓ drive	get	ride
fall	hear	steal
feed	hurt	take

1. Mary walked to school today. Rebecca _____**drove**_____ her car. Alison _____ her bicycle. Sandy _____ the bus.

2. When Alan slipped on the icy sidewalk yesterday, he _____ down and _____ his back. His back is very painful today.

3. I didn't have any money yesterday, so my roommate _____ me enough so I could pay for my lunch.

4. The children had a good time at the park yesterday. They _____ the ducks small pieces of bread.

5. Alice called the police yesterday because someone _____ her bicycle while she was in the library studying. She's very angry.

6. Dick _____ his apartment in a hurry this morning because he was late for school. That's why he _____ to bring his books to class.

7. The children _____ pictures of themselves in art class yesterday.

8. I have a cold. Yesterday I _____ terrible, but I'm feeling better today.

9. Last night I _____ a strange noise in the house around 2:00 A.M., so I _____ up to investigate.

10. My dog isn't very friendly. Yesterday she _____ my neighbor's leg. Luckily, my dog is very old and doesn't have sharp teeth, so she didn't hurt my neighbor.

☐ **EXERCISE 6—IRREGULAR VERBS:** Complete the sentences by using the SIMPLE PAST of the given verbs. *Use each verb only one time.* All of the verbs have irregular past forms.

break	*dig*	*teach*
bring	*freeze*	*think*
buy	*ring*	*wake*
catch	*rise*	*wear*
come	*sleep*	*write*

1. I dropped my favorite vase. It fell on the floor and _____ into a hundred pieces.

2. When I went shopping yesterday, I _____ some light bulbs and a cooking pot.

3. Alex _____ his book to class with him. He didn't forget it.

4. My brother and his wife _____ to our apartment for dinner last night.

5. Last night around midnight, when I was sound asleep, the telephone _____. It _____ me up.

6. The sun _____ at 6:04 this morning.

7. I _____ a letter to my folks after I finished studying yesterday evening.

8. Ms. Manning _____ chemistry at the local high school last year.

9. The police _____ the bank robbers. They are in jail now.

10. Last night I had a good night's sleep. I _____ nine hours.

11. Today Paul has on slacks and a sports jacket, but yesterday he _____ jeans and a sweatshirt to class.

12. It was really cold yesterday. The temperature was three below zero.* I nearly _____ to death when I walked home!

13. I _____ about going to Florida for my vacation, but I finally decided to go to Puerto Rico.

14. My dog _____ a hole in the yard and buried his bone.

---

* Note: –3 °F (Fahrenheit) equals –20 °C (Centigrade or Celsius).

□ **EXERCISE 7:** Complete the following dialogues. Use the words in parentheses. Give short answers to questions where necessary.

1. A: (*you, go*) _____**Did you go**_____ to class yesterday?

   B: No, _____**I didn't**_____. I (*stay*) _____**stayed**_____ home because I (*feel, not*) _____**didn't feel**_____ good.

2. A: (*you, sleep*) _____ well last night?

   B: Yes, _____. I (*sleep*) _____ very well.

3. A: (*Tom's plane, arrive*) _____ on time yesterday?

   B: Yes, _____. It (*get in*) _____ at 6:05 on the dot.

4. A: (*you, stay*) _____ home and (*study*) _____ last night?

   B: No, _____. I (*go*) _____ to a new movie, *The Valley of the Vampires*.

   A: (*you, like*) _____ it?

   B: It was okay, I guess, but I don't really like horror movies.

5. A: (*Mary, study*) _____ last night?

   B: No, _____. She (*watch*) _____ TV.

6. A: (*Mark Twain, write*) _____ Tom Sawyer?

   B: Yes, _____.

   He also (*write*) _____ Huckleberry Finn.

7. A: (*the children, go*) _____ to the zoo yesterday?

   B: Yes, _____. And they (*have*) _____ a wonderful time.

8. A: (*you, eat*) _____ breakfast this morning?

   B: No, _____ . I (*have, not*) _____ enough time. I was late for class because my alarm clock (*ring, not*) _____.

☐ **EXERCISE 8—ORAL:** Pair up with a classmate. Practice questions, short answers, and irregular verbs.

STUDENT A: Ask questions beginning with "Did you . . . ?" Listen carefully to STUDENT B's answers to make sure he or she is using the irregular verbs correctly. Look at Chart 2-4 if necessary to check the correct form of an irregular verb. Your book is open.

STUDENT B: In order to practice using irregular verbs, answer "*yes*" to all of STUDENT A's questions. Give full answers. Your book is closed.

Example: eat breakfast this morning
STUDENT A: Did you eat breakfast this morning?
STUDENT B: Yes, I did. I ate breakfast at 7:30 this morning.

PART I: (STUDENT A asks the questions.)

1. sleep well last night
2. wake up early this morning
3. eat breakfast this morning
4. take the bus to school
5. drive your car to school
6. ride your bicycle to school
7. bring your books to class
8. lose your grammar book
9. hear about the earthquake
10. say something

11. do your homework last night
12. give your friend a present
13. catch a cold last week
14. feel terrible
15. see a doctor
16. read the newspaper this morning
17. find your grammar book
18. go to a party last night
19. have a good time
20. think about me

PART II: (Switch roles. Now STUDENT B asks the questions.)

21. come to class yesterday
22. buy some books yesterday
23. fly to this city
24. run to class today
25. write your parents a letter
26. send your parents a letter
27. lend (. . .) some money
28. wear a coat yesterday
29. go to the zoo last week
30. feed the birds at the park

31. make your own dinner last night
32. leave home at eight this morning
33. drink a cup of coffee before class
34. fall down yesterday
35. hurt yourself when you fell down
36. break your arm
37. understand the question
38. speak to (. . .) yesterday
39. meet (. . .) the first day of class
40. shake hands with (. . .) when you first met him/her

□ **EXERCISE 9—ORAL (BOOKS CLOSED):** Perform the action and then describe the action, using the SIMPLE PAST. Most of the verbs are irregular; some are regular.

Example: Give (. . .) your pen. (*The student performs the action.*)
What did you do?
Response: I gave (. . .) my pen.

1. Give (. . .) your dictionary.
2. Open your book.
3. Shut your book.
4. Stand up.
5. Blow on your finger.
6. Put your book in your lap.
7. Bend your elbow.
8. Touch the tip of your nose.
9. Spell the word "happened."
10. Shake hands with (. . .).
11. Bite your finger.
12. Hide your pen.
13. Leave the room.
14. Speak to (. . .).
15. Tear a piece of paper.
16. Tell (. . .) to stand up.
17. Throw your eraser to (. . .).
18. Draw a triangle on the board.
19. Turn to page ten in your book.
20. Hold your book above your head.
21. Choose a pen, this one or that one.
22. Invite (. . .) to have lunch with you.
23. Thank (. . .) for the invitation.
24. Steal (. . .)'s pen.
25. Sell your pen to (. . .) for a (*dime*).
26. Hit your desk with your hand.
27. Stick your pen in your pocket/purse.
28. Read a sentence from your book.
29. Repeat my sentence: This book is black.
30. Hang your (*jacket*) on your chair.
31. Take (. . .)'s grammar book.
32. Write your name on the board.

□ **EXERCISE 10—ORAL (BOOKS CLOSED):** Practice using irregular verbs by answering the questions.

Example: Where did you sit in class yesterday?
Response: I sat over there.

1. What time did class begin this morning?
2. What time did the sun rise this morning?
3. What time did you get up this morning?
4. What time did you leave home this morning?
5. What did you have for breakfast?
6. What did you drink this morning?
7. Where did you put your books when you came to class this morning?
8. What did you wear yesterday?
9. What time did you wake up this morning?
10. Where did you grow up?
11. What did you buy last week?

12. What did you eat for lunch yesterday? How much did it cost?
13. Where did you sit in class yesterday?
14. When did you meet (. . .)?
15. What cities did you fly to on your way to (*the name of this city*)?

2-5 SPELLING OF -*ING* AND -*ED* FORMS

END OF VERB	DOUBLE THE CONSONANT?	SIMPLE FORM	-*ING*	-*ED*	
-*e*	NO	(a) smile hope	smiling hoping	smiled hoped	-*ing* form: Drop the -*e*, add -*ing*. -*ed* form: Just add -*d*.
Two Consonants	NO	(b) help learn	helping learning	helped learned	If the verb ends in two consonants, just add -*ing* or -*ed*.
Two Vowels + One Consonant	NO	(c) rain heat	raining heating	rained heated	If the verb ends in two vowels + a consonant, just add -*ing* or -*ed*.
One Vowel + One Consonant	YES	ONE-SYLLABLE VERBS (d) stop plan	 stopping planning	 stopped planned	If the verb has one syllable and ends in one vowel + one consonant, double the consonant to make the –*ing* or –*ed* form.★
	NO	TWO-SYLLABLE VERBS (e) vísit óffer	 visiting offering	 visited offered	If the first syllable of a two-syllable verb is stressed, do not double the consonant.
	YES	(f) preférˈ admítˈ	preferring admitting	preferred admitted	If the second syllable of a two-syllable verb is stressed, double the consonant.
-*y*	NO	(g) play enjoy	playing enjoying	played enjoyed	If the verb ends in a vowel + -*y*, keep the -*y*. Do not change it to -*i*.
		(h) worry study	worrying studying	worried studied	If the verb ends in a consonant + -*y*, keep the -*y* for the -*ing* form, but change the -*y* to -*i* to make the -*ed* form.
-*ie*		(i) die tie	dying tying	died tied	-*ing* form: Change -*ie* to -*y* and add -*ing*. -*ed* form: Just add -*d*.

★ Exceptions: Do not double **w** or **x**: *snow, snowing, snowed*
fix, fixing, fixed

□ **EXERCISE 11:** Write the -ING and -ED forms of the following verbs. (The simple past/past participle of irregular verbs is given in parentheses.)

	-ING	-ED
1. start	*starting*	*started*
2. wait		
3. hit		(hit)
4. write		(wrote/written)
5. shout		
6. cut		(cut)
7. meet		(met)
8. hope		
9. hop		
10. help		
11. sleep		(slept)
12. step		
13. tape		
14. tap		
15. rain		
16. run		(ran, run)
17. whine		
18. win		(won)
19. explain		
20. burn		
21. swim		(swam/swum)
22. aim		
23. charm		
24. cram		
25. tame		
26. choose		(chose/chosen)
27. ride		(rode/ridden)
28. remind		

☐ **EXERCISE 12:** Write the **-ING** and **-ED** forms of the following verbs.

	-ING	**-ED**
1. open	_____	_____
2. begin	_____	_____ (began/begun) _____
3. occur	_____	_____
4. happen	_____	_____
5. refer	_____	_____
6. offer	_____	_____
7. listen	_____	_____
8. admit	_____	_____
9. visit	_____	_____
10. omit	_____	_____
11. hurry	_____	_____
12. study	_____	_____
13. enjoy	_____	_____
14. reply	_____	_____
15. stay	_____	_____
16. buy	_____	_____ (bought) _____
17. try	_____	_____
18. tie	_____	_____
19. die	_____	_____
20. lie★	_____	_____

☐ **EXERCISE 13:** Write the **-ING** and **-ED** forms of the following verbs on your own paper.

1. *lift*	6. *map*	11. *drag*	16. *appear*
2. *promise*	7. *mope*	12. *use*	17. *relax*
3. *slap*	8. *smile*	13. *prefer*	18. *borrow*
4. *wave*	9. *fail*	14. *pray*	19. *cry*
5. *carry*	10. *file*	15. *point*	20. *ship*

_____

★ *Lie* is a regular verb when it means "not tell the truth." *Lie* is an irregular verb when it means "put one's body flat on a bed or another surface": *lie, lay, lain.*

2-6 THE SIMPLE PAST AND THE PAST PROGRESSIVE

THE SIMPLE PAST ——×——	(a) Mary **walked** downtown yesterday. (b) I **slept** for eight hours last night.	The simple past is used to talk about activities or situations that **began and ended** at a particular time in the past (e.g., *yesterday, last night, two days ago, in 1990*), as in (a) and (b).
THE PAST PROGRESSIVE ——×—⌣—	(c) I sat down at the dinner table at 6:00 P.M. yesterday. Tom came to my house at 6:10 P.M. I **was eating** dinner when Tom came. (d) I went to bed at 10:00. The phone rang at 11:00. I **was sleeping** when the phone rang.	The past progressive expresses an activity that **was in progress** (was occurring, was happening) at a point of time in the past (e.g., *at 6:10*) or at the time of another action (e.g., *when Tom came.*) In (c): Eating was in progress at 6:10; eating was in progress when Tom came. FORM: **was, were + -ing**.
(e) **When** *the phone rang,* I was sleeping. (f) The phone rang **while** *I was sleeping.*		**when** = at that time **while** = during that time (e) and (f) have the same meaning.
(g) *While I* **was doing** *my homework, my roommate* **was watching** *TV.*		In (g): When two actions are in progress at the same time, the past progressive can be used in both parts of the sentence.

2-7 FORMS OF THE PAST PROGRESSIVE

STATEMENT		{I-She-He-It} *was working*. {You-We-They} *were working*.
NEGATIVE		{I-She-He-It} *was not (wasn't) working*. {You-We-They} *were not (weren't) working*.
QUESTION	**Was** **Were**	{I-she-he-it} *working?* {you-we-they} *working?*
SHORT ANSWER	Yes, Yes,	{I-she-he-it} *was*. No, {I-she-he-it} *wasn't*. {you-we-they} *were*. No, {you-we-they} *weren't*.

□ **EXERCISE 14:** Complete the sentences with the words in parentheses. Use the SIMPLE PAST or the PAST PROGRESSIVE.

1. At 6:00 P.M., Bob sat down at the table and began to eat. At 6:05, Bob

   (*eat*) _____ dinner.

2. While Bob (*eat*) _____ dinner, Ann (*come*)

   _____ through the door.

3. In other words, when Ann (*come*) _____ through the

   door, Bob (*eat*) _____ dinner.

4. Bob went to bed at 10:30. At 11:00 Bob (*sleep*) _____.

5. While Bob (*sleep*) _____, the phone (*ring*) _____.

6. In other words, when the phone (*ring*) _____, Bob (*sleep*)

   _____.

7. Bob left his house at 8:00 A.M. and (*begin*)

   _____ to walk to class.

   While he (*walk*) _____

   to class, he (*see*) ★ _____

   Mrs. Smith.

_____

★Some verbs, like *see*, are not used in progressive tenses. See Chart 1-4.

8. When Bob (see) _____ Mrs. Smith, she (stand)

_____ on her front porch. She (hold) _____

_____ a broom. Mrs. Smith (wave) _____

at Bob when she (see) _____ him.

☐ **EXERCISE 15—ORAL (BOOKS CLOSED):** Perform the actions and answer the questions.

Example:	A: write on the board B: open the door
To STUDENT A:	Please write on the board. Write anything you wish. (STUDENT A writes on the board.) What are you doing?
Response:	I'm writing on the board.
To STUDENT A:	Good. Please continue.
To STUDENT B:	Open the door. (STUDENT B opens the door.) What did you just do?
Response:	I opened that door.
To STUDENT A:	(STUDENT A), thank you. You may stop now.
To STUDENT C:	Describe the two actions that just occurred, using *when*.
Response:	When (B) opened the door, (A) was writing on the board.
To STUDENT D:	Again, using *while*.
Response:	While (A) was writing on the board, (B) opened the door.

1. A: write a note to (. . .)   B: knock on the door
2. A: walk around the room   B: clap your hands once
3. A: talk to (. . .)   B: come in the room
4. A: read your book   B: tap (STUDENT A)'s shoulder
5. A: look out the window   B: ask (STUDENT A) a question
6. A: whistle   B: leave the room
7. A: look at your watch   B: ask (STUDENT A) a question
8. A: pantomime eating (pretend to eat)   B: sit down next to (STUDENT A)
9. A: pantomime sleeping   B: take (STUDENT A)'s grammar book
10. A: pantomime drinking a glass of water   B: come in the room

☐ **EXERCISE 16:** Complete the following. Use the words in parentheses. Use the SIMPLE PAST or the PAST PROGRESSIVE.

1. Sally (eat) _____ dinner last night when someone

(knock) _____ on the door.

2. I began to study at seven last night. Fred (come) _____

at seven-thirty. I (study) _____ when Fred (come)

_____ .

3. While I (*study*) _____ last night, Fred (*drop by*)

    _____ to visit me.

4. My roommate's parents (*call*) _____ him last night while

    we (*watch*) _____ TV.

5. My mother called me around five. My husband came home a little after

    that. When he (*come*) _____ home, I (*talk*) _____

    _____ to my mother on the phone.

6. Yesterday afternoon I (*go*) _____ to visit the Parker

    family. When I (*get*) _____ there around two o'clock,

    Mrs. Parker (*be*) _____ in the yard. She (*plant*)

    _____ flowers in her garden. Mr. Parker (*be*)

    _____ in the garage. He (*work*) _____

    on their car. He (*change*) _____ the oil. The children

    (*play*) _____ in the front yard. In other words, while

    Mr. Parker (*fix*) _____ the oil in the car, the children

    (*play*) _____ with a ball in the yard.

7. Yesterday Tom and Janice (*go*) _____ to the zoo around

    one o'clock. They (*see*) _____ many kinds of animals

    and (*have*) _____ a few adventures. While they (*walk*)

_____ by the elephant, it (*begin*) _____
to squirt water at them, so they (*run*) _____ behind a rock
and (*dry*) _____ themselves. Later, while they (*pass*)
_____ the giraffe area, one of the tall, purple-
tongued animals (*lower*) _____ its head toward Tom and
(*start*) _____ to nibble on his green hat. Janice said,
"Shoo!" At that point, the giraffe (*stretch*) _____
its head toward Janice and (*try*) _____ to eat her ice cream
cone. Janice (*let, not*) _____ the giraffe have the ice
cream because she (*stand*) _____ right in front of a
sign that said, "DO NOT FEED THE ANIMALS." She (*point*)
_____ at the sign and (*say*) _____ to the
giraffe, "Can't you read?"

8. A: There was a power outage in our part of town last night. (*Your lights,
    go out*) _____ too?

   B: Yes, they did. It (*be*) _____ terrible! I (*take*)
      _____ a shower when the lights went out. My
      wife (*find*) _____ a flashlight and rescued me from
      the bathroom! We couldn't cook dinner, so we (*eat*) _____
      sandwiches instead. I (*try*) _____ to study by candlelight,
      but I couldn't see well enough, so I (*go*) _____ to bed
      and (*sleep*) _____. How about you?

A: I (*read*) _____ when the lights (*go out*)

_____. I (*study*) _____ for

a history exam. Of course, I couldn't study in the dark, so I (*get up*)

_____ very early this morning and finished studying

for my test.

2-8 EXPRESSING PAST TIME: USING TIME CLAUSES

(a) ⌐time clause⌐ ⌐main clause⌐ *When I went to Chicago,* *I visited my uncle.* (b) ⌐main clause⌐ ⌐time clause⌐ *I visited my uncle* *when I went to Chicago.*	*when I went to Chicago* = a time clause★ *I visited my uncle* = a main clause★ (a) and (b) have the same meaning. A time clause can: (1) come in front of a main clause, as in (a); (2) follow a main clause, as in (b).
(c) *After Mary ate dinner,* she went to the library. (d) Mary went to the library *after she ate dinner.* (e) *Before I went to bed,* I finished my homework. (f) I finished my homework *before I went to bed.* (g) *While I was watching TV,* the phone rang. (h) The phone rang *while I was watching TV.* (i) *When the phone rang,* I was watching TV. (j) I was watching TV *when the phone rang.*	**When, after, before,** and **while** introduce time clauses. *when* *after* } + subject and verb = a time clause *before* *while* PUNCTUATION: Put a comma at the end of a time clause when the time clause comes first in a sentence (comes in front of the main clause): **time clause + comma + main clause** **main clause + NO comma + time clause**
(k) When the phone *rang,* I *answered* it.	In a sentence with a time clause introduced by **when**, both the time clause verb and the main verb can be simple past. In this case, the action in the "**when** clause" happened first. In (i): *First: the phone rang. Then: I answered it.*

★ A *clause* is a structure that has a subject and a verb.

□ **EXERCISE 17:** Combine the two sentences into one sentence by using time clauses. Punctuate carefully.

1. *First:* I got home.
   Then: I ate dinner.

   (a) After _____***I got home, I ate dinner.***_____

   (b) _____***I ate dinner***_____ after _____***I got home.***_____

2. *First:* I washed dishes.
   Then: I watched TV.

   (a) After _____

   (b) _____ after _____

3. *First:* I unplugged the coffee pot.
   Then: I left my apartment this morning.

   (a) Before _____

   (b) _____ before _____

4. *First:* I was eating dinner.
   Then: Jim came.

   (a) While _____

   (b) _____ while _____

   (c) When _____

   (d) _____ when _____

5. *First:* It began to rain.
   Then: I stood under a tree.

   (a) When _____

   (b) _____ when _____

□ **EXERCISE 18—ORAL:** Combine the two sentences into one sentence by using a time clause. Use the word in parentheses to introduce the time clause. Discuss punctuation.

1. (**before**) *First:* I did my homework.
   Then: I went to bed.

2. (**after**) *First:* Bob graduated.
   Then: He got a job.

3. (**while**) *First:* I was studying.
   Then: Amanda called me on the phone.

4. (**when**) *First:* My alarm clock rang.
   Then: I woke up.

5. (**while**) *First:* I was falling asleep last night.
   Then: I heard a strange noise.

6. (**when**) *First:* I heard a strange noise.
   Then: I turned on the light.

7. (**when**) *First:* I was eating lunch.
   Then: Eric came.

8. (**before**) *First:* I bought some flowers.
   Then: I went to the hospital to visit my friend.

☐ **EXERCISE 19—ORAL/WRITTEN:** Pair up with a classmate.

> STUDENT A: Tell STUDENT B about your activities yesterday. Think of at
> least five things you did yesterday to tell STUDENT B about.
> Also think of two or three things you didn't do yesterday.
> STUDENT B: Listen carefully to STUDENT A. Make sure that STUDENT A is
> using past tenses correctly. Ask STUDENT A questions about
> his/her activities if you wish. Take notes while STUDENT A is
> talking.

When STUDENT A finishes talking, switch roles: STUDENT B tells
STUDENT A about his/her activities yesterday.
Use the notes from the conversation to write a composition about the
other student's activities yesterday. Use time clauses.

☐ **EXERCISE 20:** Complete the sentences with the correct form of the words in parentheses.

(1)   Last Friday was a holiday. It (*be*) _____ Independence

(2) Day, so I didn't have to go to classes. I (*sleep*) _____ a little

(3) later than usual. Around ten, my friend Larry (*come*) _____

(4) over to my apartment. We (*pack*) _____ a picnic basket and

(5) then (*take*) _____ the bus to Forest Park. We (*spend*)

(6) _____ most of the day there.

(7)   When we (*get*) _____ to the park, we (*find*)

(8) _____ an empty picnic table near a pond. There were some

(9) ducks on the pond, so we (*feed*) _____ them. We (*throw*)

(10) _____ small pieces of bread on the water, and the ducks

(11) (*swim*) _____ over to get them. One duck was very clever. It

(12) (*catch*) _____ the bread in midair before it (*hit*)

(13) _____ the water. Another duck was a thief. It (*steal*)

(14) _____ bread from the beaks of other ducks. While we (*feed*)

(15) _____ the ducks, Larry and I (*meet*) _____ a

(16) man who usually (*come*) _____ to the park every day to feed

(17) the ducks. We (*sit*) _____ on a park bench and (*speak*)

(18) _____ to him for fifteen or twenty minutes.

(19)   After we (*eat*) _____ our lunch, I (*take*) _____

(20) a short nap under a tree. While I

(21) (*sleep*) _____, a

(22) mosquito (*bite*) _____

(23) my arm. When I (*wake*)

(24) _____ up, my arm

(25) itched, so I scratched it. Suddenly I

(26) (*hear*) _____ a noise

(27) in the tree above me. I (*look*)

(28) _____ up and (*see*)

(29) _____ an orange and

(30) gray bird. After a few moments, it

(31) (*fly*) _____ away.

(32)   During the afternoon, we (*do*) _____ many things. First

(33) we (*take*) _____ a long walk. When we (*get*) _____

(34) back to our picnic table, I (*read*) _____ a book, and Larry,

(35) who (*be*) _____ an artist, (*draw*) _____

(36) pictures. Later we (*play*) _____ a game of chess. Larry (*win*)

(37) _____ the first game, but I (*win*) _____ the

(38) second one. Then he (*teach*) _____ me how to play a new

(39) game, one with dice. While we (*play*) _____ this new

(40) game, one of the dice (*fall*) _____ from the picnic table onto

(41) the ground. We finally (*find*) _____ it in some tall grass.

(42)   In the evening, we (*join*) _____ a huge crowd to watch

(43) the fireworks display. The fireworks (*be*) _____ beautiful.

(44) Some of the explosions (*be*) _____ very loud, however. They

(45) (*hurt*) _____ my ears. When the display (*be*)

(46) _____ over, we (*leave*) _____. All in all, it

(47) (*be*) _____ a very enjoyable day.

☐ **EXERCISE 21—WRITTEN:** Write a composition about one of the following:

    1. Write about an enjoyable day in your life. OR:

    2. Write about an important event in your life.

2-9 EXPRESSING PAST HABIT: *USED TO*

(a) I *used to live* with my parents. Now I live in my own apartment. (b) Ann *used to be* afraid of dogs, but now she likes dogs. (c) Don *used to smoke*, but he doesn't anymore.	*Used to* expresses a past situation or habit that no longer exists at present. FORM: *used to* + *the simple form of a verb*
(d) *Did* you *use to live* in Paris?	QUESTION FORM: *did* + *subject* + *use to*
(e) I *didn't use to drink* coffee at breakfast. (f) I *never used to drink* coffee at breakfast, but now I always have coffee in the morning.	NEGATIVE FORM: *didn't use to/never used to*

☐ **EXERCISE 22:** Make sentences with a similar meaning by using *used to*. Some of the sentences are negatives, and some of them are questions.

1. *When I was a child, I was shy. Now I'm not shy.*

   → I _____ **used to be** _____ shy, but now I'm not.

2. *Now you live in this city. Where did you live before you came here?*

   → Where _____ **did you use to live** _____ ?

3. *When I lived in my hometown, I went to the beach every weekend. Now I don't go to the beach every weekend.*

   → I _____ to the beach every weekend, but now I don't.

4. *Rita worked in a law office for many years. Now she doesn't have a job.*

   → Rita _____ in a law office, but now she doesn't.

5. *Adam has a new job. He has to wear a suit every day. When he was a student, he always wore jeans.*

   → Adam _____ a suit every day, but now he does.

6. *Sara has two cats that she enjoys as pets. In the past, she hated cats. These are her first pets.*

   → Sara _____ cats. She _____ pets, but today she enjoys her two cats.

7. *Now you have a job every summer. Have you always worked during summers?*

→ What _____ in summer?

8. *When I was in high school, I wore a uniform to school.*

→ I _____ a uniform to school, but now I don't.

9. *When I was a child, I drank a lot of milk. I never drank coffee. How about you?*

→ I _____ milk with every meal. I _____

_____ coffee, but now I have at least

one cup every day. _____ a lot of

milk when you were a child?

10. *When I was a child, I watched cartoons on TV. I don't watch cartoons anymore. Now I watch news programs. How about you?*

→ I _____ cartoons on TV, but I don't

anymore. I _____ news programs,

but now I do. What _____on TV

when you were a little kid?

□ **EXERCISE 23:** Complete the sentences. Each sentence should have a form of ***used to***. Add your own words.

1. I _____***used to ride***_____ my bicycle to work, but now I take the bus.

2. What time _____***did you use to go***_____ to bed when you were a child?

3. I _____***didn't use to stay up***_____ past midnight, but now I often go to bed very late because I have to study.

4. I _____ wild and reckless when I was younger, but now I'm not.

5. Tom _____ tennis after work every day, but now he doesn't.

6. I _____ any physical exercise, but now I exercise for an hour every day.

7. When you were a child, where _____ on vacation?

8. Ann _____ most of her lunches and dinners at restaurants before she got married.

9. I used to spend a lot of time with _____, but now _____.

10. When you were a little kid, what _____ after school?

11. I _____ breakfast, but now I always have something to eat in the morning because I read that students who eat breakfast do better in school.

12. I _____, but now I don't have any pets at all.

13. I _____, but now I attend _____.

14. I live in _____ now, but I _____ in _____.

15. I didn't use to _____, but _____.

16. What _____ for fun when you were _____?

17. _____ live with my parents, but now _____.

18. _____ interested in _____, but now I am.

□ **EXERCISE 24—ORAL AND/OR WRITTEN:** Use *used to*.

1. You are an adult now. What did you use to do when you were a child that you don't do now?

2. You are living in a foreign country. What did you use to do in your own country that you don't do now?

3. Think of a particular time in your past (e.g., when you were in elementary school, when you lived in Paris, when you worked at your uncle's store). Describe a typical day in your life at that time. What did you use to do?

2-10 PREPOSITIONS OF TIME: *IN, AT,* and *ON*

<table>
<tr><td colspan="2">The prepositions in, at, and on are used in time expressions as follows:</td></tr>
<tr>
<td>(a) Please be on time in the future.
(b) I usually watch TV in the evening.</td>
<td>in the past, in the present, in the future★
in the morning, in the afternoon, in the evening</td>
</tr>
<tr>
<td>(c) We sleep at night. I was asleep at midnight.
(d) I fell asleep at 9:30 (nine-thirty).
(e) He's busy at present. Please call again.</td>
<td>at noon, at night, at midnight
at + "clock time"
at present, at the moment, at the present time</td>
</tr>
<tr>
<td>(f) I was born in October.
(g) I was born in 1975.
(h) I was born in the twentieth century.
(i) The weather is hot in (the) summer.★★</td>
<td>in + a month/a year/a century/a season</td>
</tr>
<tr>
<td>(j) I was born on October 31, 1975.
(k) I went to a movie on Thursday.
(l) I have class on Thursday morning(s).</td>
<td>on + a date/a weekday

on + weekday morning(s), afternoon(s), evening(s)</td>
</tr>
</table>

★ Possible in British English: *in future. (Please be on time in future.)*

★★ In expressions with the seasons, *the* is optional: *in (the) spring, in (the) summer, in (the) fall/autumn, in (the) winter.*

□ **EXERCISE 25—PREPOSITIONS:** Complete the sentences with *in, at,* or *on.* All of the expressions contain time expressions.

1. History is the study of events that occurred _____ the past.

2. We don't know what will happen _____ the future.

3. Newspapers report events that happen _____ the present.

4. Last year I was a junior in high school. _____ present, I am a senior in high school.

5. I am a student _____ the present time, but I will graduate next month.

6. Ms. Walker can't come to the phone right now. She's in a meeting _____ the moment.

7. I usually take a walk _____ the morning before I go to work.

8. Frank likes to take a nap _____ the afternoon.

9. Our family enjoys spending time together _____ the evening.

10. Our children always stay home _____ night.

11. I ate lunch _____ noon.

12. I got home _____ midnight.

13. I moved to this city _____ September.

14. I moved here _____ 1990.

15. I moved here _____ September 1990.

16. I moved here _____ September 3.

17. I moved here _____ September 3, 1990.

18. I moved here _____ the fall.

19. I work _____ the morning. _____ the afternoon, I have an English class.

20. _____ Wednesday, I work all day. _____ Thursday, I have an English class.

21. _____ Thursday afternoon, I have an English class.

22. My plane was supposed to leave _____ 7:07 P.M., but it didn't take off until 8:30.

CHAPTER **3**
Future Time

3-1 EXPRESSING FUTURE TIME: *BE GOING TO* AND *WILL*

FUTURE	(a) I *am going to leave* at nine tomorrow morning. (b) I *will leave* at nine tomorrow morning. (c) Marie *is going to be* at the meeting tonight. (d) Marie *will be* at the meeting tonight.	*Be going to* and *will* are used to express future time. (a) and (b) have the same meaning. (c) and (d) have the same meaning.*
(e) *I shall* leave at nine tomorrow morning. (f) *We shall* leave at nine tomorrow morning.		The use of *shall* (with *I* or *we*) to express future time is infrequent and formal.

* *Will* and *be going to* usually give the same meaning, but sometimes they express different meanings. The differences are discussed in Chart 3-4.

☐ **EXERCISE 1—ORAL (BOOKS CLOSED):** Practice using *be going to.*

STUDENT A: Make a sentence with *be going to* about *your* future activities.
STUDENT B: Ask a question about STUDENT A's sentence.
STUDENT C: Answer the question.

   Example: go/tomorrow morning
STUDENT A: I'm going to go to class tomorrow morning.
STUDENT B: What is (STUDENT A) going to do tomorrow morning?
STUDENT C: S/he's going to go to class.

1. go/tomorrow afternoon
2. write/tomorrow night
3. study/tonight
4. take/next week
5. see/later today
6. eat/in a couple of hours

7. buy/this weekend
8. go/next year
9. walk/pretty soon
10. have/after a while
11. wash/the day after tomorrow
12. travel to/sometime

☐ **EXERCISE 2—ORAL (BOOKS CLOSED):** Make sentences about *your* activities. Use present, past, or future verbs.

1. yesterday
2. tomorrow
3. right now
4. every day
5. today★
6. this morning★
7. this afternoon★
8. tonight★
9. the day before yesterday
10. the day after tomorrow
11. last week
12. this week★
13. next week
14. two days ago
15. in a few days (from now)
16. a few minutes ago

☐ **EXERCISE 3:** Complete the sentences by using *a pronoun + a form of* **be going to.**

1. I ate lunch with Alan today, and _____*I'm going to eat*_____ lunch with him tomorrow too.★★

2. Jason wasn't in class today, and _____*he isn't going to be*_____ in class tomorrow either.★★

3. The students took a quiz yesterday, and _____ another quiz today.

4. Margaret walked to school this morning, and _____ to school tomorrow morning too.

5. It isn't raining today, and according to the weather report, _____ _____ tomorrow either.

6. We're in class today, and _____ in class tomorrow too.

7. You didn't hitchhike to school today, and _____ to school tomorrow either.

★ Time expressions such as *today, this morning, this afternoon, this evening, tonight, this week, this month, this year, this semester* can be used with past, present, or future verbs.

★★ See Chart 9-5 for more information about **too** and **either**.

8. I didn't get married last year, and _____

   married this year either.

9. Peter didn't wear a clean shirt today, and _____

   a clean one tomorrow either.

☐ **EXERCISE 4: ORAL:** Complete the sentences with a *pronoun + a form of* **be going to**. Use a future time expression. Use **too** (with affirmative sentences) or **either** (with negative sentences).

> *Example:*   I didn't study last night, and . . . .
> *Response:*   I didn't study last night, and I'm not going to study tonight either.

1. I did my homework yesterday, and . . . .
2. I wasn't at home last night, and . . . .
3. We didn't have a grammar quiz today, and . . . .
4. Our teacher is in class today, and . . . .
5. It's (*cold/hot/nice*) today, and . . . .
6. I didn't go bowling today, and . . . .
7. I brought my umbrella with me today, and . . . .
8. I didn't get hit by a truck on my way to school today, and . . . .
9. The sun rose before six today, and . . . .
10. We didn't have pizza for breakfast this morning, and . . . .

3-2   FORMS WITH *WILL*

STATEMENT	{I-You-She-He-It-We-They} *will come* tomorrow.	
NEGATIVE	{I-You-She-He-It-We-They} *will not* (*won't*) *come* tomorrow.	
QUESTION	*Will* {I-you-she-he-it-we-they} *come* tomorrow?	
SHORT ANSWER	Yes, {I-you-she-he-it-we-they} *will*. No, {I-you-she-he-it-we-they} *won't*.	
CONTRACTIONS	I'll, you'll, she'll, he'll, it'll, we'll, they'll	*Will* is usually contracted with pronouns in both speech and informal writing.
	Bob + will = "Bob'll" the teacher will = "the teacher'll"	*Will* is usually contracted with nouns in speech, but usually not in writing.

□ **EXERCISE 5:** Practice using contractions with **will**. Write the correct contraction for the words in parentheses. Practice pronunciation.

1. (*I will*) _____*I'll*_____ be home at eight tonight.

2. (*We will*) _____ see you tomorrow.

3. (*You will*) _____ probably get a letter today.

4. (*She will*) Karen is tired tonight. _____ probably go to bed early.

5. (*He will*) Dennis has a cold. _____ probably stay home in bed today.

6. (*It will*) _____ probably be too cold to go swimming tomorrow.

7. (*They will*) I invited some guests for dinner. _____ probably get here around seven.

□ **EXERCISE 6:** Read the following sentences aloud. Practice contracting **will** with nouns in speech.

1. Rob will probably call tonight.
2. Dinner will be at seven.
3. Mary will be here at six tomorrow.
4. The weather will probably be a little colder tomorrow.
5. The party will start at eight.
6. Sam will help us move into our new apartment.
7. My friends will be here soon.
8. The sun will rise at 6:08 tomorrow morning.

3-3 USING *PROBABLY* WITH *WILL*

(a) Ann *will* **probably** go to the park tomorrow.	People often use **probably** with **will**. **Probably** comes between **will** and the main verb, as in (a). In a negative sentence, **probably** comes in front of **won't**, as in (b), or more formally, between **will** and **not**, as in (c).*
(b) Bob **probably** *won't* go to the park tomorrow.	
(c) FORMAL: Bob *will* **probably** *not* go to the park tomorrow.	

* See Chart 7-8 for more information about placement of midsentence adverbs such as **probably**.

□ **EXERCISE 7:** Complete the sentences. Use a *pronoun* + *will/won't*. Use *probably*.

1. I went to the library last night, and ____*I'll probably go*____ there tonight too.

2. Ann didn't come to class today, and ____*she probably won't come*____ tomorrow either.

3. I watched TV last night, and _____ TV tonight too.

4. I wasn't at home last night, and _____ at home tonight either.

5. Greg went to bed early last night, and _____ to bed early tonight too.

6. Jack didn't hand his homework in today, and _____ _____ it in tomorrow either.

7. It's hot today, and _____ hot tomorrow too.

8. My friends didn't come over last night, and _____ over tonight either.

9. The students had a quiz today, and _____ one tomorrow too.

10. Alice didn't ride her bike to school today, and _____ _____ it to school tomorrow either.

3-4 *BE GOING TO* vs. *WILL*

(a) She *is going to succeed* because she works hard. (b) She *will succeed* because she works hard.	*Be going to* and *will* are the same when they are used to make predictions about the future. (a) and (b) have the same meaning.
(c) I bought some wood because *I am going to build* a bookcase for my apartment.	*Be going to* (but not *will*) is used to express a preconceived plan. In (c): The speaker is planning to build a bookcase.
(d) This chair is too heavy for you to carry alone. *I'll help* you.	*Will* (but not *be going to*) is used to volunteer or express willingness. In (d): The speaker is happy to help.

□ **EXERCISE 8:** Complete the sentences with *be going to* or *will*.

1. A: Why did you buy this flour?

   B: I _____*'m going to*_____ make some bread.

2. A: Could someone get me a glass of water?

   B: Certainly. I _____*'ll*_____ get you one. Would you like some ice in it?

3. I arranged to borrow some money because I _____ buy a motorcycle tomorrow.

4. A: Could someone please open the window?

   B: I _____ do it.

5. A: Can I borrow this book?

   B: Sure. But I need it back soon.

   A: I _____ return it to you tomorrow. Okay?

6. A: I _____ wear a dark suit to the wedding reception. How about you?

   B: I'm not sure.

7. A: What are your vacation plans?

   B: I _____ spend two weeks on a Greek island.

8. A: Gee, I'd really like an ice cream cone, but I didn't bring any money with me.

   B: That's okay. I _____ get one for you.

   A: Thanks!

9. A: Hi, Josh. I hear that you _____ move into a
      new apartment.

   B: That's right. Sara and I found a great apartment on 45th Street.

   A: I _____ help you on moving day if you like.

   B: Hey, great! We'd really appreciate that.

10. A: So you _____ get married.

    B: That's right. On September 22nd.

    A: My congratulations.

11. A: If you can wait just a few minutes, I _____
       walk to the meeting with you.

    B: Okay. I _____ meet you by the elevator. Okay?

    A: Okay. I _____ wait for you there.

12. A: Excuse me, but . . . .

    B: I _____ be with you in a moment.

    A: Thanks.

3-5 EXPRESSING FUTURE TIME IN TIME CLAUSES AND "*IF*-CLAUSES"

(a) *Before I* **go** *to class tomorrow*, I'm going to eat breakfast.	The simple present is used in a future time clause. *Be going to* and *will* are NOT used in a future time clause.
(b) I'm going to eat dinner at 6:00 tonight. *After I* **eat** *dinner*, I'm going to study in my room.	*before* *after* *when* } + subject and verb + a time clause* *as soon as*
(c) I'll give Mary your message *when I* **see** *her tomorrow*.	In (a): The speaker is talking about two events: going to class and eating breakfast. Both events are in the future. However, the speaker uses the simple present (not *be going to* or *will*) to talk about going to class because the verb occurs in a time clause:
(d) It's raining right now. *As soon as the rain* **stops**, I'm going to walk downtown.	*Before I* **go** *to class tomorrow* . . . .
(e) Maybe it will rain tomorrow. *If it* **rains** *tomorrow*, I'm going to stay home.	When the meaning is future, the simple present (not *be going to* or *will*) is used in an "*if*-clause." *If* + *subject and verb* = an "*if*-clause"*

* See Chapter 16 for other uses of "*if*-clauses."

☐ **EXERCISE 9 — ORAL:** Combine the ideas of the two sentences into one sentence by using a time clause. Use the word in parentheses to introduce the time clause. Punctuate carefully.*

1. (*after*)   *First:* I'm going to finish my homework.
                 Then: I'm going to go to bed.

   →   **After I finish my homework, I'm going to go to bed. OR:**

          I'm going to bed after I finish my homework.

2. (*after*)   *First:* I'm going to write a letter.
                 Then: I'm going to go to bed.

3. (*when*)   *First:* I'm going to go to Chicago next week.
                 Then: I'm going to visit the art museum.

4. (*after*)   *First:* I'll go to the drug store.
                 Then: I'll go to the post office.

5. (*before*)   *First:* Ann will finish her homework.
                 Then: She will watch TV tonight.**

6. (*after*)   *First:* Jim will get home this evening.
                 Then: He's going to read the newspaper.

7. (*when*)   *First:* I'll call John tomorrow.
                 Then: I'll ask him to my party.

8. (*as soon as*) *First:* The rain will stop.
                 Then: The children are going to go outside and play.

9. (*as soon as*) *First:* The teacher will get here.
                 Then: Class will begin.

10. (*before*)   *First:* The Robertsons will get some travelers' checks.
                 Then: They will leave on vacation.

11. (*as soon as*) *First:* I will get home tonight.
                 Then: I'm going to take a hot bath.

12. (*when*)   *First:* I'm going to go shopping tomorrow.
                 Then: I'm going to buy a new pair of shoes.

---

* Notice the punctuation in the sample answer in number one. A comma is used when the time clause comes before the main clause. No comma is used when the time clause follows the main clause. See Chart 2-8 for punctuation of time clauses.

** A noun usually comes before a pronoun:
  After **Ann** eats dinner, **she** is going to study.
  Ann is going to study after **she** eats dinner.

□ **EXERCISE 10:** Complete the following sentences with your own words.

1. I'm going to eat dinner before I . . . .
2. As soon as I get home tonight, I . . . .
3. I'm going to call my friend after I . . . .
4. My life will be easy after I . . . .
5. Before I go to bed tonight, I . . . .
6. When I'm in Florida next month, I . . . .
7. I'll call you as soon as I . . . .
8. I'm going to visit my aunt and uncle when . . . .

□ **EXERCISE 11:** Combine the ideas of the two sentences into one sentence by using an "*if*-clause."

POSSIBLE CONDITION ⟶ RESULT

1. Maybe it will rain tomorrow. ⟶ I'm going to stay home.

→ ___*If it rains tomorrow, I'm going to stay home.* OR:___

___*I'm going to stay home if it rains tomorrow.**___

2. Maybe it will be hot tomorrow. ⟶ I'm going to go swimming.

3. Maybe it will snow tomorrow. ⟶ Betsy isn't going to ride her bike to school.

4. Maybe Adam will have enough time. → He'll finish his composition tonight.

5. Maybe I won't get a letter tomorrow. → I'll call my parents.

To make sentences with "if-clauses" in the following, you need to decide which sentence is the "possible condition" and which is the "result."

6. We're going to go on a picnic. Perhaps the weather will be nice tomorrow.

7. Maybe Greg won't study for his test. He'll get a bad grade.

8. I'm probably going to go to Hawaii for my vacation. Maybe I will have enough money.

9. Maybe I won't study tonight. I probably won't pass the chemistry exam.

10. I'll probably get a good grade. Maybe I will study for the test.

---

* Notice the punctuation in the example. A comma is used when the "*if*-clause" comes before the main clause. No comma is used when the "*if*-clause" follows the main clause.

☐ **EXERCISE 12—ORAL (BOOKS CLOSED):** Make sentences from the given possibilities. Use *if* and add your own ideas.

> *Example:* Maybe you'll go downtown tomorrow.
>
> *Response:* If I go downtown tomorrow, (*I'm going to buy some new clothes/I'm going to go to a department store/I can go to the post office, etc.*).

1. Maybe it'll be nice tomorrow.
2. Maybe it'll be hot/cold tomorrow.
3. Maybe it won't be nice/hot/cold tomorrow.
4. Maybe it'll rain tomorrow.
5. Maybe it won't rain tomorrow.
6. Maybe you'll be tired tonight.
7. Maybe you won't be tired tonight.
8. Maybe you'll have enough time tomorrow.

> *Example:* Maybe you'll go downtown tomorrow.
>
> STUDENT A: If I go downtown tomorrow, I'm going to buy some new boots.
>
> STUDENT B: If (. . .) buys some new boots, his/her feet will be warm this winter.

9. Maybe you'll have some free time tomorrow.
10. Maybe you won't be in class tomorrow.
11. Maybe you'll be hungry after class.
12. Maybe you'll go to (*name of a local place*) tomorrow.
13. Maybe you won't have enough money to buy (*something*) when you go shopping tomorrow.
14. Maybe (. . .) will call (. . .) on the phone tonight.

☐ **EXERCISE 13:** Following is a review of time clauses and "*if*-clauses." Complete the sentences by using a form of the words in parentheses. Read carefully for time expressions.

1. a. Before Tom (*go*) _____**goes**_____ to bed, he always (*brush*) _____**brushes**_____ his teeth.

   b. Before Tom (*go*) _____ to bed later tonight, he (*write*) _____ a letter to his girlfriend.

   c. Before Tom (*go*) _____ to bed last night, he (*take*) _____ a shower.

   d. While Tom (*take*) _____ a shower last night, the phone (*ring*) _____.

e. As soon as the phone (*ring*) _____ last night, Tom (*jump*) _____ out of the shower to answer it.

f. As soon as Tom (*get*) _____ up tomorrow morning, he (*brush*) _____ his teeth.

g. Tom always (*brush*) _____ his teeth as soon as he (*get*) _____ up.

2. a. After I (*get*) _____ home from school every afternoon, I usually (*drink*) _____ a cup of tea.

b. After I (*get*) _____ home from school tomorrow afternoon, I (*drink*) _____ a cup of tea.

c. After I (*get*) _____ home from school yesterday, I (*drink*) _____ a cup of tea.

d. While I (*drink*) _____ a cup of tea yesterday afternoon, my neighbor (*come*) _____ over, so I (*offer*) _____ her a cup of tea, too.

e. My neighbor (*drop*) _____ over again tomorrow. When she (*come*) _____, I (*make*) _____ a cup of tea for her.

3. Jane (*meet*) _____ me at the airport when my plane (*arrive*) _____ tomorrow.

4. If I (*see*) _____ Mike tomorrow, I (*tell*) _____ him about the party.

5. I go to New York often. When I (*be*) _____ in New York, I usually (*see*) _____ a Broadway play.

6. When I (*be*) _____ in New York next week, I (*stay*) _____ at the Park Plaza Hotel.

7. Cindy and I (*go*) _____ to the beach tomorrow if the weather (*be*) _____ warm and sunny.

8. As soon as the test (*be*) _____ over in class yesterday, the students (*leave*) _____ the room.

9. Jack (*watch*) _____ a football game on TV right now. As soon as the game (*be*) _____ over, he (*mow*) _____ the grass in the back yard.

10. As soon as I (*get*) _____ home every day, my children always (*run*) _____ to the door to meet me.

☐ **EXERCISE 14—WRITTEN:** Write two paragraphs. Show the time relationships by using words such as *before, after, when, while, as soon as, next, then, later, after that*.

Paragraph 1: a detailed description of your day yesterday.
Paragraph 2: a detailed description of your day tomorrow.

3-6 PARALLEL VERBS

v *and* **v** (a) Jim **makes** his bed *and* **cleans** up his room every morning.	Often a subject has two verbs that are connected by **and**. We say that the two verbs are parallel: **v** + *and* + **v** *makes* *and* *cleans* = parallel verbs
(b) Ann **is cooking** dinner *and* (*is*) **talking** on the phone at the same time. (c) I **will stay** home *and* (*will*) **study** tonight. (d) I **am going to stay** home *and* (*am going to*) **study** tonight.	It is not necessary to repeat a helping verb (an auxiliary verb) when two verbs are connected by **and**.

☐ **EXERCISE 15:** Complete the sentences with the correct forms of the words in parentheses.

1. When I (*walk*) _____ into the living room yesterday evening, Grandpa (*read*) _____ a newspaper and (*smoke*) _____ his pipe.

2. Helen will graduate next semester. She (*move*) _____ _____ to New York and (*look*) _____ for a job after she (*graduate*) _____.

3. Every day my neighbor (*call*) _____ me on the phone and (*complain*) _____ about the weather.

4. Look at Erin! She (*cry*) _____ and (*laugh*) _____ at the same time. I wonder if she is happy or sad.

5. I'm beat! I can't wait to get home. After I (*get*) _____ home, I (*take*) _____ a hot shower and (*go*) _____ to bed.

6. Yesterday my dog (*dig*) _____ a hole in the back yard and (*bury*) _____ a bone.

7. I'm tired of this cold weather. As soon as spring (*come*) _____, I (*play*) _____ tennis and (*jog*) _____ in the park as often as possible.

☐ **EXERCISE 16:** Complete the sentences by using a form of the words in parentheses.

1. It's getting late, but before I (*go*) _____ to bed, I (*finish*) _____ my homework and (*write*) _____ a couple of letters.

2. While I (*make*) _____ dinner last night, some grease (*spill*) _____ out of the frying pan and (*catch*) _____ on fire. When the smoke detector on the ceiling (*start*) _____ to buzz, my roommate (*run*) _____ into the kitchen to find out what was wrong. He (*think*) _____ that the house was on fire!

3. Mark is obsessed with video games. He (*play*) _____

video games morning, noon, and night. Sometimes he (*cut*)

_____ class to play the games. Right now he (*do, not*)

_____ very well in school. If he (*study, not*)

_____ harder and (*go*) _____ to

class every day, he (*flunk*) _____ out of

school.

4. Sometimes my daughter, Susie, has temper tantrums. She (*cry*)

_____ and (*stamp*) _____ her feet when

she (*get*) _____ angry. Yesterday when she (*get*)

_____ angry, she (*pick*) _____ up a toy

car and (*throw*) _____ it at her little brother. Luckily,

the car (*hit, not*) _____ him. Susie (*feel*)

_____ very bad. She (*apologize*) _____

to her little brother and (*kiss*) _____ him.

5. It's October now. The weather (*begin*) _____ to get

colder. It (*begin*) _____ to get cold every October. I (*like,

not*) _____ winter, but I (*think*) _____

autumn is beautiful. In a couple of weeks, my friend and I (*take*)

_____ a weekend trip to the country if the

weather (*be*) _____ nice. We (*drive*) _____

_____ through the river valley and (*enjoy*) _____

the colors of fall.

3-7 USING THE PRESENT PROGRESSIVE TO EXPRESS FUTURE TIME

(a) Don *is going to come* to the party tomorrow night. (b) Don *is coming* to the party tomorrow night. (c) We*'re going to go* to a movie tonight. (d) We*'re going* to a movie tonight. (e) I*'m going to stay* home tonight. (f) I*'m staying* home tonight. (g) Ann *is going to fly* to Chicago next week. (h) Ann *is flying* to Chicago next week. (i) Bob *is going to take* a taxi to the airport tomorrow. (j) Bob *is taking* a taxi to the airport tomorrow.	Sometimes the present progressive is used to express future time. (a) and (b) have the same meaning. The present progressive is used to express future time when the sentence concerns **a definite plan, a definite intention, a definite future activity.★**
	Verbs such as **come, go, stay, arrive, leave** are frequently used in the present progressive to express future time. Such verbs express definite plans. Verbs expressing planned means of transportation in the future are also frequently used in the present progressive; for example, **fly, walk, ride, drive, take** (*a bus, a taxi, etc.*).
(k) A: You shouldn't buy that used car. It's in terrible condition. It costs too much. You don't have enough money. You'll have to get insurance, and you can't afford the insurance. Buying that used car is a crazy idea. B: I **am buying** that used car tomorrow morning! My mind is made up. Nobody—not you, not my mother, not my father—can stop me. I*'m buying* that car, and that's it! I don't want to talk about it anymore. A: Oh well, it's your money.	Sometimes a speaker will use the present progressive when he or she wants to make **a very strong statement** about a future activity, as in (k).

★ A future meaning for the present progressive is indicated either by future time words in the sentence or by the context.

□ **EXERCISE 17:** Complete the sentences with appropriate *pronouns* + the PRESENT PROGRESSIVE.

1. I met Jane after class yesterday, and ___*I'm meeting*___ her after class again later today.

2. My friends came over last night, and _____ over this evening, too.

3. Susan didn't come to class today, and _____ to class tomorrow either.

4. We had a meeting this morning, and _____ another meeting tomorrow morning.

5. I didn't eat lunch at the cafeteria this noon, and _____ _____ lunch there tomorrow either.

6. I took a bus to work this morning, and _____ the same bus to work tomorrow morning.

7. Harry didn't go to work today, and _____ to work tomorrow either.

8. The children went to the beach today, and _____ _____ to the beach again tomorrow.

□ **EXERCISE 18:** Practice using the PRESENT PROGRESSIVE to express future time by completing the dialogues. Use the words in the list or your own words. Are there any sentences in this exercise in which the present progressive expresses present, not future, time?

call	drive	go	meet
come	fly	make	stay

1. A: What are you doing tomorrow afternoon?

   B: I _____*am going*_____ downtown. I _____*am going*_____ _____ shopping. How about you? What _____*are*_____ you _____*doing*_____ tomorrow afternoon?

   A: I _____ to a movie with Tom. After the movie, we _____ out to dinner. Would you like to come with us?

   B: No, thanks. I can't. I _____ Heidi at 6:30 at the new seafood restaurant on Fifth Street.

2. A: What courses _____ you _____ this year?

   B: I _____ English, biology, math, and psychology.

   A: What courses _____ you _____ next year?

   B: I _____ English literature, chemistry, calculus, and history.

   A: That should keep you busy!

3. A: I _____ on vacation tomorrow.

B: Where _____ you _____?

A: To San Francisco.

B: How are you getting there? _____ you

   _____ or _____ your car?

A: I _____. I have to be at the airport by seven

   tomorrow morning.

B: Do you need a ride to the airport?

A: No, thanks. I _____ a taxi. Are you planning to

   go somewhere over vacation?

B: No. I _____ here.

4. A: My sister and her husband _____ over to my

   house for dinner tomorrow night. It's my sister's birthday, so I

   _____ a special birthday dinner for her. I

   _____ her favorite food: roast beef and mashed

   potatoes.

B: _____ anyone else _____ over for the

   birthday dinner?

A: Yes. Rick and Olga Walker.

5. A: I'm going to call the doctor. You have a fever, chills, and a stomach

   ache.

B: No, don't call a doctor. I'll be okay.

A: I'm worried. I _____ the doctor! And that's it!

3-8 USING THE SIMPLE PRESENT TO EXPRESS FUTURE TIME

(a) My plane **arrives** at 7:35 *tomorrow evening.* (b) Tom's new job **starts** *next week.* (c) The semester **ends** *in two more weeks.* (d) There **is** a meeting at ten *tomorrow morning.*	The simple present can express future time when events are on a definite schedule or timetable. Only a few verbs are used in the simple present to express future time. The most common are **arrive, leave, start, begin, end, finish, open, close, be.**

□ **EXERCISE 19:** Use the SIMPLE PRESENT of the verb in parentheses *if possible.* Otherwise, use **be going to**/the PRESENT PROGRESSIVE.

1. (*start*)   The game _____ **starts** _____ (*also possible: is starting/is going to start*)

         at one tomorrow afternoon.

2. (*have*)   We ___ **are having/are going to have** ___ chicken and pasta for

         dinner tonight.

3. (*walk*)   I _____ to school tomorrow morning. I

         need the exercise.

4. (*leave*)   The bus _____ at 8:15 tomorrow morning.

5. (*begin,*   The exam _____ at 9:00 tomorrow morning

     end)   and _____ at 11:00.

6. (*open,*   Tomorrow the museum _____ at 10:00 and

     close)   _____ at 5:00. Let's go around 2:30, okay?

7. (*get*)   Have you heard the news? Laura and Jason _____

         married in August.

8. (*watch*)   I _____ the championship game on TV at

         Jim's house tomorrow.

9. (*arrive,*   Alex's plane _____ at 10:14 tomorrow

     take)   morning. I can't pick him up, so he _____

         the airport bus into the city center.

10. (*be*)   There _____ a flight to Dallas at 7:02 tomorrow

         morning.

3-9 PRESENT PLANS FOR FUTURE ACTIVITIES: USING *INTEND, PLAN, HOPE*

(a) I'm *intending*/I *intend* **to go** to Paris. (b) I'm *planning*/I *plan* **to take** a trip next month. (c) I'm *hoping*/I *hope* **to fly** to Paris next month.	*Intend*, *plan*, and *hope* are used in present tenses to express present ideas about future activities. INCORRECT: *I will intend to go to Paris next month.*
TO + THE SIMPLE FORM OF A VERB (d) I intend **to** + **go** I plan **to** + **take**	*Intend*, *plan*, and *hope* are followed by an infinitive (**to** + the simple form of a verb).*

* See Chapter 10 for more information about infinitives.

☐ **EXERCISE 20—ORAL:** Make sentences that communicate the same or a similar meaning. Use the verbs in parentheses.

1. I think that I will graduate next June. (*hope*)
   → *I am hoping/hope to graduate next June.*
2. I think that I will be at the meeting on time tomorrow. (*intend*)
3. Tom thinks that he will buy a new red bicycle tomorrow. (*plan*)
4. Jane thinks that she is going to get a good job after she graduates. (*hope*)
5. I think I will stay in London for two weeks after I leave Paris. (*plan*)
6. I think I will finish my education, get a good job, start a family, and live happily ever after. (*intend*)

3-10 IMMEDIATE FUTURE: USING *BE ABOUT TO*

(a) Ann's bags are packed, and she is wearing her coat. She *is **about to leave*** for the airport. (b) Shhh. The movie *is **about to begin***.	The idiom *be **about to do something*** expresses an activity that will happen in the **immediate future**, usually within five minutes. In (a): Ann is going to leave sometime in the next few minutes.

☐ **EXERCISE 21—ORAL:** What are the following people probably about to do?

1. Jack is holding his camera to his eye. He has his finger on the button.
   → *He's about to take a picture.*
2. Sally has her hand on the door knob.
3. Ben is putting on his coat and heading for the door.
4. Nancy has dirty hands from working in the garden. She is holding a bar of soap. She is standing at the bathroom sink.
5. Eric is on the last question of the examination.
6. Rita is holding a fly swatter and staring at a fly on the kitchen table.

□ **EXERCISE 22—WRITTEN:** Write a short paragraph on each of the following topics.

1. Write about an interesting experience you had when you were a child (six to twelve years old).
2. Write about your plans for the future.

□ **EXERCISE 23—PREPOSITIONS:** Complete the sentences with prepositions. (See Appendix 1 for a list of preposition combinations.)

1. I borrowed this dictionary _____ Pedro.

2. Could you please help me _____ these heavy suitcases?

3. Sue, I'd like to introduce you _____ Ed Jones.

4. You shouldn't stare _____ other people. It's not polite.

5. Marco Polo traveled _____ China in the thirteenth century.

6. Do you believe _____ ghosts?

7. Are you laughing _____ my mistake?

8. I admire my father _____ his honesty and intelligence.

9. I argued _____ Jack _____ politics.

10. I discussed my educational plans _____ my parents.

11. I applied _____ the University of Massachusetts. I applied _____ admission to the University of Massachusetts.

12. Joanna applied _____ a job at the automobile factory.

CHAPTER 4

Nouns and Pronouns

☐ **EXERCISE 1—PRETEST:** Identify each italicized word in the sentences as a:
- NOUN
- ADJECTIVE
- PREPOSITION or
- PRONOUN.

1. Eric is wearing a new *shirt* today.

    shirt _____*noun*_____

2. Algeria is *in* North Africa.

    in _____*preposition*_____

3. Steve is in Asia. *He* is traveling.

    he _____*pronoun*_____

4. I'm *thirsty*.

    thirsty _____*adjective*_____

5. We have class in this *room* every day.

    room _____

6. I know my *way* to Joanna's house.

    way _____

7. The *happy* children squealed with joy.

    happy _____

8. I walked to class *with* Maria.

    with _____

9. Hawaii has eight principal *islands*.

    islands _____

10. The *hungry* man stuffed his mouth with rice.

    hungry _____

11. Tokyo is the capital of *Japan*.

    Japan _____

12. Athens is a *beautiful* city.

    beautiful _____

13. My history book is *under* my desk.

    under _____

14. Do you like classical *music*?

    music _____

15. I don't eat sour oranges. I don't like *them*.

    them _____

☐ **EXERCISE 2—PRETEST (BOOKS CLOSED):** Number a piece of paper from 1 to 22. This is a spelling test. Write the plural forms of the given nouns.

Example: one chair, two . . .
Written: **chairs**

1. glass	12. roof
2. problem	13. hero
3. match	14. radio
4. bush	15. zero
5. animal	16. foot
6. sex	17. mouse
7. library	18. sheep
8. monkey	19. woman
9. family	20. child
10. wife	21. phenomenon
11. shelf	22. offspring

4-1 PLURAL FORMS OF NOUNS

SINGULAR	PLURAL	
(a) one bird one street one rose	two **birds** two **streets** two **roses**	To make most nouns plural, add **-s**.
(b) one dish one match one class one box	two **dishes** two **matches** two **classes** two **boxes**	Add **-es** to nouns ending in **-sh**, **-ch**, **-ss**, and **-x**.
(c) one baby one city	two **babies** two **cities**	If a noun ends in a consonant + **-y**, change the "**y**" to "**i**" and add **-es**. (NOTE: If **-y** is preceded by a vowel, add only **-s**: *boys, days, keys*.)
(d) one knife one shelf	two **knives** two **shelves**	If a noun ends in **-fe** or **-f**, change the ending to **-ves**. (Exceptions: *beliefs, chiefs, roofs, cuffs*.)

(e) one tomato
one zoo
one zero
	two **tomatoes**
	two **zoos**
	two **zeroes**/**zeros**
		The plural form of nouns that end in **-o** is sometimes **-oes** and sometimes **-os**.
		  -oes: *tomatoes, potatoes, heroes, echoes, mosquitoes*
		  -os: *zoos, radios, studios, pianos, solos, sopranos, photos, autos*
		  -oes or **-os**: *zeroes/zeros, volcanoes/volcanos, tornadoes/tornados*

(f) one child one foot one goose one man one mouse one tooth one woman —	two *children* two *feet* two *geese* two *men* two *mice* two *teeth* two *women* two *people*	Some nouns have irregular plural forms. (NOTE: The singular form of *people* can be *person*, *woman*, *man*, *child*. For example, one man and one child = two people.)
(g) one deer one fish one sheep one offspring one species	two *deer* two *fish* two *sheep* two *offspring* two *species*	The plural form of some nouns is the same as the singular form.
(h) one bacterium one cactus one crisis one phenomenon	two *bacteria* two *cacti* two *crises* two *phenomena*	Some nouns that English has borrowed from other languages have foreign plurals.

□ **EXERCISE 3:** Write the plural forms of the nouns.

1. one potato, two ____**potatoes**____

2. a dormitory, many _____

3. one child, two _____

4. a leaf, a lot of _____

5. a wish, many _____

6. one fish, two _____

7. an opinion, many _____

8. a mouse, several _____

9. a sandwich, some _____

10. a man, many _____

11. one woman, two _____

12. a flash, three _____

13. one tomato, a few _____

14. one tooth, two _____

15. one half, two _____

16. a tax, a lot of _____

17. a possibility, several _____

18. a thief, many _____

19. a volcano, many _____

20. a goose, a lot of _____

21. an attorney, a few _____

22. a butterfly, several _____

23. one category, two _____

24. a mosquito, a lot of _____

25. one sheep, two _____

26. a wolf, some _____

27. one stitch, two _____

28. one foot, three _____

29. one piano, two _____

30. a belief, many _____

4-2 SUBJECTS, VERBS, AND OBJECTS

(a) The **sun shines**.
    (noun) (verb)
 	
(b) **Plants grow**.
    (noun) (verb)
	An English sentence has a SUBJECT (**S**) and a VERB (**V**).
	
	The SUBJECT is a **noun**. In (a): *sun* is a noun; it is the subject of the verb *shines*.

(c) **Plants need water**.
    (noun) (verb) (noun)
 	
(d) **Bob is reading** a **book**.
    (noun) (verb) (noun)
	Sometimes a VERB is followed by an OBJECT (**O**).
	
	The OBJECT of a verb is a **noun**. In (c): *water* is the object of the verb *need*.

☐ **EXERCISE 4:** Find the SUBJECT (S) and VERB (V) of each sentence. Also find the OBJECT (O) of the verb if the sentence has an object.

                    S   V   O
  1. The <u>carpenter</u> <u>built</u> a <u>table</u>.

            S   V
  2. <u>Birds</u> <u>fly</u>.

  3. Cows eat grass.

  4. My dog barked.

  5. The dog chased the cat.

  6. Accidents happen.

  7. My roommate opened the window.

  8. Most birds build nests.

  9. Our guests arrived.

10. Teachers assign homework.

11. Steam rises.

12. Jack raised his hand.

13. Irene is watching her sister's children.

4-3 OBJECTS OF PREPOSITIONS

S V O PREP O of PREP (a) Ann put her books **on** the ***desk***. (noun) **S V PREP O of PREP** (b) A leaf fell ***to*** the ***ground***. (noun)	Many English sentences have prepositional phrases. In (a): "on the desk" is a prepositional phrase. A prepositional phrase consists of a PREPOSITION (**PREP**) and an OBJECT OF A PREPOSITION (**O of PREP**). The object of a preposition is a *noun*.

REFERENCE LIST OF PREPOSITIONS

about	*before*	*despite*	*of*	*to*
above	*behind*	*down*	*off*	*toward(s)*
across	*below*	*during*	*on*	*under*
after	*beneath*	*for*	*out*	*until*
against	*beside*	*from*	*over*	*up*
along	*besides*	*in*	*since*	*upon*
among	*between*	*into*	*through*	*with*
around	*beyond*	*like*	*throughout*	*within*
at	*by*	*near*	*till*	*without*

☐ **EXERCISE 5:** Find the SUBJECTS, VERBS, and OBJECTS in the following. Identify the PREPOSITION (PREP) and the noun that is used as the OBJECT OF THE PREPOSITION (O of PREP).

                  S   V   O   PREP   O of PREP

1. Sara saw some pictures on   the wall.

2. Sara looked at the pictures.

3. Emily waited for her friend at a restaurant.

4. The sun rises in the east.

5. Sue lost her ring in the sand at the beach.

6. The moon usually disappears from view during the day.

7. Eric talked to his friend on the phone for thirty minutes.

8. Children throughout the world play with dolls.

9. Astronauts walked on the moon in 1969.★

10. A woman in a blue suit sat beside me until the end of the meeting.

★ Note: In a typical English sentence, "**place**" (e.g., *on the moon*) is mentioned before "**time**" (e.g., *in 1969*). INCORRECT: *Astronauts walked in 1969 on the moon.*

EXERCISE 6—ORAL: Review prepositions of place by using the following phrases in sentences. Demonstrate the meaning of the preposition by some action.

> *Example:* above my head
> *Oral response:* I'm holding my hand above my head. (*The student demonstrates this action.*)

1. across the room	11. below the window
2. against the wall	12. beside my book
3. among my books and papers	13. near the door
4. between two pages of my book	14. far from the door
5. around my wrist	15. off my desk
6. at my desk	16. out the window
7. on my desk	17. under my desk
8. in the room	18. through the door
9. into the room	19. throughout the room
10. behind me	20. toward(s) the door

4-4 USING ADJECTIVES TO DESCRIBE NOUNS

(a) Bob is reading a **good** book. (adjective + noun)	Words that describe nouns are called *adjectives*. In (a): *good* is an adjective; it describes the book.
(b) The **tall** woman wore a **new** dress. (c) The **short** woman wore an **old** dress. (d) The **young** woman wore a **short** dress.	We say that adjectives "modify" nouns. "Modify" means "change a little." An adjective changes the meaning of a noun by giving more information about it.
(e) Roses are **beautiful** flowers. INCORRECT: Roses are beautifuls flowers.	Adjectives are neither singular nor plural. They do NOT have a plural form.
(f) He wore a **white** shirt. INCORRECT: He wore a shirt white. (g) Roses *are* **beautiful**. (h) His shirt *was* **white**.	Adjectives can come immediately before nouns, as in (f). Adjectives can also follow main verb *be*, as in (g) and (h).

□ **EXERCISE 7:** Find the ADJECTIVES (ADJ) in the sentences. Also discuss subjects, verbs, and objects.

Adj.

1. The students wrote long compositions.

2. Deserts are dry.

3. The audience laughed at the funny joke.

4. Sensible people wear comfortable shoes.

5. Knives are sharp.

6. Crocodiles have big teeth.

7. Dark places frighten small children.

8. Steve cleaned the shelves of the refrigerator with soapy water.

9. The local police searched the stolen car for illegal drugs.

10. Before the development of agriculture, primitive people gathered wild plants for food.

4-5   USING NOUNS AS ADJECTIVES

(a) I have a **flower** garden. (b) The **shoe** store also sells socks. (c) INCORRECT: a flowers garden INCORRECT: the shoes store	Sometimes words that are usually used as nouns are used as adjectives. For example, *flower* is usually a noun, but in (a) it is used as an adjective to modify *garden*. When a noun is used as an adjective, it is singular in form, NOT plural.

☐ **EXERCISE 8:** Identify the nouns. Use a noun in the first sentence as an adjective in the second sentence.

      NOUN   NOUN   NOUN   NOUN

1. My garden has vegetables. It is a _____ *vegetable* _____ garden.*

2. The program is on television. It's a _____ program.

3. He climbs mountains. He is a _____ climber.

---

* When one noun modifies another noun, the spoken stress is usually on the first noun: a **vegetable** garden.

4. The lesson concerned history. It was a _____ lesson.

5. Tom works for the government. He is a _____ worker.

6. The soup has beans. It is _____ soup.

7. The factory makes automobiles. It's an _____ factory.

8. Janet forecasts the weather. She's a _____ forecaster.

9. This book is about grammar. It's a _____ book.

10. An album that contains photographs is called a _____ album.

□ **EXERCISE 9:** The following sentences have many mistakes in the use of nouns.
- Find each noun.
- Decide if the noun should be plural.
- Write the correct plural form as necessary.

Do not change any of the words in the sentences.

1. The mountain in Chile are beautiful.

→ ***The mountains in Chile are beautiful.***

2. Cat hunt mouse.

3. Mosquito are small insect.

4. Everyone has eyelash.

5. Goose are larger than duck.

6. What are your favorite radio program?

7. Forest sometimes have fire. Forest fire endanger wild animal.

8. Sharp kitchen knife can be dangerous weapon.

9. There are many different kind of people in the world.

10. I applied to several foreign university because I want to study abroad next year.

11. Ted lives with three other university student.

12. The offspring of animal like horse, zebra, and deer can run soon after they are born.

13. I like to read book and magazine article about true personal experience.

14. Many modern device require battery to work. Flashlight, pocket calculator, portable radio, tape recorder, and many kind of toy often need battery.

□ EXERCISE 10: Find the nouns. Make them plural if necessary.

Whales

(1)   ~~Whale~~ look like fish, but they aren't. They are mammal. Mouse, tiger,

(2) and human being are other examples of mammal. Whale are intelligent

(3) animal like dog and chimpanzee. Even though they live in sea, ocean, and

(4) river, whale are not fish. Fish lay egg and do not feed their offspring.

(5) Mammal give birth to live offspring and feed them.

(6)   There are many kind of whale. Most whale are huge creature. The

(7) largest whale are called blue whale. They can grow to 100 foot (30 meter) in

(8) length and can weigh 150 ton (135,000 kilogram). Blue whale are much

(9) larger than elephant and larger than any of the now extinct dinosaur. The

RELATIVE SIZES OF A BLUE WHALE AND AN AFRICAN ELEPHANT

(10) heart of an adult blue whale is about the size of a compact car. Its main

(11) blood vessel, the aorta, is large enough for a person to crawl through.

(12)   Human being have hunted and killed whale since ancient times. Aside

(13) from people, whale have no natural enemy. Today many people are trying to

(14) stop the hunting of whale.

4-6 PERSONAL PRONOUNS: SUBJECTS AND OBJECTS

<table>
<tr><th colspan="6">PERSONAL PRONOUNS</th></tr>
<tr><td>SUBJECT PRONOUNS:</td><td>I</td><td>we</td><td>you</td><td>she, he, it</td><td>they</td></tr>
<tr><td>OBJECT PRONOUNS:</td><td>me</td><td>us</td><td>you</td><td>her, him, it</td><td>them</td></tr>
</table>

S (a) **Kate** is married. **She** has two children. O (b) **Kate** is my friend. I know **her** well. (c) Mike has **a new blue bicycle**. He bought **it** yesterday.	A pronoun refers to a noun. It is used in place of a noun. In (a): "she" is a pronoun. It refers to "Kate." It is used in place of the noun "Kate." In (b): "her" is a pronoun. It refers to "Kate." **She** is a subject pronoun; **her** is an object pronoun. A pronoun is used in the same ways as a noun: as a subject or as an object of a verb or preposition. A pronoun can refer to a single noun, as in (a) and (b). A pronoun can also refer to a noun phrase. In (c): "it" refers to the whole noun phrase "a new blue bicycle."
S (d) *[Eric and I]* are good friends. O (e) Ann met *[Eric and me]* at the museum. O of **PREP** (f) Ann walked between *[Eric and me]*.	Sometimes nouns and pronouns are connected by **and**. The choice of a pronoun after **and** can be troublesome.* If the pronoun is used as part of the subject, use a subject pronoun (e.g., *I*), as in (d). If it is part of the object, use an object pronoun, (e.g., *me*) as in (e) and (f).

<table>
<tr><td>SINGULAR PRONOUNS:</td><td>I</td><td>me</td><td>you</td><td>she, he, it</td><td>her, him</td></tr>
<tr><td>PLURAL PRONOUNS:</td><td>we</td><td>us</td><td>you</td><td>they</td><td>them</td></tr>
</table>

(g) **Mike** is in class. **He** is taking a test. (h) The **students** are in class. **They** are taking a test. (i) **Kate and Tom** are married. **They** have two children.	*Singular* = one. *Plural* = more than one. Singular pronouns refer to singular nouns, plural pronouns to plural nouns. In (g): "Mike" is singular (one person), so a singular pronoun (*he*) is used. In (h): "students" is plural, so a plural pronoun (*they*) is used.

*Pronoun usage after **and** can be troublesome for native speakers, too!

☐ **EXERCISE 11:** Choose the correct words in italics.

1. Ms. Lee wrote a note on my test paper. ⟨*She*,⟩ *Her* wanted to talk to

   I, ⟨*me*⟩ after class.

2. Nick ate dinner with *I, me*.

3. Nick ate dinner with Betsy and *I, me*.

4. *I, me* had dinner with Nick last night.

5. Betsy and *I, me* had dinner with Nick last night.

6. Nick ate dinner with *we, us*.

7. Nick ate dinner with the Robertsons and   *we, us*.

8. My brother drove Emily and   *I, me*   to the store. He didn't come in.
   He waited for   *we, us*   in the car.   *We, Us*   hurried.

9. A: I want to get tickets for the soccer game.

   B: You'd better get   *it, them*   right way.   *It, They*   *is, are*
       selling fast.

10. Alex bought a ticket to the soccer game. He put   *it, them*   in his pocket
    and forgot about   *it, them*.   The next day, he put his shirt in the wash.
    The ticket came out of the washing machine and dryer crumpled and
    nearly illegible. But when Alex took   *it, them*   to the game, the ticket
    taker accepted   *it, them*   and let Alex in.

11. Please take these food scraps and give   *it, them*   to the dog.

12. I talked to Jennifer and Mike. I told   *they, them*   about the surprise
    birthday party for Lizzy.   *They, them*   won't tell   *she, her*   about
    it, them.   *She, Her*   is really going to be surprised!

13. Ted invited   *I, me*   to go to the game with   *he, him*.

14. Ted invited Adam and   *I, me*   to go to the game with Tina and   *he, him*.

15. Between you and   *I, me*,   I think Brian made a bad decision when he
    quit his job. Brian and   *I, me*   see things differently.

4-7 POSSESSIVE NOUNS

SINGULAR: (a) I know the **student's** name.		An apostrophe (') and an **-s** are used with nouns to show possession. Notice the patterns:
PLURAL: (b) I know the **students'** names.		
PLURAL: (c) I know the **children's** names.		

SINGULAR	the student ⟶ the **student's** name my baby ⟶ my **baby's** name a man ⟶ a **man's** name	SINGULAR POSSESSIVE NOUN: noun + apostrophe (') + **-s**

PLURAL	the students ⟶ the **students'** names
	my babies ⟶ my **babies'** names
	men ⟶ **men's** names
	the children ⟶ the **children's** names
		PLURAL POSSESSIVE NOUN:
		    noun + **-s** + apostrophe (')
		IRREGULAR PLURAL* POSSESSIVE NOUN:
		    noun + apostrophe (') + **-s**

*An irregular plural noun is a plural noun that does not end in **-s**: *children, men, people, women*. See Chart 4-1.

☐ **EXERCISE 12:** Use the correct possessive form of the noun in italics to complete the sentence.

1. *student*   One student asked several questions. I answered the
    student's questions.

2. *students*   Many students had questions after the lecture. I answered the
    students' questions.

3. *daughter*   We have one child, a girl. Our _____
    bedroom is right next to ours.

4. *daughters*   We have two children, both girls. They share a bedroom. Our
    _____ bedroom is next to ours.

5. *man*   Keith is a _____ name.

6. *woman*   Heidi is a _____ name.

7. *men*   Keith and Jeremy are _____ names.

8. *women*   Emily and Colette are _____ names.

9. *people*   It's important to be sensitive to other _____
    feelings.

10. *person*   I always look straight into a _____ eyes
    during a conversation.

11. *earth*   The _____ surface is about seventy per cent water.

12. *elephant*   An _____ skin is gray and wrinkled.

13. *teachers*   We have class in this building, but all of the _____
    offices are in another building.

14. *teacher*   My grammar _____ husband is an
    engineer.

15. *enemy*   Two soldiers, each faceless and nameless to the other, fought
    to the death on the muddy river bank. At the end, the winner
    could not help but admire his _____
    courage and wonder why he'd had to die.

16. *enemies*   Through the years in public office, he made many political
    enemies. He made a list of his _____
    names so that he could get revenge when he achieved
    political power.

4-8 POSSESSIVE PRONOUNS AND ADJECTIVES

This pen belongs to me. (a) It's **mine**. (b) It is **my** pen.		(a) and (b) have the same meaning; they both show possession. "Mine" is a possessive pronoun; "my" is a possessive adjective.
POSSESSIVE PRONOUNS (c) I have **mine**. (d) You have **yours**. (e) She has **hers**. (f) He has **his**. (g) We have **ours**. (h) You have **yours**. (i) They have **theirs**. (j) ——————	POSSESSIVE ADJECTIVES I have **my** pen. You have **your** pen. She has **her** pen. He has **his** pen. We have **our** pens. You have **your** pens. They have **their** pens. I have a book. **Its** cover is black.	A **possessive pronoun** is used alone, without a noun following it. A **possessive adjective** is used only with a noun following it. In (j): the possessive **its** is used only with a noun following it. Note that possessive **its** has no apostrophe.*

*__its__ = possessive adjective
__it's__ = it is (or it has when used in the present perfect)

☐ **EXERCISE 13:** Choose the correct words in italics.

1. Children should obey *his, their* parents.

2. A: Excuse me. Is this *my, mine* dictionary or *your, yours*?

   B: This one is *my, mine*. *Your, Yours* is on *your, yours* desk.

3. The bird cleaned *its, it's* feathers with *its, it's* beak.

4. A: What kind of bird is that?

   B: *Its, It's* a crow.

5. Paula had to drive my car to work. *Hers, Her* had a flat tire.

6. Julie fell off her bicycle and broke *hers, her* arm.

7. Fruit should be a part of *your, yours* daily diet. *It, They*   *is, are* good for *you, them*.

8. a. Adam and Amanda are married. *They, Them* live in an apartment building.

b. *Their, There, They're★* apartment is on the fifth floor.

c. We live in the same building. *Our, Ours* apartment has one bedroom, but *their, theirs* has two.

d. *Their, There, They're* sitting in the kitchen of *their, there, they're* apartment right now.

e. *Their, There, They're* sitting *their, there, they're* now because *their, there, they're* waiting for a phone call from *their, there, they're* son.

4-9 *A FRIEND OF* + POSSESSIVE

(a) Do you know Greg Smith? He is *a friend of mine*.★ (b) We ate dinner with *a friend of Bill's*. INCORRECT: *a friend of Bill*	*A friend of* + *a possessive noun/pronoun* is a special or idomatic expression. It is used to identify another person as one friend among many friends. In (a): *a friend of mine* = one of my friends, but not my only friend. In (b): *a friend of Bill's* = one of Bill's friends; Bill has other friends. In (d): The expression can also be used in the plural.
(c) The Smiths are *friends* of mine.	

★*He is my friend* may give the idea that the speaker has only one friend. A speaker would normally say *He is one of my friends* or *He is a friend of mine*.

★*Their, there,* and *they're* have the same pronunciation (but not meaning).

    Their = possessive adjective. *There* = expression of place. *They're* = *They are*.

☐ **EXERCISE 14—ORAL (BOOKS CLOSED):** Make sentences with *a friend of/friends of.*

> *Example:* You have a friend (in Chicago). You wrote a letter to this person.
> *Response:* I wrote a letter to a friend of mine in Chicago.
>
> *Example:* (...) has a friend (in Miami). He wrote a letter to this person.
> *Response:* Pedro wrote a letter to a friend of his in Miami.

1. (...) has a friend in (*a city*). He/She wrote a letter to this person.
2. You have a good friend in (*a city*). You wrote a letter to this person.
3. (...) and (...) have friends in (*a city*). They visited them.
4. You have a good friend. You want to introduce me to this person.
5. You and I have a mutual friend. We ran into this person at (*name of a place*).
6. (...) has a good friend. You met this person.
7. You have a friend. You invited this person to spend the weekend with your family.
8. (...) and (...) have some friends. They usually have dinner with these people.

4-10 REFLEXIVE PRONOUNS

myself	(a) *I saw **myself** in the mirror.*	Reflexive pronouns end in *-self/-selves*. They are used when the subject (e.g., *I*) and the object (e.g., *myself*) are the same person. The action of the verb is pointed back to the subject of the sentence. INCORRECT: *I saw me in the mirror.*
yourself	(b) *You* (one person) saw ***yourself**.*	
herself	(c) *She* saw ***herself**.*	
himself	(d) *He* saw ***himself**.*	
itself	(e) *It* (e.g, the kitten) saw ***itself**.*	
ourselves	(f) *We* saw ***ourselves**.*	
yourselves	(g) *You* (plural) saw ***yourselves**.*	
themselves	(h) *They* saw ***themselves**.*	
(i) Greg lives **by himself**. (j) I sat **by myself** on the park bench.		***By** + a reflexive pronoun* = alone. In (i): Greg lives alone, without family or roommates.
(k) I **enjoyed myself** at the fair.		***Enjoy** and a few other verbs are commonly followed by a reflexive prounoun. See the list below.

VERBS AND PHRASES COMMONLY FOLLOWED BY A REFLEXIVE PRONOUN

believe in yourself	*hurt yourself*	*take care of yourself*
blame yourself	*give yourself (something)*	*talk to yourself*
cut yourself	*introduce yourself*	*teach yourself*
enjoy yourself	*kill yourself*	*tell yourself*
feel sorry for yourself	*pinch yourself*	*work for yourself*
help yourself	*be proud of yourself*	*wish yourself (luck)*

☐ **EXERCISE 15—ORAL (BOOKS CLOSED):** Using a mirror in the classroom, describe who is looking at whom.

> *Example:* (*Spyros*) holds the mirror and looks into it.
> TEACHER: What is (Spyros) doing?
> STUDENT A: He is looking at himself in the mirror.
> TEACHER: What are you doing, Spyros?
> SPYROS: I am looking at myself in the mirror.
> TEACHER: Tell Spyros what he is doing.
> STUDENT B: Spyros, you are looking at yourself in the mirror.

> *Example:* (. . .) and (. . .) hold the mirror and look into it.
> TEACHER: What are (Min Sok) and (Ivonne) doing?
> Etc.

☐ **EXERCISE 16:** Complete the sentences with reflexive pronouns.

1. Are you okay, Heidi? Did you hurt _____**yourself**_____ ?

2. David was really embarrassed when he had to go to the job interview with a bandage on his face. He had cut _____ while he was shaving.

3. Do you ever talk to _____? Most people talk to _____ sometimes.

4. It is important for all of us to have confidence in our own abilities. We need to believe in _____.

5. Sara is self-employed. She doesn't have a boss. She works for

_____.

6. Steve, who is on the wrestling team, wishes _____ good luck before each match.

7. There's plenty of food on the table. Would all of you please simply help _____ to the food?

8. Brian, don't blame _____ for the accident. It wasn't your fault. You did everything you could to avoid it.

9. I couldn't believe my good luck! I had to pinch _____ to make sure I wasn't dreaming.

10. A newborn puppy can't take care of _____.

11. I know Nicole and Paul have had some bad luck, but it's time for them to stop feeling sorry for _____ and get on with their lives.

12. Jane and I ran into someone she knew. I'd never met this person before. I waited for Jane to introduce me, but she forgot her manners. I finally introduced _____ to Jane's friend.

☐ **EXERCISE 17—ORAL/WRITTEN:** Make up sentences with reflexive pronouns. Use imaginary situations.

Example: pinch herself
Response: When Graciela won the lottery, she pinched herself to make sure she wasn't dreaming.

Example: wish myself
Response: Last week I took my first lesson in skydiving. Before I jumped out of the airplane, I wished myself good luck.

1. talk to himself
2. hurt myself
3. enjoy themselves
4. take care of herself
5. cut himself
6. wish yourself
7. be proud of yourselves
8. blame ourselves
9. feel sorry for myself
10. introduce herself
11. believe in myself
12. pinch yourself

4-11 SINGULAR FORMS OF *OTHER*: *ANOTHER* vs. *THE OTHER*

ANOTHER

(a) There is a large bowl of apples on the table. Paul is going to eat one apple. If he is still hungry after that, he can eat ***another*** apple. There are many apples to choose from.	***Another*** means "one more out of a group of similar items, one in addition to the one(s) I've already talked about." ***Another*** is a combination of *an* + *other*, written as one word.

THE OTHER

(b) There are two apples on the table. Paul is going to eat one of them. Sara is going to eat ***the other*** apple.	***The other*** means "the last one in a specific group, the only one that remains from a given number of similar items."
(c) Paul ate one apple. Then he ate ***another*** apple. (d) Paul ate one apple. Then he ate ***another*** one. (e) Paul ate one apple. Then he ate ***another***.	***Another*** and ***the other*** can be used as an adjective in front of a noun (e.g., *apple*) or in front of the word *one*.
(f) Paul ate one apple. Sara ate ***the other*** apple. (g) Paul ate one apple. Sara ate ***the other*** one. (h) Paul ate one apple. Sara ate ***the other***.	***Another*** and ***the other*** can also be used alone as a pronoun, as in (e) and (h).

☐ **EXERCISE 18:** Complete the sentences with *another* or *the other*.

1. There are many kinds of animals in the world. The elephant is one kind. The tiger is _____*another*_____.

2. There are two colors on this page. One is white. _____*The other*_____ is black.

3. Alex's bicycle was run over by a truck and destroyed. He needs to get _____ one.

4. The Smiths have two bicycles. One belongs to Mr. Smith. _____ bike belongs to Mrs. Smith.

5. There are three books on my desk. Two of them are dictionaries. _____ one is a telephone directory.

6. The puppy chewed up my telephone directory, so I went to the telephone company to get _____ phone book.

7. Vietnam is a country in Southeast Asia. Thailand is _____.

8. It rained yesterday, and from the looks of those dark clouds, we're going to have _____ rainstorm today.

9. Nicole and Michelle are identical twins. The only way you can tell them apart is by looking at their ears. One of them has pierced ears and _____ doesn't.

10. Of the fifty states in the United States, forty-nine are located on the North American continent. Where is _____ located?

11. I have two brothers. One is named Nick. _____ is named Matt.

12. There are five names in this list. One is Adam. _____ is Greg. _____ is Nick. _____ one of the names is Eric. _____ name on the list (the last of the five) is Jessica.

People I need to call

✓ Adam
Greg
Eric
Nick
Jessica

4-12 PLURAL FORMS OF *OTHER: OTHER(S)* vs. *THE OTHER(S)*

OTHER(S)

one apple
other apples
other apples
others etc.

There are many apples in Paul's kitchen. Paul is holding one apple.
 	
(a) There are **other** *apples* in a bowl.
          _(adjective + noun)
 	
(b) There are **other** *ones* on a plate.
          _(adjective + ones)
 	
(c) There are **others** on a chair.
          _(pronoun)
	***Other**(s)* (without *the*) means "several more out of a group of similar items, several in addition to the one(s) I've already talked about."
	The adjective ***other*** (without an *-s*) can be used with a plural noun (e.g., *apples*) or with the word *ones*.
	Others (with an *-s*) is a plural **pronoun**; it is not used with a noun.
	In (c): ***others** = **other apples***.

THE OTHER(S)

one apple
the other apples

There are four apples on the table. Paul is going to take one of them.
 	
(d) Sara is going to take ***the other*** *apples*.
                  _(adjective + noun)
 	
(e) She is going to take ***the other*** *ones*.
                  _(adjective + ones)
 	
(f) She is going to take ***the others***.
                  _(pronoun)
	***The other**(s)* means "the last ones in a specific group, the remains from a given number of similar items."
	The other (without an *-s*) can be used as an adjective in front of a noun or the word *ones*, as in (d) and (e).
	The others (with an *-s*) is a plural **pronoun**; it is not used with a noun.
	In (f): ***the others** = **the other apples***.

☐ **EXERCISE 19:** Complete the sentences with *other(s)* or *the other(s)*.

1. There are many kinds of animals in the world. The elephant is one kind.

   Some _____ *others* _____ are tigers, horses, and whales.

2. There are many kinds of animals in the world. The elephant is one kind.

   Some _____ *other* _____ kinds are tigers, horses, and whales.

3. There are three colors in the U.S. flag. One of the colors is red.

   _____ *The others* _____ are white and blue.

4. There are three colors in the U.S. flag. One of the colors is red.

   _____ *The other* _____ colors are white and blue.

5. There are four seasons. Spring and summer are two.

   _____ are fall and winter.

6. Spring and summer are two of the four seasons. _____

   seasons are fall and winter.

7. There are many kinds of geometric figures. Some are circles.

   _____ figures are squares. Still _____

   are rectangular.

8. There are four geometric figures in the above drawing. One is a square.

   _____ figures are a rectangle, a circle, and a triangle.

9. Of the four geometric figures in the drawing, only the circle has curved

   lines. _____ have straight lines.

10. Some ships are fueled by petroleum. _____ are

    propelled by atomic power.

11. Some boats are used for pleasure. _____ boats are used for commercial fishing.

12. Many people like to get up very early in the morning. _____ like to sleep until noon.

13. Out of the twenty students in the class, eighteen passed the exam. _____ failed.

14. Out of the twenty students in the class, only two failed the exam. _____ students passed.

4-13 SUMMARY OF FORMS OF *OTHER*

	ADJECTIVE	PRONOUN	
SINGULAR	another apple	another	Notice that the word ***others*** (*other* + final *-s*) is used only as a plural pronoun.
PLURAL	other apples	others	
SINGULAR	the other apple	the other	
PLURAL	the other apples	the others	

☐ **EXERCISE 20:** Complete the sentences with correct forms of *other*: **another, other, others, the other, the others.**

1. Jake has only two suits, a blue one and a gray one. His wife wants him to buy ____*another*____ one.

2. Jake has two suits. One is blue, and _____ is gray.

3. Some suits are blue. _____ are gray.

4. Some suits have two buttons. _____ suits have three buttons.

5. Our physical education class was divided into two groups. Half of the students stayed inside and played basketball. _____ students went outside and played soccer.

6. If you really hate your job, why don't you look for _____ one? You don't have to be a dishwasher all your life. There are lots of _____ jobs in the world.

7. An automobile consists of many parts. The motor is one, and the steering wheel is _____. _____ parts are the brakes, the trunk, and the fuel tank.

8. Some people keep dogs as pets. _____ have cats. Still _____ people have fish or birds as pets. Can you name _____ kinds of animals that people keep for pets?

9. When I was a kid, I had two pets. One was a black dog. _____ was an orange cat.

10. When I walked into the classroom on the first day, the room was empty. I sat down at a desk and wondered if I was in the right room. Soon _____ student came and took a seat. Then a few _____ followed, and the room slowly began to fill.

11. The students in our class had two choices: basketball or soccer. Half of the students played basketball. _____ played soccer.

12. Here, children. I have two coins. One is for you, Tommy. _____ is for you, Jimmy.

13. My boyfriend gave me a ring. I tried to put it on my ring finger, but it didn't fit. So I had to put it on _____ finger.

14. People have two thumbs. One is on the right hand. _____ is on the left hand.

15. The telephone and the automobile are twentieth-century inventions. _____ are the computer, television, and the airplane. Can you name _____ twentieth-century inventions?

□ **EXERCISE 21—ORAL (BOOKS CLOSED):** Complete the sentences or answer the questions using a form of ***other***.

          Example: Please give me your pen.
To STUDENT A: Would you please give me your pen? Thank you.
To STUDENT B: I now have two pens, (STUDENT A's) pen and my pen. I'm holding a total of two pens. Mine is one. Is (STUDENT A's) pen another or the other?
      Response: The other.
To STUDENT C: Please give me your pen. Now I'm holding three pens. Mine is one. Is (STUDENT A's) the other or another?
      Response: Another.
To STUDENT C: And your pen? Another or the other?
      Response: The other.

1. To STUDENTS A and B: Please write your names on the board.
To STUDENT C: There are two names on the board. (. . .) is one of the names. (. . .) is . . . .
To STUDENT D: Please write your name on the board.
To STUDENT E: There are three names on the board. (. . .) is one of the names. (. . .) is . . . . (. . .) [the last of the three names] is . . . .
[Students should continue to write their names on the board and discuss them in terms of *another, other, the others,* etc.]

2. What is one name in this class? And another? And others? And still another? And still others?

3. You have two hands. One is your right hand. Is your left hand another or the other?

4. Look at your right hand. You have five fingers. Your thumb is one finger. Your index finger is . . . . Your middle finger is . . . . Your ring finger is . . . . And your little finger, the last of the five, is . . . .

5. To STUDENTS A and B: Would you please come and stand in front of the class?
To STUDENT C: There are only two people standing in front of the class. One of them is (. . .). How would you describe (. . .), using a form of *other*?
[Continue by having more students join the group in front of the class and discuss who is *another, others, the other, the others,* etc.]

4-14 CAPITALIZATION

CAPITALIZE:		
1. The first word of a sentence	(a) **W**e saw a movie last night. **It** was very good.	*Capitalize* = use a big letter, not a small letter.
2. The names of people	(b) I met **G**eorge **A**dams yesterday.	
3. Titles used with the names of people	(c) I saw **D**octor (**Dr.**) Smith. Do you know **P**rofessor (**Prof.**) Alston?	COMPARE: I saw a **d**octor. I saw **D**octor Wilson.
4. Months, days, holidays	(d) I was born in **A**pril. Bob arrived last **M**onday. It snowed on **T**hanksgiving **D**ay.	NOTE: Seasons are not capitalized: *spring, summer, fall/autumn, winter*
5. The names of places: city state/province country continent	(e) He lives in **C**hicago. She was born in **C**alifornia. They are from **M**exico. Tibet is in **A**sia.	COMPARE: She lives in a **c**ity. She lives in New York **C**ity.
ocean lake river desert mountain	They crossed the **A**tlantic **O**cean. Chicago is on **L**ake **M**ichigan. The **N**ile **R**iver flows north. The **S**ahara **D**esert is in Africa. We visited the **R**ocky **M**ountains.	COMPARE: They crossed a **r**iver. They crossed the Yellow **R**iver.
school business	I go to the **U**niversity of **F**lorida. I work for the **G**eneral **E**lectric **C**ompany.	COMPARE: I go to a **u**niversity. I go to the **U**niversity of Texas.
street, etc. building park, zoo	He lives on **G**rand **A**venue. We have class in **R**itter **H**all. I went jogging in **F**orest **P**ark.	COMPARE: We went to a **p**ark. We went to Central **P**ark.
6. The names of courses	(f) I'm taking **C**hemistry 101 this term.	COMPARE: I'm reading a book about **p**sychology. I'm taking **P**sychology 101 this term.
7. The names of languages and nationalities	(g) She speaks **S**panish. We discussed **J**apanese customs.	Words that refer to the names of nations, nationalities and languages are always capitalized.
8. The names of religions	(h) **B**uddism, **C**hristianity, **H**induism, **I**slam, and **J**udaism are major religions in the world. Talal is a **M**oslem.	Words that refer to the names of religions are always capitalized.
9. The pronoun ''I.''	(i) Yesterday **I** fell off my bicycle.	The pronoun ''I'' is always capitalized.

☐ **EXERCISE 22:** Add capital letters where necessary.

W   **T**

1. we're going to have a test next tuesday.

2. do you know richard smith? he is a professor at this university.

3. i know that professor smith teaches at the university of arizona.

4. the nile river flows into the mediterranean sea.

5. john is a catholic. ali is a moslem.

6. anna speaks french. she studied in france for two years.

7. i'm taking a history course this semester.

8. i'm taking modern european history 101 this semester.

9. we went to vancouver, british columbia, for our vacation last summer.

10. venezuela is a spanish-speaking country.

11. canada is in north america.*

12. canada is north of the united states.

13. the sun rises in the east.

14. the mississippi river flows south.

☐ **EXERCISE 23:** Add capital letters where necessary.

1. We don't have class on saturday.

2. I'm taking biology 101 this semester.

3. I'm taking history, biology, english, and calculus this semester.

4. We went to a zoo. We went to brookfield zoo in chicago.

5. I live on a busy street. I live at 2358 olive street.

6. We went to canada last summer. We went to montreal in july.

7. I like vietnamese food.

8. The religion of saudi arabia is islam.

9. She works for the xerox corporation. It is a very large corporation.

10. Pedro is from latin america.

---

*When **north, south, east,** and **west** refer to the direction on a compass, they are not capitalized: *Japan is **east** of China.*

When they are part of a geographical name, they are capitalized: *Japan is in the Far **East**.*

11. My uncle lives in st. louis. I'm going to visit uncle bill next spring.

12. On valentine's day (february 14), sweethearts give each other presents.

13. We went to a park. We went to woodland park.

14. Are you going to go to the university of oregon or oregon state university?

15. Alice goes to a university in oregon.

☐ **EXERCISE 24—PREPOSITIONS:** Complete the sentences with prepositions. (See Appendix 1 for a list of preposition combinations.)

1. Tom paid ___*for*___ his airplane ticket in cash.

2. Joan graduated _____ high school two years ago.

3. I waited _____ the bus.

4. Jim is a waiter. He waits _____ customers at a restaurant.

5. I have a different opinion. I don't agree _____ you.

6. I arrived _____ this city last month.

7. I arrived _____ the airport around eight.

8. I listened _____ the news on TV last night.

9. This exercise consists _____ verbs that are followed by certain prepositions.

10. Jack invited me _____ his party.

11. I complained _____ the landlord _____ the leaky faucet in the kitchen.

12. Did you talk _____ Professor Adams _____ your grades?

CHAPTER *5*
Modal Auxiliaries

5-1 THE FORM OF MODAL AUXILIARIES

The verbs in the list below are called *modal auxiliaries*. They are helping verbs that express a wide range of meanings (ability, permission, possibility, necessity, etc.). Most of the modals have more than one meaning.

AUXILIARY + THE SIMPLE FORM OF A VERB	
can	(a) I *can speak* English.
could	(b) He *couldn't come* to class.
may	(c) It *may rain* tomorrow.
might	(d) It *might rain* tomorrow.
should	(e) Mary *should study* harder.
had better	(f) I *had better study* tonight.
must	(g) Joe *must see* a doctor today.
will	(h) I *will be* in class tomorrow.
would	(i) *Would* you please *close* the door?

Can, *could*, *may*, *might*, *should*, *had better*, *must*, *will*, and *would* are followed by the simple form of a verb.

They are not followed by *to*:
  CORRECT: *I can speak English.*
  INCORRECT: *I can to speak English.*

The main verb never has a final *-s*.
  CORRECT: *Olga can speak English.*
  INCORRECT: *Olga can speaks English.*

AUXILIARY + *TO* + THE SIMPLE FORM OF A VERB	
have to	(j) I *have to study* tonight.
have got to	(k) I *have got to study* tonight.
ought to	(l) Kate *ought to study* harder.

Have, *have got*, and *ought* are followed by an infinitive (*to* + *the simple form of a verb*).

□ **EXERCISE 1:** Add *to* where necessary. If no *to* is necessary, write Ø in the blank.

1. I have _____***to***_____ go downtown tomorrow.

2. Tom can _____**Ø**_____ play soccer.

3. Could you please _____ open the window?

4. The students must _____ learn all of the irregular verbs.

5. Sally has _____ do her history report tonight.

6. I think you should _____ take better care of yourself.

7. I ought _____ go to the post office this afternoon.

8. Would you _____ speak more slowly, please?

9. We may _____ go to Argentina for our vacation.

10. Will you please _____ mail this letter for me?

11. Tom and I might _____ play tennis after work tomorrow.

12. You had better _____ see a doctor.

13. We can _____ go shopping tomorrow.

14. The students have _____ take a test next Friday.

15. I have got _____ go to the post office this afternoon.

16. Shouldn't you _____ save a little money for a rainy day?

17. Poor Edward. He has _____ go to the hospital for an operation.

18. Alex! Stop! You must not _____ run into the street when there's traffic!

19. May I please _____ have the salt and pepper? Thanks.

20. You'd better not _____ come to the meeting late. The boss will _____ be angry if you're late.

21. I've had a lot of trouble sleeping the last few nights. I've got _____ get a good night's sleep! I can barely _____ stay awake in class.

5-2 EXPRESSING ABILITY: *CAN* AND *COULD*

(a) Bob *can play* the piano.* (b) You *can buy* a screwdriver at a hardware store.	*Can* expresses *ability* in the present or future.
(c) I $\left\{ \begin{array}{l} \textit{can't} \\ \textit{cannot} \\ \textit{can not} \end{array} \right\}$ understand that sentence.	The negative form of *can* may be written: *can't*, *cannot*, or *can not*.
(d) Our son *could talk* when he was two years old.	The past form of *can* is *could*.
(e) They $\left\{ \begin{array}{l} \textit{couldn't} \\ \textit{could not} \end{array} \right\}$ come to class yesterday.	The negative of *could*: *couldn't* or *could not*.

*Notice: CORRECT: *Bob can play the piano.*
              INCORRECT: *Bob can to play the piano.*
              INCORRECT: *Bob can plays the piano.*

☐ **EXERCISE 2:** Complete the sentences with *can* and *can't*.

1. A cat _____ *can* _____ climb trees, but it _____ *can't* _____ fly.

2. A fish _____ walk, but it _____ swim.

3. A dog _____ bark, but it _____ sing.

4. You _____ buy stamps at the post office, but you _____ buy shoes there.

5. A tiny baby _____ cry, but it _____ talk.

6. I _____ write with a pen, but I _____ write with a paper clip.

7. I _____ read a book by moonlight, but I _____ read in sunlight.

8. Trees _____ produce oxygen, but rocks _____.

9. Fish _____ live in air, but they _____ live in water.

10. You _____ store water in a glass jar, but you _____ store it in a paper bag.

11. You _____ drive from the Philippines to Australia, but you _____ drive from Italy to Austria.

12. You _____ ride on the back of a cat, but you _____ ride on the back of a horse.

13. Jack's friends are going to the park to play soccer. Jack wants to play too, but he has a broken toe, so he's on crutches. Jack _____ go to the park and watch the game, but he _____ play in the game.

14. Laurie has to go to the airport. The airport is 25 miles (40 kilometers) from her house. She _____ walk to the airport. It's too far. She _____ take a bus, however.

☐ **EXERCISE 3—ORAL (BOOKS CLOSED):** Use *can*.

1. What abilities and talents do you have? Tell the class about some of the things you can do. Can you swim? Whistle? Play the piano? Cook?

2. Tell the class about some abilities or talents that you don't have—things that you can't do.

3. Ask a classmate if he or she has a certain ability or talent.

   Example: STUDENT A: (...), can you play pool?
   STUDENT B: Yes, I can. OR: No, I can't.

4. (...) wants to go to the zoo. Tell him/her what he/she can see at the zoo.

5. (...) wants to buy a hammer. Tell him/her where he/she can get a hammer. A wristwatch? Some bananas? Tennis balls? A haircut?

6. (...) has to go to the airport tomorrow. How can he/she get there?

7. (...) is bored on weekends. Tell him/her some things he/she can do on weekends in (*this city*).

8. (...) wants to go out to eat tonight. Where can he/she get a good meal?

9. (...) is interested in science. What are some of the courses he/she can take at a university?

10. What are some things you can find in (a library, a computer room, a language lab, etc.)?

11. (...) has four days to take a trip somewhere. She/He is going to drive her/his friend's car. Where can she/he go? Where can't she/he go?

12. The temperature is around _____ degrees today. It's a (cold, hot, nice, etc.) day. (...) and (...) don't have class later today. They don't want to go home. Where can/can't they go?

13. (...) is going to a dinner party at a fancy restaurant tonight. He/She doesn't know what to wear. Suggest to him/her things that he/she can and can't wear.

14. You are going to a department store this afternoon. You have (a certain amount of money). You intend to spend all of it. What can and can't you buy?

☐ EXERCISE 4—ORAL (BOOKS CLOSED): Use *could*.

1. What could you do when you were a child that you can't do now?
2. What could you do when you were living in your own country or hometown that you can't do now?
3. What did you want to do yesterday or last week but couldn't do? Why couldn't you do it?
4. Who has missed class recently? When? Why?
5. Who has had a cold or the flu recently? What couldn't you do when you were sick?

5-3 EXPRESSING POSSIBILITY: *MAY* AND *MIGHT*
EXPRESSING PERMISSION: *MAY* AND *CAN*

(a) It **may rain** tomorrow. (b) It **might rain** tomorrow. (c) A: Why isn't John in class? B: I don't know. He $\left\{ \begin{array}{l} \textbf{\textit{may}} \\ \textbf{\textit{might}} \end{array} \right\}$ be sick today.	**May** and **might** express *possibility* in the present or future. They have the same meaning. There is no difference in meaning between (a) and (b).
(d) It **may not rain** tomorrow. (e) It **might not rain** tomorrow.	Negative: **may not** and **might not**. (Do not contract **may** and **might** with **not**.)
(f) **Maybe** it will rain tomorrow. (g) **Maybe** John is sick. (h) John **may be** sick.	**Maybe** (spelled as one word) is an adverb meaning "perhaps." Notice (f) and (g). **May be** (spelled as two words) is a verb form, as in (h): the auxiliary **may** + the main verb **be**.
(i) Yes, children, you **may have** a cookie after dinner. (j) Okay, kids, you **can have** a cookie after dinner.	**May** is also used to give *permission*. Often **can** is used to give *permission*, too. (i) and (j) have the same meaning, but **may** is more formal than **can**.
(k) You **may not** have a cookie. You **can't have** a cookie.	**May not** and **cannot** (**can't**) are used to deny permission (i.e., to say "no").

☐ EXERCISE 5—ORAL (BOOKS CLOSED): Answer the questions. Include at least three possibilities in the answer to a question, using *may, might,* and *maybe* as in the example.

      Example: What are you going to do tomorrow?
      Response: I don't know. I *may* go downtown. Or I *might* go to the
                   laundromat. *Maybe* I'll study all day. Who knows?

1. What are you going to do tomorrow night?
2. What's the weather going to be like tomorrow?
3. What is (. . .) going to do tonight?
4. I'm taking something out of my briefcase/purse/pocket/wallet. It's small and I'm holding it in my fist. What is it?
5. What does (. . .) have in her purse?
6. What does (. . .) have in his pants pockets?
7. (. . .) isn't in class today. Where is he/she?

8. You have another class after this one. What are you going to do in that class?

9. We have a vacation (*during a certain time*). What are you going to do during vacation?

10. What are you going to do this weekend?

11. What is (. . .) going to do after class today?

12. What are you going to do after you graduate?

□ EXERCISE 6—ORAL: Make sentences with *may, might,* and *maybe* based on given situations. Notice: Some of the situations are future, and some of them are present.

1. You don't have any special plans for this coming weekend. (*I may . . . . Or I might . . . . Maybe I'll . . . .*)

2. It's midnight. Your roommate/spouse isn't home. Where is he/she?

3. (. . .) wants to buy a sandwich. The sandwich costs (*a certain amount of money*). (. . .) has only (*a lesser amount of money*) in her/his pocket. What is she/he going to do?

4. Your friends are coming to your home for dinner. What are you going to make (i.e., cook) for them?

5. You want to go on a picnic tomorrow, but the weather forecaster predicts rain for tomorrow. What are you going to do if you can't go on a picnic?

6. It is late at night. You hear a strange noise. What is it?

7. What is your (younger sister/younger brother/daughter/son/niece/nephew) going to be when she or he grows up?

8. Look at the picture. What is the man's occupation? What is the woman's occupation?

5-4 USING *COULD* TO EXPRESS POSSIBILITY

(a) A: Why isn't Greg in class?
   B: I don't know. He ***could be*** sick.
 	
(b) Look at those dark clouds. It
   could start raining any minute.
	Could can mean *past ability* (see Chart 5-2). But that is not its only meaning. Another meaning of ***could*** is *possibility*.
	In (a): "He *could* be sick" has the same meaning as "He *may/might* be sick," i.e., "It is possible that he is sick."
	In (a), ***could*** expresses a **present** possibility.
	In (b), ***could*** expresses a **future** possibility.

☐ **EXERCISE 7—ORAL (BOOKS CLOSED):** Listen to the clues; then make guesses. Use ***could, may,*** and ***might***.

> *Example:* made of metal and you keep it in a pocket
> TEACHER: I'm thinking of something made of metal that you can find in my pocket. What could it be?
> STUDENTS: It could be a pen. It could be some keys. It might be a paper clip. It may be a small pocket knife. It could be a coin.
> TEACHER: (...) was right! I was thinking of the keys in my pocket.

1. has wheels and a motor
2. is made of plastic and can be found in my purse/pocket
3. is brown, is made of leather, and is in this room
4. is flat and rectangular
5. is white, hard, and in this room

6. is played with a ball on a large field
7. has (*three*) stories/storeys and is made of (*brick*)
8. has four legs and is found on a farm
9. is green and we can see it out that window
10. is sweet and you can eat it

5-5 ASKING FOR PERMISSION: *MAY I, COULD I, CAN I*

POLITE QUESTION	POSSIBLE ANSWERS	
(a) ***May I*** please borrow your pen? (b) ***Could I*** please borrow your pen? (c) ***Can I*** please borrow your pen?	Yes. Yes. Of course. Yes. Certainly. Of course. Certainly.	People use ***may I, could I,*** ★ and ***can I*** to ask polite questions. The questions ask for someone's permission. (a), (b), and (c) have basically the same meaning. Note: ***can I*** is less formal than ***may I*** and ***could I***.
	Sure. (*informal*) Okay. (*informal*) Uh-huh. (*meaning* "yes")	***Please*** can come at the end of the question: *May I borrow your pen, please?* ***Please*** can be omitted from the question: *May I borrow your pen?*

★In a polite question, ***could*** is NOT the past form of ***can***.

□ **EXERCISE 8:** Following are some phone conversations. Complete the dialogues. Use *may I, could I,* or *can I* + a verb from the list. Note: The caller is SPEAKER B.

           help   leave   speak/talk   take

1. A: Hello?
   B: Hello. Is Dick there?
   A: Yes, he is.
   B: _____ to him?
   A: Just a minute. I'll get him.

2. A: Hello. Dean Black's office.
   B: _____ to Dean Black?
   A: May I ask who is calling?
   B: Susan Abbott.
   A: Just a moment, Ms. Abbott. I'll connect you.

3. A: Hello?
   B: Hi. This is Bob. _____ to Steve?
   A: Sure. Hang on.

4. A: Good afternoon. Dr. Anderson's office. _____
      _____ you?
   B: Yes. I'd like to make an appointment with Dr. Anderson.
   A: Fine. Is Friday morning at ten all right?
   B: Yes. Thank you.
   A: Your name?

5. A: Hello?
   B: Hello. _____ to Emily?
   A: She's not at home right now. _____ a message?
   B: No thanks. I'll call later.

6. A: Hello?
   B: Hello. _____ to Mary?
   A: She's not here right now.
   B: Oh. _____ a message?
   A: Certainly. Just a minute. I have to get a pen.

7. A: Hello?
   B: Hello. _____ to Jack?
   A: Who?
   B: Jack. Jack Butler.
   A: There's no one here by that name. I'm afraid you have the wrong
      number.
   B: Is this 221–3892?
   A: No, it's not.
   B: Oh. I'm sorry.
   A: That's okay.

□ **EXERCISE 9—ORAL (BOOKS CLOSED):** Ask a classmate a polite question. Use *may I, could I,* or *can I.*

> *Example:* (...) has a book. You want to see it for a minute.
> STUDENT A: May/Could/Can I (please) see your book for a minute?
> STUDENT B: Of course./Sure./etc.
> STUDENT A: Thank you./Thanks.

1. (...) has a dictionary. You want to see it for a minute.
2. (...) has a pen. You want to use it for a minute.
3. (...) has a calculator. You want to borrow it.
4. (...) has a camera. You want to see it for a minute.
5. You want to see something that a classmate has.
6. You want to use something that a classmate has.
7. You want to borrow something that a classmate has.
8. You are at a restaurant. (...) is your waiter/waitress. You have finished your meal. You want the check.
9. You are at (...)'s house. You want to use the phone.
10. (...) is carrying some heavy packages. What are you going to say to him/her?
11. You are speaking to one of your teachers. You want to leave class early today.
12. You're in a store. Your bill is (*a certain amount of money*). You have only (*a lesser amount of money*). What are you going to say to your friend?
13. You have a job at (*name of a local store*). A customer walks to your counter. What are you going to say to the customer?

5-6 ASKING FOR ASSISTANCE: *WOULD YOU, COULD YOU, WILL YOU, CAN YOU*

POLITE QUESTION	POSSIBLE ANSWERS*	
(a) **Would you** please open the door? (b) **Could you** please open the door? (c) **Will you** please open the door? (d) **Can you** please open the door?	Yes. Yes. Of course. Yes. Certainly. Of course. Certainly. I'd be happy to. I'd be glad to. Of course. I'd be happy/glad to. Certainly. I'd be happy/glad to. Sure. (*informal*) Okay. (*informal*) My pleasure. (*informal*) Uh-huh. (*meaning* "yes")	People use **would you**, **could you**, **will you**, and **can you** to ask polite questions. The questions ask for someone's help or cooperation. (a), (b), (c), and (d) have basically the same meaning. The use of **can**, as in (d), is less formal than the others. NOTE: **May** is NOT used when **you** is the subject of a polite question. INCORRECT: *May you please open the door?*

*Answers to polite questions are usually affirmative. Examples of possible polite negative responses follow:
   I'm sorry, but (I can't, I don't have enough time, my arms are full, etc.).
   I'd like to, but (I can't, I don't have enough time, my arms are full, etc.).

□ **EXERCISE 10:** Complete the dialogues. Use a polite question with *would you/could you/will you/can you* in each. Use the expressions in the list or your own words.

> answer the phone for me   say that again
> get the door for me   turn it down
> open the window   turn the volume up
> pick some up

1. TEACHER: It's getting hot in here. ___**Would/Could/Will/Can you**___
    ___**please open the window?**___

    STUDENT: ___**Of course, I'd be happy to./Sure./etc.**___

    TEACHER: ___**Thank you./Thanks.**___

    STUDENT: You're welcome.

2. FRIEND A: The phone is ringing, but my hands are full. _____

    _____

    FRIEND B: _____

    FRIEND A: _____

    FRIEND B: No problem.

3. ROOMMATE A: I'm trying to study, but the radio is too loud. _____

    _____

    ROOMMATE B: _____

    ROOMMATE A: _____

    ROOMMATE B: That's okay. No problem.

4. SISTER: I'm trying to listen to the news on television, but I can't hear it. _____

    BROTHER: _____

    SISTER: _____

    BROTHER: Don't mention it.

5. HUSBAND: Honey, I'm out of razor blades. When you go to the store, _____

    WIFE: _____

    HUSBAND: _____

    WIFE: Anything else?

6. STRANGER A: Excuse me. _____

    STRANGER B: _____

    STRANGER A: _____

    STRANGER B: You're welcome.

7. PERSON A: Hi.

    PERSON B: Hi. Walabaxitinpundoozit?

    PERSON A: Excuse me? _____

    PERSON B: Walabaxitinpundoozit.

    PERSON A: I'm sorry, but I don't understand.

□ **EXERCISE 11—ORAL (BOOKS CLOSED):** Ask a classmate a polite question.

> *Example:* You want someone to open the door.
> STUDENT A: (. . .), would/could/will/can you please open the door?
> STUDENT B: Certainly./Sure./I'd be happy to./etc.
> STUDENT A: Thank you./Thanks.

You want someone to . . .

1. close the door.
2. lend you his/her eraser.
3. tell you the time.
4. hand you (*something*).
5. shut the window.
6. lend you a quarter.
7. help you.
8. spell (*a particular word*) for you.
9. hold your books for a minute.
10. give (*something*) to (. . .).

11. (. . .) is at your apartment. The phone is ringing, but your hands are full. You want him/her to answer it for you.
12. You and (. . .) are on vacation together. You'd like to have a picture of the two of you together. You see a stranger who looks friendly. You want her to take a picture of you.

13. You wrote a letter to a university. You want your teacher to read it and correct the mistakes.

14. (...) is going to the library. You want him/her to return a book for you.

15. (...) and you are at (*name of a nearby restaurant*). You want (...) to lend you (*a certain amount of money*).

5-7 EXPRESSING ADVICE: *SHOULD, OUGHT TO, HAD BETTER*

(a) My clothes are dirty. I { *should* *ought to* *had better* } *wash* them.		***Should***, ***ought to***, and ***had better*** have basically the same meaning. They mean: "*This is a good idea. This is good advice.*"
(b) You need your sleep. You ***shouldn't*** stay up late.		Negative: ***should*** + ***not*** = ***shouldn't***.*
(c) ***I'd*** better ***You'd*** better ***He'd*** better ***She'd*** better study tonight. ***We'd*** better ***They'd*** better		Contraction of ***had*** = ***'d***. NOTE: Usually ***had*** is the past form of ***have***. However, in the expression ***had better***, ***had*** is used as part of an idiom and the meaning is not past. The meaning is present or future.

*****Ought to*** is usually not used in the negative.

The negative of ***had better*** is ***had better not***, and it often carries a warning of bad consequences.

You had better not be late! If you are late, you will get into a lot of trouble.

☐ **EXERCISE 12:** Complete the sentences. Use ***shouldn't*** + the expressions in the list or your own words.

be cruel to animals	give too much homework
be late for an appointment	miss any classes
drive a long distance	smoke
exceed the speed limit	throw trash out of your car window

1. If you are tired, you ___**shouldn't drive a long distance.**___

2. Cigarette smoking is dangerous to your health. You _____

3. A good driver _____

4. A teacher _____

5. A student _____

6. Animals have feelings, too. You _____

7. It is important to be punctual. You _____

8. Littering is against the law. You _____

FINE FOR
LITTERING
$300.

☐ **EXERCISE 13:** Complete the dialogues. Use ***should, ought to,*** or ***had better***. Choose
from the expressions in the list or use your own words.

borrow some money	*marry somebody who is rich*
call the landlord and complain	*put cotton in your ears*
call the police	*see a dentist*
drink a glass of water	*send her a dozen roses*
find a new apartment	*soak it in cold water*
find a new girlfriend	*speak English outside of class every day*
get a job	*take it back to the store*
go back to the restaurant and ask if	*use a dictionary when he writes*
someone found them	*watch TV a lot*
hold your breath	

1. A: I have a toothache. This tooth hurts. What should I do?★

   B: _____***You should/ought to/had better see a dentist.***_____

2. A: I have the hiccups. What should I do?

   B: _____

3. A: Ali wants to improve his English. What should he do?

   B: _____

4. A: I don't have any money. I'm broke. I can't pay my rent. I don't have
   enough money to pay my bills. What should I do?

   B: _____

———————

★***Should***, not ***ought to*** or ***had better***, is usually used in a question. The answer, however,
can contain ***should***, ***ought to***, or ***had better***, as in the example answer in number one.

5. A: Someone stole my bicycle. What should I do?

   B: _____

6. A: I cut my finger. I got blood on my sweater. My finger is okay, but I'm worried about my sweater. What should I do?

   B: _____

7. A: Tom's spelling isn't very good. He makes a lot of mistakes when he writes compositions. What should he do?

   B: _____

8. A: Ann bought a new tape recorder. After two days, it stopped working. What should she do?

   B: _____

9. A: The refrigerator in my apartment doesn't work. The stove doesn't work. The air conditioner doesn't work. And there are cockroaches in the kitchen. What should I do?

   B: _____

10. A: I asked Mary to marry me. She said no. What should I do?

    B: _____

11. A: I left my sunglasses at a restaurant yesterday. What should I do?

    B: _____

12. A: My husband/wife snores. I can't get to sleep at night. What should I do?

    B: _____

☐ **EXERCISE 14—ORAL:** Discuss problems and give advice.

> STUDENT A: Think of a problem. It can be your problem or a friend's problem. Tell your classmates about the problem and then ask them for advice.
>
> OTHER STUDENTS: Give STUDENT A some advice. Use ***should/ought to/had better***.

Example: A: I can't study at night because the dorm is too noisy. What should I do?
B: You ought to study at the library.
C: You shouldn't stay in your dorm room in the evening.
D: You'd better get some ear plugs.
E: (Etc.)

5-8 EXPRESSING NECESSITY: *HAVE TO, HAVE GOT TO, MUST*

(a) I have a very important test tomorrow. I { *have to* / *have got to* / *must* } *study* tonight.	*Have to*, *have got to*, and *must* have basically the same meaning. They express the idea that something is *necessary*.
	Have to is used much more frequently than *must* in everyday speech and writing.* *Have got to* is generally used only in informal speech and writing.
(b) I *have to* (''hafta'') *go* downtown today. (c) Rita *has to* (''hasta'') *go* to the bank. (d) I've *got to* (''gotta'') *study* tonight.	Usual pronunciation: *have to* = ''hafta'' *has to* = ''hasta'' (*have*) *got to* = ''gotta''
(e) I *had to study* last night.	The past form of *have to*, *have got to*, and *must* (meaning necessity) is *had to*.

*Must means that something is **very** necessary; there is no other choice. *Must* is used much less frequently than *have to* in everyday speech and writing. *Must* is a ''strong'' word.

☐ **EXERCISE 15:** Complete the sentences. Use *have to*, *has to*, or *had to* in each.

1. I went downtown yesterday because _____*I had to go to City Hall.*_____

2. I can't go to the movie tonight because _____

3. I couldn't go to Pete's party last Saturday because _____

4. Josh can't go downtown with us this afternoon because _____

5. When I was in high school, _____

6. If you want to travel abroad, _____

7. I'm sorry I was absent from class yesterday, but _____

8. Erica can't come to class tomorrow because _____

9. I need a car because _____

10. When I worked in my uncle's restaurant, _____

11. If you want to enter the university, _____

12. We wanted to go on a picnic yesterday, but we couldn't because _____

_____

13. I wanted to _____ yesterday, but _____

_____ instead.

□ **EXERCISE 16—ORAL (BOOKS CLOSED):** Practice using *have to, have got to, must,* and *should.*

> *Example:* Tell me something you have to do this evening.
> STUDENT A: I have to go to a meeting.
> TEACHER: What does (STUDENT A) have to do this evening?
> STUDENT B: He/She has to go to a meeting.
> TEACHER: How about you, (...)? Tell me something you have to do this evening.

1. Use *have to*:
   a. Tell me something you have to do today or tomorrow.
   b. Tell me something you have to do every day.
   c. Tell me something you had to do yesterday or last week.

2. Use *have got to*:
   d. Tell me something you have got to do today or tomorrow.
   e. Tell me something you've got to do tonight.
   f. Tell me something you've got to do after class today.

3. Use *must* or *should*:
   g. Tell me something very important that you must do today or tomorrow.
   h. Tell me something that you should do today or tomorrow (but which you may or may not do).
   i. Tell me something a driver must do, according to the law.
   j. Tell me something a good driver should always do.
   k. Tell me something a person should do in order to stay healthy.
   l. Tell me something a person must do to stay alive. (If a person doesn't do this, he or she will die.)
   m. I don't have a driver's license for this state/province, but I want to get one. Tell me something I must do to get a driver's license.

5-9 EXPRESSING LACK OF NECESSITY: *DO NOT HAVE TO* EXPRESSING PROHIBITION: *MUST NOT*

(a) I finished all of my homework this afternoon. I *don't have to study* tonight. (b) Tomorrow is a holiday. Mary *doesn't have to go* to class.	*Don't/doesn't have to* expresses the idea that something is *not necessary.*
(c) Children, you *must not play* with matches! (d) We *must not use* that door. The sign says: PRIVATE: DO NOT ENTER.	*Must not* expresses *prohibition.* (DO NOT DO THIS!)
(e) You *mustn't play* with matches.	*Must + not = mustn't.* (Note: The first "t" is not pronounced.)

☐ **EXERCISE 17:** Complete the sentences with **don't/doesn't have to** or **must not**.

1. The soup is too hot. You _____**must not**_____ eat it yet. Wait for it to cool.

2. You _____**don't have to**_____ have soup for lunch. You can have a sandwich if you like.

3. Liz finally got a car, so now she usually drives to work. She _____ _____ take the bus.

4. Tommy, you _____ say that word. That's not a nice word.

5. Mr. Moneybags is very rich. He _____ work for a living.

6. If you are in a canoe, you _____ stand up and walk around. If you do, the canoe will probably tip over.

7. According to the rules of the game, one player _____ hit or trip another player.

8. The review class before the final exam is optional. We _____ go unless we want to.

9. Most vegetables can be eaten raw. You _____ cook them.

10. You _____ use a pencil to write a check because someone could change the amount you have written on it.

11. When the phone rings, you _____ answer it. It's up to you.

12. When you have a new job, you _____ be late the first day. In fact, it is a good idea to be a few minutes early.

13. A: You _____ tell Jim about the surprise birthday party. Do you promise?

    B: I promise.

14. A: Did Professor Adams make an assignment?

    B: Yes, she assigned Chapters 4 and 6, but we _____ read Chapter 5.

15. A: I _____ forget to set my alarm for 5:30.

    B: Why do you have to get up at 5:30?

    A: I'm going to meet Ron at 6:00. We're going fishing.

16. A: Listen to me carefully, Annie. If a stranger offers you a ride, you _____ get in the car. Never get in a car with a stranger. Do you understand?

    B: Yes, Mom.

17. A: Do you have a stamp?

    B: Uh-huh. Here.

    A: Thanks. Now I _____ go to the post office to buy stamps.

18. A: Children, your mother and I are going to go out this evening. I want you to be good and follow these rules: You must do everything the baby-sitter tells you to do. You _____ go outside after dark. It's Saturday night, so you _____ go to bed at eight. You can stay up until eight-thirty. And remember: you _____ pull the cat's tail. Okay?

    B: Okay, Dad.

5-10 MAKING LOGICAL CONCLUSIONS: *MUST*

(a) A: Nancy is yawning. B: She ***must be*** sleepy.	In (a): SPEAKER B is making a logical guess. He bases his guess on the information that Nancy is yawning. His logical conclusion, his "best guess," is that Nancy is sleepy. He uses ***must*** to express his logical conclusion.
(b) LOGICAL CONCLUSION: Amy plays tennis every day. She ***must like*** to play tennis. (c) NECESSITY: If you want to get into the movie theater, you ***must buy*** a ticket.	COMPARE: ***Must*** can express: • a logical conclusion, as in (b). • necessity, as in (c).
(d) NEGATIVE LOGICAL CONCLUSION: Eric ate everything on his plate except the pickle. He ***must not like*** pickles. (e) PROHIBITION: There are sharks in the ocean near our hotel. We ***must not go*** swimming there.	COMPARE: ***Must not*** can express: • a negative logical conclusion, as in (d). • prohibition, as in (e).

☐ **EXERCISE 18:** Make logical conclusions. Use ***must*** or ***must not***.

1. Tim has been working in the hot sun for the last hour. He just drank one glass of water. Right now he is refilling his glass. (*thirsty?*)
   → Tim ____ **must be thirsty.** ____

2. I am at Eric's apartment door. I've knocked on the door and have rung the doorbell several times. Nobody has answered the door. (*at home?*)
   → Eric ____ **must not be at home.** ____

3. Brian has a red nose and has been coughing and sneezing. (*have a cold?*)
   → Brian _____

4. Sally looks tired. She's been coughing and sneezing. (*feel well?*)
   → Sally _____

5. Adam has already eaten one sandwich. Now he's making another sandwich. (*hungry?*)
   → Adam _____

6. When Joe takes a problem to his grandmother, she always knows how to help him solve it. (*very wise?*)
   → Joe's grandmother _____

7. Kate has a full academic schedule, plays on the volleyball team, has the lead in the school play, is a cheerleader, takes piano lessons, and has a part-time job at the ice cream store. (*have a lot of spare time? busy all the time?*)
   → Kate _____

8. David goes to the video store and rents three movies every night. (*like movies a lot? spend much time with his friends and family in the evenings?*)

   → David _____

9. Jennifer reads all the time. She sits in a corner and reads even when people come to visit her. (*love books? like books better than people?*)

   → Jennifer _____

10. Jake called Betsy and asked her to go to a movie. Betsy told him that she had to study. She has just hung up, and now she's going to get ready for bed and go to sleep. (*want to go to a movie? be tired? want to hurt Jake's feelings?*)

    → Betsy _____

11. The teacher just asked Jason a question. Jason is looking down at the floor and not answering. His ears are getting red. (*know the answer? be embarrassed?*)

    → Jason _____

12. Debbie just got home from school. She slammed the front door, threw her books on the floor, and ran to her room. Now her parents can hear music through Debbie's closed door. (*be upset? want to be alone? want to talk to her parents right now? like loud music?*)

    → Debbie _____

13. A crow is a large black bird. It is a scavenger. That means that it eats dead and rotting animal remains. A crow that lives near a beach looks for shellfish left behind when the tide goes out. It first tries to open a shellfish with its beak, but if it can't, it picks the shellfish up and flies over a hard surface such as a paved road or sidewalk. From this height, it drops the shellfish so that the shell will crack open. After that, it flies down to claim its dinner. (*smart birds?*)

    → Crows _____

5-11 GIVING INSTRUCTIONS: IMPERATIVE SENTENCES

COMMAND
  (a) *General:* **Open** the door!
      Soldier: Yes, sir!
REQUEST
  (b) *Teacher:* **Open** the door, please.
      Student: Okay, I'd be happy to.
DIRECTIONS
  (c) *Barbara:* Could you tell me how to get to the
             post office?
      Stranger: Certainly. **Walk two blocks down**
          this street. Turn left and *walk* three
          more blocks. It's on the right hand
          side of the street.
	Imperative sentences are used to give commands, make polite requests, and give directions.
	The difference between a command and a request lies in the speaker's tone of voice and the use of ***please***.
	Please can come at the beginning or end of a request:
	    Open the door, please.
	    Please open the door.

(d) ***Close*** the window.
  (e) Please ***sit*** down.
  (f) ***Be*** quiet!
  (g) ***Don't walk*** on the grass.
  (h) Please ***don't wait*** for me.
  (i) ***Don't be*** late.
	The simple form of a verb is used in imperative sentences. The understood subject of the sentence is ***you*** (meaning the person the speaker is talking to): (*You*) *close the window.*
	Negative form:
	  Don't + *the simple form of a verb.*

□ **EXERCISE 19:** Complete the dialogues with imperative sentences. Try to figure out something the first speaker might say in the given situation.

1.   THE TEACHER: ***Read this sentence, please./Look at page 33./etc.***
      THE STUDENT: Okay.

2.   THE DOCTOR: _____
      THE PATIENT: All right.

3.   THE MOTHER: _____
      THE SON: I will. Don't worry.

4.   MRS. JONES: _____
      THE CHILDREN: Yes, ma'am.

5.   THE GENERAL: _____
      THE SOLDIER: Yes, sir! Right away, sir!

6.   THE FATHER: _____
      THE DAUGHTER: Okay, Dad.

7.   A FRIEND: _____
      A FRIEND: Why not?

8.   THE WIFE: _____
      THE HUSBAND: Okay.

9. THE HUSBAND: _____

   THE WIFE: Why?

10. THE BOSS: _____

    THE EMPLOYEE: I'll do it immediately.

11. THE FATHER: _____

    THE SON: Okay. I won't.

☐ **EXERCISE 20—ORAL:** Use imperative sentences.

1. Using an imperative sentence, tell another classmate to perform some action in the classroom.

   (STUDENT A to B: *Write your name on the board.* [STUDENT B writes on the board.]

   STUDENT B to C: *Change desks.* [STUDENT C changes desks.]

   STUDENT C to D: *etc.*)

2. Using an imperative sentence, tell a classmate either what to do or what NOT to do in classroom.

   (STUDENT A to B: *Don't interrupt while another student is speaking.*

   STUDENT B to C: *Raise your hand if you want to speak.*

   STUDENT C to D: *etc.*)

3. Tell your listeners what to do in their daily lives to help preserve the earth's environment and natural resources. (*Recycle aluminum cans. Walk instead of driving your car. . . .etc.*)

4. Direct a classmate whose eyes are closed (or who is blindfolded) from one spot in the room to another. Make sure your classmate doesn't bump into any tables or chairs or other people! (*Take two steps straight ahead. Now turn to your left and take one step . . . .etc.*)

5. Give a classmate explicit directions on how to get to a place that is near the classroom building. Don't name the place. Let your classmate figure out which place you are thinking about from listening to your directions. (*Go out the main door. Turn left and . . . etc.*)

☐ **EXERCISE 21—WRITTEN:** Write about one of the following.

1. Give general advice to people who want to (*choose one*):

   a. improve their health.   e. find a job.

   b. get good grades.   f. live life fully every day.

   c. improve their English.   g. get married.

   d. make a good first impression.

   Tell your readers: Do this. Don't do that. You should do this. You shouldn't do that. You ought to do this. You have to do this. You don't have to do that. You must do this. You must not do that. You can do this. You had better do that, etc.

2. One of your friends wants to come to this city. He/She wants to go to school here or get a job here. Write your friend a letter. Give your friend advice about coming to this city to study or work.

3. Explain how to get a date for Saturday night.

5-12 MAKING SUGGESTIONS: *LET'S* AND *WHY DON'T*

(a) A: It's hot today. ***Let's go*** to the beach. B: Okay. Good idea. (b) A: It's hot today. ***Why don't we go*** to the beach? B: Okay. Good idea.	***Let's*** (*do something*) and ***why don't we*** (*do something*) have the same meaning. They are used to make suggestions about activities for you and me. ***Let's*** = *let us*.
(c) A: I'm tired. B: ***Why don't you take*** a nap? A: That's a good idea. I think I will.	People use ***why don't you*** (*do something*) to make a friendly suggestion, to give friendly advice.

☐ **EXERCISE 22:** Complete the dialogues. Use *let's* or *why don't we.*

1. A: The weather's beautiful today. _____

   B: Good idea.

2. A: I'm bored.

   B: Me too. _____

   A: Great idea!

3. A: Are you hungry?

   B: Yes. Are you?

   A: Yes. _____

   B: Okay.

4. A: What are you going to do over spring break?

   B: I don't know. What are you going to do?

   A: I haven't made any plans.

   B: _____

   A: That sounds like a terrific idea, but I can't afford it.

   B: Actually, I can't either.

5. A: I need to go shopping.

    B: So do I.

    A: _____

    B: I can't go then. _____

    A: Okay. That's fine with me.

6. A: Do you have any plans for this weekend?

    B: Not really.

    A: I don't either. _____

    B: Okay. Good idea.

7. A: What time should we leave for the airport?

    B: _____

    A: Okay.

8. A: What should we do tonight?

    B: _____

    A: Sounds okay to me.

9. A: _____

    B: Let's not. _____ instead.

    A: Okay.

□ EXERCISE 23—ORAL: Give suggestions. Use *"Why don't you . . . ?"*

1. I'm thirsty.
2. I'm sleepy.
3. I have a headache.
4. I have a toothache.
5. It's too hot in this room.
6. Brrr. I'm cold.
7. I'm broke.
8. I'm hungry.
9. I have to take a science course next semester. What should I take?
10. Tomorrow is my sister's birthday. What should I give her?
11. I'd like to go to (. . .)'s party tonight, but I should probably stay home and study. What do you think I should do?
12. I'm going to take a vacation this summer. Where should I go?

□ **EXERCISE 24:** Make sentences by combining one of the ideas in Column A with one of the ideas in Column B. Use *if* with the ideas in Column A.*

Example: *If you need some help when you move into your new apartment, please call me.*

COLUMN A (*conditions*)

✓1. You may need some help when you move into your new apartment.

2. The weather may be nice tomorrow.

3. You may have a problem with your visa.

4. I may not be at the airport when your plane gets in.

5. Matt may want to lose some weight.

6. You may be tired.

7. Sara may not get better soon.

8. You may not know the answer to a question on the test.

9. Alice may call while I'm out.

10. You may be hungry.

COLUMN B (*suggestions*)

1. Guess.

2. You should see the International Student Advisor.

3. Why don't you take a nap?

4. Wait for me by the United Airlines counter.

5. Please take a message.

6. I could make a sandwich for you.

7. He should stop eating candy.

✓8. Please call me.

9. She should see a doctor.

10. Let's go sailing.

---

*Use the simple present in the "**if**-clause." (See Chart 3-2.) Do not use **may** in the "**if**-clause."

5-13 STATING PREFERENCES: *PREFER, LIKE . . . BETTER, WOULD RATHER*

(a) I *prefer* apples *to* oranges. (b) I *prefer* watching TV *to* studying.	*prefer* + NOUN + *to* + NOUN *prefer* + -ING VERB + *to* + -ING VERB
(c) I *like* apples *better than* oranges. (d) I *like* watching TV *better than* studying.	*like* + NOUN + *better than* + NOUN *like* + -ING VERB + *better than* + -ING VERB
(e) Ann *would rather have* an apple *than* (*have*) an orange. (f) *I'd rather visit* a big city *than live* there.	In (e) and (f): *would rather* and *than* are followed immediately by the simple form of a verb (e.g., *have, visit, live*).*
(g) *I'd/You'd/She'd/He'd/We'd/They'd* rather have an apple.	Contraction of *would* = *'d*.
(h) *Would you rather* have an apple *or* an orange?	In (h): In a polite question, *would rather* can be followed by *or* to offer someone a choice.

*INCORRECT: *Ann would rather has an apple.*
INCORRECT: *I'd rather visit a big city than to live there.*
INCORRECT: *I'd rather visit a big city than living there.*

☐ **EXERCISE 25:** Complete the sentences with *than* or *to*.

1. When I'm hot and thirsty, I **prefer** cold drinks _____ **to** _____ hot drinks.

2. When I'm hot and thirsty, I **like** cold drinks **better** _____ **than** _____ hot drinks.

3. When I'm hot and thirsty, I **'d rather have** a cold drink _____ **than** _____ a hot drink.

4. I **prefer** chicken _____ beef.

5. I **like** chicken **better** _____ beef.

6. I **'d rather** eat chicken _____ beef.

7. When I choose a book, I **prefer** nonfiction _____ fiction.

8. I **like** rock 'n roll **better** _____ classical music.

9. Tina **would rather lie** on the beach _____ **go** swimming.

10. Tina **likes lying** on the beach **better** _____ **going** swimming.

11. Tina **prefers lying** on the beach _____ **going** swimming.

12. My parents **would rather work** _____ **retire.** They enjoy their jobs.

13. Do you **like** fresh vegetables **better** _____ frozen or canned vegetables?

14. I **would rather take** a picture of a wild animal _____ **kill** it with a gun.

15. Mr. Kim **prefers** tea _____ coffee with his evening meal.

16. I **prefer visiting** my friends in the evening _____ **watching** TV by myself.

17. My brother **would rather read** a book in the evening _____ **visit** with friends.

18. My sister **likes** her math class **better** _____ her biology class.

□ **EXERCISE 26—ORAL (BOOK CLOSED):** Answer the questions **in complete sentences.**

Example: Which do you prefer, apples or oranges?
Response: I prefer (oranges) to (apples).

Example: Which do you like better, bananas or strawberries?
Response: I like (bananas) better than (strawberries).

Example: Which would you rather have right now, an apple or a banana?
Response: I'd rather have (a banana).

1. Which do you like better, rice or potatoes?
2. Which do you prefer, rice or potatoes?
3. Which would you rather have for dinner tonight, rice or potatoes?
4. Which do you prefer, fish or beef?
5. Which do you like better, fish or beef?
6. Which would you rather have for dinner tonight, fish or beef?
7. Which do you like better, Chinese food or Mexican food?
8. Which do you prefer, tea or coffee?
9. Would you rather have a cup of tea after class or a cup of coffee?
10. Which do you like better, hot weather or cold weather?
11. Which do you prefer, rock music or classical music?
12. What kind of music would you rather listen to, rock or classical?

13. Name two vegetables. Which do you prefer?
14. Name two kinds of fruit. Which do you like better?
15. Name two sports. Which do you like better?
16. Name two sports that you play. Which sport would you rather play this afternoon?
17. Name two TV programs. Which do you like better?
18. Name two movies. Which one would you rather see?

☐ **EXERCISE 27—ORAL (BOOKS CLOSED):** Answer the questions in complete sentences. Use *would rather . . . than . . . .*

Would you rather. . .

1. have a cup of coffee or (have) a cup of tea right now?
2. be a doctor or (be) a dentist?
3. be married or (be) single?
4. live in an apartment or (live) in a house?*
5. go to Moscow or (go) to London for your vacation?
6. visit Niagara Falls or (visit) the Grand Canyon?
7. take a nap or go downtown this afternoon?
8. watch TV or read a good book?
9. study chemistry or (study) accounting?
10. be a plumber or (be) a carpenter?
11. go to a football game or (go) to a soccer game?
12. take a long walk this afternoon or go swimming?
13. after dinner, wash the dishes or dry the dishes?
14. go to (*name of a place in this city*) or go to (*name of a place in this city*)?
15. have straight hair or (have) curly hair?
16. be a student or (be) a teacher?
17. have six children or (have) two children?
18. take your vacation in Greece or (take your vacation) in Brazil?
19. have a car or (have) an airplane?
20. be a bird or (be) a fish?

---

*It is possible but not necessary to repeat a preposition after *than.*
    CORRECT: I'd rather live in an apartment *than in a house.*
    CORRECT: I'd rather live in an apartment *than a house.*

1. A: Do you feel like going to a show tonight?

   B: Not really. I'd rather _____

2. A: Which do you like better, _____ or _____

   B: I like _____ better _____

3. A: What are you going to do this weekend?

   B: I may _____, but I'd rather _____

4. A: What kind of music do you like?

   B: All kinds. But I prefer _____ to _____

5. A: What are you going to do tonight?

   B: I should _____, but I'd rather _____

6. A: Let's go on a picnic next Saturday.

   B: That sounds good, but I'd rather _____

7. A: I like _____ better _____

   B: Oh? Why?

   A: _____

8. A: Are you going to _____ tonight?

   B: I'd like to, but I can't. I have to _____,

   but I'd much rather _____

☐ **EXERCISE 29—PREPOSITIONS:** Complete the sentences with prepositions. This exercise contains prepositions that follow adjectives. (See Appendix 1 for a list of preposition combinations.)

1. Alex is afraid ____**of**____ snakes.

2. I don't understand that sentence. It isn't clear _____ me.

3. Mark Twain is famous _____ his novels about life on the Mississippi in the nineteenth century.

4. I'm hungry _____ some chocolate ice cream.

5. Our daughter graduated from the university. We're very proud _____ her.

6. A lot of sugar isn't good _____ you. Sugar is especially bad _____ your teeth.

7. Who was responsible _____ the accident?

8. My coat is similar _____ yours, but different _____ Ben's.

9. Some people aren't friendly _____ strangers.

10. My daughter is crazy _____ horses. She is very interested _____ horses.

11. Sara knows what she's talking about. She's sure _____ her facts.

12. Are you aware _____ the number of children who die each day throughout the world? According to one report, 40,000 children die each day throughout the world, mostly due to malnutrition and lack of minimal medical care.

CHAPTER 6
Asking Questions

6-1 YES/NO QUESTIONS AND SHORT ANSWERS

YES/NO QUESTIONS	SHORT ANSWER (+ LONG ANSWER)	
(a) **Do you know** Jim Smith?	**Yes, I do**. (I know Jim Smith.) **No, I don't**. (I don't know Jim Smith.)	A *yes/no question* is a question that can be answered by ''yes'' or ''no'' (or their equivalents, such as ''yeah'' or ''nah,'' and ''uh huh'' or ''huh uh'').
(b) **Did it rain** last night?	**Yes, it did**. (It rained last night.) **No, it didn't**. (It didn't rain last night.)	
(c) **Are you studying** English?	**Yes, I am**.★ (I'm studying English.) **No, I'm not**. (I'm not studying English.)	
(d) **Was Ann** in class?	**Yes, she was**. (Ann was in class.) **No, she wasn't**. (Ann wasn't in class.)	
(e) **Will Rob be** here soon?	**Yes, he will**.★ (Rob will be here soon.) **No, he won't**. (Rob won't be here soon.)	
(f) **Can you swim**?	**Yes, I can**. (I can swim.) **No, I can't**. (I can't swim.)	

★NOTE: In an affirmative answer (*yes*), a helping verb is not contracted with the subject.
     In (c): CORRECT: *Yes, I am*. (The spoken emphasis is on **am**.)
             INCORRECT: *Yes, I'm*.
     In (e): CORRECT: *Yes, he will*. (The spoken emphasis is on **will**.)
             INCORRECT: *Yes, he'll*.

☐ **EXERCISE 1:** In the following dialogues, the long answer is given in parentheses. Look at the long answer, and then make the appropriate YES/NO QUESTION and SHORT ANSWER to complete each dialogue. Do not use a negative verb in the question.

1. A: _____***Do you know my brother?***_____

   B: No, _____***I don't.***_____ (I don't know your brother.)

2. A: _____

   B: Yes, _____ (Jane eats lunch at the cafeteria every day.)

3. A: _____

   B: No, _____ (That pen doesn't belong to me.)

4. A: _____

   B: Yes, _____ (The students in this class speak English well.)

5. A: _____

   B: Yes, _____ (I slept well last night.)

6. A: _____

   B: No, _____ (Ann and Jim didn't come to class yesterday.)

7. A: _____

   B: Yes, _____ (I'm studying my grammar book.)

8. A: _____

   B: No, _____ (The children aren't watching TV.)

9. A: _____

   B: Yes, _____ (Tim Wilson is in my astronomy class.)

10. A: _____

    B: No, _____ (It wasn't foggy yesterday.)

11. A: _____

    B: No, _____ (I won't be at home tonight.)

12. A: _____

    B: No, _____ (Jason isn't going to be at work tomorrow.)

13. A: _____

    B: Yes, _____ (Karen will finish her work before she
                                              goes to bed.)

14. A: _____

    B: No, _____ (I can't play the piano.)

15. A: _____

    B: Yes, _____ (Some birds can swim under water.)

16. A: _____

    B: Yes, _____ (You should make an appointment to see
                                              the doctor.)

17. A: _____

    B: Yes, _____ (You need to make an appointment to see
                                              the doctor.)

18. A: _____

    B: Yes, _____ (I have a bicycle.)*

19. A: _____

    B: No, _____ (Greg doesn't have a roommate.)

20. A: _____

    B: Yes, _____ (I have to study tonight.)

□ EXERCISE 2—ORAL (BOOKS CLOSED): Answer the questions. Use short answers.

    Example: Do you know how to swim?
    Response: Yes, I do. OR: No, I don't.

    Example: Is (. . .) wearing blue jeans today?
    Response: Yes, s/he is. OR: No, s/he isn't.

1. Is (. . .) in class today?
2. Does (. . .) have a mustache?
3. Is (. . .) wearing a sweater today?
4. Was (. . .) in class yesterday?
5. Did (. . .) come to class yesterday?
6. Is (. . .) from (*name of a country*)?
7. Does (. . .) speak (*name of a language*)?
8. Are you going downtown tomorrow?
9. Will you be in class tomorrow?
10. Can you play the piano?

---

*In American English, a form of **do** is usually used when **have** is the main verb:
    Do you have a car?

In British English, a form of **do** with main verb **have** is not necessary:
    Have you a car?

11. Do you know how to play the violin?
12. Are we going to have a test tomorrow?
13. Can turtles swim?
14. Should people smoke cigarettes?
15. Did you watch TV last night?
16. Do you have a bicycle?
17. Will class begin at (*time*) tomorrow?

18. Does class begin at (*time*) every day?
19. Do giraffes eat meat?
20. Were all of the students in class yesterday?
21. Should I speak more slowly?
22. Is English grammar easy?
23. Was this exercise difficult?

☐ **EXERCISE 3—ORAL (BOOKS CLOSED):** Make questions and give short answers.

> *Example:* (...) is wearing jeans today.
> STUDENT A: Is (...) wearing jeans today?
> STUDENT B: Yes, s/he is.
>
> *Example:* (...) isn't wearing jeans today.
> STUDENT A: Is (...) wearing jeans today?
> STUDENT B: No, s/he isn't.

1. (...) has curly hair.
2. (...) doesn't have a mustache.
3. (...) is going to be in class tomorrow.
4. (...) won't be in class tomorrow.
5. (...) studied at the library last night.
6. (...) can't play the piano.
7. (...) has to study tonight.
8. (...) went to a party last night.
9. (...) is wearing earrings.
10. (...) has dark eyes.
11. (...)'s grammar book isn't open.

12. (...) should close his/her grammar book.
13. That book belongs to (...).
14. (...) and (...) came to class yesterday.
15. (...) wasn't in class yesterday.
16. This book has an index.
17. Most books have indexes.
18. This exercise is easy.
19. (...) will be at home tonight.
20. An ostrich can't fly.

6-2 YES/NO QUESTIONS AND INFORMATION QUESTIONS

<table>
<tr><td colspan="6">A yes/no question = a question that may be answered by "yes" or "no."
    A: Does Ann live in Montreal?
    B: Yes, she does. OR: No, she doesn't.
An information question = a question that asks for information by using a question word: where,
    when, why, who, whom, what, which, whose, how.
    A: Where does Ann live?
    B: In Montreal.</td></tr>
<tr>
<td>(QUESTION WORD)</td>
<td>HELPING VERB</td>
<td>SUBJECT</td>
<td>MAIN VERB</td>
<td>(REST OF SENTENCE)</td>
<td rowspan="4">The same subject-verb word order is used in both yes/no and information questions:

HELPING VERB + SUBJECT + MAIN VERB</td>
</tr>
<tr>
<td>(a)
(b) Where</td>
<td>Does
does</td>
<td>Ann
Ann</td>
<td>live
live?</td>
<td>in Montreal?</td>
</tr>
<tr>
<td>(c)
(d) Where</td>
<td>Is
is</td>
<td>Sara
Sara</td>
<td>studying
studying?</td>
<td>at the library?</td>
</tr>
<tr>
<td>(e)
(f) When</td>
<td>Will
will</td>
<td>you
you</td>
<td>graduate
graduate?</td>
<td>next year?</td>
</tr>
<tr>
<td>(g)
(h) Who(m)*</td>
<td>Did
did</td>
<td>they
they</td>
<td>see
see?</td>
<td>Jack?</td>
<td rowspan="2">In (i) and (j): Main verb be in simple present and simple past (am, is, are, was, were) precedes the subject. It has the same position as a helping verb.</td>
</tr>
<tr>
<td>(i)
(j) Where</td>
<td>Is
is</td>
<td>Heidi
Heidi?</td>
<td></td>
<td>at home?</td>
</tr>
<tr>
<td>(k)
(l)</td>
<td></td>
<td>Who
What</td>
<td>came
happened</td>
<td>to dinner?
yesterday?</td>
<td>When the question word (e.g., who or what) is the subject of the question, the usual question word order is not used. No form of do is used. Notice (k) and (l).</td>
</tr>
</table>

*See Chart 6-3 for a discussion of who(m).

□ **EXERCISE 4—ORAL:** Make questions from the following sentences. Make (a) a YES/NO QUESTION and (b) an INFORMATION QUESTION with where.

    Example: I live there.
    Response: (a) Do you live there?
               (b) Where do you live?

1. She lives there.
2. The students live there.
3. Bob lived there.
4. I'm living there.
5. Mary is living there.
6. I was living there.

7. He was living there.
8. They are going to live there.
9. John will live there.

10. The students can live there.
11. Alice should live there.
12. Tom has to live there.*

☐ **EXERCISE 5:** Make information questions. Use *where, why, when,* or *what time.*

1. A: ____***When/What time** did you get up this morning?***____
   B: At 7:30. (I got up at 7:30 this morning.)

2. A: _____
   B: At the cafeteria. (I ate lunch at the cafeteria today.)

3. A: _____
   B: At 12:15. (I ate lunch at 12:15.)

4. A: _____
   B: Because the food is good. (I eat lunch at the cafeteria because the food is good.)

5. A: _____
   B: In Chicago. (My aunt and uncle live in Chicago.)

6. A: _____
   B: Next week. (I'm going to visit my aunt and uncle next week.)

7. A: _____
   B: Around six. (I'll get home around six tonight.)

8. A: _____
   B: At the library. (George is going to study at the library tonight.)

9. A: _____
   B: Because it's quiet. (George studies at the library because it's quiet.)

10. A: _____
    B: At that corner. (You can catch a bus at that corner.)

11. A: _____
    B: Ten o'clock. (I have to leave at ten o'clock.)

12. A: _____
    B: In Japan. (I was living in Japan in 1988.)

---

*In a question, a form of **do** is used with **have to**.
   Do you have to go there? Where do you have to go?
   Does she have to go there? Where does she have to go?

A question with **what time usually asks about time on a clock. The answer can be *7:30, a quarter past ten, around five o'clock,* etc.
   A question with **when** can be answered by any time expression: *7:30, around five o'clock, last night, next week, in a few days, yesterday,* etc.

13. A: _____

    B: Because they're working on an exercise. (The students are writing in their books because they're working on an exercise.)

14. A: _____

    B: Around seven. (You should call me around seven.)

15. A: _____

    B: Because she's flying her kite in the park. (Yoko is absent because she's flying her kite in the park.)

□ **EXERCISE 6:** Make information questions. Use *where, why, when, what time,* or *what.*

1. A: _____

    B: Tomorrow. (I'm going to go downtown tomorrow.)

2. A: _____

    B: Because I didn't feel good. (I stayed home yesterday because I didn't feel good.)

3. A: _____

    B: To a movie. (I went to a movie last night.)

4. A: _____

    B: At a hardware store. (You can buy a hammer at a hardware store.)

5. A: _____

    B: At 1:10. (Class begins at 1:10.)

6. A: _____

    B: Because I need to buy some stamps. (I have to go to the post office because I need to buy some stamps.)

7. A: _____

    B: Next June. (My daughter will graduate from college next June.)

8. A: _____

    B: At Lincoln Elementary School. (My children go to school at Lincoln Elementary School.)

9. A: _____

    B: Four years ago. (I met the Smiths four years ago.)

10. A: _____

    B: "Try." ("Attempt" means "try.")

11. A: _____

    B: An amphibian. (A frog is an amphibian.)

12. A: _____

    B: An animal that can live on land or in water. (An amphibian is an animal that can live on land or in water.)

13. A: _____
    B: Mostly insects. (Frogs eat mostly insects.)

14. A: _____
    B: "Job or profession." ("Occupation" means "job or profession.")

15. A: _____
    B: Because I need to know it in order to study in the United States.
       (I'm studying English because I need to know it in order to study in
       the United States.)

☐ **EXERCISE 7—ORAL:** Pair up with a classmate. Practice asking questions with *why*.

STUDENT A's book is open. STUDENT B's book is closed.
STUDENT A: Say the sentence in the book. (Then listen carefully to B's
            question with *why* and make sure it is correct.)
STUDENT B: Ask a question using *why*.★
STUDENT A: Make up an answer to the question.

Example: A: I'm tired today.
            B: Why are you tired today?
            A: Because I stayed up late last night.

1. A: I was absent from class yesterday.
2. A: I'm going to the bank after class.
3. A: I went downtown yesterday.
4. A: I took a taxi to school today.
5. A: I need to go to the drugstore.
6. A: I'm going to buy a new dictionary.

_____
★In normal daily conversation, the second speaker (STUDENT B) would usually ask only
"Why?" or "Why not?" However, to practice question word order, STUDENT B should
ask the full question in this exercise.

Example: A: I didn't study last night.

  B: Why didn't you study last night?
  (*Notice: Use a negative verb in the question with* **why.**)

  A: Because I was tired.

7. A: I didn't do my homework last night.

8. A: I'm not coming to class tomorrow.

9. A: I can't come to your party this weekend.

10. A: I didn't eat breakfast this morning.

11. A: I won't be in class tomorrow.

12. A: I don't like the weather in this city.

6-3 USING *WHO, WHO(M),* AND *WHAT*

QUESTION	ANSWER	
(a) **Who** came? S	**Someone** came. S	In (a): **Who** is used as the subject (**S**) of a question. In (b): **Who(m)** is used as the object (**O**) in a question. **Whom** is used in formal English. In everyday spoken English, **who** is usually used instead of **whom**: FORMAL: *Whom did you see?* INFORMAL: *Who did you see?*
(b) **Who(m)** did you see? O S	I saw **someone**. S O	
(c) **What** happened? S	**Something** happened. S	**What** can be used as either the subject or the object in a question. Notice in (a) and (c): When **who** or **what** is used as the subject of a question, usual question word order is not used; no form of **do** is used. CORRECT: *Who came?* INCORRECT: *Who did come?*
(d) **What** did you see? O S	I saw **something**. S O	

☐ **EXERCISE 8:** Make questions. Use *what, who,* or *who(m).*

1. A: _____ ***What did you see?*** _____

   B: An accident. (I saw an accident.)

2. A: _____

   B: An accident. (Mary saw an accident.)

WHO

WHAT

3. A: _____
   B: Mary. (Mary saw an accident.)

4. A: _____
   B: John. (Mary saw John.)

WHO   WHO(M)

5. A: _____
   B: Mary. (Mary saw John.)

6. A: _____
   B: An accident. (An accident happened.)

7. A: _____
   B: A new coat. (Alice bought a new coat.)

8. A: _____
   B: Alice. (Alice bought a new coat.)

9. A: _____
   B: A map of the world. (I'm looking at a map of the world.)*

10. A: _____
    B: Jane. (I'm looking at Jane.)

11. A: _____
    B: The secretary. (I talked to the secretary.)

12. A: _____
    B: His problems. (Tom talked about his problems.)

13. A: _____
    B: The board. (The teacher looked at the board.)

14. A: _____
    B: The teacher. (The teacher looked at the board.)

15. A: _____
    B: The students. (The teacher looked at the students.)

---

*A preposition may come at the beginning of a question in very formal English:
   At what are you looking?
   At whom (NOT *who)* are you looking?
In everyday English, a preposition usually does not come at the beginning of a question.

□ **EXERCISE 9—ORAL:** In spoken English, *is*, *are*, *did*, and *will* are often contracted with question words. Listen to your teacher say the following questions and practice saying them yourself.

1. Where is my book?★
2. What is in that drawer?★
3. Why is Mary absent?
4. Who is that man?★
5. Who are those men?
6. Where are you going?
7. What are you doing?

8. Where did Bob go last night?
9. What did you say?
10. Why did you say that?
11. Who did you see at the party?
12. Where will you be?
13. When will you arrive?
14. Who will meet you at the airport?

□ **EXERCISE 10:** Make any appropriate question for the given answer.

1. A: _____
   B: Yesterday.

2. A: _____
   B: A new pair of shoes.

3. A: _____
   B: Mary.

4. A: _____
   B: Six-thirty.

5. A: _____
   B: To the zoo.

6. A: _____
   B: Because I was tired.

7. A: _____
   B: A sandwich.

8. A: _____
   B: I don't know.

9. A: _____
   B: Tomorrow.

10. A: _____
    B: My brother.

★Often *is* is contracted with *where*, *what*, and *who* in informal writing as well as in spoken English.
Where's my pen?
What's that?
Who's he?

6-4   USING *WHAT* + A FORM OF *DO*

What + *a form of do* is used to ask questions about activities. (Examples of forms of *do: am doing, will do, are going to do, did,* etc.)	

QUESTION	ANSWER
(a) *What **does** Bob **do** every morning?* →	He *goes to class.*
(b) *What **did** you **do** yesterday?* →	I *went downtown.*
(c) *What **is** your roommate **doing**?* →	She's *studying.*
(d) *What **are** you **going to do** tomorrow?* →	I'm *going to go to the beach.*
(e) *What **do** you **want to do** tonight?* →	I *want to go to a movie.*
(f) *What **would** you **like to do** tomorrow?* →	I *would like to visit Jim.*
(g) *What **will** you **do** tomorrow?* →	I'll *go downtown.*
(h) *What **should** I **do** about my headache?* →	You *should take an aspirin.*

☐ **EXERCISE 11:** Make questions. Use *what* + *a form of do.*

1 A: ___***What are you doing?***___ right now?
   B: I'm studying.

2. A: _____ last night?
   B: I studied.

3. A: _____ tomorrow?
   B: I'm going to visit my relatives.

4. A: _____ tomorrow?
   B: I want to go to the beach.

5. A: _____ tomorrow?
   B: I need to go to the library.

6. A: _____ tomorrow?
   B: I would like to go to a movie.

7. A: _____ tomorrow?
   B: I'm planning to stay home and relax most of the day.

8. A: _____ in class every day?
   B: I study English.

9. A: _____ (for a living)?★
   B: I'm a teacher. (I teach.)

★*What do you do?* has a special meaning. It means *What is your occupation, your job?* Another way of asking the same question: *What do you do for a living?*

10. A: _____ if it snows tomorrow
    and you can't get to the airport?
    B: I'll cancel my reservation and book a flight for the next day.

11. A: _____ to improve my English?
    B: You should speak English as much as possible.

12. A: _____ after class yesterday?
    B: He (Steve) went to the post office.

13. A: _____ after class yesterday?
    B: She (Jane) went swimming.

14. A: _____ when he stopped you
    for speeding?
    B: He (the police officer) gave me a ticket.

15. A: _____ ?
    B: She (Yoko) is writing in her book.

16. A: _____ in the winter?
    B: It (a bear) hibernates.

17. A: I have the hiccups. _____ ?
    B: You should drink a glass of water.

18. A: Mike is in trouble with the law. _____?
    B: He should see a lawyer.

19. A: _____?
    B: He (my husband) is a businessman. He works for General Electric.

20. A: _____?
    B: She (my wife) is a computer programmer. She works for the
    telephone company.

☐ **EXERCISE 12—ORAL (BOOKS CLOSED):** Ask a classmate a question. Use *what* + *do*.

    Example: tomorrow
STUDENT A: What are you going to do tomorrow?/What do you want to do tomorrow?/What would you like to do tomorrow?/etc.
STUDENT B: (*Answer the question.*)

1. last night
2. right now
3. next Saturday
4. this afternoon
5. tonight
6. yesterday
7. every day
8. yesterday afternoon
9. this morning
10. last weekend
11. on weekends
12. tomorrow afternoon
13. after class yesterday
14. after class today
15. every morning
16. the day after tomorrow

6-5 USING *WHAT KIND OF*

QUESTION	ANSWER	

(a) ***What kind of*** *shoes* did you buy? ⟶	Boots.
	Sandals.
	Tennis shoes.
	Loafers.
	Running shoes.
	High heels.
	(etc.)
		What kind of asks for information about a specific type (a specific kind) in a general category.
		
		In (a):
		general category = shoes
		specific kinds = boots
		               sandals,
		               tennis shoes,
		               etc.

(b) ***What kind of*** *fruit* do you like best? ⟶	Apples. Bananas. Oranges. Grapefruit. Grapes. Strawberries. (etc.)	

☐ **EXERCISE 13:** Complete each question. Give other possible answers to the question.

1. A: What kind of _____*shoes*_____ are you wearing?

   B: Boots. (*Other possible answers:* _____*loafers / running shoes / etc.*_____)

2. A: What kind of _____*meat*_____ do you eat most often?

   B: Beef. (*Other possible answers:* _____*chicken / lamb / pork / etc.*_____)

3. A: What kind of _____ do you like best?

   B: Rock 'n roll. (*Other possible answers:*_____)

4. A: What kind of _____ would you like to have?

   B: A Mercedes-Benz. (*Other possible answers:* _____)

5. A: What kind of _____ do you like to read?

   B: Science fiction. (*Other possible answers:*_____)

6. A: What kind of _____ do you like best?

   B: Chocolates. (*Other possible answers:*_____)

7. A: What kind of _____ do you prefer to use?

   B: A Macintosh.* (*Other possible answers:*_____)

8. A: What kind of _____ do you have?

   B: _____. (*Other possible answers:*_____)

☐ **EXERCISE 14—ORAL (BOOKS CLOSED):** Answer the questions.

1. What kind of music do you like best?
2. What kind of shoes are you wearing?
3. What kind of food do you like best?
4. What kind of books do you like to read?
5. Who has a car? What kind of car do you have?**
6. I'm going to buy a car. What kind of car should I buy?
7. Who is wearing a watch? What kind of watch do you have?
8. Who has a camera? What kind of camera do you have?
9. Who had a sandwich yesterday/for lunch today? What kind of sandwich did you have?

---

*"Macintosh" is a brand name of a type of computer.

When a question with ***what kind of* involves manufactured products, the answer may either name a particular brand or describe the product's particular attributes (qualities).

    A: What kind of car do you have?   *A: What kind of car do you have?*
    B: A Ford.   *B: A four-door station wagon.*

10. Who had soup yesterday/for lunch today? What kind of soup did you have?

11. Who has a TV? A VCR? What kind?

12. What kind of government does your country have?

13. What kind of job would you like to have?

14. What kind of person would you like to marry?

15. What kind of products can we recycle?

6-6 USING *WHICH*

(a) *Tom:* May I borrow a pen from you? *Ann:* Sure. I have two pens. This pen has black ink. That pen has red ink. ***Which (pen/one) do you want?*** *Tom:* That one. Thanks. (b) ***Which pen*** do you want? (c) ***Which one*** do you want? (d) ***Which*** do you want?	In (a): Ann uses ***which*** (not *what*) because she wants Tom to choose. ***Which*** is used when the speaker wants someone to make a choice, when the speaker is offering alternatives: *this one or that one; these or those.* (b), (c), and (d) have the same meaning.
(e) *Sue:* I like these earrings, and I like those earrings. *Bob:* ***Which (earrings/ones) are you going to buy?*** *Sue:* I think I'll get these. (f) ***Which earrings*** are you going to buy? (g) ***Which ones*** are you going to buy? (h) ***Which*** are you going to buy?	***Which*** can be used with either singular or plural nouns. (f), (g), and (h) have the same meaning.

□ **EXERCISE 15:** Make questions. Use *which* or *what*.

1. A: I have two books. ___*Which book/Which one/Which do you want?*___

   B: That one. (I want that book.)

2. A: _____*What did you buy when you went shopping?*_____

   B: A book. (I bought a book when I went shopping.)

3. A: Could I borrow your pen for a minute?

   B: Sure. I have two. _____

   A: That one. (I would like that one.)

4. A: _____

   B: A pen. (Chris borrowed a pen from me.)

5. A: Do you like this tie?

   B: Yes.

   A: Do you like that tie?

   B: It's okay.

   A: _____

   B: This one. (I'm going to buy this one.)

6. A: _____

   B: A tie. (Tony got a tie when he went shopping.)

7. A: These shoes are comfortable, and so are those shoes. _____

   _____ I can't decide.

   B: These. (You should buy these shoes.)

8. A: There are flights to Atlanta at 7:30 A.M. and 8:40 A.M. _____

   B: The 7:30 flight. (I'm going to take the 7:30 flight.)

9. A: _____

   B: "Very big." ("Huge" means "very big.")

10. A: _____

    B: "Fast." (The meaning of "rapid" is "fast.")

11. A: Would you please hand me a sharp knife?

    B: I'd be happy to. _____

    A: That one. (I'd like that one.)

12. A: Are you a student in the English program?

    B: Yes, I am.

    A: _____

    B: The beginning class. (I'm in the beginning class.)*

13. A: Did you enjoy your trip to Europe?

    B: Yes, I did. Very much.

    A: _____

    B: I visited Poland, Germany, Czechoslovakia, and Italy.

    A: _____

    B: Poland. (I enjoyed visiting Poland the most.)

---

*The differences between *what class* and *which class* and between *what country* and *which country* are often very small.

6-7 USING *WHOSE*

QUESTION	ANSWER	
(a) **Whose** (**book**) is this? (b) **Whose** (**books**) are those? (c) **Whose car** did you borrow?	It's John's (book). They're mine (OR: my books). I borrowed Karen's (car).	**Whose** asks about possession. Notice in (a): the speaker of the question may omit the noun (*book*) if the meaning is clear to the listener.
COMPARE: (d) **Who's** that? (e) **Whose** is that?	Mary Smith. Mary's.	**Who's** and **whose** have the same pronunciation. **Who's** = a contraction of **who is**. **Whose** = asks about possession.*

*See Charts 4-7 and 4-8 for ways of expressing possession.

☐ **EXERCISE 16:** Make questions with **whose** or **who**. The things near Susan belong to her. The things near Eric belong to him.

1. A: _____**Whose basketball is**_____ this?
   B: Susan's. (It's Susan's basketball.)

2. A: _____**Who is**_____ this?
   B: Susan. (This is Susan.)

3. A: _____ that?
   B: Eric's. (It's Eric's notebook.)

4. A: _____ these?
   B: Eric's. (They're Eric's tapes.)

5. A: _____ that?
   B: Eric. (That is Eric.)

6. A: _____ those?
   B: Susan's. (They're Susan's clothes.)

7. A: _____ that?
   B: Susan's. (It's Susan's coat.)

8. A: _____ in a gym?
   B: Susan. (Susan is in a gym.)

9. A: _____ sitting down?
   B: Eric. (Eric is sitting down.)

10. A: _____ hair is longer?
    B: Eric's. (Eric's hair is longer than Susan's.)

11. A: _____
    B: Pedro's. (I borrowed Pedro's umbrella.)

12. A: _____
    B: Linda's. (I used Linda's book.)

13. A: _____
    B: Nick's. (Nick's book is on the table.)

14. A: _____
    B: Nick. (Nick is on the phone.)

15. A: _____
    B: Pat's. (That's Pat's house.)

16. A: _____
    B: Pat. (Pat is living in that house.)

17. A: _____
    B: Sue Smith. (That's Sue Smith.) She's a student in my class.

18. A: _____
    B: Sue's. (That's Sue's.) This one is mine.

□ EXERCISE 17—ORAL: Ask questions with *whose.*

STUDENT A: Pick up, touch, or point to an object in the classroom. Ask a
question with *whose.*
STUDENT B: Answer the question.

Example: (*Student A picks up a book.*)
STUDENT A: Whose (book) is this?
STUDENT B: It's Maria's (book).

Example: (Student A points to some books.)
STUDENT A: Whose (books) are those?
STUDENT B: They're Kim's (books).

☐ **EXERCISE 18—ORAL:** Ask and answer questions about possession. Follow the pattern in the examples. Talk about things in the classroom.

    Example: pen
STUDENT A: Is this your pen?/Is this (pen) yours?
STUDENT B: No, it isn't.
STUDENT A: Whose is it?
STUDENT B: It's Ali's.

    Example: pens
STUDENT A: Are these Yoko's (pens)?/Are these (pens) Yoko's?
STUDENT B: No, they aren't.
STUDENT A: Whose are they?
STUDENT B: They're mine.

  1. dictionary   5. bookbag   9. purse
  2. books   6. briefcase   10. calculator
  3. notebook   7. glasses   11. things
  4. papers   8. backpack   12. stuff*

☐ **EXERCISE 19—WRITTEN:** Make questions for the given answers. Use any appropriate question word. Write **both** the question (A:) and the answer (B:). Use your own paper.

      Example: A: ...? B: I'm reading.
  Written dialogue: **A: What are you doing?**
                   B: I'm reading.

1. A: ...? B: They're mine.   7. A: ...? B: Jazz.
2. A: ...? B: I'm going to study.   8. A: ...? B: Because I didn't feel good.
3. A: ...? B: A Toyota.   9. A: ...? B: This one, not that one.
4. A: ...? B: Mr. Miller.   10. A: ...? B: You should buy that shirt.
5. A: ...? B: It's Bob's.   11. A: ...? B: A couple of days ago.
6. A: ...? B: It means "small."   12. A: ...? B: I would like to go to India.

Stuff is used in informal spoken English to mean miscellaneous things. For example, when a speaker says, "This is my stuff," the speaker may be referring to pens, pencils, books, papers, notebooks, clothes, etc. (Note: **stuff** is a noncount noun; it never has a final **-s**.)

6-8 USING *HOW*

QUESTION	ANSWER	
(a) *How* did you get here? ————⟶	I drove./By car. I took a taxi./By taxi. I took a bus./By bus. I flew./By plane. I took a train./By train. I walked./On foot.	*How* has many uses. One use of *how* is to ask about means (ways) of transportation.
(b) *How old* are you? ——————⟶ (c) *How tall* is he? ——————⟶ (d) *How big* is your apartment? ——⟶ (e) *How sleepy* are you? —————⟶ (f) *How hungry* are you? ————⟶ (g) *How soon* will you be ready? ——⟶ (h) *How well* does he speak English? ⟶ (i) *How quickly* can you get here? ⟶	Twenty-one. About six feet. It has three rooms. Very sleepy. I'm starving. In five minutes. Very well. I can get there in 30 minutes.	*How* is often used with adjectives (e.g., *old*, *big*) and adverbs (e.g., *well*, *quickly*).

☐ **EXERCISE 20:** Make questions with *how*.

1. A: _____*How old is your daughter?*_____
   B: Ten. (My daughter is ten years old.)

2. A: _____
   B: Very important. (Education is very important.)

3. A: _____
   B: By bus. (I get to school by bus.)

4. A: _____
   B: Very, very deep. (The ocean is very, very deep.)

5. A: _____
   B: Very heavy. (My suitcase is very heavy.) I can hardly lift it.

6. A: _____
   B: By plane. (I'm going to get to Denver by plane.)

7. A: _____
   B: Very well. (Roberto speaks English very well.)

8. A: _____
   B: It's 29,028 feet high. (Mt. Everest is 29, 028 feet high.)★

9. A: _____
   B: I'm starving! When's dinner? (I'm very hungry.)

★29,028 feet = 8,848 meters.

10. A: _____
    B: I walked. (I walked to school today.)

11. A: _____
    B: By express mail. (You should send that letter by express mail.)

12. A: _____
    B: It's not very safe at all. (That neighborhood isn't very safe at night.)

13. A: _____
    B: Not very. (The test wasn't very difficult.)

14. A: _____
    B: About 5½ feet. (Mary is about 5½ feet tall.)*

15. A: _____
    B: Not very fast. Usually about 55 miles per hour. (I don't drive very
       fast.)**

6-9 USING *HOW OFTEN*

QUESTION	ANSWER	*How often* asks about frequency.
(a) *How often* do you go shopping?	Every day. Once a week. About twice a week. Every other day or so.* Three times a month.	
(b) *How many times a day* do you eat? *How many times a week* do you go shopping? *How many times a month* do you go to the bank? *How many times a year* do you take a vacation?	Three or four. Two. Once. Once or twice.	Other ways of asking *how often*: *how many times* { a day a week a month a year

Every other day means Monday yes, Tuesday no, Wednesday yes, Thursday no, etc. *Or so* means *approximately*.

☐ EXERCISE 21—ORAL: Ask and answer questions about frequency.

STUDENT A: Ask a question with *how often* or *how many times a day/week/month/year*.

STUDENT B: Answer the question. (Possible answers are suggested in the list of frequency expressions.)

_____

*5 ½ feet = 165 cm.

**55 mph = 88 kilometers per hour.

FREQUENCY EXPRESSIONS

a lot	*every*
occasionally★	*every other*
once in a while	*once a*
not very often	*twice a* } day/week/month/year
hardly ever	*three times a*
almost never	*ten times a*
never	

Example: eat lunch at the cafeteria

STUDENT A: How often do you eat lunch at the cafeteria?

STUDENT B: About twice a week.

1. go to a movie
2. watch TV
3. go out to eat
4. cook your own dinner
5. play cards
6. read a newspaper
7. get your hair cut
8. write a letter to your parents
9. see a dentist
10. buy a toothbrush
11. wake up during the night
12. go to a laundromat
13. go swimming
14. be late for class
15. attend a wedding
16. see a falling star

6-10   USING *HOW FAR*

(a) *It is* 289 miles *from* St. Louis *to* Chicago.★★ (b) *It is* 289 miles { *from* St. Louis *to* Chicago. *from* Chicago *to* St. Louis. *to* Chicago *from* St. Louis. *to* St. Louis *from* Chicago.	The most common way of expressing distance: *It is* + *distance* + *from/to* + *to/from.* In (b): All four expressions with *from* and *to* have the same meaning.
(c) A: *How far is it* from St. Louis to Chicago? B: 289 miles. (d) A: *How far do you* live from school? B: Four blocks.	*How far* is used to ask questions about distance.
(e) *How many miles* is it from St. Louis to Chicago? (f) *How many kilometers* is it to Montreal from here? (g) *How many blocks* is it to the post office?	Other ways to ask *how far:* *how many miles* *how many kilometers* *how many blocks*

★★1 mile = 1.609 kilometers.
  1 kilometer = 0.614 mile.

★*Notice: Occasionally* is spelled with *two* ''c's'' but only *one* ''s.''

☐ **EXERCISE 22:** Make questions.

1. A: _____
   B: 237 miles. (It's 237 miles from New York City to Washington, D.C.)

2. A: _____
   B: 257 kilometers. (It's 257 kilometers from Montreal to Quebec.)

3. A: _____
   B: 919 miles. (It's 919 miles to Chicago from New Orleans).

4. A: _____
   B: Six blocks. (It's six blocks to the post office.)

5. A: _____
   B: Two and a half blocks. (It's two and a half blocks to the bookstore from here.)

6. A: _____
   B: About three miles. (I live about three miles from school.)

7. A: Karen is really into physical fitness. She jogs every day.

   B: Oh? _____
   A: Five miles. (She jogs five miles every day.)
   B: That's great. I usually don't even walk five miles a day.

8. A: I had a terrible day yesterday.
   B: What happened?
   A: I ran out of gas while I was driving to work.

   B: _____ before you ran out of gas?
   A: To the junction of I-90 and 480. (I got to the junction of I-90 and 480.) Luckily, there was a gas station about half a mile down the road.

☐ **EXERCISE 23—ORAL:** In small groups, look at a map of your area and ask each other questions with **how far.**

6-11 EXPRESSING LENGTH OF TIME: *IT + TAKE*

IT + TAKE + (SOMEONE) + TIME EXPRESSION + INFINITIVE*				
(a) *It*	takes		*six hours*	*to drive*	to Chicago from here.
(b) *It*	took	*Janet*	*a long time*	*to finish*	her composition.

*An infinitive = *to* + *the simple form of a verb.* See Chart 10-1.

□ **EXERCISE 24:** Make sentences using *it* + *take* to express length of time.

1. I drove to Los Angeles. (*Length of time: three days*)

   It took me three days to drive to Los Angeles.

2. I walk to class. (*Length of time: twenty minutes*)

   _____

3. George finished the test. (*Length of time: an hour and a half*)

   _____

4. We will drive to the airport. (*Length of time: forty-five minutes*)

   _____

5. Ann made a dress. (*Length of time: six hours*)

   _____

6. Alan hitchhiked to Alaska. (*Length of time: two weeks*)

   _____

7. Jennifer puts on her makeup. (*Length of time: five minutes*)

   _____

8. I wash my clothes at the laundromat. (*Length of time: two hours*)

   _____

6-12 USING *HOW LONG*

QUESTION	ANSWER	
(a) *How long* *does it take* to drive to Chicago from here?	Two days.	*How long* asks for information about length of time.
(b) *How long* did you study last night?	Four hours.	
(c) *How long* will you be in Florida?	Ten days.	
(d) *How many days* will you be in Florida?	Ten.	Other ways of asking *how long*: *how many* + { *minutes* *hours* *days* *weeks* *months* *years* }

□ **EXERCISE 25:** Make questions using *how long*.

1. A: _____**How long did it take you to drive to New York?**_____

   B: Five days. (It took me five days to drive to New York.)

2. A: _____

   B: Twenty minutes. (It takes me twenty minutes to walk to class.)

3. A: _____

   B: Two hours. (It took Mike two hours to finish his composition.)

4. A: _____

   B: Thirty minutes. (It will take us thirty minutes to drive to the stadium.)

5. A: _____

   B: For a week. (Mr. McNally is going to be in the hospital for a week.)

6. A: _____

   B: Four years. (I'll be at the University of Maryland for four years.)

7. A: _____

   B: About an hour. (It takes about an hour to bake a cake.)

   A: How about cookies? _____

   B: Oh, it depends. Maybe thirty minutes. (It takes maybe thirty minutes to bake cookies.)

8. A: _____

   B: Five days. (I was out of town for five days.)

   A: How about Amy? _____

   B: A week. (She was out of town for a week.)

9. A: _____

   B: About fifteen minutes. (It takes me about fifteen minutes to change a flat tire.)

   A: How about the oil? _____

   B: Not long. Maybe twenty minutes. (It takes me maybe twenty minutes to change the oil.)

10. A: _____

    B: A long time. (It takes a long time to learn a second language.)

    A: How about a computer language? _____

    B: That takes a long time, too. (It takes a long time to learn a computer language.)

□ **EXERCISE 26:** Make questions. Use any appropriate question words.

1. A: _____*What are you going to do this weekend?*_____

   B: I'm going to go to a baseball game. (I'm going to go to a baseball game this weekend.)

2. A: There are two games this weekend, one on Saturday and one on Sunday. _____

   B: The one on Sunday. (I'm going to go to the one on Sunday.)

3. A: _____

   B: No, I didn't. (I didn't go to the game yesterday.)

4. A: _____

   B: Sara and Jim. (Sara and Jim went to the game yesterday.)

5. A: _____

   B: About once a month. (I go to a baseball game about once a month.)

6. A: _____

   B: Bob. (I'm going to go to the game with Bob on Sunday.)

7. A: _____

   B: At the corner of Fifth and Grand. (The stadium is at the corner of Fifth and Grand.)

8. A: _____

   B: Six miles. (It's six miles to the stadium from here.)

9. A: _____

   B: Twenty minutes. (It takes twenty minutes to get there.)

10. A: _____

    B: One o'clock. (The game starts at one o'clock.)

11. A: _____

    B: Because I have fun. (I like to go to baseball games because I have fun.)

12. A: _____

    B: I yell, enjoy the sunshine, eat peanuts, and drink beer. (I yell, enjoy the sunshine, eat peanuts, and drink beer when I go to a baseball game.)

☐ **EXERCISE 27—ORAL (BOOKS CLOSED):** Make questions. Use question words.

Example: I'm studying English grammar.
Response: What are you doing? OR: What are you studying?

1. I studied last night.
2. I studied at the library.
3. I studied for two hours at the library last night.
4. I'm going to study tonight.
5. I'm going to study at home.
6. I'm going to study with (. . .).
7. We're going to study together because we have a test tomorrow.
8. I saw (. . .) yesterday.
9. (. . .) called me last night.
10. I talked to (. . .) last night.
11. I go to the library twice a week.
12. The library is two blocks from here.
13. I live in (*name of this city*).
14. I was born in (*name of town*).
15. I grew up in (*name of town*).
16. I stayed home yesterday because I didn't feel good.
17. I'm looking at the board.
18. I'm looking at (. . .).
19. That is (. . .)'s pen.
20. I want this pen, not that one.
21. (. . .) is wearing (*kind of shoes*).
22. I'm going to wear jeans tomorrow.
23. I'm going to write a letter to (. . .).
24. (. . .) wrote me a letter.
25. It's (*distance*) to (*name of city*) from here.
26. I have a (*kind of car*).
27. It takes (*length of time*) to drive to (*name of city*) from here.
28. I drive to (*name of city*) once or twice a year.
29. "Glad" means "happy."
30. The first oil well in history was drilled near Titusville, Pennsylvania, in the year 1859.

6-13 MORE QUESTIONS WITH *HOW*

QUESTION	ANSWER	
(a) ***How do you spell*** "coming"? (b) ***How do you say*** "yes" in Japanese? (c) ***How do you say/pronounce*** this word?	C-O-M-I-N-G. *Hai.* _____	To answer (a): Spell the word. To answer (b): Say the word. To answer (c): Pronounce the word.
(d) ***How are you getting along?*** (e) ***How are you doing?*** (f) ***How's it going?***	Great. Fine. Okay. So-so.	In (d), (e), and (f): How is your life? Is your life okay? Do you have any problems? NOTE: (f) is often used in greetings: *Hi, Bob. How's it going?*
(g) ***How do you feel?*** ***How are you feeling?***	Terrific! Wonderful! Great! Fine. Okay. So-so. A bit under the weather. Not so good. Terrible! Lousy. Awful!	The questions in (g) ask about health or about general emotional state.
(h) ***How do you do?***	How do you do?	***How do you do?*** is used by both speakers when they are introduced to each other in a somewhat formal situation.*

 *A: *Dr. Erickson, I'd like to introduce you to a friend of mine, Dick Brown. Dick, this is my biology professor, Dr. Erickson.*
  B: ***How do you do**, Mr. Brown?*
  C: ***How do you do**, Dr. Erickson? I'm pleased to meet you.*

☐ **EXERCISE 28—ORAL (BOOKS CLOSED):** Ask another student how to spell the given word.

>   *Example:* country
> STUDENT A: How do you spell "country"?
> STUDENT B: C-O-N-T-R-Y
> STUDENT A: Yes, that's right. OR: No, that isn't right. The correct spelling is C-O-U-N-T-R-Y.

1. together	4. planned	7. different
2. purple	5. rained	8. foreign
3. daughter	6. neighbor	9. studying

10. bought	13. beginning	16. occasionally
11. people	14. intelligent	17. family
12. beautiful	15. writing	18. Mississippi

□ **EXERCISE 29—ORAL:** Ask your classmates how to say these words in their native languages:

Example: yes
STUDENT A: How do you say "yes" in Japanese?
STUDENT B: *Hai.*

1. Yes.   3. Thank you.
2. No.   4. I love you.

□ **EXERCISE 30—ORAL:** Ask your classmates how to pronounce these words.

Example:
STUDENT A: How do you pronounce number 9?
STUDENT B: (STUDENT B *pronounces the word.*)
STUDENT A: Good. OR: No, I don't think that's right.

GROUP A:	(1)	(2)	(3)	(4)	(5)	(6)	(7)	(8)	(9)	(10)
	beat	bit	bet	bite	bait	bat	but	boot	boat	bought

GROUP B:	(1)	(2)	(3)	(4)	(5)	(6)	(7)	(8)	(9)	(10)
	zoos	Sue's	shoes	chews	choose	chose	those	toes	doze	dose

□ **EXERCISE 31—WRITTEN:** Make questions for the given answers. Write **both** the question (A:) and the answer (B:). Use your own paper.

Example: A: ...? B: I'm reading.
Written dialogue: **A: What are you doing?**
                      B: I'm reading.

1. A: ...?	B: It means "big."	10. A: ...?	B: Because I....
2. A: ...?	B: Three days ago.	11. A: ...?	B: This one, not that one.
3. A: ...?	B: Once a week.	12. A: ...?	B: 100 (miles/kilometers).
4. A: ...?	B: Fine.	13. A: ...?	B: I'm going to study.
5. A: ...?	B: By bus.	14. A: ...?	B: A bit under the weather.
6. A: ...?	B: Mine.	15. A: ...?	B: How do you do?
7. A: ...?	B: Nonfiction.	16. A: ...?	B: Two hours.
8. A: ...?	B: B-E-A-U-T-I-F-U-L.	17. A: ...?	B: Six o'clock.
9. A: ...?	B: The park.	18. A: ...?	B: Mary.

6-14 USING *HOW ABOUT* AND *WHAT ABOUT*

(a) A: We need one more player. B: ***How about (what about)* Jack?** Let's ask him if he wants to play. (b) A: What time should we meet? B: ***How about (what about)* three o'clock?**	*How about* and *what about* have the same meaning and usage. They are used to make suggestions or offers. *How about* and *what about* are followed by a noun (or pronoun) or the *-ing* form of a verb.
(c) A: What should we do this afternoon? B: ***How about* going** to the zoo? (d) A: ***What about* asking** Sally over for dinner next Sunday? B: Okay. Good idea.	Note: *How about* and *what about* are used in informal spoken English frequently, but are usually not used in writing.
(e) A: I'm tired. ***How about you?*** B: Yes, I'm tired too. (f) A: Are you hungry? B: No. ***What about you?*** A: I'm a little hungry.	*How about you?* and *What about you?* are used to ask a question that refers to the information or question that immediately preceded. In (e): *How about you? = Are you tired?* In (f): *What about you? = Are you hungry?*

□ **EXERCISE 32—ORAL (BOOKS CLOSED):** Respond by using *how about* or *what about*.

Example: I'm looking for a good book to read. Do you have any suggestions?

Response: How about (What about) *Tom Sawyer* by Mark Twain? It's a good book.

1. You and I are having dinner together this evening, (. . .). What time should we get together?
2. I can't figure out what to give my sister for her birthday.
3. I'm hungry, but I'm not sure what I want to eat.
4. We have a whole week of vacation. Where should we go?
5. What time should I call you?
6. Where should we go for dinner tonight?
7. I've already asked (. . .) and (. . .) to my party. Who else should I ask?
8. Some friends are coming to visit me this weekend. They said they wanted to see some of the interesting places in the city. I'm wondering where I should take them.

□ **EXERCISE 33:** Complete the dialogues by using ***how about you*** or ***what about you*** and an appropriate response.

Example: A: What are you going to do over vacation?

B: I'm staying here. _____ ***What about (How about) you?***

A: _____ ***I'm going to Texas to visit my sister.***

1. A: Did you like the movie?

    B: It was okay, I guess. _____

    A: _____

2. A: Are you going to summer school?

    B: I haven't decided yet. _____

    A: _____

3. A: Do you like living in the dorm?

    B: Sort of. _____

    A: _____

4. A: What are you going to have?

    B: Well, I'm not really hungry. I think I might have just a salad.

    _____

    A: _____

5. A: Where are you planning to go to school next year?

    B: I've been accepted by the state university. _____

    A: _____

6. A: Are you married?

    B: _____

    A: _____

☐ **EXERCISE 34—ORAL:** Pair up with another member of the class. One of you will be
STUDENT A and the other will be STUDENT B. During your conversation, find
out as much information about each other on the given topics as you can.

STUDENT A: The following questions are conversation openers. Glance at a
question quickly, then look up—directly into the eyes of
STUDENT B—and initiate the conversation. After the two of you
have explored the topic, go on to the next question (or make
up one of your own).

STUDENT B: Do not look at your text. Answer STUDENT A's questions. Then
ask *How about you?* or *What about you?* to continue the
conversation.

1. How long have you been living in (this city or country)?
2. How do you like living here?
3. Where are you staying?
4. What are you going to do after class today?

5. What are your plans for this evening?

6. What are you going to do this weekend?

7. What are you planning to do at the end of this term/semester?

8. Do you come from a large family?

9. What kind of sports do you enjoy?

10. Do you speak a lot of English outside of class?

6-15 TAG QUESTIONS

AFFIRMATIVE	**NEGATIVE**	A tag question is a question that is added onto the end of a sentence. An auxiliary verb is used in a tag question.
(a) *You **know** Bob Wilson,*	***don't** you?*	
(b) *Mary **is** from Chicago,*	***isn't** she?*	In (a), (b), and (c): When the main verb is affirmative, the tag question is negative.
(c) *Jerry **can play** the piano,*	***can't** he?*	
NEGATIVE	**AFFIRMATIVE**	In (c), (d), and (e): When the main verb is negative, the tag question is affirmative.
(d) *You **don't know** Jack Smith,*	***do** you?*	
(e) *Mary **isn't** from New York,*	***is** she?*	
(f) *Jerry **can't speak** Arabic,*	***can** he?*	

Notice in the following: I (the speaker) use a tag question because I expect you (the listener) to agree with me. I give my idea while asking a question at the same time.*

THE SPEAKER'S IDEA	THE SPEAKER'S QUESTION	EXPECTED ANSWER
(g) I think that you know Bob Wilson.	You **know** Bob Wilson, **don't** you?	**Yes,** I **do.**
(h) I think that you don't know Jack Smith.	You **don't know** Jack Smith, **do** you?	**No,** I **don't.**
(i) I think that Mary is from Chicago.	Mary **is** from Chicago, **isn't** she?	**Yes,** she **is.**
(j) I think that Mary isn't from New York.	Mary **isn't** from New York, **is** she?	**No,** she **isn't.**
(k) I think that Jerry can play the piano.	Jerry **can play** the piano, **can't** he?	**Yes,** he **can.**
(l) I think that Jerry can't speak Arabic.	Jerry **can't speak** Arabic, **can** he?	**No,** he **can't.**

*COMPARE: *A yes/no question:*
   A: Do you know Bob Wilson? (*The speaker has no idea. The speaker is simply looking for information.*)
   B: Yes, I do. OR: No, I don't.

   A tag question:
   A: You know Bob Wilson, don't you? (*The speaker believes that you know Bob Wilson. The speaker wants to make sure that his/her idea is correct.*)
   B: Yes, I do. (*The speaker expects you to answer **yes.** You can, however, answer **no** if you do not know Bob Wilson.*)

☐ **EXERCISE 35:** Add tag questions and give the expected answers.

1. A: You are a student, _____ ***aren't you?*** _____

   B: _____ ***Yes, I am.*** _____

2. A: Erica lives in the dorm, _____

   B: _____

3. A: You don't live in the dorm, _____

   B: _____

4. A: Ted came to class yesterday, _____

   B: _____

5. A: Kathy will be in class tomorrow, _____

   B: _____

6. A: Mr. Lee is at home now, _____

   B: _____

7. A: Our teacher didn't give us a homework assignment, _____

   B: _____

8. A: You can speak Spanish, _____

   B: _____

9. A: Tim and Brian can't speak Arabic, _____

   B: _____

10. A: You should write a letter to your father, _____

    B: _____

11. A: It snows a lot in Minneapolis, _____

    B: _____

12. A: You weren't at home last night around nine, _____

    B: _____

13. A: This is your pen,* _____

    B: _____

14. A: That is Mike's dictionary, _____

    B: _____

15. A: Those are your gloves, _____

    B: _____

16. A: These are Jean's glasses, _____

    B: _____

_____

*When **this** or **that** is used in the first part of the sentence, **it** is used in the tag question:
This is your book, isn't it?
When **these** or **those** is used in the first part of the sentence, **they** is used in the tag
question: *These are your shoes, aren't they?*

17. A: This isn't a hard exercise, _____

    B: _____

18. A: That was an easy test, _____

    B: _____

☐ **EXERCISE 36—ORAL (BOOKS CLOSED):** Ask and answer tag questions.

        Example: You think that someone in this room lives in an apartment.
STUDENT A: (Ali), you live in an apartment, don't you?
STUDENT B: Yes, I do. OR: No, I don't.

        Example: You think that someone in this room lives in an apartment.
STUDENT A: (Ali), (Maria) lives in an apartment, doesn't she?
STUDENT B: Yes, she does. OR: No, she doesn't. OR: I don't know.

You think that someone in this room . . . .

1. lives in the dorm
2. doesn't live in an apartment
3. lives in an apartment
4. doesn't live in the dorm
5. was in class yesterday
6. wasn't in class yesterday
7. came to class yesterday
8. didn't come to class yesterday
9. is married
10. isn't married
11. can speak (*language*)
12. is from (*country*)
13. can't speak (*language*)
14. isn't from (*country*)
15. likes to play (*name of a sport*)
16. will be in class tomorrow
17. can whistle
18. knows (*name of a person*)
19. wore blue jeans to class yesterday
20. has brown eyes

☐ **EXERCISE 37—ORAL:** Ask and answer tag questions.

STUDENT A: Make a statement about a classmate by beginning a sentence
        with *I think that* (name of a classmate) . . . .
STUDENT B: Change that supposition into a sentence with a tag question.
STUDENT C: Answer the question.

    Example:

STUDENT A: *I think that Juan is from Venezuela.* What do you think?
STUDENT B: I'll ask him. Juan, you're from Venezuela, aren't you?
STUDENT C: Yes, I am./Yes, that's right. OR: No, I'm not./No, what makes
        you think that?

NOTE: If a questioner gets an unexpected answer, s/he will often show surprise. Notice the ways STUDENT B expresses surprise:

STUDENT B: You're from Venezuela, aren't you?
STUDENT C: Venezuela? No. I'm from Colombia.
STUDENT B: *Oh?/Really?/You are? Hmm. I wonder why I thought you were from Venezuela.*

Make suppositions about the following topics or any topic of your own choosing. Begin with *I think that* (name of classmate) . . . .

1. hometown
2. place of residence
3. field of study
4. previous English study
5. clothes worn yesterday
6. transportation to school
7. activities before and/or after class
8. contents of a pocket/bookbag/briefcase
9. size and composition of family
10. presence in class yesterday
11. length of time in this city/country
12. etc.

□ **EXERCISE 38—PREPOSITIONS:** Complete the sentences with prepositions. (See Appendix 1 for a list of preposition combinations.)

1. What's the matter _____ you? What's wrong?

2. We can go out for dinner, or we can eat at home. It doesn't matter _____ me.

3. To make this recipe, you have to separate the egg whites _____ the yolks.

4. I don't know anything _____ astrology.

5. I'm looking forward _____ my vacation next month.

6. Dennis dreamed _____ his friend last night.

7. Right now I'm doing an exercise. I'm looking _____ my book.

8. Jim can't find his book. He's looking _____ it.

9. Jim is searching _____ his book.

10. I asked the waitress _____ another cup of coffee.

11. I asked Rebecca _____ her trip to Japan.

12. Does this pen belong _____ you?

CHAPTER 7

The Present Perfect and the Past Perfect

7-1 THE PAST PARTICIPLE

	SIMPLE FORM	SIMPLE PAST	**PAST PARTICIPLE**	
				The **past participle** is one of the principal parts of a verb. (See Chart 2-3.)
REGULAR VERBS	finish stop wait	finished stopped waited	**finished** **stopped** **waited**	The past participle is used in the PRESENT PERFECT tense and the PAST PERFECT tense.★
IRREGULAR VERBS	see make put	saw made put	**seen** **made** **put**	The past participle of regular verbs is the same as the simple past form: both end in **-ed**. See Chart 2-4 for a list of irregular verbs.

★The past participle is also used in the passive. See Chapter 11.

☐ **EXERCISE 1:** Write the PAST PARTICIPLE.

SIMPLE FORM	SIMPLE PAST	PAST PARTICIPLE				
1. finish	finished	*finished*	10. fly	flew	_____
			11. come	came	_____
2. see	saw	*seen*	12. study	studied	_____
3. go	went	_____	13. stay	stayed	_____
4. have	had	_____	14. begin	began	_____
5. meet	met	_____	15. start	started	_____
6. call	called	_____	16. write	wrote	_____
7. fall	fell	_____	17. eat	ate	_____
8. do	did	_____	18. cut	cut	_____
9. know	knew	_____	19. read	read	_____
			20. be	was/were	_____

7-2 FORMS OF THE PRESENT PERFECT

STATEMENT: **HAVE/HAS** + **PAST PARTICIPLE** (a) I **have finished** my work. (b) The students **have finished** Chapter 5. (c) Jim **has eaten** lunch.	The basic form of the present perfect: **have or has** + **the past participle**. Use **have** with *I, you, we, they,* or a plural noun (e.g., *students*). Use **has** with *she, he, it,* or a singular noun (e.g., *Jim*).
(d) **I've/You've/We've/They've** eaten lunch. (e) **She's/He's** eaten lunch. (f) **It's** been cold for the last three days.	With pronouns, **have** is contracted to apostrophe + **ve** ('ve) and **has** to apostrophe + **s** ('s).
NEGATIVE: **HAVE/HAS** + **NOT** + **PAST PARTICIPLE** (g) I **have not** (**haven't**) **finished** my work. (h) Ann **has not** (**hasn't**) **eaten** lunch.	*have + not = haven't* *has + not = hasn't*
QUESTION: **HAVE/HAS** + **SUBJECT** + **PAST PARTICIPLE** (i) **Have you finished** your work? (j) **Has Jim eaten** lunch? (k) How long **have you lived** here?	In a question, the helping verb (*have* or *has*) precedes the subject.

(l) A: Have you seen that movie?
    B: *Yes, I* **have**. OR: *No, I* **haven't**.
(m) A: Has Jim eaten lunch?
    B: *Yes, he* **has**. OR: *No, he* **hasn't**.
	The helping verb (*have* or *has*) is used in a short answer to a yes/no question.
	The helping verb in the short answer is not contracted with the pronoun.

7-3 MEANINGS OF THE PRESENT PERFECT

(time?)	(a) Jim **has** already **eaten** lunch. (b) Ann **hasn't eaten** lunch yet. (c) **Have** you ever **eaten** at that restaurant? (d) I**'ve** never **eaten** there.	The present perfect expresses activities or situations that occurred (or did not occur) "before now," at some unspecified time in the past.★
	(e) Pete **has eaten** at that restaurant many times. (f) I**'ve been** to that theater five or six times. (g) I**'ve had** three tests so far this week.	The present perfect expresses activities that were repeated several or many times in the past. The exact times are unspecified.
	(h) Erica **has lived** in this city *since 1989*. (i) I **have known** Ben *for ten years*. (j) We**'ve been** in class *since ten o'clock this morning*.	When the present perfect is used with **since** or **for**, it expresses situations that began in the past and continue to the present.

★If the exact time is specified, the simple past tense is used. (See Chart 7-4.)

SPECIFIC TIME: Jim **ate** lunch *at 12:00/two hours ago/yesterday.*

UNSPECIFIED TIME: Jim **has** already **eaten** lunch. (*at some unspecified time before now*)

☐ **EXERCISE 2:** Complete the sentences. Use the words in parentheses. Use the PRESENT PERFECT. Discuss the meaning of the present perfect.

1. (*I, meet*) _____*I've (I have) met*_____ Ann's husband. I met him at a party last week.

2. (*I, finish*) _____ my work. I finished it two hours ago.

3. (*she, fly*) Ms. Parker travels to Washington, D.C., frequently. _____ there many times.

4. (*they, know*) Bob and Jane are old friends. _____ _____ each other for a long time.

5. (*it, be*) I don't like this weather. _____ cold and cloudy for the last three days.

6. (*you, learn*) Your English is getting better. _____ _____ a lot of English since you came here.

7. (we, be)   My wife and I came here two months ago. _____

_____ in this city for two months.

8. (he, finish)   Rob can go to bed now. _____

his homework.

9. (he, be)   Matt is at home in bed. _____ sick

for three days.

10. (she, be)   Kate is falling behind in her schoolwork. _____

_____ absent from class a lot lately.

☐ **EXERCISE 3:** When speakers use the present perfect, they often contract *have* and *has* with nouns in everyday speech. Listen to your teacher say these sentences in normal contracted speech and practice saying them yourself.

1. Bob has been in Chicago since last Tuesday. (*"Bob's been in . . . ."*)
2. Jane has been out of town for two days.
3. The weather has been terrible lately.
4. My parents have been married for forty years.
5. Mike has already eaten breakfast.
6. My friends have moved into a new apartment.
7. My roommate has been in bed with a cold for the last couple of days.
8. My aunt and uncle have lived in the same house for twenty-five years.

☐ **EXERCISE 4:** Complete the sentences. Use the words in parentheses. Use the PRESENT PERFECT. Discuss the meaning of the present perfect.

1. (I, write, not)   _____ ***I haven't written*** _____ my sister a letter in

a long time. I should write her soon.

2. (I, write, never)*   _____ ***I've never written*** a letter to the President of the

United States.

3. (he, finish, not)   Greg is working on his composition, but _____

_____ it yet. He'll probably finish it in a

couple of hours.

4. (I, meet, never)   _____ Nancy's parents. I

hope I get the chance to meet them soon.

_____

Never has the same usual position as other frequency adverbs. (See Chart 7-8.) With the present perfect, **never comes between the helping verb (*have* or *has*) and the main verb.

5. (*Ron, never, be*) _____ in Hong Kong, but

he would like to go there someday.

6. (*Linda, be, not*) _____ in class for the last

couple of days. I hope she's okay.

7. (*they, come, not*) The children are late. _____

home from school yet. I hope nothing's wrong.

8. (*we, finish, not*) _____ this exercise yet.

9. (*Alice, go, never*) _____ to the Museum of

Science and Industry in Chicago, but she would like to.

10. (*I, call, not*) _____ Irene yet. I'll call

her tomorrow.

7-4 USING THE SIMPLE PAST vs. THE PRESENT PERFECT

SIMPLE PAST: (a) I ***finished*** my work *two hours ago*. PRESENT PERFECT: (b) I ***have already**** **finished** my work.	In (a): I finished my work at a specific time in the past (*two hours ago*). In (b): I finished my work at an unspecified time in the past (sometime before now).
SIMPLE PAST: (c) I ***was*** in Europe *last year/three years ago/in 1989/in 1985 and 1989/when I was ten years old*. PRESENT PERFECT: (d) I ***have been*** in Europe *many times/several times/a couple of times/once/*(no mention of time).	The simple past expresses an activity that occurred at a specific time (or times) in the past, as in (a) and (c). The present perfect expresses an activity that occurred at an unspecified time (or times) in the past, as in (b) and (d).

*****Already*** has the same usual placement as frequency adverbs. (See Chart 7-8.) ***Already*** means "before." (See Chart 7-9.)

☐ **EXERCISE 5:** Complete the sentences with the words in parentheses. Use the PRESENT PERFECT or the SIMPLE PAST.

1. A: Have you ever been in Europe?

B: Yes, I _____ ***have*** _____. I (*be*) _____ ***have been*** _____ in Europe

several times. In fact, I (*be*) _____ ***was*** _____ in Europe last year.

2. A: Have you ever eaten at Al's Steak House?

    B: Yes, I _____. I (*eat*) _____ there many times. In fact, my wife and I (*eat*) _____ there last night.

3. A: Have you ever talked to Professor Alston about your grades?

    B: Yes, I _____. I (*talk*) _____ to him about my grades a couple of times. In fact, I (*talk*) _____ to him after class yesterday about the F I got on the last test.

4. A: What European countries (*you, visit*) _____?

    B: I (*visit*) _____ Hungary, Germany, and Switzerland. I (*visit*) _____ Hungary in 1988. I (*be*) _____ in Germany and Switzerland in 1990.

5. A: (*Bob, have, ever*) _____ a job?

    B: Yes, he _____. He (*have*) _____ lots of part-time jobs. Last summer he (*have*) _____ a job at his uncle's waterbed store.

☐ **EXERCISE 6:** Complete the sentences with the words in parentheses. Use the PRESENT PERFECT or the SIMPLE PAST. Use the present perfect with *already*.*

  1. A: Are you going to finish your work before you go to bed?

    B: I (*finish, already*) ____**have already finished**____ it. I (*finish*) ____**finished**____ my work two hours ago.

  2. A: Is Jim going to eat lunch with us today?

    B: No. He (*eat, already*) _____. He (*eat*) _____ lunch an hour ago.

  3. A: Do you and Erica want to go to the movie at the Bijou with us tonight?

    B: No thanks. We (*see, already*) _____ it. We (*see*) _____ it last week.

---

*In informal spoken English, the simple past is often used with *already*. Practice using the present perfect with *already* in this exercise.

4. A: When are you going to write your paper for Dr. Roth?

   B: I (*write, already*) _____ it. I (*write*)

   _____ it two days ago.

5. A: When is Jane going to call her parents and tell them about her

   engagement?

   B: She (*call, already*) _____ them. She (*call*)

   _____ them last night.

6. A: This is a good book. Would you like to read it when I'm finished?

   B: Thanks, but I (*read, already*) _____ it. I

   (*read*) _____ it a couple of months ago.

☐ **EXERCISE 7—ORAL:** Ask and answer questions using the PRESENT PERFECT.

STUDENT A: Use **ever** in the question. **Ever** comes between the subject (*you*)
and the main verb.★

STUDENT B: Give a short answer first and then a complete sentence answer.

Use
{
many times
several times
a couple of times
once in my lifetime
never
}
in the complete sentence.

Example: be in Florida★★

STUDENT A: Have you ever been in Florida?

STUDENT B: Yes, I have. I've been in Florida many times. OR: No, I
haven't. I've never been in Florida.

1. be in Europe	9. ride a horse
2. be in Africa	10. ride a motorcycle
3. be in the Middle East	11. ride an elephant
4. be in Asia	12. ride in a taxi
5. eat Chinese food	13. be in (*name of a city*)
6. eat Italian food	14. be in (*name of a state/province*)
7. eat (*a certain kind of*) food	15. be in (*name of a country*)
8. eat at (*name of a restaurant*)	16. be in love

★In these questions, **ever** means *in your lifetime, at any time(s) in your life before now.*

★★When using the present perfect, a speaker might also use the idiom **be to** (*a place*): *Have
you ever been to Florida?*

17. play soccer	21. walk to (*a place in this city*)	
18. play baseball	22. stay up all night	
19. play pool	23. go to (*a place in this city*)	
20. play a video game	24. use a computer	

☐ **EXERCISE 8:** Write the SIMPLE PAST and the PAST PARTICIPLES of these irregular verbs.

1. see	*saw*	*seen*	7. drive	_____	_____
2. eat	_____	_____	8. ride	_____	_____
3. give	_____	_____	9. write	_____	_____
4. fall	_____	_____	10. bite	_____	_____
5. take	_____	_____	11. hide	_____	_____
6. shake	_____	_____			

☐ **EXERCISE 9—ORAL:** Ask and answer questions using the PRESENT PERFECT in order to practice using past participles of irregular verbs.

STUDENT A: Ask a question beginning with "Have you ever...?"
STUDENT B: Answer the question.

Example: eat at the student cafeteria
STUDENT A: Have you ever eaten at the student cafeteria?
STUDENT B: Yes, I have. I've eaten there many times. In fact, I ate breakfast there this morning. OR: No, I haven't. I usually eat all my meals at home.

1. ride a horse	7. drive a semi (a very large truck)
2. take a course in chemistry	8. eat raw fish
3. write a poem	9. hide money under your mattress
4. give the teacher an apple	10. fall down stairs
5. shake hands with (. . .)	11. see the skeleton of a dinosaur
6. bite into an apple that had a worm inside	

☐ **EXERCISE 10:** Write the SIMPLE PAST and the PAST PARTICIPLES.

1. break _____ _____   8. throw _____ _____

2. speak _____ _____   9. blow _____ _____

3. steal _____ _____   10. fly _____ _____

4. get _____ _____   11. drink _____ _____

5. wear _____ _____   12. sing _____ _____

6. draw _____ _____   13. swim _____ _____

7. grow _____ _____   14. go _____ _____

☐ **EXERCISE 11—ORAL:** Ask questions beginning with "Have you ever...?" and give answers.

1. fly in a private plane
2. break your arm
3. draw a picture of a mountain
4. swim in the ocean
5. speak to (...) on the phone
6. go to a costume party

11. sing (*name of a song*)
12. drink carrot juice
13. throw a football
14. blow a whistle

7. wear a costume to a party
8. get a package in the mail
9. steal anything
10. grow tomatoes

□ **EXERCISE 12:** Write the SIMPLE PAST and the PAST PARTICIPLES.

1. have _____ _____
2. make _____ _____
3. build _____ _____
4. lend _____ _____
5. send _____ _____
6. spend _____ _____
7. leave _____ _____

8. lose _____ _____
9. sleep _____ _____
10. feel _____ _____
11. meet _____ _____
12. sit _____ _____
13. win _____ _____
14. hang★ _____ _____

□ **EXERCISE 13—ORAL:** Ask questions beginning with ''Have you ever...?'' and give answers.

1. lose the key to your house
2. meet (. . .)
3. have the flu
4. feel terrible about something
5. send a telegram
6. sit on a cactus

10. sleep in a tent

11. make a birthday cake
12. build sand castles

7. leave your sunglasses at a restaurant
8. spend one whole day doing nothing
9. lend (. . .) any money

13. win money at a racetrack
14. hang a picture on the wall

★***Hang*** is a regular verb (*hang, hanged, hanged*) when it means to kill a person by putting a rope around his/her neck. ***Hang*** is an irregular verb when it refers to hanging a thing (on the wall, in a closet, on a hook, etc.).

☐ **EXERCISE 14:** Write the SIMPLE PAST and the PAST PARTICIPLES.

1. sell _____ _____   9. think _____ _____

2. tell _____ _____   10. teach _____ _____

3. hear _____ _____   11. catch _____ _____

4. hold _____ _____   12. cut _____ _____

5. feed _____ _____   13. hit _____ _____

6. read _____ _____   14. quit★ _____ _____

7. find _____ _____   15. put _____ _____

8. buy _____ _____

☐ **EXERCISE 15—ORAL:** Ask questions beginning with ''Have you ever. . . ?'' and give answers.

1. teach a child to count to ten
2. hold a newborn baby
3. find any money on the sidewalk
4. cut your own hair
5. think about the meaning of life
6. hear strange noises at night
7. read *Tom Sawyer* by Mark Twain
8. feed pigeons in the park
9. tell a little white lie
10. quit smoking
11. buy a refrigerator
12. sell a car
13. hit another person with your fist
14. put off doing your homework
15. catch a fish

★**Quit** can be used as a regular verb in British English: *quit, quitted, quitted.*

7-5 USING *SINCE* AND *FOR*

SINCE		
(a) I *have been* here { since eight o'clock. since Tuesday. since May. since 1989. since January 3, 1988. since the beginning of the semester. since yesterday. since last month.		*Since* is followed by the mention of *a specific point in time*: an hour, a day, a month, a year, etc. *Since* expresses the idea that an activity began at a specific time in the past and continues to the present. The present perfect also expresses the idea that an activity began in the past and continues to the present.
(b) INCORRECT: I am living here since May. (c) INCORRECT: I live here since May. INCORRECT: I am here since May. (d) INCORRECT: I lived here since May. INCORRECT: I was here since May. (e) CORRECT: **I *have lived* here *since* May.**★ CORRECT: **I *have been* here *since* May.**		The *present perfect* is used in sentences with *since*. In (b): The present progressive is NOT used. In (c): The simple present is NOT used. In (d): The simple past is NOT used.
MAIN CLAUSE (present perfect)	*SINCE* CLAUSE (simple past)	*Since* may also introduce a time clause (i.e., a subject and verb may follow *since*). Notice in the examples: The present perfect is used in the main clause; the simple past is used in the "*since* clause."
(f) I *have lived* here	since I *was* a child.	
(g) Al *has met* many people	since he *came* here.	
FOR		
(h) I *have been* here { for ten minutes. for two hours. for five days. for about three weeks. for almost six months. for many years. for a long time.		*For* is followed by the mention of a *length of time*: two minutes, three hours, four days, five weeks, etc. Note: If the noun ends in *-s* (*hours, days, weeks*, etc.), use *for* in the time expression, not *since*.
(i) I *have lived* here *for two years*. I moved here two years ago, and I still live here. (j) I *lived* in Chicago *for two years*. I don't live in Chicago now.		In (i): The use of the present perfect in a sentence with *for* + *a length of time* means that the action began in the past and continues to the present. In (j): The use of the simple past means that the action began and ended in the past.

★ALSO CORRECT: *I have been living* here *since May.* See Chart 7-6 for a discussion of the present perfect progressive.

□ **EXERCISE 16:** Complete the sentence "I have been here . . . ." by using *since* or *for* with the given expressions.

I have been here . . .

1. __*for*__ two months.
2. __*since*__ September.
3. _____ 1988.
4. _____ last year.
5. _____ two years.
6. _____ last Friday.
7. _____ 9:30.
8. _____ three days.
9. _____ the first of January.
10. _____ almost four months.
11. _____ the beginning of the term.
12. _____ the semester started.
13. _____ a couple of hours.
14. _____ fifteen minutes.
15. _____ yesterday.
16. _____ about five weeks.

□ **EXERCISE 17:** Complete the sentences.

1. I've been in this building ......
   - since __*nine o'clock this morning.*__
   - for __*27 minutes.*__

2. We've been in class ....
   - since _____
   - for _____

3. I've been in this city ....
   - since _____
   - for _____

4. I've had a driver's license ......
   - since _____
   - for _____

5. I've had this book ....
   - since _____
   - for _____

□ **EXERCISE 18—ORAL (BOOKS CLOSED):** Answer the questions. STUDENT A should use *since* in his/her answer; STUDENT B should use *for*.

Example: How long have you had this book?
STUDENT A: I've had this book **since** (the beginning of the term).
To B: How long has (. . .) had this book?
STUDENT B: S/he has had this book **for** (five weeks).

1. How long have you been in (*this country/city*)?
2. How long have you been at (*this school*)?
3. How long have you been up today?
4. How long have you known (. . .)?

5. Where do you live? How long have you lived there?
6. How long have you had your wristwatch?
7. Who has a car/bicycle? How long have you had it?
8. How long have you been in this room today?
9. Who is wearing new clothes? What? How long have you had it/them?
10. Who is married? How long have you been married?

☐ **EXERCISE 19:** Add tag questions to the following and give the expected responses.
(See Chart 6-14 if necessary.)

1. A: You've already seen that movie, _____*haven't you?*_____
   B: _____*Yes, I have.*_____

2. A: Alex hasn't called, _____*has he?*_____
   B: _____*No, he hasn't.*_____

3. A: You talked to Mike last night, _____*didn't you?*_____
   B: _____*Yes, I did.*_____

4. A: Jessica has already left for Kansas City, _____
   B: _____

5. A: Steve left for Kansas City yesterday, _____
   B: _____

6. A: You've already eaten lunch, _____
   B: _____

7. A: You didn't eat at the cafeteria, _____
   B: _____

8. A: You usually bring a sack lunch to school, _____
   B: _____

9. A: Rita and Philip have been married for five years, _____
   B: _____

10. A: Kathy has already finished her work, _____
    B: _____

11. A: Janet has a car, _____*
    B: _____

---

*In American English, a form of *do* is usually used with main verb *have* in questions and negatives: *You have a bike, don't you?*
Principally British: *You have a bike, haven't you?*

12. A: We have to hand in our assignments today, _____

     B: _____

13. A: Jack doesn't have to join the army, _____

     B: _____

14. A: You used to live in Los Angeles, _____

     B: _____

15. A: You studied tag questions in Chapter 6, _____

     B: _____

16. A: You haven't forgotten about them, _____

     B: _____

☐ **EXERCISE 20:** Complete the sentences with the words in parentheses. Use the PRESENT PERFECT or the SIMPLE PAST.

1. Carol and I are old friends. I (*know*) _____ her

   since I (*be*) _____ a freshman in high school.

2. Maria (*have*) _____ a lot of problems since she

   (*come*) _____ to this country.

3. I (*have, not*) _____ any problems since I (*come*)

   _____ here.

4. Since the semester (*begin*) _____, we (*have*) _____

   _____ four tests.

5. Mike (*be*) _____ in school since he (*be*) _____

   _____ six years old.

6. My mother (*be, not*) _____ in school since she

   (*graduate*) _____ from college in 1968.

7. Since we (*start*) _____ doing this exercise, we (*complete*)

   _____ six sentences.

8. My name is Surasuk Jutukanyaprateep. I'm from Thailand. Right now

   I'm studying English at this school. I (*be*) _____ at this

   school since the beginning of January. I (*arrive*) _____

here January 2, and my classes (*begin*) _____ January 6.

Since I (*come*) _____ here, I (*do*) _____

many things, and I (*meet*) _____ many people. I (*go*)

_____ to several parties. Last Saturday I (*go*)

_____ to a party at my friend's house. I (*meet*)

_____ some of the other students from Thailand at the

party. Of course, we (*speak*) _____ Thai, so I (*practice,*

not) _____ my English that night. There (*be*)

_____ only people from Thailand at the party. However,

since I (*come*) _____ here, I (*meet*) _____

a lot of other people. I (*meet*) _____ students from

Latin America, Africa, the Middle East, and Asia. I enjoy meeting

people from other countries.

☐ **EXERCISE 21—ORAL (BOOKS CLOSED):** Answer the questions.

(To the teacher: Ask a question that prompts the use of the present perfect, and then immediately follow up with a related question that prompts the use of the simple past.)

Example: What countries have you been in?
Response: Well, I've been in England, and I've been in Mexico.
  Teacher: Oh? When were you in England?
Response: I was in England three years ago.
  Teacher: How about you, (. . .)? What countries have you been in?
    etc.

1. What countries have you been in?

2. What cities (*in the United States, in Florida, etc.*) have you been in?

3. What are some of the things you have done since you came to (*this city*)?

4. Who are some of the people you have met since you came to (*this city*)?

5. What have we studied in this class since (*the beginning of the term*)?

6. What have we done in class today since (*nine o'clock*)?

7-6 THE PRESENT PERFECT PROGRESSIVE

(a) I *have been studying* English at this school since May. (b) Adam *has been sleeping* for two hours.	Form of the present perfect progressive: *have/has* + *been* + *ing* The present perfect progressive expresses how long an activity has been in progress.
(c) How long *have you been studying* English here? (d) How long *has Adam been sleeping*?	Question form: *have/has* + *subject* + *been* + *-ing*
COMPARE (e) and (f). PRESENT PROGRESSIVE: (e) I *am sitting* in class right now.	The present progressive expresses an activity that is in progress (is happening) right now.
PRESENT PERFECT PROGRESSIVE: (f) I *have been sitting* in class { since 9 o'clock. for 45 minutes.	The present perfect progressive expresses the duration (the length of time) an activity is in progress. Time expressions with *since* and *for* are used with the present perfect progressive.

☐ **EXERCISE 22:** Complete the sentences. Use the PRESENT PROGRESSIVE or the PRESENT PERFECT PROGRESSIVE.

1. Mark isn't studying right now. He (*watch*) _____
   TV. He (*watch*) _____ TV since seven o'clock.

2. Kate is standing at the corner. She (*wait*) _____
   for the bus. She (*wait*) _____ for the bus
   for twenty minutes.

3. Right now we're in class. We (*do*) _____ an
   exercise. We (*do*) _____ this exercise for
   a couple of minutes.

4. Scott and Rebecca (*talk*) _____ on the phone
   right now. They (*talk*) _____ on the
   phone for over an hour.

5. I (*sit*) _____ in class right now. I (*sit*)
   _____ since ten minutes after one.

6. A: You look busy right now. What (*you, do*) _____?
   B: I (*work*) _____ on my physics experiment.
   It's a long and difficult experiment.

A: How long (*you, work*) _____ on it?

B: I started planning it last January. I (*work*) _____

on it since then.

☐ **EXERCISE 23—ORAL (BOOKS CLOSED):** Answer the questions. Use *since* or *for* in your answer.

1. How long have you been sitting in class?
2. How long have you been studying English?
3. How long have you been living in (*this city*)?
4. Who lives in an apartment/a dormitory? How long have you been living there?
5. I am standing up/sitting down. How long have I been standing up/sitting down?
6. I began to teach English in (*year*). How long have I been teaching English?
7. I began to work at this school in (*month or year*). How long have I been working here?
8. We're doing an exercise. How long have we been doing this exercise?
9. Who drives? How long have you been driving?
10. Who drinks coffee? How old were you when you started to drink coffee? How long have you been drinking coffee?
11. Who smokes? When did you start? How long have you been smoking?
12. How long have you been wearing glasses?

7-7 THE PRESENT PERFECT vs. THE PRESENT PERFECT PROGRESSIVE

PRESENT PERFECT: (a) Rita **has talked** to Josh on the phone many times. PRESENT PERFECT PROGRESSIVE: (b) Rita **has been talking** to Josh on the phone for twenty minutes.	The present perfect is used to express repeated actions in the past, as in (a). The present perfect progressive is used to express the *duration* of an activity that is in progress, i.e., how long something has continued to the present time. In (b): Their conversation began 20 minutes ago and has continued since that time. It has been in progress for 20 minutes. It is still in progress.
PRESENT PERFECT: (c) I **have lived** here for two years. PRESENT PERFECT PROGRESSIVE: (d) I **have been living** here for two years.	With some verbs (e.g., *live, work, teach*), duration can be expressed by either the present perfect or the present perfect progressive. (c) and (d) have essentially the same meaning.

□ **EXERCISE 24:** Complete the sentences. Use the PRESENT PERFECT or the PRESENT PERFECT PROGRESSIVE. In some sentences, either form is possible.

1. The post office isn't far from here. I (*walk*) _____ there many times.

2. I'm tired. We (*walk*) _____ for more than an hour. Let's stop and rest for a while.

3. Mr. Alvarez (*work*) _____ at the power company for fifteen years. He likes his job.

4. I (*read*) _____ this chapter in my chemistry text three times, and I still don't understand it!

5. My eyes are getting tired. I (*read*) _____ _____ for two hours. I think I'll take a break.

6. Mrs. Jackson (*teach*) _____ kindergarten for twenty years. She's one of the best teachers at the elementary school.

7. Debbie is writing a letter to her boyfriend. She (*write*) _____ _____ it since she got home from class. It's going to be a long letter!

8. I (*write*) _____ my folks at least a dozen letters since I left home and came here.

□ **EXERCISE 25:** Following is a general review of verb tenses. Complete the sentences by using the proper forms of the words in parentheses.

1. A: (*you, have*) _____**Do you have**_____ any plans for vacation?

   B: Yes, I do. I (*plan*) _____**am planning**_____ to go to New Orleans.

   A: (*you, be, ever*) _**Have you ever been**_ there before?

   B: Yes, I have. I (*be*) _____**was**_____ in New Orleans two months ago. My brother (*live*) _____**lives/is living**_____ there, so I (*go*) _____**go**_____ there often.

2. A: Where's Jessica?

   B: She (*study*) _____ at the library.

   A: When (*she, get*) _____ back home?

   B: In an hour or so. Probably around five o'clock.

A: How long (*she, study*) _____ at the library?

B: Since two o'clock this afternoon.

A: (*she, study*) _____ at the library every day?

B: Not every day, but often.

3. A: Shhh. Irene (*talk*) _____ on the phone long-distance.

B: Who (*she, talk*) _____ to?

A: Her brother. They (*talk*) _____ for

almost an hour. I think her brother is in some kind of trouble.

B: That's too bad. I hope it's nothing serious.

4. A: (*you, know*) _____ Don's new

address?

B: Not off the top of my head. But I (*have*) _____ it at

home in my address book. When I (*get*) _____ home

this evening, I (*call*) _____ and (*give*) _____

you his address.

A: Thanks. I'd appreciate it.

5. A: Where's Juan? He (*be*) _____ absent from class for

the last three days. (*anyone, see*) _____ him lately?

B: I have. I (*see*) _____ him yesterday. He has a bad

cold, so he (*be*) _____ home in bed since the weekend.

He (*be, probably*) _____ back in class tomorrow.

6. A: How long (*you, have to*) _____ wear glasses?

B: Since I (*be*) _____ ten years old.

A: (*you, be*) _____ nearsighted or farsighted?

B: Nearsighted.

7. A: Let's go to a restaurant tonight.

B: Okay. Where should we go?

A: (*you, like*) _____ Thai food?

B: I don't know. I (*eat, never*) _____ any. What's it like?

A: It's delicious, but it can be pretty hot!

B: That's okay. I (*love*) _____ really hot food.

A: There (be) _____ a Thai restaurant downtown. I (go) _____ there a couple of times. The food is excellent.

B: Sounds good. I (be, never) _____ to a Thai restaurant, so it (be) _____ a new experience for me. After we (get) _____ there, can you explain the menu to me?

A: Sure. And if I can't, our waiter or waitress can.

8. A: (you, smoke) _____?

B: Yes, I do.

A: How long (you, smoke) _____?

B: Well, let me see. I (smoke) _____ since I (be) _____ seventeen. So I (smoke) _____ for almost four years.

A: Why (you, start) _____?

B: Because I (be) _____ a dumb, stupid kid.

A: (you, want) _____ to quit?

B: Yes. I (plan) _____ to quit very soon. In fact, I (decide) _____ to quit on my next birthday. My twenty-first birthday is two weeks from now. On that day, I (smoke) _____ my last cigarette.

A: That's terrific! You (feel) _____ much better after you (stop) _____ smoking.

B: (you, smoke, ever) _____?

A: No, I haven't. I (have, never) _____ a cigarette in my life. When I (be) _____ ten years old, I (smoke) _____ one of my uncle's cigars. My sister and I (sneak) _____ a couple of his cigars out of the house and (go) _____ behind the garage to smoke them. Both of us (get) _____ sick. I (have, not) _____ anything to smoke since then.

B: That's smart.

7-8 MIDSENTENCE ADVERBS

(a) I **always** get up at 6:30. (b) You **probably** know the right answer.	Some adverbs typically occur in the middle of a sentence, not at the beginning or end of a sentence. These adverbs, such as **always**, are called "midsentence adverbs."

<table>
<tr>
<td colspan="2">

LIST OF COMMON MIDSENTENCE ADVERBS

FREQUENCY ADVERBS   OTHER MIDSENTENCE ADVERBS

positive
- ever
- always
- almost always
- usually★
- often★
- frequently★
- generally★
- sometimes★
- occasionally★

already★
finally
just
probably

---

negative
- seldom
- rarely
- hardly ever
- almost never
- never
- not ever

</td>
<td>

The adverbs in the list usually occur in the middle of a sentence. When these adverbs occur in the middle of a sentence, they have special positions, as shown in examples (c) through (h) below.

The adverbs with an asterisk (★) may also occur at the beginning or end of a sentence.
> I **sometimes** get up at 6:30.
> **Sometimes** I get up at 6:30.
> I get up at 6:30 **sometimes**.

The other adverbs in the list (without asterisks) rarely occur at the beginning or end of a sentence. Their usual position is in the middle of a sentence.

</td>
</tr>
</table>

(c) He **always** comes to class. She **finally** finished her work.	In (c): In a STATEMENT, midsentence adverbs come in front of simple present and simple past verbs (except **be**).
(d) They are **always** on time for class. He was **probably** at home last night.	In (d): Midsentence adverbs follow **be** in the simple present (am, is, are) and simple past (was, were).
(e) I will **always** remember her. She is **probably** sleeping. They have **finally** finished their work.	In (e): Midsentence adverbs come between a helping verb and a main verb.
(f) Do **you always** eat breakfast? Did **Tom finally** finish his work? Is **she usually** on time for class?	In (f): In a QUESTION, the adverbs come directly after the subject.
(g) She **usually doesn't** eat breakfast. I **probably won't** go to the meeting.	In (g): In a NEGATIVE sentence, most adverbs come in front of the negative verb (except **always** and **ever**).
(h) She **doesn't always** eat breakfast. He **isn't ever** on time for class.	In (h): **Always** and **ever** follow a negative helping verb or negative **be**.
(i) CORRECT: She never eats meat. (j) INCORRECT: She doesn't never eat meat.	Negative adverbs (seldom, rarely, hardly ever, never) are NOT used with a negative verb.

☐ **EXERCISE 26:** Add the word in italics to the sentence. Put the word in its usual midsentence position.

always

1. *always*   Tom studies at home in the evening.
                                    ^

2. *always*   Tom is at home in the evening.

3. *always*   You can find Tom at home in the evening.

4. *usually*   The mail comes at noon.

5. *usually*   The mail is here by noon.

6. *probably*   The mail will be here soon.

7. *often*   Ann stays home at night.

8. *often*   Ann is at home at night.

9. *probably*   Ann will stay home tonight.

10. *finally*   Jack wrote me a letter.

11. *finally*   The semester is over.

12. *finally*   I have finished my composition.

13. *always*   Does Tom study at home in the evening?

14. *always*   Is Tom at home in the evening?

15. *always*   Can you find Tom at home in the evening?

16. *usually*   Do you study at the library?

17. *ever*   Is the teacher absent?

18. *just*   What did you say?

19. *usually*   When do you go to bed?

20. *generally*   What time do you eat lunch?

21. *occasionally*   My son stays overnight with a friend.

22. *frequently*   We have company for dinner.

23. *sometimes*   Do you feel homesick?

24. *already*   I have read that book.

25. *already*   The mail is here.

☐ **EXERCISE 27—ORAL:** Add the given words to the sentence. Put the adverbs in their usual midsentence position. Make any necessary changes in the sentence.

     1. Jack doesn't shave in the morning.
         a. usually → *Jack usually doesn't shave in the morning.*
         b. often → *Jack often doesn't shave in the morning.*

c. frequently   g. always   j. hardly ever
d. generally   h. ever   k. rarely
e. sometimes   i. never   l. seldom
f. occasionally

2. I don't eat breakfast.
   a. generally   d. usually   g. occasionally
   b. always   e. never   h. rarely
   c. seldom   f. ever   i. hardly ever

3. Jane doesn't come to class on time.
   a. never   d. occasionally   f. hardly ever
   b. usually   e. always   g. ever
   c. seldom

4. My roommate isn't home in the morning.
   a. usually   d. ever   g. frequently
   b. generally   e. never   h. hardly ever
   c. always   f. seldom

☐ **EXERCISE 28:** Add the word(s) in italics to the sentence. Put the word in its usual midsentence position. Make any necessary changes.

1. *probably*   Brian knows the answer.

2. *usually*   Is Pat at home in the evening?

3. *finally*   They have finished their work.

4. *seldom*   Jack doesn't write letters.

5. *generally*   I don't stay up late. I go to bed early.

6. *probably*   Susan won't come to the party. She will stay home.

7. *never*   You shouldn't allow children to play with matches.

8. *hardly ever*   Jerry isn't in a bad mood.

9. *frequently*   My chemistry lecturer came to class late last semester.

10. *seldom*   The temperature doesn't drop below freezing in Miami.

11. *always*   Rita rides the bus to school.

12. *always*   I don't ride the bus to school.

13. *usually*   Tom doesn't ride the bus to school.

14. *never*   Paul doesn't ride his bike to his office.

15. *often*   Our classroom is too hot.

Respond in complete sentences.

> *Example:* What is something that you always do in the morning?
> *Response:* I always drink a cup of coffee.

What is something that . . .

1. you seldom do?
2. you will probably do tomorrow?
3. you probably won't do tomorrow?
4. you are probably going to do next week?
5. you hardly ever do?
6. you almost always do before you go to bed?
7. you have never done?
8. your roommate/spouse occasionally does?
9. a lazy person seldom does?
10. is always or usually expensive?
11. a polite person usually does?
12. a polite person never does?
13. drivers generally do?
14. your classmates sometimes do?
15. you have already done?
16. you just did?
17. I frequently do in class?
18. I usually don't do in class?
19. you rarely eat?
20. people in your country always or usually do to celebrate the New Year?
21. you usually do, but don't always do?
22. you usually don't do?

7-9 USING *ALREADY, YET, STILL,* AND *ANYMORE*

ALREADY	(a) The mail came an hour ago. **The mail is *already* here.**	Idea of ***already***: Something happened before now, before this time. *Position: midsentence.*★
YET	(b) I expected the mail an hour ago, but **it hasn't come *yet*.**	Idea of ***yet***: Something did not happen before now (up to this time), but it may happen in the future. *Position: end of sentence.*
STILL	(c) It was cold yesterday. **It is *still* cold today.** (d) I could play the piano when I was a child. **I can *still* play the piano.** (e) The mail didn't come an hour ago. **The mail *still* hasn't come.**	Idea of ***still***: A situation continues to exist from past to present without change. *Position: midsentence.*★
ANYMORE	(f) I lived in Chicago two years ago, but then I moved to another city. **I don't live in Chicago *anymore*.**	Idea of ***anymore***: A past situation does not continue to exist at present; a past situation has changed. ***Anymore*** has the same meaning as ***any longer***. *Position: end of sentence.*

NOTE: ***Already*** is used in *affirmative* sentences.
    Yet and ***anymore*** are used in *negative* sentences.
    Still is used in either *affirmative or negative* sentences.

★See Chart 7-8 for the usual positions of midsentence adverbs.

□ **EXERCISE 30:** Complete the sentences with *already, yet, still,* or *anymore.*

1. It's 1:00 P.M. I'm hungry. I haven't eaten lunch _____ **yet** _____.

2. It's 1:00 P.M. I'm not hungry. I've _____ eaten lunch.

3. Eric was hungry, so he ate a candy bar a few minutes ago. But he's

   _____ hungry, so he's going to have another candy bar.

4. I used to eat lunch at the cafeteria every day, but now I bring my lunch

   to school in a paper bag instead. I don't eat at the cafeteria

   _____.

5. It started raining an hour ago. We can't go for a walk because it's

   _____ raining. I hope it stops soon.

6. Look! The rain has stopped. It isn't raining _____. Let's

   go for a walk.

7. I didn't understand this chapter in my biology book when I read it

   yesterday. Since then, I've read it three times, but I _____

   don't understand it!

8. I don't have to study tonight. I've _____ finished all my

   homework.

9. I started a letter to my parents yesterday, but I haven't finished it

   _____. I'll finish it later today and put it in the mail.

10. I started a letter to my parents yesterday. I thought about finishing it

    last night before I went to bed, but I didn't. I _____

    haven't finished it.*

□ **EXERCISE 31:** *Yet* and *still* are frequently used in questions. Complete the following
dialogues by using *yet* or *still.*

1. A: Is Mary home _____?

   B: No, but I'm expecting her soon.

2. A: Is Mary _____ in class?

   B: Yes, she is. Her class doesn't end until 11:30.

---

*In negative sentences, *still* and *yet* express similar meanings. The meanings of *I haven't
finished it yet* and *I still haven't finished it* are similar.

3. A: Has Dennis graduated _____?

B: No. He's still in school.

4. A: I'm hungry. How about you? Did you eat _____?

B: No. Did you?

A: Nope. Let's go eat lunch.

5. A: Do you _____ live on Fifth Street?

B: Not anymore. I moved.

6. A: Has Karen found a new apartment _____?

B: Not that I know of. She's still living on Elm Street.

7. A: Do you _____ love me?

B: Of course I do! I love you very much.

8. A: Is the baby _____ sleeping?

B: Yes. Shhh. We don't want to wake him up.

9. A: Is the baby asleep _____?

B: I think so. I don't hear anything from the nursery. I put him down for his nap fifteen minutes ago, so I'm pretty sure he's asleep by now.

□ **EXERCISE 32:** Complete the dialogues by using *already, yet, still,* or *anymore.*

1. A: Has Rob found a new job _____?

B: No. He _____ works at the bookstore.

2. A: When is your sister going to come to visit you?

B: She's _____ here. She got here yesterday.

3. A: Do you _____ live on Pine Avenue?

B: No, I don't live there _____. I moved to another apartment closer to school.

4. A: Is Anne home _____?

B: No, she isn't. I'm getting worried. She was supposed to be home at eight. It's almost nine and she _____ isn't here.

A: Don't worry. She'll probably be here any minute.

5. A: I'm going to have another sandwich.

   B: What? You just ate three sandwiches!

   A: I know, but I'm not full _____. I'm
   _____ hungry.

6. A: Would you like to see today's newspaper?

   B: Thanks, but I've _____ read it.

7. A: Did you try to call Peter again?

   B: Yes, but the line was _____ busy. I'll try again in a
   few minutes.

8. A: How does Dick like his job at the hardware store?

   B: He doesn't work there _____. He found a new job.

9. A: Is your younger sister a college student?

   B: No. She's _____ in high school.

10. A: When are you going to make Tommy's birthday cake?

    B: I've _____ made it.

11. A: How did you do on your calculus exam?

    B: I haven't taken it _____. The exam is tomorrow. I'm
    _____ studying for it.

☐ **EXERCISE 33:** Using the given information, add *already, yet, still,* or *anymore* to the
sentences in italics.

1. I finished my work two hours ago. *In other words, I have finished my
   work.*

   → ***In other words, I have already finished my work.***

2. Ann didn't finish her work yesterday. She's doing it now. *In other words,
   she hasn't finished it.*

   → ***In other words, she hasn't finished it yet.***

   → ***In other words, she still hasn't finished it.****

---

*Reminder: In negative sentences, *yet* and *still* often express a similar meaning.

3. I expected Mike to come home an hour ago, but he didn't come. *In other words, he isn't home.*

4. I was hungry an hour ago, but I didn't eat anything. *In other words, I'm hungry.*

5. Erica used to work at the drugstore, but she quit her job. *In other words, she doesn't work there.*

6. Susan has been working at the bookstore for a year. She has tried to find a different job, but she hasn't found one yet. *In other words, she is working at the bookstore.*

7. We're late. The movie started half an hour ago. *In other words, the movie has started.*

8. Greg started smoking four years ago. *In other words, he smokes. He hasn't quit.*

9. We studied Chapter 6 last week. *In other words, we've studied Chapter 6. We haven't studied Chapter 8.*

10. When I was a child, I used to read comic books. But they are for kids. *In other words, I don't read comic books.*

11. We started this exercise ten minutes ago. *In other words, we haven't finished it. We are doing this exercise.*

12. When we were little, my sister and I could speak a little French. I don't remember French, but my sister does. *In other words, I can't speak French. My sister, however, can speak French because she practices using it.*

□ **EXERCISE 34—WRITTEN:** Write about one (or both) of the following topics.

1. Think of two or three important events that have occurred in your life in the past year or two. In a paragraph for each, briefly tell your reader about these events and give your opinions and/or predictions.

2. Think of two or three important events that have occurred in the world in the past year or two. In a paragraph for each, briefly tell your reader about these events and give your opinions and/or predictions.

7-10 USING THE PAST PERFECT

COMPARE (a) THE PRESENT PERFECT AND (b) THE PAST PERFECT:		
PRESENT PERFECT before now ✗ — now ✗	(a) I am not hungry now. I *have* already *eaten*.	The present perfect expresses an activity that *occurred "before now," at an unspecified time in the past.*
PAST PERFECT before 1:00 ✗ — 1:00 pm ✗	(b) I was not hungry at 1:00 P.M. I *had* already *eaten*.	The past perfect expresses an activity that *occurred before another time in the past.* In (b): I ate at noon. I was not hungry at 1:00 P.M. because I had already eaten before 1:00 P.M.

COMPARE (c) THE PAST PROGRESSIVE AND (d) THE PAST PERFECT:		
PAST PROGRESSIVE began eating ✗ — Bob came ✗ *eating in progress*	(c) I *was eating* when Bob came.	The past progressive expresses an activity that was *in progress* at a particular time in the past. In (c): I began to eat at noon. Bob came at 12:10. My meal was in progress when Bob came.
PAST PERFECT finished eating ✗ — Bob came ✗	(d) I *had eaten* when Bob came.	The past perfect expresses an activity that was *completed before a particular time in the past.* In (d): I ate at noon. Bob came at 1:00 P.M. My meal was completed before Bob came.

☐ **EXERCISE 35:** Complete the sentences with the words in parentheses. Use the PRESENT PERFECT or the PAST PERFECT.

1. I am not hungry. I (*eat, already*) _____*I have already eaten.*_____.

2. I was not hungry. I (*eat, already*) _____*I had already eaten.*_____.

3. It's ten o'clock. I (*finish, already*) _____
   my homework, so I'm going to go to bed.

4. Last night I went to bed at ten o'clock. I (*finish, already*) _____
   _____ my homework.

5. By the time* I went to bed last night, I (*finish, already*) _____
   _____ my homework.

6. I was late. The party (*start, already*) _____
   by the time I got there.

7. We're late. The party (*start, already*) _____.

8. Carol missed her plane yesterday because of a traffic jam on her way to
   the airport. By the time she got to the airport, her plane (*leave, already*)
   _____.

☐ **EXERCISE 36:** Complete the sentences with the words in parentheses. Use the PAST PROGRESSIVE or the PAST PERFECT.

1. When I left for school this morning, it (*rain*) _____*was raining*_____,
   so I used my umbrella.

2. By the time class was over this morning, the rain (*stop*) __*had stopped*__,
   so I didn't need my umbrella anymore.

3. Last night I started to study at 7:30. Dick came at 7:35. I (*study*)
   _____ when Dick came.

4. Last night I started to study at 7:30. I finished studying at 9:00. Dick
   came at 9:30. By the time Dick came, I (*finish*) _____
   my homework.

_____
*by the time = *before*

5. When I walked into the kitchen after dinner last night, my wife (*wash*) _____ the dishes, so I picked up a dish towel to help her.

6. By the time I walked into the kitchen after dinner, my husband (*wash, already*) _____ the dishes and (*put*) _____ them away.

☐ **EXERCISE 37:** Complete the sentences with the words in parentheses.

1. A: (*you, enjoy*) _____**Did you enjoy**_____ the concert last night?

   B: Very much. I (*go, not*) _____**hadn't gone**_____ to a concert in a long time.

2. A: (*you, see*) _____ John yesterday?

   B: Yes, I did. It (*be*) _____ good to see him again. I (*see, not*) _____ him in a long time.

3. A: Hi, Jim! It's good to see you again. I (*see, not*) _____ _____ you in weeks.

   B: Hi, Sue! It (*be*) _____ good to see you again, too. I (*see, not*) _____ you since the end of last semester. How's everything going?

4. A: (*you, get*) _____ to class on time yesterday morning?

   B: No. By the time I (*get*) _____ there, it (*begin, already*) _____ .

5. A: (*you, go*) _____ out to eat last night?

   B: No. By the time I (*get*) _____ home, my husband (*make, already*) _____ dinner for us.

   A: How (*be*) _____ it?

   B: Terrific. We (*have*) _____ chicken, rice, and a salad. While we (*eat*) _____ , George Drake (*stop*) _____ by to visit us, so we (*invite*) _____ him to join us for dinner. But he (*eat, already*) _____ his dinner, so he (*be, not*) _____ hungry.

A: What (you, do) _____ after dinner?

B: I wanted to go a movie—*Galaxy Invaders*. But George and my

husband (see, already) _____ it, so

we (go) _____ to *Ghost Ship* instead. It (be)

_____ pretty good.

☐ **EXERCISE 38—PREPOSITIONS:** Complete the sentences with prepositions.
(See Appendix 1 for a list of preposition combinations.)

1. I apologized _____ Ann _____ stepping on her toe.

2. I thanked Sam _____ helping me fix my car.

3. My grandfather doesn't approve _____ gambling.

4. Please forgive me _____ forgetting your birthday.

5. My friend insisted _____ taking me to the airport.

6. Please excuse me _____ being late.

7. Children depend _____ their parents for love and support.

8. In my composition, I compared this city _____ my hometown.

9. Umbrellas protect people _____ rain.

10. We're relying _____ Jason to help us move into our new apartment.

11. We had mice in the house, so we set some traps to get rid _____

    them.

12. What happened _____ your finger? Did you cut it?

CHAPTER 8
Count/Noncount Nouns and Articles

8-1 COUNT AND NONCOUNT NOUNS

	SINGULAR	PLURAL	
COUNT NOUN	*a* chair *one* chair	chairs *two* chairs *three* chairs *some* chairs *several* chairs *a lot of* chairs *many* chairs *a few* chairs	Some nouns are called COUNT NOUNS: (1) In the singular, they can be preceded by *a/an* or *one*. (2) They have a plural form: *-s* or *-es*.★
NONCOUNT NOUN	furniture *some* furniture *a lot of* furniture *much* furniture *a little* furniture	Ø	Some nouns are called NONCOUNT NOUNS: (1) They are NOT immediately preceded by *a/an* or *one*. (2) They do NOT have a plural form (no final *-s* is added).

★See Chart 4-1.

☐ **EXERCISE 1:** Notice the expressions of quantity (*two, some, a lot of*, etc.) that are used with count nouns and noncount nouns in Chart 8-1. Draw a line through the expressions of quantity that **cannot** be used to complete the sentences.

NONCOUNT NOUNS: *fruit* .... *mail* ...... *traffic*
COUNT NOUNS: *apples* ..... *letters* ..... *cars*

1. I ate _____ **fruit**.
   a. some
   ~~b. several~~
   c. a little
   ~~d. a few~~
   ~~e. too many~~
   f. too much
   g. a lot of
   ~~h. two~~

2. I ate _____ **apples**.
   a. some
   b. several
   c. a little
   d. a few
   e. too many
   f. too much
   g. a lot of
   h. two

3. I get _____ **mail** every day.
   - a. a lot of
   - b. some
   - c. a little
   - d. a few
   - e. too much
   - f. too many
   - g. several
   - h. three

4. I get _____ **letters** every day.
   - a. a lot of
   - b. some
   - c. a little
   - d. a few
   - e. too much
   - f. too many
   - g. several
   - h. three

5. There is _____ **traffic** in the street.
   - a. several
   - b. some
   - c. too many
   - d. a little
   - e. a lot of
   - f. a few
   - g. too much
   - h. five

6. There are _____ **cars** in the street.
   - a. several
   - b. some
   - c. too many
   - d. a little
   - e. a lot of
   - f. a few
   - g. too much
   - h. five

8-2 NONCOUNT NOUNS

(a) I bought **some furniture**.
(b) I got **some mail** yesterday.
	A noncount noun* is NOT preceded by **a/an**, **one**, **two**, **three**, etc.
	    INCORRECT: *I bought a furniture.*
	A noncount noun does NOT have a plural form.
	    INCORRECT: *I bought some furnitures.*

INDIVIDUAL PARTS (COUNT NOUNS)		THE WHOLE (A NONCOUNT NOUN)	
(c)	chairs tables beds etc.	furniture	Noncount nouns usually refer to a whole group of things that is made up of many individual parts, a whole category made up of different varieties. For example, some common noncount nouns are *furniture*, *mail*, *money*, *fruit*, and *jewelry*.

(d)	letters
	postcards
	bills
	etc.
		mail	A language is not always logical. For instance:
			    *I had some **corn** for dinner.* (noncount)
			    *I had some **peas** for dinner.* (count)
			Both **corn** and **peas** express a larger whole made up of smaller parts, but **corn** is a noncount noun and **pea** is a count noun.

(e)	pennies nickels dollars etc.	money	**Vegetables** *are good for you.* (count) **Fruit** *is good for you.* (noncount) Both **vegetables** and **fruit** describe whole categories of food, but one is count and the other noncount.

(f)	apples
	bananas
	oranges
	etc.
		fruit	Logically, you can count furniture. But in grammar, you cannot count furniture. For example: *I see a table and a bed.*
			    CORRECT: *I see some furniture.*
			    INCORRECT: *I see two furnitures.*

(g)	rings bracelets necklaces etc.	jewelry	

A noncount noun is also sometimes called a *mass noun*.

```
┌─────────────────────────────────────────────────────────────────────────┐
│ SOME COMMON NONCOUNT NOUNS: WHOLE GROUPS MADE UP OF INDIVIDUAL PARTS       │
│ A. clothing          B. homework          F. grammar                      │
│    equipment            housework            slang                        │
│    food                 work                 vocabulary                   │
│    fruit                                                                  │
│    furniture         C. advice            G. corn                         │
│    garbage              information          dirt                         │
│    hardware             news                 dust                         │
│    jewelry                                   flour                        │
│    machinery         D. history              grass                        │
│    mail                 literature           hair                         │
│    makeup               music                pepper                       │
│    money                poetry               rice                         │
│      cash                                    salt                         │
│      change          E. English, Arabic, Chinese, etc.   sand             │
│    postage              (names of languages)  sugar                       │
│    scenery                                   wheat                        │
│    stuff                                                                  │
│    traffic                                                                │
└─────────────────────────────────────────────────────────────────────────┘
```

☐ **EXERCISE 2:** Complete the sentences with the correct form, **singular or plural**, of the given nouns. When necessary, choose the correct word in parentheses in some of the sentences.

1. *chair*　　　I bought some _____*chairs*_____.

2. *furniture*　I bought some _____*furniture*_____.

3. *fruit*　　　There (is,) are) a lot of _____*fruit*_____ on the table.

4. *vegetable*　There (is, (are)) a lot of _____*vegetables*_____ on the table.

5. *clothing*　 I have a lot of _____ in my closet.

6. *dress*　　　Mary has a lot of _____ in her closet.

7. *information*　There (is, are) a lot of _____ in an encyclopedia.

8. *fact*　　　　There (is, are) a lot of _____ in an encyclopedia.

9. *grammar*　 I know a lot of _____.

10. *vocabulary*　I'm learning a lot of new _____.

11. *word*　　　I'm learning a lot of new _____.

12. *slang*　　　I want to learn some American _____.

13. *idiom*   I know a lot of English _____.

14. *traffic*   There (is, are) a lot of _____ in the street.

15. *car*   There (is, are) a lot of _____ on the road.

16. *literature*   I like to read good _____.

17. *novel*   I like to read good _____.

18. *poem*   I like to read _____.

19. *poetry*   I like to read _____.

20. *mail*   Did you get any _____ today?

21. *letter*   Did you get any _____ today?

22. *sand*   I got some _____ in my shoes at the beach.

23. *dust*   There (is, are) a lot of _____ under the bed.

24. *homework*   I have a lot of _____ to do tonight.

25. *assignment*   The teacher gives us a lot of _____.

26. *penny*   Tommy had four _____ in his pocket.

27. *money*   He has some _____ in his pocket.

28. *coin*   I need some _____ for the vending
                   machine.

                   I want to get a can of soda pop.

29. *change*   I need some _____ for the vending
                   machine.

30. *garbage*   The street is very dirty. There (is, are) some
                   _____ in the street.

☐ **EXERCISE 3:** Complete the sentences with the **singular or plural** form of the given
   nouns. When necessary, choose the correct word in parentheses in some of the
   sentences.

1. *machinery*   It takes a lot of _____ to build a road.

2. *machine*   There (is, are) a lot of washing _____ in a
                 laundromat.

3. *equipment*   There (is, are) a lot of _____ in the
                 chemistry lab.

4. *tool*   There (is, are) a lot of _____ in the garage.

5. *hardware*   That store sells a lot of _____.

6. *ring*   Marie wears a lot of _____ and

   bracelet   _____.

7. *jewelry*   Marie wears a lot of _____.

8. *jewel*   A crown has a lot of _____.

9. *suggestion*   Can you give me some _____?

10. *advice*   Can you give me some _____?

11. *information*   I need some _____.

12. *news*   There (isn't, aren't) any interesting _____ in today's paper.

13. *lake*   We saw a lot of _____ and

   mountain   _____ on our vacation.

14. *scenery*   We saw a lot of beautiful _____ on our vacation.

15. *plant*   Ann has a lot of _____ in her apartment.

16. *grass*   When we went on a picnic, we sat on the _____.

17. *rice*   People in my country eat a lot of _____.

18. *English*   Ahmed's children know a lot of _____.

19. *song*   The children learned a lot of new _____ in nursery school.

20. *music*   I enjoy listening to _____.

21. *thing*   Whose _____ (is, are) (this, these)?

22. *stuff*   Whose _____ (is, are) (this, these)?

23. *corn*   Rebecca had some _____ for dinner.

24. *pea*   Jack had some _____ with his dinner.

25. *makeup*   My aunt has a drawer full of _____.

26. *bread*   My uncle always has _____ with his dinner.

27. *sandwich*   People in Canada often have _____ for lunch.

28. *toast*   We had eggs and _____ for breakfast.

8-3 MORE NONCOUNT NOUNS

(a) LIQUIDS		SOLIDS and SEMI-SOLIDS				GASES
beer	milk	bread	meat	chalk	rubber	air
blood	oil	butter	beef	copper	silver	fog
coffee	shampoo	cheese	chicken	cotton	soap	oxygen
cream	soup	ice	fish	glass	tin	pollution
gasoline	tea	ice cream	ham	gold	toothpaste	smog
honey	water	lettuce	lamb	iron	wood	smoke
juice	wine	toast	pork	paper	wool	steam

(b) NATURAL PHENOMENA (things that occur in nature)		
weather	lightning	darkness
rain	thunder	light
snow	humidity	sunshine

(c) ABSTRACTIONS (An abstraction is something that has no physical form. A person cannot touch it.)					
anger	enjoyment	happiness	ignorance	luck	recreation
beauty	entertainment	hate	intelligence	patience	research
confidence	experience	health	justice	peace	stupidity
courage	fun	help	knowledge	poverty	time
cowardice	generosity	honesty	laughter	pride	violence
education	greed	hospitality	love	progress	wealth

□ **EXERCISE 4:** Complete the sentences with the correct form, **singular or plural**, of the given nouns. Choose the correct word in parentheses as necessary.

1. *snow* It's winter. There (is, are) a lot of _____ **snow** _____ on the ground.

2. *weather* There (is, are) a lot of cold _____ in Alaska.

3. *sunshine* _____ (is, are) a source of vitamin D.

4. *knowledge* Prof. Nash has a lot of _____ about that subject.

5. *fun* We had a lot of _____ on the picnic.

6. *luck* I want to wish you good _____.

7. *idea* Emily has a lot of good _____.

8. *intelligence* I admire Emily for her _____.

9. *gold* _____ (is, are) expensive.

10. *diamond* _____ (is, are) expensive, too.

11. *movie* I like to go to _____.

12. *entertainment*   What do you do for _____ on weekends?

13. *game*   Children like to play _____.

14. *generosity*   Thank you for your _____.

15. *help*   Could you give me some _____ with this?

16. *patience*   Teaching children to read requires _____.

17. *patient*   Doctors take care of _____.

18. *confidence*   You can do it! I have _____ in you.

19. *progress*   Mr. Fernandez's English is improving. He's making a lot of _____.

20. *courage*   Be brave. You must have _____.

21. *pollution*   Automobiles are the biggest source of _____ in most cities.

22. *forest*   The destruction of rain _____ throughout much of the world is harming the earth's environment.

23. *peace*   There have been many conflicts and wars throughout the history of the world, but almost all people prefer _____.

24. *hospitality*   Thank you for your _____.

25. *beef*   The _____ we had for dinner last night (was, were) very good.

26. *fog*   During the winter months along the coast, there (is, are) usually a lot of _____ in the morning.

☐ **EXERCISE 5:** Complete the sentences with *much* or *many* and the **singular or plural** form of the noun. Choose the correct word in parentheses as necessary.

REMINDER: Use *many* with count nouns: *many apples.*
                 Use *much* with noncount nouns: *much fruit.*

1. *apple*   How _____ ***many apples*** _____ did you buy?

2. *fruit*   How _____ ***much fruit*** _____ did you buy?

3. *mail*   How _____ did you get yesterday?

4. *letter*   How _____ did you get yesterday?

5. *postage*   How _____ do I need for this
package?

6. *stamp*   How _____ did you buy?

7. *English*   Anna's husband doesn't know _____.

8. *slang*   Sometimes I can't understand my roommate because he
uses too _____.

9. *word*   How _____ (is, are) there in your dictionary?

10. *coffee*   Louise drinks too _____.

11. *sandwich*   Billy has a stomach ache. He ate too

_____.

12. *sugar*   You shouldn't eat too _____.

13. *course*   How _____ are you taking this semester?

14. *homework*   How _____ do you have to do tonight?

15. *news*   There (isn't, aren't) _____ in the paper today.

16. *article*   How _____ (is, are) there on
the front page of today's paper?

17. *fun*   I didn't have _____ at the party. It
was boring.

18. *star*   How _____ (is, are) there in the universe?

19. *sunshine*   There (isn't, aren't) _____ in Seattle
in winter.

20. *pollution*   (Is, Are) there _____ in Miami?

21. *luck*   We didn't have _____ when we went fishing.

22. *kind*   There (is, are) _____ of flowers.

23. *violence*   I think there (is, are) too _____
on television.

24. *makeup*   I think that Mary wears too _____.

25. *car*   How _____ pass in front of this
building in 30 seconds?

26. *traffic*   (Is, Are) there _____ in front of
your apartment building?

☐ **EXERCISE 6:** Complete the sentences by using *a few* or *a little* and the given noun. Use the plural form of the noun when necessary.

REMINDER: Use *a few* with a count noun: *a few songs.*
Use *a little* with a noncount noun: *a little music.*

1. *music* I feel like listening to _____ **a little music** _____ tonight.

2. *song* We sang _____ **a few songs** _____ at the party.

3. *time* I'm not finished with my work. I need _____ **a little** _____ more _____ **time** _____ .

4. *desk* We need _____ more _____ in our classroom.

5. *help* Do you need _____ with that?

6. *apple* I bought _____ at the market.*

7. *fruit* I bought _____ at the market.

8. *advice* I need _____ .

9. *money* If I accept that job, I'll make _____ more _____ .

10. *coin* Annie put _____ in her pocket.

11. *information* Could you give me _____ ?

12. *hour* Don's plane will arrive in _____ more _____ .

13. *toothpaste* Tommy, put just _____ on your toothbrush, not half the tube!

14. *laughter* We need to be able to see the humor in a situation even when we're unhappy. _____ never hurts.

15. *laugh* Greg's joke produced _____ in the audience, but most of the people didn't think it was funny.

16. *grammar* Pedro already knew _____ English _____ before he took this course.

17. *flower* I picked _____ from my garden.

18. *progress* I've made _____ in the last couple of weeks.

_____

I bought a few apples. = I bought a small number of apples.
I bought a little apple. = I bought one apple and it was small, not large.

19. *chicken*   I'm still hungry. I think I'll have _____ more

_____.

20. *chicken*   When I was a child, we raised _____

in our back yard.

8-4   NOUNS THAT CAN BE COUNT OR NONCOUNT

Quite a few nouns can be used as either noncount or count nouns. Examples of both noncount and count usages for some common nouns follow:

NOUN	USED AS **NONCOUNT** NOUN	USED AS A **COUNT** NOUN
glass	(a) Windows are made of **glass**.	(b) I drank **a glass** of water.
		(c) Janet wears **glasses** when she reads.
hair	(d) Rita has brown **hair**.	(e) There's **a hair** on my jacket.
iron	(f) **Iron** is a metal.	(g) I pressed my shirt with **an iron**.
light	(h) I opened the curtain to let in **some light**.	(i) Please turn off **the lights** (*lamps*).
paper	(j) I need **some paper** to write a letter.	(k) I wrote **a paper** for Prof. Lee.
		(l) I bought **a paper** (*a newspaper*).
time	(m) How **much time** do you need to finish your work?	(n) How **many times** have you been in Mexico?
work	(o) I have **some work** to do tonight.	(p) That painting is **a work** of art.
coffee	(q) I had **some coffee** after dinner.	(r) **Two coffees**, please.
chicken *fish* *lamb*	(s) I had **some chicken/some fish/some lamb** for dinner.	(t) She drew a picture of **a chicken/a fish/a lamb**.

☐ **EXERCISE 7:** Complete the sentences with the given words. Choose words in parentheses as necessary.

1. *lamb* Joe, would you like (a, some) _____ for dinner tonight?

2. *lamb* _____ (is, are) born in the springtime.

3. *time* It took a lot of _____ to write my composition.

4. *time* I really like that movie. I saw it three _____.

5. *paper* Students in Prof. Young's literature class have to write a lot of _____.

6. *paper* Students who take thorough lecture notes use a lot of _____.

7. *paper* *The New York Times* is (a, some) famous _____.

8. *work* Rodin's statue of "The Thinker" is one of my favorite _____ of art.

9. *work* I have a lot of _____ to do tomorrow.

10. *light* If _____ accidentally (gets, get) in a darkroom, (it, they) can ruin photographic negatives.

11. *light* There (is, are) a lot of fluorescent _____ on the ceilings of the school building.

12. *hair* Erin has straight _____, and Sara has curly _____.

13. *hair* Brian has a white cat. When I stood up from Brian's sofa, my black slacks were covered with short, white _____.

14. *coffee* We'd like two cheese sandwiches and two _____, please.

15. *coffee* I don't drink a lot of _____. I prefer tea.

16. *glass* I wear _____ because I'm nearsighted.

17. *glass* In some countries, people use _____ for their tea; in other countries, they use cups.

18. *glass*   Framed paintings are usually covered with _____ to protect them.

19. *iron*   _____ (is, are) necessary to animal and plant life.

20. *iron*   _____ (is, are) used to make clothes look neat.

8-5   USING UNITS OF MEASURE WITH NONCOUNT NOUNS

(a) I had some tea. (b) I had **two cups of** tea. (c) I ate some toast. (d) I ate **one piece of** toast.	To mention a specific quantity of a noncount noun, speakers use units of measure such as *two cups of* or *one piece of*. A unit of measure usually describes the container (e.g., *a cup of, a bowl of*) the amount (*a pound of, a quart of*),★ or the shape (*a bar of soap, a sheet of paper*).

★Weight measure: *one pound = 0.45 kilograms/kilos*   Liquid measure: *one quart = 0.95 litres/liters*
four quarts = one gallon = 3.8 litres/liters

☐ **EXERCISE 8:** Use the words in the list to complete the sentences. Use the plural form if necessary. Some sentences have more than one possible completion.

bar	gallon	piece	sheet
bottle	glass	pound	spoonful
bowl	loaf	quart	tube
cup			

1. I drank a _____*cup*_____ of coffee.

2. I bought two _____*pounds*_____ of cheese.

3. I bought a _____ of milk at the supermarket.

4. I drank a _____ of orange juice.

5. I had a _____ of toast and an egg for breakfast.

6. I put ten _____ of gas in my car.

7. I had a _____ of soup for lunch.

8. I need a _____ of chalk.

9. I drank a _____ of beer.

10. I bought a _____ of margarine.

11. There are 200 _____ of lined paper in my notebook.

12. There is a _____ of fruit on the table.

13. I used two _____ of bread to make a sandwich.

14. I bought one _____ of bread at the store.

15. I put a _____ of honey in my tea.

16. I need to buy a new _____ of toothpaste.

17. There is a _____ of soap in the bathroom.

18. Let me give you a _____ of advice.

19. I just learned an interesting _____ of information.

20. There were a dozen* _____ of mail for me in my mailbox today.

21. A three-piece suit is made up of three _____ of clothing: slacks, a jacket, and a vest.

□ **EXERCISE 9—ORAL (BOOKS CLOSED):** Ask and answer questions with *how much* and *how many.*

> *Example:* (. . .) has two children.
> STUDENT A: How many children does (. . .) have?
> STUDENT B: Two.

1. There are (25) students in this class.
2. (. . .) gets a lot of mail every day.
3. There are 50 states in the United States.
4. I drink (two) cups of coffee every day.**
5. I bought one pound of butter.
6. There are ten provinces in Canada.
7. There are 256 pages in this book.
8. I have (twenty dollars).
9. (. . .) cooked two cups of rice.
10. There are (around 25) desks in this room.
11. I use very little salt on my food.
12. (. . .) knows very few students in his/her (chemistry) class.
13. A round-trip ticket from here to (Chicago) costs ($430).
14. There are approximately 22,000 different kinds of fish in the world.
15. I know a lot of English vocabulary.
16. (. . .) invited ten people to his/her house for dinner.
17. There are (about five) pieces of chalk in the chalk tray.
18. (. . .) bought ten gallons of gas(oline)/petrol.

---

*A dozen = twelve. It is followed by a plural noun: *a dozen eggs.*
**There are two possible questions:
> *How much coffee do you drink every day?*
> *How many cups of coffee do you drink every day?*

8-6 GUIDELINES FOR ARTICLE USAGE

	USING *A* OR Ø (NO ARTICLE)		USING *A* OR *SOME*
SINGULAR COUNT NOUNS	(a) *A dog* makes a good pet. (b) *A banana* is yellow. (c) *A pencil* contains lead.	A speaker uses *a* with a singular count noun when s/he is making a generalization. In (a): The speaker is talking about any dog, all dogs, dogs in general.	(j) I saw *a dog* in my yard. (k) Mary ate *a banana*. (l) I need *a pencil*.
PLURAL COUNT NOUNS	(d) Ø *Dogs* make good pets. (e) Ø *Bananas* are yellow. (f) Ø *Pencils* contain lead.	A speaker uses no article (Ø) with a plural count noun when s/he is making a generalization.★ In (d): The speaker is talking about any dog, all dogs, dogs in general. Note: (a) and (d) have the same meaning.	(m) I saw *some dogs* in my yard. (n) Mary bought *some bananas*. (o) Bob has *some pencils* in his pocket.
NONCOUNT NOUNS	(g) Ø *Fruit* is good for you. (h) Ø *Coffee* contains caffeine. (i) I like Ø *music*.	A speaker uses no article (Ø) with a noncount noun when s/he is making a generalization.★ In (g): The speaker is talking about any fruit, all fruit, fruit in general.	(p) I bought *some fruit*. (q) Bob drank *some coffee*. (r) Would you like to listen to *some music*?

★Sometimes a speaker uses an expression of quantity (e.g., *almost all, most, some*) when s/he makes a generalization: *Almost all dogs make good pets. Most dogs are friendly. Some dogs have short hair.*

	USING *THE*	
A speaker uses *a* with a singular count noun when s/he is talking about one thing (or person) that is not specific.	(s) Did you feed *the dog*? (t) I had a banana and an apple. I gave *the banana* to Mary. (u) *The pencil* on that desk is Jim's. (v) *The sun* is shining. (w) Please close *the door*. (x) Mary is in *the kitchen*.	*The* is used in front of: singular count nouns: *the dog* plural count nouns: *the dogs* noncount nouns: *the fruit* A speaker uses *the* (not *a*, Ø, or *some*) when the speaker and the listener are thinking about the same specific thing(s) or person(s).
In (j): The speaker is saying, "I saw one dog (not two dogs, some dogs, many dogs). It wasn't a specific dog (e.g., your dog, the neighbor's dog, that dog). It was only one dog out of the whole group of animals called dogs."		In (s): The speaker and the listener are thinking about the same specific dog. The listener knows which dog the speaker is talking about: the dog that they own, the dog that they feed every day. There is only one dog that the speaker could possibly be talking about.
A speaker often uses *some*** with a plural count noun when s/he is talking about things (or people) that are not specific.	(y) Did you feed *the dogs*? (z) I had some bananas and some apples. I gave *the bananas* to Mary. (aa) *The pencils* on that desk are Jim's. (bb) Please turn off *the lights*.	In (t): A speaker uses *the* when s/he mentions a noun the second time. First mention: *I had a banana* . . . Second mention: *I gave the banana* . . . In the second mention, the listener now knows which banana
In (m): The speaker is saying, "I saw more than one dog. They weren't specific dogs (e.g., your dogs, the neighbor's dogs, those dogs). The exact number of dogs isn't important (two dogs, five dogs); I'm simply saying that I saw an indefinite number of dogs."		the speaker is talking about: the banana the speaker had (not the banana John had, not the banana in that bowl).
A speaker often uses *some*** with a noncount noun when s/he is talking about something that is not specific.	(cc) *The fruit* in this bowl is ripe. (dd) I drank some coffee and some milk. *The coffee* was hot. (ee) I can't hear you. *The music* is too loud. (ff) *The air* is cold today.	
In (p): The speaker is saying, "I bought an indefinite amount of fruit. The exact amount isn't important information (e.g., two pounds of fruit, four bananas and two apples). And I'm not talking about specific fruit (e.g., that fruit, the fruit in that bowl.)"		

*In addition to *some*, a speaker might use *several, a few, a lot of,* etc. with a plural count noun, or *a little, a lot of,* etc. with a noncount noun. (See Chart 8-1.)

□ **EXERCISE 10:** Discuss SPEAKER A's use of articles in the following dialogues. Why does SPEAKER A use *a*, *some*, *the*, or Ø? Discuss what both SPEAKER A and SPEAKER B are thinking about.

DIALOGUE 1:

A: **A dog** makes a good pet.   B: I agree.

DIALOGUE 2:

A: I saw **a dog** in my yard.

DIALOGUE 4:

A: **Dogs** make good pets.   B: I agree.

DIALOGUE 5:

A: I saw **some dogs** in my yard.

DIALOGUE 7:

A: **Fruit** is good for you.   B: I agree.

DIALOGUE 8:

A: I ate **some fruit**.

DIALOGUE 3:

B: Oh?

A: Did you feed *the dog*?

B: Yes.

DIALOGUE 6:

B: Oh?

A: Did you feed *the dogs*?

B: Yes.

DIALOGUE 9:

B: Oh?

A: *The fruit* in this bowl is ripe.

B: Good.

□ **EXERCISE 11:** Here are some conversations. Try to decide whether the speakers probably use *the* or *a/an*.* Are the speakers thinking about the same objects or persons?

1. A: Do you have ____*a*____ car?

    B: No. But I have ____*a*____ bicycle.

2. A: Do you need ____*the*____ car today, honey?

    B: Yes. I have a lot of errands to do. Why don't I drive you to work today?

    A: Okay. But be sure to fill ____*the*____ car up with gas sometime today.

3. A: Did you have a good time at _____ party last night?

    B: Yes.

    A: So did I. I'm glad that you decided to go with me.

4. A: What did you do last night?

    B: I went to _____ party.

    A: Oh? Where was it?

5. A: I bought _____ table yesterday.

    B: Oh? I didn't know you went shopping for furniture.

6. A: Have you seen my keys?

    B: Yes. They're on _____ table next to _____ front door.

7. A: Is Mr. Jones _____ graduate student?

    B: No. He's _____ professor.

8. A: Where's _____ professor?

    B: She's absent today.

9. A: Would you like to go to _____ zoo this afternoon?

    B: Sure. Why not?

10. A: Does San Diego have _____ zoo?

    B: Yes. It's world famous.

11. A: Where do you live?

    B: We live on _____ quiet street in the suburbs.

***A** is used in front of nouns that begin with a consonant sound: *a book, a dog, a pencil*. **An** is used in front of nouns that begin with a vowel sound: *an apple, an elephant, an idea, an opinion, an uncle, an hour.*

12. A: I'm hungry and I'm tired of walking. How much farther is it to

          _____ restaurant?

    B: Just a couple of blocks. Let's cross _____ street here.

    A: Are you sure you know where you're going?

13. A: Did Bob find _____ job?

    B: Yes. He's working at _____ restaurant.

    A: Oh? Which one?

14. A: Did you feed _____ cat?

    B: Yes. I fed him a couple of hours ago.

15. A: Does Jane have _____ cat?

    B: No, she has _____ dog. She doesn't like cats.

16. A: Where's Dennis?

    B: He's in _____ kitchen.

17. A: Do you like your new apartment?

    B: Yes. It has _____ big kitchen.

☐ **EXERCISE 12:** Complete the sentences with the given nouns. Use *the* for specific statements. Do not use *the* for general statements.

1. *flowers*   a. _____ **The flowers** _____ in that vase are beautiful.

             b. _____ **F lowers** _____ are beautiful.

2. *mountains*   a. _____ are beautiful.

             b. _____ in Colorado are beautiful.

3. *water*   a. _____ consists of hydrogen and

             oxygen.

             b. I don't want to go swimming today. _____

             is too cold.

4. *information*   a. _____ in that book is inaccurate.

             b. An encyclopedia is a source of _____.

5. *health*   a. _____ is more important than

             money.

             b. Doctors are concerned with _____

             of their patients.

6. *men*
   women

   a. _____ generally have stronger muscles than _____.

   b. At the party last night, _____ sat on one side of the room and _____ sat on the other.

7. *problems*

   a. Everyone has _____.

   b. Irene told me about _____ she had with her car yesterday.

8. *happiness*

   a. I can't express _____ I felt when I heard the good news.

   b. Everyone seeks _____.

9. *vegetables*

   a. _____ are good for you.

   b. _____ we had for dinner last night were overcooked.

10. *gold*

   a. _____ is a precious metal.

   b. _____ in Mary's ring is 24 karats.

☐ **EXERCISE 13:** Add *the* if necessary. Otherwise, make the symbol Ø to show that no article is necessary.

1. Please pass me ___**the**___ butter.

2. ___**Ø**___ butter is a dairy product.

3. John, where's _____ milk? Is it in _____ refrigerator or on _____ table?

4. _____ milk comes from cows and goats.

5. Tom usually has _____ wine with dinner.

6. Dinner's ready. Shall I pour _____ wine?

7. I'm studying _____ English. I'm studying _____ grammar.

8. _____ grammar in this chapter isn't easy.

9. _____ chemistry is my favorite subject.

10. Do you like _____ weather in this city?

11. _____ copper is used in electrical wiring.

12. _____ air is free.

13. _____ air is humid today.

14. _____ windows are closed. Please open them.

15. _____ windows are made of _____ glass.

16. We usually have _____ meat for dinner.

17. _____ meat we had for dinner last night was tough.

18. People used to use _____ candles for _____ light, but now they use _____ electricity.

☐ **EXERCISE 14:** Use *a/an/some* or *the* in the following. REMINDER: Use *the* when a noun is mentioned for the second time.

1. Yesterday I saw ___*a*___ dog and ___*a*___ cat. ___*The*___ dog was chasing ___*the*___ cat. _____ cat was chasing _____ mouse. _____ mouse ran into _____ hole, but _____ hole was very small. _____ cat couldn't get into _____ hole, so it ran up _____ tree. _____ dog tried to climb _____ tree too, but it couldn't.

2. Yesterday I bought _____ clothes. I bought _____ suit, _____ shirt, and _____ tie. _____ suit is gray and comes with a vest. _____ shirt is pale blue, and _____ tie has black and gray stripes.

3. Yesterday I saw _____ man and _____ woman. They were having _____ argument. _____ man was yelling at _____ woman, and _____ woman was shouting at _____ man. I don't know what _____ argument was about.

4. I had _____ soup and _____ sandwich for lunch. _____ soup was too salty, but _____ sandwich was pretty good.

5. A: I saw _____ accident yesterday.

   B: Oh? Where?

   A: On Grand Avenue. _____ man in _____ Volkswagen drove
   through a stop sign and hit _____ bus.

   B: Was anyone hurt in _____ accident?

   A: I don't think so. _____ man who was driving _____
   Volkswagen got out of his car and seemed to be okay. His car was
   only slightly damaged. No one in _____ bus was hurt.

6. A: What did you do last weekend?

   B: I went on _____ picnic Saturday and saw _____ movie
   Sunday.

   A: Did you have fun?

   B: _____ picnic was fun, but _____ movie was boring.

☐ **EXERCISE 15:** Complete the sentences with *a*, *an*, *some*, *the*, or Ø.

1. A: Do you like ___Ø___ fruit?

   B: Very much.

2. A: I'm hungry.

   B: Would you like _____ fruit? How about _____ apple?

3. A: _____ fruit we bought at the market was fresh.

   B: That's the best place to buy _____ fruit.

4. _____ gas is expensive nowadays.

5. _____ gas at Mack's Service Station is cheaper than _____ gas
   at the Shell Station.

6. I need _____ gas. Let's stop at the next service station.

7. Kathy bought _____ radio. She likes to listen to _____ music
   when she studies.

8. A: Would you please turn _____ radio down? _____ music is
   too loud.

   B: No problem.

9. A: Do you see _____ man who is standing next to Janet?

   B: Yes. Who is he?

   A: He's _____ president of this university.

10. A one-dollar bill has the picture of _____ president of the United States. It's the picture of George Washington.

11. A: What did you buy when you went shopping?

    B: I bought _____ blouse and _____ jewelry.

    A: What color is _____ blouse?

    B: Red.

12. A: Where's my bookbag?

    B: It's on _____ floor over there, in _____ corner next to _____ sofa.

13. We need to buy _____ furniture. I'd like to get _____ sofa and _____ easy chair.

14. _____ furniture is expensive these days.

15. _____vegetarian doesn't eat _____ meat.

16. Last week I read _____ book about _____ life of Gandhi.

17. I enjoy _____ life.

18. A: Let's go swimming in _____ lake today.

    B: That sounds like _____ good idea.

19. _____ lake is a body of _____ water that is smaller than _____ sea but larger than _____ pond. _____ ocean is larger than _____ sea.

20. During our vacation in Florida, we walked along _____ beach in front of our hotel and looked at _____ ocean.

21. People can drink _____ fresh water. They can't drink _____ seawater because it contains _____ salt.

22. I had _____ interesting experience yesterday. _____ man in _____ blue suit came into my office and handed me _____ bouquet of _____ flowers. I had never seen _____ man before in my life, but I thanked him for _____ flowers. Then he walked out _____ door.

8-7 USING EXPRESSIONS OF QUANTITY AS PRONOUNS

Expressions of quantity are words that describe the number or amount of a noun.
  Examples of common expressions of quantity: *some, any, many, much, a lot (of), a few,*
                                                    a little, two, a couple (of), three, several, etc.
Expressions of quantity are usually used in front of a noun (e.g., *some paper, a lot of fruit*).
They can also be used alone—without a noun—when the meaning is clear, i.e., when both
speaker and listener know what the expression of quantity refers to. These expressions
function as pronouns.	

(a) A: I need some yellow paper.
     B: I don't have **any**. Ask Matt. I think he
        has **some**.
	In (a): *any* and ***some*** are used without a noun.
	It is clearly understood that:
	   any = *any yellow paper*
	   some = *some yellow paper*****

(b) A: I understand you're a baseball fan.
        Have you gone to a lot of baseball
        games?
     B: Yes. I've gone to ***many***. I saw ***three*** just
        last week.
	In (b): *many* = *many baseball games*
	       three = *three baseball games*

*In general, *any* is used in negative sentences; *some* is used in affirmative sentences.

□ **EXERCISE 16—ORAL:** What do the italicized expressions of quantity refer to?

1. There are 25 desks in room 204. How *many* are there in room 207?
   many = *many desks*

2. A: I'm hungry. Do we have any apples?
   B: I think there are *some* in the refrigerator.

3. A: I'm hungry. Do we have any bread?
   B: I think there is *some* in the refrigerator.

4. A: Do you have any envelopes?
   B: I think there are *some* in the upper right-hand drawer of my desk. If
      you can't find *any* there, look on the bookcase next to my desk.

5. A: Do you take sugar in your coffee?
   B: No, but I usually add *a little* to my tea.

6. A: Amy, do you have any lined paper for a three-ring notebook?
   B: How *much* do you need?
   A: I don't really need *a lot*.* *A little* will do. I need just a few sheets.

7. A: There aren't any erasers for the chalkboard in this room.
   B: I can borrow *a couple* from the classroom next door.*

---

*Note: *of* is not included when ***a lot*** and ***a couple*** function alone as pronouns. ***Of*** is
    included if ***a lot*** or ***a couple*** is followed by a noun/pronoun:
        *Eric has **a lot of** friends. I have met **a lot of** them.*
        *I don't have many friends, but Eric has **a lot**. (no **of**)*

8. A: I need some blank floppy disks. Do you have *any*?
   B: Only *two*. How *many* do you need?
   A: Maybe *four* or *five*.
   B: Ask Janet. She usually keeps *a few* in the supply cabinet.
   A: Would Janet also know where to find some blank cassette tapes?
   B: I'm sure there are *some* in the supply cabinet. How *many* do you need?
   A: Just *a couple*.

8-8 NONSPECIFIC OBJECT PRONOUNS: *SOME, ANY,* AND *ONE*

(a) A: I need *some blank tapes*. (nonspecific) 　　B: I don't have **any**, but Jack has **some**. (b) A: Where are *the blank tapes* that were on my desk? (specific) 　　B: Rita has **them**.	Object pronouns for PLURAL COUNT NOUNS: 　nonspecific → **some** or **any** 　specific → **them** In (a): The speakers are not talking about specific tapes. In (b): The speakers are talking about specific tapes, the tapes SPEAKER A left on her desk.
(c) A: I need *a blank tape*. (nonspecific) 　　B: I think you can get **one** from Jack. (d) A: Where's *the blank tape* that was on my desk? (specific) 　　B: Rita has **it**.	Object pronouns for SINGULAR COUNT NOUNS: 　nonspecific → **one** 　specific → **it, her, him**
(e) A: Would you like *some coffee*? (nonspecific) 　　B: No thanks, I just had **some**. I don't want **any** right now. (f) A: Your cup is empty. What happened to *your coffee*? (specific) 　　B: I drank **it**.	Object pronouns for NONCOUNT COUNT NOUNS: 　nonspecific → **some** or **any** 　specific → **it**

☐ **EXERCISE 17:** Complete the sentences by choosing the correct words in italics.

1. A: I need a red pen. Do you have (*one,*) *it* that I could borrow?

   B: No. See if Joy has (*one,*) *it*.

2. A: Where's my grammar book? I need *one, it.*

   B: I don't know. Did you lend *one, it* to someone? Ask Joy if she has *one, it.*

3. A: I need a Korean–English dictionary. Where can I get *one, it?*

   B: At the university bookstore.

4. A: I see you have a Korean–English dictionary. May I borrow *one, it*?

   B: Sure. Here. I'm not using it right now.

5. A: Where can I get some new running shoes at a good price?

   B: You can probably find *some, them* at Sam's Sport Shop.

6. A: Where'd you get those new running shoes? They look comfortable.

   B: I found *some, them* at Sam's Sport Shop.

7. A: Where did you get this photograph of a tiger?

   B: I took *one, it* myself when I was in Nepal.

8. A: Have you ever seen a tiger in the wild?

   B: Yes. I saw *one, it* when I visited the national park in southern Nepal.

9. A: The cafeteria has a different hot soup every day.

   B: That sounds good on a cold day like today. I think I'll have *some, it* for lunch.

10. A: This soup is delicious! Is it homemade?

    B: Yes. I made *some, it* yesterday.

    A: Do you make soup often?

    B: I made *some, it* last week and the week before that, too. About once a week, I guess.

11. A: Did you look over your paper carefully for mistakes?

    B: Yes, but I didn't find *any, them.* Maybe you can find *some, them.*

    A: Maybe you didn't make *any, them.*

12. A: The mistakes on your paper are marked in red ink.

    B: I'll correct *some, them* right away.

13. A: Do you have a bicycle?

    B: Not yet, but I've been planning to get *one, it* for quite a while.

14. A: Did you ride your bicycle to school today?

    B: Yes. I parked *one, it* in the bike racks by the library.

□ **EXERCISE 18—ERROR ANALYSIS:** All of the following sentences contain mistakes. Can you find the mistakes and correct them?

1. There are a lot of informations in that book.

2. The oil is a natural resource.

3. Lions are wild animal.

4. I was late because there were too many traffics.

5. I drank two waters.

6. Our teacher gives us too many homeworks.

7. Ann knows a lot of vocabularies.

8. I had a egg for breakfast.

9. There is many kind of trees in the world.

10. I'm studying the English.

11. I'm living in United State.

12. Only twelve student were in class yesterday.

13. I need some advices.

14. We all have a few problem in the life.

□ **EXERCISE 19—WRITTEN:** Write about one (or both) of the following topics.

1. Look around your room, apartment, house. Tell your reader what you see. Indicate quantity (*some, a lot of, two, etc.*) and position (*in the corner, next to the bed, etc.*).

2. Think of someone you admire. Tell your reader why you admire this person.

□ **EXERCISE 20—PREPOSITIONS:** Complete the sentences with prepositions. (See Appendix 1 for a list of preposition combinations.)

1. Shhh. I'm trying to concentrate _____ this math problem.

2. My opinion is different _____ yours. I disagree _____ you.

3. How did the bank robbers escape _____ jail?

4. What did you tell your parents _____ the dent in their new car? Did you tell them that you hit a parking meter when you were trying to parallel park?

5. The Jordans lost everything when their house burned down. I feel very

   sorry _____ them. I'm sorry _____ the fire.

6. We're hoping _____ good weather tomorrow so we can go sailing.

7. Did you hear _____ the earthquake in Turkey?

8. I heard _____ my sister last week. She wrote me a letter.

9. I spoke _____ Dr. Rice _____ my problem.

10. I'm not accustomed _____ cold weather.

11. When you divide 2 _____ 6, the answer is 3.

12. When you subtract 1 _____ 6, the answer is 5.

13. When you multiply 6 _____ 3, the answer is 18.★

14. When you add 6 _____ 4, the answer is 10.★★

CHAPTER 9

Connecting Ideas

□ **EXERCISE 1—PREVIEW:** Add PUNCTUATION (commas and periods) and CAPITAL LETTERS if necessary. Do not change or add any words. Identify SUBJECTS (S) and VERBS (V).

1. Butterflies are insects all insects have six legs.

>   **S**   **V**   **S**   **V**
> → *Butterflies are insects. All insects have six legs.*

2. Ants and butterflies are insects.

3. Ants butterflies cockroaches bees and flies are insects.

4. Butterflies and bees are insects spiders are different from insects.

5. Spiders have eight legs so they are not called insects.

6. Most insects have wings but spiders do not.

7. Bees are valuable to us they pollinate crops and provide us with honey.

8. Some insects bite us and carry diseases.

9. Insects can cause us trouble they bite us carry diseases and eat our food.

10. Insects are essential to life on earth the plants and animals on earth could not live without them insects may bother us but we have to share this planet with them.

11. We have to share the earth with insects because they are essential to plant and animal life.

12. Because insects are necessary to life on earth it is important to know about them.

9-1 CONNECTING IDEAS WITH *AND*

When ***and*** connects only two items within a sentence, NO COMMAS are used. When ***and*** connects three or more items in a series in a sentence, commas are used.	

(a) I saw a *cat* ***and*** a *mouse*.	In (a): ***and*** connects two nouns:
(b) I saw a *cat*, a *mouse*, ***and*** a *rat*.	*cat + mouse* = NO COMMAS
I saw a *cat*, a *mouse*, a *rat*, ***and*** a *dog*.	In (b): ***and*** connects three or more nouns, so commas are used.★
(c) I *opened* the door ***and*** *walked* into the room.	In (c): NO COMMAS are used because ***and*** connects only two verbs (*opened + walked*).
(d) I *opened* the door, *walked* into the room, ***and*** *sat* down at my desk.	In (d): Commas are used because ***and*** connects three verbs (*opened + walked + sat*).
(e) Their flag is *green* ***and*** *black*.	In (e): ***and*** connects two adjectives (NO COMMAS).
(f) Their flag is *green*, *black*, ***and*** *yellow*.	In (f): ***and*** connects three adjectives (commas).

When ***and*** connects two sentences, a comma is usually used.	

(g) I opened the door. She opened the window.	In (g): Two complete sentences (also called independent clauses) are separated by a period, NOT a comma.★★
(h) INCORRECT: I opened the door, she opened the window.	(h) is incorrect because it has a comma between the two independent clauses.
(i) I opened the door, ***and*** she opened the window.	In (i): When ***and*** connects two independent clauses, a comma is usually used.

★In a series of three or more items, the comma before ***and*** is optional.
  ALSO CORRECT: *I saw a cat, a mouse and a rat.*

★★Notice that a capital letter ("S" not "s") follows the period in (g). The first word in a new sentence is capitalized. See Chart 4-14 for more information about capitalization. Also note that a *period* is called a *full stop* in British English.

☐ **EXERCISE 2:** Add COMMAS where appropriate.

1. My aunt puts milk and sugar in her tea. (*no commas*)

2. My aunt puts milk sugar and lemon in her tea.

   → ***My aunt puts milk, sugar, and lemon in her tea.***

3. Tom ate a sandwich and drank a glass of milk.

4. Tom made a sandwich poured a glass of milk and sat down to eat his lunch.

5. Cats and dogs are animals.

6. Cows goats and horses are farm animals.

7. Giraffes anteaters tigers and kangaroos are wild animals.

8. The river is wide and deep.

9. The river is wide deep and dangerous.

10. Doctors save lives and relieve suffering.

11. Doctors save lives relieve suffering and cure diseases.

12. The restaurant served a five-course dinner: soup fish entreé salad and dessert.

13. I had fish and a salad for dinner last night.

14. The children played games sang songs drew pictures and had a piece of birthday cake.

15. An invitation should include your name address the date the time the purpose of the party and any special activities such as swimming or dancing.

□ **EXERCISE 3:** Add COMMAS and PERIODS where appropriate. CAPITALIZE as necessary.

1. I talked he listened.
   → ***I talked. He listened.***

2. I talked and he listened.
   → ***I talked, and he listened.*** *

3. I talked to Ryan about his school grades and he listened to me carefully.
   → ***I talked to Ryan about his school grades, and he listened to me carefully.***

4. I talked to Ryan about his grades he listened carefully and promised to improve them.
   → ***I talked to Ryan about his school grades. He listened carefully and promised to improve them.***

5. The river rose it flooded the towns in the valley.

6. The river rose and flooded the towns in the valley.

7. The river rose and it flooded the towns in the valley.

8. The river rose it flooded the towns and farms in the valley.

9. The river and streams rose they flooded the towns and farms in the valley.

---

*Sometimes the comma is omitted when ***and*** connects two very short independent clauses. ALSO CORRECT: *I talked and he listened.* In longer sentences, the comma is important and usual.

10. Rome is an Italian city it has a mild climate and many interesting attractions.

11. You should visit Rome its climate is mild and there are many interesting attractions.

12. The principal metals used to make coins are gold silver copper and nickel.

13. Coins are made of metal and last for a long time paper money has a short life span.

14. Collecting stamps can teach a youngster about some of the famous people and events in a country's history.

15. The United States is bounded by two oceans and two countries the oceans are the Pacific to the west and the Atlantic to the east and the countries are Canada to the north and Mexico to the south.

9-2 CONNECTING IDEAS WITH *BUT* AND *OR*

(a) I *went* to bed *but couldn't sleep.* (b) Is a lemon *sweet or sour?* (c) Did you order *coffee, tea, or milk?*	***And***, ***but***, and ***or*** are called "conjunctions." ***But*** and ***or*** are used in the same ways as ***and*** (see 9-1). Notice: Only (c) uses commas.
(d) I dropped the vase, ***but*** it didn't break. (e) Do we have class on Monday, ***or*** is Monday a holiday?	Commas are usually used when ***but*** or ***or*** connects two complete sentences.* (*I dropped the vase* = a complete sentence.) (*it didn't break* = a complete sentence.)

*Sometimes with *but*, a period is used instead of a comma.
ALSO POSSIBLE: *I dropped the vase. But it didn't break.*

☐ **EXERCISE 4:** Add *and, but,* or *or*. Add COMMAS if necessary.

1. I washed my shirt ___*, but*___ it didn't get clean.

2. Would you like some water ___*or*___ some fruit juice?

3. I washed my face *,* brushed my teeth ___*, and*___ took a shower.

4. I invited the Carters to dinner _____ they couldn't come.

5. You can have chicken fish _____ beef for dinner.

6. The flight attendants served dinner _____ I didn't eat.

7. I was hungry _____ didn't eat on the plane. The food didn't look appetizing.

8. Jennifer wore boots jeans a long-sleeved shirt _____ gloves when she worked in her garden.

9. Golf _____ tennis are popular sports.

10. Sara is a good tennis player _____ she's never played golf.

11. Which would you prefer? Would you like to play tennis _____ golf Saturday morning?

12. Who called whom? Did Bob call you _____ did you call Bob?

□ **EXERCISE 5:** Add COMMAS, PERIODS, and CAPITAL LETTERS as appropriate.

1. Cats are mammals turtles are reptiles.

   → ***Cats are mammals. Turtles are reptiles.***

2. Cats are mammals but turtles are reptiles.

3. Cows are farm animals but zebras are wild animals.

4. Cows and horses are farm animals but zebras and giraffes are wild animals.

5. Cows and horses are farm animals zebras giraffes and lions are wild animals.

6. Cars use roads trains run on tracks.

7. Cars use roads but trains run on tracks.

8. Cars buses and trucks use roads but trains run on tracks.

9. Most vegetables grow above the ground but some are roots and grow under the ground corn beans and cabbage grow above the ground but carrots and beets grow under the ground.

10. A good office has modern equipment such as computers intercoms and copying machines but the most important part of a good office is the people who work there.

9-3 CONNECTING IDEAS WITH *SO*

(a) The room was dark, *so* I turned on a light.	*So* can be used as a conjunction. It is preceded by a comma. It connects the ideas in two independent clauses. *So* expresses **results**:
(b) I didn't study, *so* I failed the exam.	cause: *the room was dark* result: *I turned on a light*

☐ **EXERCISE 6:** Add *so* or *but*. Add COMMAS where appropriate.

1. It began to rain _____*, so*_____ I opened my umbrella.

2. It began to rain _____*, but*_____ I didn't have my umbrella with me.

3. I didn't have an umbrella _____ I got wet.

4. I didn't have an umbrella _____ I didn't get wet because I was wearing my raincoat.

5. The water was cold _____ I didn't go swimming.

6. The water was cold _____ I went swimming anyway.

7. Scott's directions to his apartment weren't clear _____ George got lost.

8. The directions weren't clear _____ I found Scott's apartment anyway.

9. My friend lied to me _____ I still like and trust her.

10. My friend lied to me _____ I don't trust her anymore.

☐ **EXERCISE 7:** Add COMMAS, PERIODS, and CAPITAL LETTERS as appropriate. Don't change any of the words or the order of the words.

1. James has a cold he needs to rest and drink plenty of fluids so he should go to bed and drink water fruit juices or soda pop he needs to sleep a lot so he shouldn't drink fluids with caffeine such as tea or coffee.

   → *James has a cold. He needs to rest and drink plenty of fluids, so he should go to bed and drink water, fruit juice, and soda pop. He needs to sleep a lot, so he shouldn't drink fluids with caffeine such as tea and coffee.*

2. My friend and I were tired so we went home early we had wanted to stay until the end of the game but it got too late for us both of us had to get up early in the morning and go to our jobs.

3. The normal pulse for an adult is between 60 and 80 beats per minute but exercise nervousness excitement and a fever will all make a pulse faster the normal pulse for a child is around 80 to 90.

4. Many famous explorers throughout history set out on their hazardous journeys in search of gold silver jewels or other treasures but some explorers wanted only to discover information about their world.

5. Edward Fox was a park ranger for thirty-five years during that time, he was hit by lightning eight times the lightning never killed him but it severely burned his skin and damaged his hearing.

6. The Indian Ocean is bordered on four sides by the continents of Africa Asia Australia and Antarctica some of the important ports are Aden Bombay Calcutta and Rangoon.

7. The Indian Ocean has many fish and shellfish but it has less commercial fishing than the Atlantic or the Pacific the climate of the Indian Ocean is tropical so fish spoil quickly out of the water it is difficult and expensive for commercial fishing boats to keep fish fresh.

9-4   USING AUXILIARY VERBS AFTER *BUT* AND *AND*

(a) I *don't like coffee,* **but** my husband *does.* (b) I *like tea,* **but** my husband *doesn't.* (c) I *won't be here tomorrow,* **but** Sue *will.* (d) I *'ve seen that movie,* **but** Joe *hasn't.* (e) He *isn't here,* **but** she *is.*★	After **but** and **and**, often a main verb is not repeated. Instead, only an auxiliary verb is used. The auxiliary is a substitute for the main verb phrase. The auxiliary after **but** and **and** has the same tense or modal as the main verb. In (a): *does = likes coffee.* The auxiliary *does* (simple present) is the substitute for the main verb phrase (simple present).
(f) I *don't like coffee,* **and** Ed *doesn't* either. (g) I *like tea,* **and** Kate *does* too. (h) I *won't be here,* **and** he *won't* either. (i) I *'ve seen that movie,* **and** Pat *has* too. (j) He *isn't here,* **and** Anna *isn't* either.	

	Notice in the examples:
	
	  negative + **but** *+ affirmative*
	affirmative + **but** *+ negative*
	
	  negative + **and** *+ negative*
	affirmative + **and** *+ affirmative*

★A verb is not contracted with a pronoun at the end of a sentence after **but** and **and**:
  CORRECT: . . . *but she is.*
  INCORRECT: . . . *but she's.*

☐ **EXERCISE 8:** Practice using auxiliary verbs after **but** and **and**.

1. Dan didn't study for the test, but Amy _____**did**_____ .

2. Alice doesn't come to class every day, but Julie _____.

3. Jack went to the movie last night, but I _____.

4. I don't live in the dorm, but Rob and Jim _____.

5. Rob lives in the dorm, and Jim _____ too.

6. I don't live in the dorm, and Carol _____ either.

7. My roommate was at home last night, but I _____.

8. Ted isn't here today, but Alex _____.

9. Ted isn't here today, and Linda _____ either.

10. The teacher is listening to the tape, and the students _____ too.

11. Susan won't be at the meeting tonight, but I _____.

12. Susan isn't going to go to the meeting tonight, but I _____.

13. I'll be there, but she _____.

14. I'll be there, and Mike _____ too.

15. I can speak French, and my wife _____ too.

16. I haven't finished my work yet, but Erica _____.

17. I didn't finish my work last night, but Erica _____.

18. Jane would like a cup of coffee, and I _____ too.

☐ **EXERCISE 9:** Complete the sentences by using the names of your classmates and appropriate auxiliary verbs.

1. ___*Kunio*___ has a mustache, but ___*Kutaiba doesn't*___.

2. ___*Maria*___ doesn't have brown eyes, but ___*Boris does*___.

3. _____ isn't in class today, but _____.

4. _____ is here today, but _____.

5. _____ can speak Spanish, but _____.

6. _____ can't speak Japanese, but _____.

7. _____ stayed home last night, but _____.

8. _____ didn't come to class yesterday, but _____.

9. _____ will be at home tonight, but _____.

10. _____ won't be on time, but _____.

11. _____ isn't wearing jeans today, but _____.

12. _____ has long hair, but _____.

13. _____ has lived here for a long time, but _____.

14. _____ lives in an apartment, but _____.

15. _____ doesn't have a car, but _____.

☐ **EXERCISE 10:** Complete the sentences by using the names of your classmates. Add *too* (if the auxiliary verb is affirmative) or *either* (if the auxiliary verb is negative) to the end of the sentences.

1. ___*Carlos*___ has a pen with blue ink, and ___*Yoko does too*___.

2. ___*Ali*___ doesn't speak Chinese, and ___*Roberto doesn't either*___.

3. _____ isn't married, and _____.

4. _____ sits in the same seat every day, and _____.

5. _____ is wearing jeans today, and _____.

6. _____ walked to class today, and _____.

7. _____ was in class yesterday, and _____.

8. _____ didn't call me last night, and _____.

9. _____ isn't married, and _____.

10. _____ comes to class every day, and _____.

11. _____ has brown eyes, and _____.

12. _____ has been here for over a month, and _____.

13. _____ doesn't have a beard, and _____.

14. _____ can't speak Arabic, and _____.

15. _____ will be in class tomorrow, and _____.

9-5 USING *AND + TOO, SO, EITHER, NEITHER*

AND . . . TOO	(a) Sue likes milk, AND + S + *aux* + TOO ⌐and⌐ ⌐Tom⌐ ⌐does⌐ ⌐too.⌐	(a) and (b) have the same meaning. Notice in (b): After *and so* . . ., the auxiliary verb (*aux*) comes before the subject (S).
AND SO . . .	(b) Sue likes milk, AND + SO + *aux* + S ⌐and⌐ ⌐so⌐ ⌐does⌐ ⌐Tom.⌐	
AND . . . EITHER AND NEITHER . . .	(c) Mary doesn't like milk, AND + S + *aux* + EITHER ⌐and⌐ ⌐John⌐ ⌐doesn't⌐ ⌐either.⌐ (d) Mary doesn't like milk, AND + NEITHER + *aux* + S ⌐and⌐ ⌐neither⌐ ⌐does⌐ ⌐John.⌐	(c) and (d) have the same meaning. Notice in (d): After *and neither* . . ., the auxiliary verb comes before the subject. Notice in (c): A negative auxiliary verb is used with *and . . . either*. In (d): An affirmative auxiliary verb is used with *and neither* . . . .

(e) A: I'm hungry.
    B: *I am too*.
(g) A: I don't like hot dogs.
    B: *I don't either*.
	(f) A: I'm hungry.
	    B: *So am I*.
	(h) A: I don't like hot dogs.
	    B: *Neither do I*.
		And is usually not used when there are two speakers.
		(e) and (f) have the same meaning.
		(g) and (h) have the same meaning.

(i) A: I'm hungry.
    B: *Me too*. (informal)
	(j) A: I don't like hot dogs.
	    B: *Me neither*. (informal)
		Me too and *me neither* are often used in informal spoken English.

□ **EXERCISE 11:** Complete the sentences by using the word in italics and an appropriate auxiliary.

1. Tom Jack has a mustache, and so _____**does Tom**_____.

Jack has a mustache, and _____**Tom does**_____ too.

2. Brian Alex doesn't have a mustache, and neither _____.

Alex doesn't have a mustache, and _____ either.

3. *I*   Sara was at home last night, and so _____.

                Sara was at home last night, and _____ too.

4. *Oregon*   California is on the West Coast, and so _____.

                California is on the West Coast, and _____ too.

5. *Jean*   I went to a movie last night, and so _____.

                I went to a movie last night, and _____ too.

6. *Jason*   I didn't study last night, and neither _____.

                I didn't study last night, and _____ either.

7. *Dick*   Jim can't speak Arabic, and neither _____.

                Jim can't speak Arabic, and _____ either.

8. *Laura*   I like to go to science fiction movies, and so _____.

                I like to go to science fiction movies, and _____ too.

9. *Alice*   I don't like horror movies, and neither _____.

                I don't like horror movies, and _____ either.

10. *porpoises*   Whales are mammals, and so _____.

                Whales are mammals, and _____ too.

BLUE WHALE

PORPOISE

11. *I*   Karen hasn't seen that movie yet, and neither _____.

                Karen hasn't seen that movie yet, and _____ either.

12. *my brother* I have a car, and so _____.

                I have a car, and _____ too.

13. *Erin*   Rob won't join us for lunch, and neither _____.

                Rob won't join us for lunch, and _____ either.

Complete the sentences by using the names of your classmates and appropriate auxiliaries.

1. ____*Maria*____ wasn't in class yesterday, and neither ____*was Jin Won*____.

2. _____ is wearing slacks today, and so _____.

3. _____ lives in an apartment, and so _____.

4. _____ can't speak Chinese, and neither _____.

5. _____ stayed home and studied, and so _____.

6. _____ doesn't have a mustache, and neither _____.

7. _____ will be in class tomorrow, and so _____.

8. _____ isn't married, and neither _____.

9. _____ has dimples, and so _____.

10. _____ has been in class all week, and so _____.

□ EXERCISE 13: Complete the dialogues by agreeing with SPEAKER A's idea. Use *so* or *neither*. Use *I*.

1. A: I'm tired.

   B: ____*So am I.*____

2. A: I didn't enjoy the movie last night.

   B: ____*Neither did I.*____

3. A: I've never been in France.★

   B: ____*Neither have I.*____

4. A: I always have a cup of coffee in the morning.

   B: _____

5. A: I don't feel like going to class today.

   B: _____

6. A: I've never been in Brazil.

   B: _____

7. A: I need to go to the bank today.

   B: _____

★*Never* makes a sentence negative.

8. A: I studied last night.

   B: _____

9. A: I didn't eat breakfast this morning.

   B: _____

10. A: I should stay home and study tonight.

    B: _____

11. A: I have a roommate.

    B: _____

12. A: I've never visited Vancouver, British Columbia.

    B: _____

13. A: I don't have a car.

    B: _____

14. A: I have to go downtown this afternoon.

    B: _____

15. A: I can't speak Hungarian.

    B: _____

16. A: But I can speak English.

    B: _____

□ **EXERCISE 14—ORAL (BOOKS CLOSED):** Respond to the statements by using *so* or *neither*.

Example: Los Angeles is in California.
Response: So is (San Francisco).

1. (. . .) speaks (*language*).
2. (. . .) doesn't speak (*language*).
3. (. . .) is wearing (jeans) today.
4. (. . .) isn't wearing (jeans) today.
5. (. . .) came to class yesterday.
6. (. . .) has been in (*this city*) for (*time*).
7. (. . .) can't speak (*language*).
8. (*A city*) is in (*this state/province*).
9. The United States is in North America.
10. (Niagara Falls) is a famous landmark.
11. Ants are insects.
12. A bicycle has two wheels.
13. Mercury is a planet.
14. Snakes don't have legs.
15. Chickens lay eggs.
16. Copper is a metal.
17. Coffee contains caffeine.
18. The sun is a source of energy.
19. Pencils aren't expensive.
20. Paper burns.

9-6 CONNECTING IDEAS WITH *BECAUSE*

(a) He drank water *because* he was thirsty.	***Because*** expresses a cause; it gives a reason. Why did he drink water? Reason: he was thirsty.
(b) MAIN CLAUSE: *He drank water.*	A main clause is a complete sentence: *He drank water.* = a complete sentence.
(c) ADVERB CLAUSE: *because he was thirsty*	An adverb clause is NOT a complete sentence: *because he was thirsty* = NOT a complete sentence. ***Because*** introduces an adverb clause: ***because*** + *subject* + *verb* = *an adverb clause.*

main clause   adverb clause
(d) ⌐He drank water⌐ ⌐*because he was thirsty.*⌐
            (no comma)
 	
      adverb clause   main clause
(e) ⌐*Because he was thirsty,*⌐ ⌐he drank water.⌐
           (comma)
	An adverb clause is connected to a main clause, as in (d) and (e).*
	In (d): **main clause + *no* comma + adverb clause**.
	In (e): **adverb clause + comma + main clause**.
	
	(d) and (e) have exactly the same meaning.

(f) INCORRECT: He drank water. Because he was thirsty.	(f) is incorrect: *because he was thirsty* cannot stand alone as a sentence that starts with a capital letter and ends with a period. It has to be connected to a main clause as in (d) and (e).

*See Chart 2-8 for a discussion of other adverb clauses. "Time clauses" are adverb clauses that are introduced by *when, after, before,* and *while.*

☐ **EXERCISE 15:** Combine each pair of sentences in two different orders. Use ***because***.

1. We didn't have class. The teacher was absent.

    → ***We didn't have class because the teacher was absent.***

    → ***Because the teacher was absent, we didn't have class.***

2. The children were hungry. There was no food in the house.

3. The bridge is closed. We can't drive to the other side of the river.

4. My car didn't start. The battery was dead.

5. Debbie woke up in the morning with a sore throat. She had cheered loudly at the basketball game.

☐ **EXERCISE 16:** Complete the sentences with *so* or *because*. Add COMMAS where appropriate. CAPITALIZE as necessary.

1. a. He was hungry _____**, so**_____ he ate a sandwich.

   b. _____**Because**_____ he was hungry **,** he ate a sandwich.

   c. He ate a sandwich _____**because**_____ he was hungry.

2. a. _____ my sister was tired she went to bed.

   b. My sister went to bed _____ she was tired.

   c. My sister was tired _____ she went to bed.

3. a. _____ human beings have opposable thumbs they can easily pick things up and hold them.

   b. Human beings have opposable thumbs _____ they can easily pick things up and hold them.

   c. Human beings can easily pick things up and hold them _____ they have opposable thumbs.

4. a. Schoolchildren can usually identify Italy easily on a world map _____ it is shaped like a boot.

   b. _____ Italy has the distinctive shape of a boot schoolchildren can usually identify it easily.

   c. Italy has the distinctive shape of a boot _____ schoolchildren can usually identify it easily on a map.

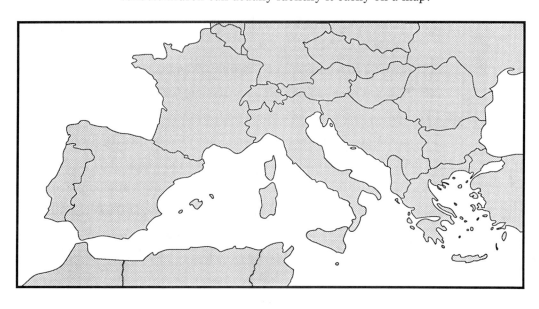

□ **EXERCISE 17:** Add COMMAS, PERIODS, and CAPITAL LETTERS as appropriate. Don't change any of the words or the order of the words.

1. Jim was hot he sat in the shade.

2. Jim was hot and tired he sat in the shade.

3. Jim was hot and tired so he sat in the shade.

4. Jim was hot tired and thirsty.

5. Because he was hot Jim sat in the shade.

6. Because he was hot and thirsty Jim drank some tea.

7. Because he was hot and thirsty Jim sat in the shade and drank some tea.

8. Because they were hot and thirsty Jim and Susan sat in the shade and drank tea.

9. Jim and Susan sat in the shade and drank tea because they were hot and thirsty.

10. Jim sat in the shade drank tea and fanned himself because he was hot tired and thirsty.

11. Because Jim was hot he stayed under the shade of the tree but Susan went back to work.

12. Mules are domestic animals they are the offspring of a horse and a donkey mules are called ''beasts of burden'' because they can work hard and carry heavy loads.

13. Because mules are strong they can work under harsh conditions but they need proper care.

14. A wolf howls because it is separated from its pack or its pup has died.

15. Ann had been looking for an apartment for two weeks yesterday she went to look at an apartment on Fifth Avenue she rented it because it was in good condition and had a nice view of the city she was glad to find a new apartment.

16. The word ''matter'' is a chemical term matter is anything that has weight this book your finger water a rock air and the sun are all examples of matter radio waves and heat are not matter because they do not have weight happiness daydreams and fear have no weight and are not matter.

9-7 CONNECTING IDEAS WITH *EVEN THOUGH/ALTHOUGH*

(a) ***Even though*** *I was hungry*, I did not eat. I did not eat ***even though*** *I was hungry*. (b) ***Although*** *I was hungry*, I did not eat. I did not eat ***although*** *I was hungry*.	*Even though* and *although* introduce an adverb clause. (a) and (b) have the same meaning. They mean: *I was hungry, but I did not eat.*
COMPARE: (c) *Because* I was hungry, *I ate.* (d) *Even though* I was hungry, *I did not eat.*	*Because* expresses an expected result. *Even though/although* expresses an unexpected or opposite result.

☐ **EXERCISE 18:** Complete the sentences by using *even though* or *because*.

1. _____***Even though***_____ the weather is cold, Rick isn't wearing a

    coat.

2. _____ the weather is cold, Ben is wearing a coat.

3. _____ Tim is fairly tall, he can't reach the ceiling.

4. _____ Matt is very tall, he can reach the ceiling.

5. _____ Dan isn't as tall as Matt, he can't reach the

    ceiling.

6. _____ Nick isn't tall, he can reach the ceiling by

    standing on a chair.

TIM   MATT   DAN   NICK

7. _____ Jane was sad, she smiled.

8. _____ Jane was sad, she cried.

9. _____ her street is dangerous, Carol doesn't go out alone after dark.

10. _____ his street is dangerous, Steve often goes out alone after dark.

11. Tony sings at weddings _____ he has a good voice.

12. George sings loudly _____ he can't carry a tune.

13. Louie didn't iron his shirt _____ it was wrinkled.

14. Eric ironed his shirt _____ it was wrinkled.

15. Kate went to a dentist _____ she had a toothache.

16. Colette didn't go to a dentist _____ she had a toothache.

17. Jennifer went to a dentist _____ she didn't have a toothache. She just wanted a checkup.

18. I would like to raise tropical fish _____ it's difficult to maintain a fish tank in good condition.

19. The baby shoved the pills into his mouth _____ they looked like candy. _____ he ingested several pills, he didn't get sick. Today many pill bottles have child-proof caps _____ children may think pills are candy and poison themselves.

20. _____ our friends live on an island, it is easy to get there _____ there is a bridge from the mainland.

☐ **EXERCISE 19—ORAL (BOOKS CLOSED):** Answer "yes" or "no," as you wish. Answer in a complete sentence using either *because* or *even though*. Change the wording as you wish.

Example: Last night you were tired. Did you go to bed early?

Response: Yes, I went to bed early because I was tired. OR:
Yes, because I was tired, I went to bed before nine. OR:
No, I didn't go to bed early even though I was really sleepy. OR:
No, even though I was really tired, I didn't go to bed until after midnight.

1. Last night you were tired. Did you stay up late?
2. You are thirsty. Do you want (a glass of water)?
3. You're hungry. Do you want (a candy bar)?
4. Vegetables are good for you. Do you eat a lot of them?
5. Space exploration is exciting. Would you like to be an astronaut?
6. Guns are dangerous. Do you want to own one?
7. (A local restaurant) is expensive/inexpensive. Do you eat there?
8. (A local delicacy) is/are expensive. Do you buy it/them?
9. The (name of a local) river is/isn't polluted. Do you want to swim in it?
10. Who (in this room) can't swim? Do you want to go to (the beach/the swimming pool) with (. . .) and me this afternoon?
11. Who loves to go swimming? Do you want to go to (the beach/the swimming pool) with (. . .) and me this afternoon?
12. What are the winters like here? Do you like living here in winter?
13. (A recent movie) has had good reviews. Do you want to see it?
14. Are you a good artist? Do you want to draw a picture of me on the board?
15. Where is your family? Are you going to go there (over the next holiday)?

☐ **EXERCISE 20—WRITTEN:** Complete the following with your own words. Pay attention to proper punctuation.

1. I like our classroom even though . . . .
2. I like my (*apartment, dorm room, etc.*) because . . . .
3. . . . even though I don't . . . .
4. . . . because I don't . . . .
5. Even though I didn't . . . , ...
6. Because I didn't . . . , ...
7. . . . because . . . salty.
8. . . . even though . . . very hot.
9. Because . . . , the world is a better place.
10. Even though . . . , I can usually communicate what I mean.
11. People put up fences because . . . .
12. Even though the government has built large apartment complexes, ...
13. Even though most people in the world desire peace, ...
14. . . . because life is hard.
15. Even though . . . , life has many joys.
16. . . . because . . . .
17. Even though . . . , ...
18. Because . . . , I . . . , but . . . .

☐ **EXERCISE 21—ERROR ANALYSIS:** Correct the errors in the following sentences. Pay special attention to punctuation.

1. Even though I was sick, but I went to work.

   → ***Even though I was sick, I went to work.***

   → ***I was sick, but I went to work.***

2. Gold silver and copper. They are metals.

3. The students crowded around the bulletin board. Because their grades were posted there.

4. I'd like a cup of coffee, and so does my friend.

5. I like coffee, but my friend does.

6. Even I am very exhausted, I didn't stop working until after midnight last night.

7. The teacher went too the meeting, and too of the students did two.

8. Although I like chocolate, but I can't eat it because I'm allergic to it.

9. Many tourists visit my country. Warm weather all year. Many interesting landmarks.

10. Because the weather in my country is warm and comfortable all year so many tourists visit it in the winter.

11. I like to eat raw eggs for breakfast and everybody else in my family too.

12. A hardware store sells tools and nails and plumbing supplies and paint and etc.★

13. Because the war broke out in late September we had to cancel our October trip even though we already had our passports visas airplane tickets and hotel reservations.

14. Many of us experience stress on our jobs my job is stressful because my workplace is not pleasant or comfortable it is noisy hot and dirty even though I try to do my best my boss is unhappy with my work and always gives me bad performance reports I need to find another job.

★***Etc.*** is an abbreviation of the Latin *et cetera*. It means "and other things of a similar nature." The word ***and*** is NOT used in front of ***etc.***
  INCORRECT: *The farmer raises cows, sheep, goats,* ***chickens, and etc.***
  INCORRECT: *The farmer raises cows, sheep, goats,* ***and chickens, etc.***
  Also, notice the spelling: *etc.* NOT *ect.*

9-8 PHRASAL VERBS (SEPARABLE)

(a) We **put off** our trip.	In (a): **put off** = a phrasal verb.* A *phrasal verb* = a verb and a particle that together have a special meaning. For example, **put off** means "postpone." A *particle* = a preposition (e.g., *off, on*) or an adverb (e.g., *away, back*) that is used in a phrasal verb.
(b) We *put off our trip.* (c) We *put our trip off.* (d) I *turned on the light.* (e) I *turned the light on.*	Many phrasal verbs are **separable.**** In other words, a NOUN can either follow or come between (separate) the verb and the particle. (b) and (c) have the same meaning. (d) and (e) have the same meaning.
(f) We *put it off.* (g) I *turned it on.*	If a phrasal verb is **separable**, the PRONOUN always comes between the verb and the particle; the pronoun never follows the particle. INCORRECT: *We put off it.* INCORRECT: *I turned on it.*

SOME COMMON PHRASAL VERBS (SEPARABLE)

figure out . . . . *find the solution to a problem*
hand in . . . . *give homework, test papers, etc., to a teacher*
hand out . . . . *give something to this person, then that person, then another person, etc.*
look up . . . . *look for information in a dictionary, a telephone directory, an encyclopedia, etc.*
make up . . . . *invent a story*
pick up . . . . *lift*
put down . . . . *stop holding or carrying*
put off . . . . *postpone*
put on . . . . *put clothes on one's body*
take off . . . . *remove clothes from one's body*
throw away⎫ . . . . *put in the trash, discard*
throw out ⎭
turn off . . . . *stop a machine or a light*
turn on . . . . *start a machine or a light*
wake up . . . . *stop sleeping*
write down . . . . . . *write a note on a piece of paper*

*Phrasal verbs are also called *two-word verbs* and *three-word verbs*.
Some phrasal verbs are **nonseparable. Chart 9-9 will discuss nonseparable phrasal verbs. See Appendix 2 for a list of phrasal verbs.

☐ **EXERCISE 22:** Complete the sentences with the following particles: *away, down, in, off, on, out, up.*

1. Before I left home this morning, I put _____ my coat.

2. When I got to class this morning, I took my coat _____.

3. The students handed their homework _____.

4. Johnny made a story _____. He didn't tell the truth.

5. The weather was bad, so we put _____ the picnic until next week.

6. Alice looked a word _____ in her dictionary.

7. Alice wrote the definition _____.

8. My roommate is messy. He never picks _____ his clothes.

9. The teacher handed the test papers _____ at the beginning of the class period.

10. A strange noise woke _____ the children in the middle of the night.

11. When some friends came to visit, Chris stopped watching TV. He turned the television set _____.

12. It was dark when I got home last night, so I turned the lights _____.

13. Peggy finally figured _____ the answer to the arithmetic problem.

14. When I was walking through the airport, my arms got tired. So I put my suitcases _____ for a minute and rested.

15. I threw _____ yesterday's newspaper.

☐ **EXERCISE 23:** Complete the sentences with pronouns and particles.

1. A: Did you postpone your trip to Puerto Rico?

   B: Yes, we did. We put _____*it off*_____ until next summer.

2. A: Is Pat's phone number 322–4454 or 322–5545?

   B: I don't remember. You'd better look _____. The telephone directory is in the kitchen.

3. A: Is Mary still asleep?

   B: Yes. I'd better wake _____. She has a class at nine.

4. A: Do you want to keep these newspapers?

   B: No. Throw _____.

5. A: I'm hot. This sweater is too heavy.

   B: Why don't you take _____?

6. A: Is that story true?

   B: No. I made _____.

7. A: When does the teacher want our compositions?

   B: We have to hand _____ tomorrow.

8. A: I made an appointment with Dr. Armstrong for three o'clock next Thursday.

   B: You'd better write _____ so you won't forget.

9. A: Do you know the answer to this problem?

   B: No. I can't figure _____.

10. A: Johnny, you're too heavy for me to carry. I have to put _____.

    B: Okay, Mommy.

11. A: Where are the letters I put on the kitchen table?

    B: I picked _____ and took them to the post office.

12. A: How does this tape recorder work?

    B: Push this button to turn _____, and push that button to turn _____.

13. A: I have some papers for the class. Ali, would you please hand _____ for me?

    B: I'd be happy to.

14. A: Timmy, here's your hat. Put _____ before you go out. It's cold outside.

    B: Okay, Dad.

9-9 PHRASAL VERBS (NONSEPARABLE)

(a) I *ran into Bob* at the bank yesterday. (b) I saw Bob yesterday. I *ran into him* at the bank.	If a phrasal verb is **nonseparable**, a noun or pronoun follows (never precedes) the particle. INCORRECT: *I ran Bob into at the bank.* INCORRECT: *I ran him into at the bank.*

SOME COMMON PHRASAL VERBS (NONSEPARABLE)
call on . . . . *ask to speak in class*
get over . . . . *recover from an illness*
run into . . . . *meet by chance*
get on . . . . *enter* } *a bus, an airplane, a train, a subway, a bicycle*
get off . . . . *leave*
get in . . . . *enter* } *a car, a taxi*
get out of . . . . . . *leave*

□ **EXERCISE 24:** Complete the sentences with particles. Discuss the meaning of the phrasal verbs in the sentences.

1. When I raised my hand in class, the teacher called _____ me.

2. While I was walking down the street, I ran _____ an old friend.

3. Fred feels okay today. He got _____ his cold.

4. Last week I flew from Chicago to Miami. I got _____ the plane in Chicago. I got _____ the plane in Miami.

5. Sally took a taxi to the airport. She got out _____ the taxi in front of her apartment building. She got _____ the taxi at the airport.

6. I take the bus to school every day. I get _____ the bus at the corner of First Street and Sunset Boulevard. I get _____ the bus just a block away from the classroom building.

□ **EXERCISE 25—ORAL (BOOKS CLOSED):** Complete the sentences.

Example: Yesterday I cleaned my closet. I found an old pair of shoes that I don't ever wear anymore. I didn't keep the shoes. I threw . . . .

Response: them away/out.

1. The teacher gave us some important information in class yesterday. I didn't want to forget it, so I wrote . . . .
2. When I raised my hand in class, the teacher called . . . .
3. I was carrying a suitcase, but it was too heavy, so I put . . . .
4. I didn't know the meaning of a word, so I looked . . . .
5. I was sleepy last night, so I didn't finish my homework. I put . . . .
6. It was dark when I got home, so I turned . . . .
7. (. . .) isn't wearing his/her hat right now. When s/he got to class, s/he took . . . .
8. My pen just fell on the floor. Could you please pick . . . ?
9. I saw (. . .) at a concert last night. I was surprised when I ran . . . .
10. When you finish using a stove, you should always be careful to turn . . . .
11. When I finished my test, I handed . . . .
12. Is (. . .) sleeping?! Would you please wake . . . ?
13. What's the answer to this problem? Have you figured . . . ?
14. I don't need this piece of paper anymore. I'm going to throw . . . .

15. I had the flu last week, but now I'm okay. I got . . . .
16. I told a story that wasn't true. I made . . . .
17. Name some means of transportation that you get on.
18. Name some that you get in.
19. Name some that you get off.
20. Name some that you get out of.
21. Name some things that you turn on.
22. Name some things that you turn off.

CHAPTER *10*

Gerunds and Infinitives

10-1 GERUNDS AND INFINITIVES: INTRODUCTION

(a) I enjoy ⌐noun⌐ music.	**S V O** *I enjoy **something**. (something* = the object of the verb.) The object of a verb is usually a noun or pronoun, as in (a). The object of a verb can also be a gerund. A gerund is *the **-ing** form of a verb.*★ It is used as a noun. In (b): ***listening*** is a gerund. It is the object of the verb ***enjoy***.
(b) I enjoy ⌐gerund⌐ ***listening*** to music.	
(c) I enjoy ⌐gerund phrase⌐ ***listening to music***.	
(d) I want ⌐noun⌐ a sandwich.	**S V O** *I want **something**. (something* = the object of the verb.) In (d): The object of the verb is a noun (*a sandwich*). The object of a verb can also be an infinitive. An infinitive is **to** + *the simple form of a verb.* In (e): ***to eat*** is an infinitive. It is the object of the verb ***want***.
(e) I want ⌐infinitive⌐ ***to eat*** a sandwich.	
(f) I want ⌐infinitive phrase⌐ ***to eat** a sandwich*.	
(g) I *enjoy **going*** to the beach.	Some verbs (e.g., *enjoy*) are followed by gerunds. (See 10-2.)
(h) Ted *wants **to go*** to the beach.	Some verbs (e.g., *want*) are followed by infinitives. (See 10-4.)
(i) It *began **raining***. It *began **to rain***.	Some verbs (e.g., *begin*) are followed by either gerunds or infinitives. (See 10-5.)

★The ***-ing*** form of a verb can be used as a present participle:
　　*I **am listening** to the teacher right now.* (***listening*** = a present participle, used in the present progressive)
　The ***-ing*** form of a verb can be used as a gerund:
　　*I **enjoy** listening to music.* (***listening*** = a gerund, used as the object of the verb ***enjoy***)

10-2 VERB + GERUND

COMMON VERBS FOLLOWED BY GERUNDS		Gerunds are used as the objects of the verbs in the list. The list also contains phrasal verbs (e.g., *put off*) that are followed by gerunds.
enjoy	(a) I *enjoy working* in my garden.	
finish	(b) Bob *finished studying* at midnight.	
stop*	(c) It *stopped raining* a few minutes ago.	These verbs are NOT followed by infinitives.* For example:
quit	(d) David *quit smoking*.	INCORRECT: *I enjoy to work.*
mind	(e) Would you *mind opening* the window?	INCORRECT: *Bob finished to study.*
		INCORRECT: *I'm thinking to go to Hawaii.*
postpone	(f) I *postponed doing* my homework.	
put off	(g) I *put off doing* my homework.	
keep	(h) *Keep working.* Don't stop.	
keep on	(i) *Keep on working.* Don't stop.	
consider	(j) I'm *considering going* to Hawaii.	
think about	(k) I'm *thinking about going* to Hawaii.	
discuss	(l) They *discussed getting* a new car.	See Chart 2-5 for the spelling of *-ing* verb forms.
talk about	(m) They *talked about getting* a new car.	
(n) I considered *not going* to class.		Negative form: *not* + gerund.

*The object following *stop* is a gerund, NOT an infinitive. INCORRECT: *It stopped to rain.*
But in a special circumstance, *stop* can be followed by an infinitive of purpose: *in order to* (see Chart 10-11). *While I was walking down the hall, I dropped my pen. I **stopped to pick** it up. = I **stopped walking in order to pick** it up.*

☐ **EXERCISE 1:** Complete the sentences by using gerunds. Add a preposition after the gerund if necessary.

1. It was cold and rainy yesterday, so we postponed __*going to/visiting*__ the botanical gardens.

2. The Porter's house is too small. They're considering __*buying/*__ __*moving into/renting*__ a bigger house.

3. We discussed _____ Colorado for our vacation.

4. When Martha finished _____ the floor, she dusted the furniture.

5. Sometimes students put off _____ their homework.

6. We had a blizzard yesterday, but it finally stopped _____ around ten P.M.

7. I quit _____ comic books when I was twelve years old.

8. I'm thinking about _____ a biology course next

semester.

9. Beth doesn't like her job. She's talking about _____

a different job.

10. I enjoy _____ sports.

11. I'm considering _____ New York City.

12. A: Are you listening to me?

B: Yes. Keep _____. I'm listening.

13. A: Do you want to take a break?

B: No. I'm not tired yet. Let's keep on _____ for

another hour or so.

14. A: Would you mind _____ the window?

B: Not at all. I'd be glad to.

□ **EXERCISE 2:** Complete the sentences in the dialogues. Use the expressions in the list or
your own words. Be sure to use a gerund in each sentence.

buy a new car	*rain*
do my homework	*read a good book*
do things	*repeat that*
get a Toyota	*smoke*
go to the zoo on Saturday	*tap your fingernails on the table*
help him	*try*

1. A: Would you like to go for a walk?

B: Has it stopped _____ ***raining*** _____?

A: Yes.

B: Let's go.

2. A: I've been having a lot of trouble with my old Honda the last couple

of months. It's slowly falling apart. I'm thinking about _____

_____.

B: Do you think you'll get another Honda?

A: No. I'm considering _____.

3. A: What do you usually do in your free time in the evening?

   B: I enjoy _____.

4. A: Good news! I feel great. I don't cough any more, and I don't run out of breath when I walk up a hill.

   B: Oh?

   A: I quit _____.

   B: That's wonderful!

5. A: I've been working on this math problem for the last half hour, and I still don't understand it.

   B: Well, don't give up. Keep _____. If at first you don't succeed, try, try again.

6. A: Are you a procrastinator?

   B: A what?

   A: A procrastinator. That's someone who always postpones _____

   _____.

   B: Oh. Well, sometimes I put off _____.

7. A: What are you doing?

   B: I'm helping Teddy with his homework.

   A: When you finish _____, could you help me in the kitchen?

   B: Sure.

8. A: Could you please stop doing that?

   B: Doing what?

   A: Stop _____. It's driving me crazy.

9. A: Do you have any plans for this weekend?

   B: Henry and I talked about _____.

10. A: I didn't understand what you said. Would you mind _____

    _____?

    B: Of course not. I said, "Three free trees."

10-3 GO + -ING

(a) **Did** you **go shopping** yesterday?
 (b) I **went swimming** last week.
 (c) Bob **hasn't gone fishing** in years.
	Go is followed by a gerund in certain idiomatic expressions about activities.
	 Notice: There is no **to** between **go** and the gerund.
	   INCORRECT: *Did you go to shopping?*
	   CORRECT: *Did you go shopping?*

COMMON EXPRESSIONS WITH *GO* + -*ING*

go boating	*go hiking*	*go sightseeing*
go bowling	*go jogging*	*go skating*
go camping	*go running*	*go (water) skiing*
go dancing	*go sailing*	*go skydiving*
go fishing	*go (window) shopping*	*go swimming*

☐ **EXERCISE 3—ORAL:** Answer the questions. Use the expressions with **go** + -**ing** in Chart 10-3.

1. Ann often goes to the beach. She spends hours in the water. What does she like to do?
   → *She likes to go swimming.*

2. Nancy and Frank like to spend the whole day on a lake with poles in their hands. What do they like to do?

3. Last summer Adam went to a national park. He slept in a tent and cooked his food over a fire. What did Adam do last summer?

4. Tim likes to go to stores and buy things. What does he like to do?

5. Laura takes good care of her health. She runs a couple of miles every day. What does Laura do every day? (*Note: There are two possible responses.*)

6. On weekends in the winter, Fred and Jean sometimes drive to a resort in the mountains. They like to race down the side of a mountain in the snow. What do they like to do?

7. Joe is a nature lover. He likes to take long walks in the woods. What does Joe like to do?

8. Sara prefers indoor sports. She goes to a place where she rolls a thirteen-pound ball at some wooden pins. What does Sara often do?

9. Liz and Greg know all the latest dances. What do they probably do a lot?

10. The Taylors are going to go to a little lake near their house tomorrow. The lake is completely frozen now that it's winter. The ice is smooth. What are the Taylors going to do tomorrow?

11. Barbara and Alex live near the ocean. When there's a strong wind, they like to spend the whole day in their sailboat. What do they like to do?

12. Tourists often get on buses that take them to see interesting places in an area. What do tourists do on buses?

13. Colette and Ben like to jump out of airplanes. They don't open their parachutes until the last minute. What do they like to do?

14. What do you like to do for exercise and fun?

10-4 VERB + INFINITIVE

(a) Tom **offered to lend** me some money.	Some verbs are followed by an infinitive:
(b) I've **decided to buy** a new car.	AN INFINITIVE = **to** + *the simple form of a verb.*
(c) I've **decided not to keep** my old car.	Negative form: **not** + *infinitive.*

COMMON VERBS FOLLOWED BY INFINITIVES

want	*hope*	*decide*	*seen*	*learn (how)*
need	*expect*	*promise*	*appear*	*try*
would like	*plan*	*offer*	*pretend*	
would love	*intend*	*agree*		*(can't) afford*
	mean	*refuse*	*forget*	*(can't) wait*

□ **EXERCISE 4:** Complete the sentences by using INFINITIVES. Add a PREPOSITION after the infinitive if necessary.

1. I'm planning ____*to go to/to visit/to drive to*____ Chicago next week.

2. I've decided _____ a new apartment.

3. Jack promised not _____ late for the wedding.

4. I forgot _____ some milk when I went to the grocery store.

5. I would like _____ the Grand Canyon.

6. My husband and I would love _____ Arizona.

7. I need _____ my homework tonight.

8. What time do you expect _____ Chicago?

9. I want _____ a ball game on TV after dinner tonight.

10. You seem _____ in a good mood today.

11. Susie appeared _____ asleep, but she wasn't. She was only pretending.

12. Susie pretended _____ asleep. She pretended not _____ me when I spoke to her.

13. The Millers can't afford _____ a house.

14. George is only seven, but he intends _____ a doctor when he grows up.

15. My friend offered _____ me a little money.

16. Tommy doesn't like peas. He refuses _____ them.

17. My wife and I wanted to do different things this weekend. Finally, I agreed _____ a movie with her Saturday, and she agreed _____ the football game with me on Sunday.

18. I hope _____ all of my courses this term. So far my grades have been pretty good.

19. I try _____ class on time every day.

20. I can't wait _____ my family again! It's been a long time!

21. I'm sorry. I didn't mean _____ you.

22. I learned (how) _____ when I was around six or seven.

10-5 VERB + GERUND OR INFINITIVE

(a) It began *to rain*. (b) It began *raining*.	Some verbs are followed by either an infinitive or a gerund. Usually there is no difference in meaning. (a) and (b) have the same meaning.

COMMON VERBS FOLLOWED BY EITHER A GERUND OR AN INFINITIVE

begin	*like**	*hate*
start	*love**	*can't stand*
continue		

*COMPARE: ***Like*** and ***love*** can be followed by either a gerund or an infinitive:
I like going/to go to movies. I love playing/to play chess.

Would like and ***would love*** are followed by infinitives:
I would like to go to a movie tonight. I'd love to play a game of chess right now.

☐ **EXERCISE 5—ORAL:** Use the given words to make sentences with GERUNDS and INFINITIVES.

1. start + snow around midnight

   → *It started snowing around midnight. It started to snow around midnight.*

2. continue + work even though everyone else stopped

3. like + listen to music while I'm studying

4. love + go to baseball games

5. hate + talk to pushy salespeople

6. can't stand + wait in lines for a long time

☐ **EXERCISE 6:** Complete the sentences with the INFINITIVE or GERUND form of the words in parentheses.

1. I need (study) ____*to study*____ tonight.

2. I enjoy (cook) ____*cooking*____ gourmet meals.

3. Ellen started (talk) ____*to talk/talking*____ about her problem.

4. Bud and Sally have decided (get) _____ married.

5. We finished (eat) _____ around seven.

6. Are you planning (take) _____ a vacation this year?

7. I like (meet) _____ new people.

8. The Wilsons went (*camp*) _____ in Yellowstone National Park last summer.

9. My roommate offered (*help*) _____ me with my English.

10. I'd just begun (*watch*) _____ a movie on TV when the phone rang.

11. Please stop (*crack*) _____ your knuckles!

12. Did you remember (*feed*) _____ the cat this morning?

13. I won't be late. I promise (*be*) _____ on time.

14. I'm considering (*move*) _____ to a new apartment.

15. What time do you expect (*arrive*) _____ in Denver?

16. Some children hate (*go*) _____ to school.

17. I forgot (*lock*) _____ the door when I left my apartment this morning.

18. I don't mind (*live*) _____ with four roommates.

19. Don't put off (*write*) _____ your composition until the last minute.

20. Ken had to quit (*jog*) _____ because he hurt his knee.

21. The company will continue (*hire*) _____ new employees as long as new production orders keep (*come*) _____ in.

22. That's not what I meant! I meant (*say*) _____ just the opposite.

23. I want (*go*) _____ (*shop*) _____ this afternoon.

24. Alex seems (*want*) _____ (*go*) _____ (*sail*) _____ this weekend.

☐ **EXERCISE 7:** Complete the sentences with the INFINITIVE or GERUND form of the words in parentheses.

1. Cindy intends (*go*) _____ to graduate school next year.

2. Pierre can't afford (*buy*) _____ a new car.

3. Janice is thinking about (*look*) _____ for a new job.

4. My boss refused (give) _____ me a raise, so I quit.

5. Mr. Carter continued (read) _____ his book even though the children were making a lot of noise.

6. Shhh. My roommate is trying (take) _____ a nap.

7. Dick appears (have) _____ a lot of money.

8. Eric agreed (meet) _____ us at the restaurant at seven.

9. Have you discussed (change) _____ your major with your academic advisor?

10. I haven't heard from Stacy in a long time. I keep (hope) _____ that I'll get a letter from her soon.

11. My wife can't stand (sleep) _____ in a room with all of the windows closed.

12. Sam's tomato crop always failed. Finally he quit (try) _____ (grow) _____ tomatoes in his garden.

13. Would you like (go) _____ (dance) _____ tonight?

14. The Knickerbockers talked about (build) _____ a new house.

15. Children like (play) _____ make-believe games. Yesterday Jason pretended (be) _____ a doctor, and Bobby pretended (be) _____ a patient.

16. My cousin offered (take) _____ me to the airport.

17. I'm planning (go) _____ (shop) _____ tomorrow.

18. Would you mind (pass) _____ this note to Joanna? Thanks.

19. Tim expects (go) _____ (fish) _____ this weekend.

20. When Tommy broke his toy, he started (cry) _____.

21. Jerry likes (go) _____ to professional conferences.

22. Would you like (go) _____ to Sharon's house next Saturday?

23. I expect (be) _____ in class tomorrow.

24. I enjoy (teach) _____ .

25. I enjoy (be) _____ a teacher.

□ **EXERCISE 8—ORAL:** Pair up with another student.

STUDENT A: Read the cues. Your book is open.
STUDENT B: Complete the sentences with either **to go** or **going** + *the name of a place.*

Example:
STUDENT A: I expect . . . .
STUDENT B: to go (to Mack's Bar and Grill for dinner tonight).
STUDENT A: I like . . . .
STUDENT B: to go (to Hawaii). OR: . . . going (to Hawaii).

Switch roles halfway through: STUDENT A *becomes* STUDENT B *and vice versa.*

1. I expect . . . .
2. I like . . . .
3. I would like . . . .
4. I enjoy . . . .
5. I'd love . . . .
6. I promised . . . .
7. I can't stand . . . .
8. I intend . . . .
9. I am thinking about . . . .
10. Are you considering . . . .
11. I refuse . . . .
12. I've always wanted . . . .
13. I can't afford . . . .
14. I'd enjoy . . . .
15. I don't need . . . .
16. I'm going to try . . . .
17. I hate . . . .
18. I love . . . .
19. My friend and I discussed . . . .
20. I've decided . . . .
21. My friend and I postponed . . . .
22. Sometimes I put off . . . .
23. Yesterday I forgot . . . .
24. I can't wait . . . .
25. My friend and I agreed . . . .
26. Would you mind . . . .

□ **EXERCISE 9:** Complete the sentences with a form of the words in parentheses.

1. I enjoy (get) _____ up early in the morning.

2. I enjoy (watch) _____ the sunrise.

3. I enjoy (get) _____ up early in the morning and (watch)

_____ the sunrise.

4. I enjoy (get) _____ up early in the morning, (watch)

_____ the sunrise, and (listen) _____ to

the birds.

5. I want (stay) _____ home tonight.

6. I want (*relax*) _____ tonight.

7. I want (*stay*) _____ home and (*relax*)* _____ tonight.

8. I want (*stay*) _____ home, (*relax*) _____ , and (*go*) _____ to bed early tonight.

9. Mr. and Mrs. Brown are thinking about (*sell*) _____ their old house and (*buy*) _____ a new one.

10. Kathy plans (*move*) _____ to New York City, (*find*) _____ a job, and (*start*) _____ a new life.

☐ **EXERCISE 10:** Complete the sentences with a form of the words in parentheses.

1. Have you finished (*paint*) _____ your apartment yet?

2. Steve needs (*go*) _____ to the shopping mall tomorrow and (*buy*) _____ winter clothes.

3. Don't forget (*call*) _____ the dentist's office this afternoon.

4. Do you enjoy (*go*) _____ to an expensive restaurant and (*have*) _____ a gourmet dinner?

5. Most nonsmokers can't stand (*be*) _____ in a smoke-filled room.

6. Let's postpone (*go*) _____ abroad until the political situation improves.

7. The children promised (*stop*) _____ (*make*) _____ so much noise.

8. How do you expect (*pass*) _____ your courses if you don't study?

9. Kevin is thinking about (*quit*) _____ his job and (*go*) _____ back to school.

---

*When infinitives are connected by **and**, it is not necessary to repeat **to**:
   *I need **to stay** home **and** (to) **study** tonight.*

10. Linda plans (*leave*) _____ for Chicago on Tuesday and (*return*) _____ on Friday.

11. I often put off (*wash*) _____ the dinner dishes until the next morning.

12. Shhh. I'm trying (*concentrate*) _____. I'm doing a problem for my accounting class, and I can't afford (*make*) _____ any mistakes.

13. I'm sleepy. I'd like (*go*) _____ home and (*take*) _____ a nap.

14. When are you going to start (*do*) _____ the research for your term paper?

15. Why did Marcia refuse (*help*) _____ us?

16. Don't forget (*unplug*) _____ the coffee pot, (*turn off*) _____ all the lights, and (*lock*) _____ the door before you leave for work this morning.

17. Sometimes when I'm listening to someone who is speaking English very fast, I nod my head and pretend (*understand*) _____.

18. After Isabel got a speeding ticket and had to pay a big fine, she decided (*stop*) _____ (*drive*) _____ over the speed limit on interstate highways.

19. Khalid tries (*learn*) _____ at least 25 new words every day.

20. I considered (*drive*) _____ to Minneapolis. Finally I decided (*fly*) _____.

21. Our teacher agreed (*postpone*) _____ the test until Friday.

22. I've been trying (*reach*) _____ Carol on the phone for the last three days, but she's never at home. I intend (*keep*) _____ (*try*) _____ until I finally get her.

Make sentences from the given words.
Use **I**. Use any tense.

> *Example:* *want* and *go*
> *Response:* I want to go (to New York City next week).

1. *plan* and *go*	16. *promise* and *come*
2. *consider* and *go*	17. *finish* and *study*
3. *offer* and *lend*	18. *would mind* and *help*
4. *like* and *visit*	19. *hope* and *go*
5. *enjoy* and *read*	20. *think about* and *go*
6. *intend* and *get up*	21. *quit* and *drink*
7. *decide* and *get*	22. *expect* and *stay*
8. *seem* and *be*	23. *stop* and *eat*
9. *put off* and *write*	24. *refuse* and *lend*
10. *forget* and *go*	25. *agree* and *lend*
11. *can't afford* and *buy*	26. *postpone* and *go*
12. *try* and *learn*	27. *begin* and *study*
13. *need* and *learn*	28. *continue* and *walk*
14. *would love* and *take*	29. *talk about* and *go*
15. *would like* and *go* and *swim*	30. *keep* and *try* and *improve*

10-6   UNCOMPLETED INFINITIVES

(a) I've never met Rita, but *I'd like **to**.*	In (a): *I'd like **to*** = an uncompleted infinitive; *I'd like **to meet Rita*** = the understood completion. An infinitive phrase is not completed following ***to*** when the meaning is clearly understood to repeat the idea that came immediately before. Uncompleted infinitives follow the verbs in Charts 10-4 and 10-5.
(b) INCORRECT: I've never met Rita, but I'd like.	
(c) INCORRECT: I've never met Rita, but I'd like it.	
(d) INCORRECT: I've never met Rita, but I'd like to do.	
(e) I don't want to leave, but *I have **to**.*	Uncompleted infinitives are also common with these auxiliaries: *have to, be going to, used to,* and *ought to.*
(f) Sam doesn't go to school here, but *he used **to**.*	

□ **EXERCISE 12:** Complete the sentences with the words in parentheses. Use any
appropriate tense. Discuss the understood meaning of the uncompleted
infinitives.

1. A: Why didn't you go to the concert?

   B: I (*want, not*) ___**didn't want to**___ .

2. I haven't written my parents yet this week, but I (*intend*)

    _____.

3. A: Did Jane enjoy the play?

    B: She (*seem*) _____.

4. I'd like to buy fresh flowers for my desk every day, but I can't (*afford*)

    _____.

5. I've never eaten at that restaurant, but I (*would like*)

    _____.

6. A: Want to go to the jazz festival with us tomorrow night?

    B: I (*would love*) _____!

7. A: Are you going to the historical society meeting?

    B: Yes, I (*plan*) _____. And you?

8. Oh! I'm sorry I closed the door in your face! I (*mean, not*)

    _____!

9. I don't play with toys anymore, but I (*use*) _____.

10. A: Have you called Jennifer yet?

    B: That's the fourth time you've asked me. I (*be going*)

    _____! I (*be going*) _____!

    Don't be a nag!

11. Tina doesn't feel like going to the meeting, but she (*have*)

    _____.

12. A: Are you planning to go to the market?

    B: No, but I suppose I (*ought*) _____.

10-7 PREPOSITION + GERUND

(a) Kate *insisted **on coming*** with us.	A preposition is followed by a gerund, not an
(b) We're excited ***about going*** to Tahiti.	infinitive.
(c) I *apologized **for being*** late.	In (a): preposition (*on*) + gerund (*coming*)

□ **EXERCISE 13:** Complete the sentences. Use PREPOSITIONS* and GERUNDS.

1. Bill interrupted me. He apologized ____*for*____ that.

   → Bill apologized _____*for interrupting*_____ me.

2. I like to learn about other countries and cultures. I'm interested
   _____ that.

   → I'm interested _____ about other countries
   and cultures.

3. I helped Ann. She thanked me _____ that.

   → Ann thanked me _____ her.

4. Jessica wanted to walk to work. She insisted _____ that.

   → We offered Jessica a ride, but she insisted _____
   to work.

5. Nick lost my car keys. I forgave him _____ that.

   → I forgave Nick _____ my car keys when he
   borrowed my car.

6. Sara wanted to go to a movie, but James didn't want to. They argued
   _____ that.

   → Sara and James argued _____ to a movie.

7. Jake cuts his own hair. Instead _____ that, he should go to a
   barber.

   → Instead _____
   his own hair, Jake should go to a barber.

8. Mr. and Mrs. Reed have always saved for
   a rainy day. They believe _____ that.

   → Mr. and Mrs. Reed believe _____
   _____ for a rainy day.

9. I may fall on my face and make a fool of
   myself. I'm worried _____ that.

   → I'm worried _____ on my face and

---

*If necessary, refer to Appendix 1 for a list of preposition combinations.

_____ a fool of myself when I walk up the steps to
receive my diploma.

10. The children are going to go to Disneyland. They're excited _____
that.

→ The children are excited _____ to
Disneyland.

11. Their parents are going to Disneyland, too. They are looking forward
_____ that.

→ Their parents are looking forward _____
there, too.

10-8 USING *BY* AND *WITH* TO EXPRESS HOW SOMETHING IS DONE

(a) Pat turned off the tape recorder **by pushing** the stop button.	**By** + *a gerund* is used to express how something is done.
(b) Mary goes to work **by bus**. (c) Andrea stirred her coffee **with a spoon**.	**By** or **with** followed by a noun is also used to express how something is done.

BY IS USED FOR MEANS OF TRANSPORTATION AND COMMUNICATION:

by	*by subway*★★	*by mail*	*by air*
(air)plane★	*by taxi*	*by (tele)phone*	*by land*
by boat	*by train*	*by fax*	*by sea*
by bus	*by foot* (OR *on foot*)		
by car			

OTHERS:

by chance
by choice
by mistake
by check (but *in cash*)
by hand★★★

WITH IS USED FOR INSTRUMENTS OR PARTS OF THE BODY:

I cut down the tree *with an ax* (by using an ax).
I swept the floor *with a broom*.
She pointed to a spot on the map *with her finger*.

★*airplane* = American English   *aeroplane* = British English
★★*by subway* = American English   *by underground, by tube* = British English
★★★The expression **by hand** is usually used to mean that something was made by a person, not by a machine: *This rug was made **by hand**.* (A person, not a machine, made this rug.) COMPARE: *I touched his shoulder **with my hand**.*

□ **EXERCISE 14:** Complete the following by using *by* + a GERUND. Use the words in the list or your own words.

eat	smile	watch
drink	wag	wave
guess	wash	✔ write
grow		

1. Students practice written English ___**by writing**___ compositions.

2. We clean our clothes _____ them in soap and water.

3. I save money on food _____ my own vegetables.

4. Khalid improved his English _____ a lot of TV.

5. We show other people we are happy _____.

6. We satisfy our hunger _____ something.

7. We quench our thirst _____ something.

8. I figured out what "quench" means _____.

9. Alex caught my attention _____ his arms in the air.

10. My dog shows me she is happy _____ her tail.

Complete the following with your own words. Use **by** *and* GERUNDS.

11. Students show teachers they want to say something _____ _____ their hands.

12. You can destroy bacteria in meat _____ it.

13. You can cook an egg _____ it, _____ it, or _____ it.

14. After work, I relax _____ or _____.

15. Each of you, in your own small way, can help conserve the world's natural resources _____.

□ **EXERCISE 15:** Complete the sentences with *by* or *with*.

1. I opened the door ___**with**___ a key.

2. I went to Cherryville ___**by**___ bus.

3. I dried the dishes _____ a dishtowel.

4. I went from Portland to San Francisco _____ train.

5. Paul dug a hole _____ a shovel.

6. Ted drew a straight line _____ a ruler.

7. Is there any way you could touch the ceiling _____ your foot?

8. Some advertisers try to reach target audiences _____ mail.

9. Rebecca tightened the screw in the corner of her eyeglasses _____ her fingernail.

10. I called Bill "Paul" _____ mistake.

11. The fastest way to send a copy of a piece of paper halfway around the world is _____ fax.

12. The chef sliced the partially frozen meat into thin strips _____ a razor-sharp knife.

10-9 USING GERUNDS AS SUBJECTS; USING *IT* + INFINITIVE

(a) ***Riding*** horses is fun. (b) *It* is fun *to ride* horses.	(a) and (b) have the same meaning. In (a): A gerund (*riding*) is the subject of the sentence.* Notice: The verb (*is*) is singular because a gerund is singular. In (b): The word *it* is used as the subject of the sentence. The word *it* has the same meaning as the infinitive phrase at the end of the sentence: *it* means *to ride horses*.
(c) ***Coming*** to class on time is important. (d) *It* is important *to come* to class on time.	

*It is also correct (but less common) to use an infinitive as the subject of a sentence: *To ride horses is fun.*

☐ **EXERCISE 16—ORAL:** Make sentences with the same meaning by using *it* + INFINITIVE.

1. Having good friends is important. → *It is important to have good friends.*
2. Playing tennis is fun.
3. Being polite to other people is important.
4. Learning about other cultures is interesting.
5. Walking alone at night in that part of the city is dangerous.
6. Is learning a second language difficult?
7. Is riding a motorcycle easy?
8. Having a cold isn't much fun.
9. Learning a second language takes a long time.
10. Cooking a soft-boiled egg takes three minutes.

□ **EXERCISE 17—ORAL:** Make sentences with the same meaning by using a GERUND as the subject.

1. It is important to get daily exercise.
   → *Getting daily exercise is important.*
2. It is fun to meet new people.
3. It is easy to cook rice.
4. It is boring to spend the whole weekend in the dorm.
5. It is relaxing to take a long walk.
6. Is it difficult to learn a second language?
7. It isn't hard to make friends.
8. It is wrong to cheat during a test.
9. Is it dangerous to smoke cigarettes?
10. Is it expensive to live in an apartment?
11. It isn't easy to live in a foreign country.
12. It takes time to make new friends.

□ **EXERCISE 18—ORAL:** Answer the questions.

STUDENT A: Use *it* + *infinitives*.
STUDENT B: Use *gerunds*.

1. Which is easier: to make money or to spend money?
   → A: *It is easier to spend money than (it is) to make money.*
   → B: *Spending money is easier than making money.*
2. Which is more fun: to study at the library or to go to a movie?
3. Which is more difficult: to write English or to read English?
4. Which is easier: to write English or to speak English?
5. Which is more expensive: to go to a movie or to go to a concert?
6. Which is more interesting: to talk to people or to watch people?
7. Which is more comfortable: to wear shoes or to go barefoot?
8. Which is more satisfying: to give gifts or to receive them?
9. Which is more dangerous: to ride in a car or to ride in an airplane?
10. Which is more important: to come to class on time or to get an extra hour of sleep in the morning?
11. Which is better: to light one candle or to curse the darkness?

10-10 *IT* + INFINITIVE: USING *FOR (SOMEONE)*

(a) *You* should study hard. (b) It is important **for you** to study hard. (c) *Mary* should study hard. (d) It is important **for Mary** to study hard. (e) *We* don't have to go to the meeting. (f) It isn't necessary **for us** to go to the meeting. (g) *A dog* can't talk. (h) It is impossible **for a dog** to talk.	(a) and (b) have a similar meaning. Notice the pattern in (b): *it is* + *adjective* + **for** (*someone*) + *infinitive phrase*

□ **EXERCISE 19:** Use the given information to complete each sentence. Use *for* (*someone*) and an INFINITIVE PHRASE in each completion.

1. *Students should do their homework.*

    It's important _____ **for students to do their homework.** _____

2. *Teachers should speak clearly.*

    It's important _____

3. *We don't have to hurry.*

    There's plenty of time. It isn't necessary _____

4. *A fish can't live out of water for more than a few minutes.*

    It's impossible _____

5. *Students have to budget their time carefully.*

    It's necessary _____

6. *A child usually can't sit still for a long time.*

    It's difficult _____

7. *My family always eats turkey on Thanksgiving Day.*

    It's traditional _____

8. *People can take vacation trips to the moon.*

Will it be possible _____ within the next fifty years?

9. *I usually can't understand Mr. Allen.*

It's hard _____ He talks too fast.

10. *I can understand our teacher.*

It's easy _____

11. *The guests usually wait until the hostess begins to eat.*

At a formal dinner party, it's customary _____

After she takes the first bite, the guests also start to eat.

12. *The bride usually feeds the groom the first piece of wedding cake.*

It's traditional _____

10-11 INFINITIVE OF PURPOSE: USING *IN ORDER TO*

Why did you go to the post office? (a) I went to the post office *because I wanted to mail a letter.* (b) I went to the post office *in order to mail a letter.* (c) I went to the post office *to mail a letter.*	***In order to*** expresses purpose. ***In order to*** answers the question "Why?"
	In (c): ***in order*** is frequently omitted. (a), (b) and (c) have the same meaning.
(d) I went to the post office *for some stamps.* (e) I went to the post office *to buy some stamps.* (f) INCORRECT: I went to the post office for to buy some stamps. (g) INCORRECT: I went to the post office for buying some stamps.	***For*** is also used to express purpose, but it is a preposition and is followed by a noun phrase, as in (d).

□ **EXERCISE 20:** Add *in order* to the sentences whenever possible.

1. I went to the bank to cash a check.

   → *I went to the bank in order to cash a check.*

2. I'd like to see that movie.

   → (*No change. The infinitive does not express purpose.*)

3. Sam went to the hospital to visit a friend.

4. I need to go to the bank today.

5. I need to go to the bank today to deposit my pay check.

6. On my way home from school, I stopped at the drugstore to buy some shampoo.

7. Carmen looked in her dictionary to find the correct spelling of a word.

8. Masako went to the cafeteria to eat lunch.

9. Jack and Linda have decided to get married.

10. Pedro watches TV to improve his English.

11. I didn't forget to pay my rent.

12. Kim wrote to the university to ask for a catalog.

13. Sally touched my shoulder to get my attention.

14. Donna expects to graduate next spring.

15. Jerry needs to go to the bookstore to buy a spiral notebook.

□ **EXERCISE 21:** Complete the sentences by using *to* or *for*.

1. I went to Chicago ___*for*___ a visit.

2. I went to Chicago ___*to*___ visit my aunt and uncle.

3. I take long walks _____ relax.

4. I take long walks _____ relaxation.

5. I'm going to school _____ a good education.

6. I'm going to school _____ get a good education.

7. I'm not going to school just _____ have fun.

8. I'm not going to school just _____ fun.

9. I went to the store _____ some bread and milk.

10. I went to the store _____ get some bread and milk.

11. I turned on the radio _____ listen to the news.

12. I listened to the radio _____ news about the earthquake in Peru.

13. We wear coats in the winter _____ keep warm.

14. We wear coats in the winter _____ warmth.

☐ **EXERCISE 22—ORAL (BOOKS CLOSED):** Answer "why-questions" in your own words. Show purpose by using an infinitive phrase or a "*for*-phrase."

Example: Yesterday you turned on the TV. Why?
Response: Yesterday I turned on the TV (to listen to the news, for the latest news about the earthquake, etc.).

1. You went to the supermarket. Why?
2. You need to go to the bookstore.
3. You went to the post office.
4. You have to go to the library.
5. You went to the health clinic.
6. You reached into your pocket/purse.
7. You came to this school.
8. You borrowed some money from (. . .).
9. You stopped at the service station.
10. You play (*soccer, tennis, etc.*).
11. You had to go out last night.
12. You're going to go to (*Chicago*).

☐ **EXERCISE 23—ORAL:** Combine the given ideas to make sentences using infinitives of purpose. Begin each of your sentences with "*Yesterday I. . . .*"

Example: go shopping/go downtown
Response: *Yesterday I went downtown (in order) to go shopping.*

1. call the dentist's office/make an appointment
   → *Yesterday I . . . .*
2. study for a test/go to the library
3. get rid of my headache/take an aspirin
4. go to the laundromat/wash my clothes
5. have to run/get to class on time
6. go to (*name of a place*)/eat lunch
7. make a reservation to go to . . . /call the travel agency
8. ask the teacher a question/stay after class
9. write a letter to my parents/ask them for some money
10. listen to a baseball game/turn on the radio

11. get a cup of coffee between classes/borrow some money from (. . .)

12. stand in the doorway of a store/get out of the rain while I was waiting for the bus

10-12   USING INFINITIVES WITH *TOO* AND *ENOUGH*

<table>
<tr>
<td>
TOO + ADJECTIVE + (FOR SOMEONE) + INFINITIVE
(a) A piano is too heavy   to lift.
(b) That box is too heavy   for me   to lift.
(c) That box is too heavy   for Bob   to lift.
</td>
<td rowspan="2">
Infinitives often follow expressions with too.
Too comes in front of an adjective.
In the speaker's mind, the use of too implies a negative result.
COMPARE:
The box is too heavy. I can't lift it.
The box is very heavy, but I can lift it.
</td>
</tr>
<tr>
<td>
ENOUGH + NOUN + INFINITIVE
(d) I don't have enough <i>money</i> to <i>buy</i> that car.
(e) Did you have enough <i>time</i>   to <i>finish</i> the test?
</td>
</tr>
<tr>
<td>
ADJECTIVE + ENOUGH + INFINITIVE
(f) Jimmy isn't <i>old</i> enough to <i>go</i> to school.
(g) Are you <i>hungry</i> enough to <i>eat</i> three sandwiches?
</td>
<td>
Infinitives often follow expressions with enough.
Enough comes in front of a noun.*
Enough follows an adjective.
</td>
</tr>
</table>

*Enough can also follow a noun: *I don't have **money** enough to buy that car.* In everyday English, however, **enough** usually comes in front of a noun.

□ **EXERCISE 24:** Make sentences by putting the following in the correct order.

1. time/to go to the park tomorrow/I don't have/enough

I don't have enough time to go to the park tomorrow.

2. to touch the ceiling/too/I'm/short

_____

3. to pay his bills/money/Tom doesn't have/enough

_____

4. for me/this tea is/hot/to drink/too

_____

5. to eat breakfast this morning/time/I didn't have/enough

_____

6. enough/to stay home alone/old/Susie isn't

_____

7. too/to stay home alone/young/Susie is

_____

8. late/to go to the movie/for us/too/it's

_____

☐ **EXERCISE 25—ORAL:** Combine the sentences. Use **too**.

    1. We can't go swimming today. It's very cold.
      → *It's too cold (for us) to go swimming today.*
    2. I couldn't finish my homework last night. I was very sleepy.
    3. This jacket is very small. I can't wear it.
    4. Mike couldn't go to his aunt's housewarming party. He was very busy.
    5. I live far from school. I can't walk there.
    6. Some movies are very violent. Children shouldn't watch them.

Combine the sentences. Use **enough.**

    7. I can't reach the top shelf. I'm not that tall.
      → *I'm not tall enough to reach the top shelf.*
    8. I can't lift a horse. I'm not that strong.
    9. It's not warm today. We can't go outside in shorts and sandals.
   10. I didn't stay home and miss work. I wasn't really sick, but I didn't feel good all day.

☐ **EXERCISE 26:** Complete the following sentences. Use INFINITIVES in the completions.

    1. The weather is too cold _____

    2. Timmy is two years old. He's too young _____

    3. Timmy isn't old enough _____

    4. That suitcase is too heavy _____

5. Ann isn't strong enough _____

6. Last night I was too tired _____

7. Yesterday I was too busy _____

8. A Mercedes-Benz is too expensive _____

9. I don't have enough money _____

10. Yesterday I didn't have enough time _____

11. A teenager is old enough _____

12. This coffee is too hot _____

13. I know enough English _____

14. The test was too long _____

15. I'm too short _____

16. I'm not tall enough _____

☐ **EXERCISE 27—ERROR ANALYSIS:** All of the following sentences contain mistakes. Find and correct the mistakes.

1. Do you enjoy to go to the zoo?
   (*Correction: Do you enjoy going to the zoo?*)

2. I went to the store for getting some toothpaste.

3. Did you go to shopping yesterday?

4. I usually go to the cafeteria for to get a cup of coffee in the morning,

5. Bob needed to went downtown yesterday.

6. I cut the rope by a knife.

7. I thanked him for drive me to the airport.

8. Is difficult to learn a second language.

9. It is important getting an education.

10. Timmy isn't enough old to get married.

11. Do you want go to swimming tomorrow?

12. I went to the bank for cashing a check.

13. I was to sleepy to finish my homework last night.

14. Is easy this exercise to do.

15. Last night too tired no do my homework.

16. I've never gone to sailing, but I would like.

☐ **EXERCISE 28 — ORAL:** Form small groups. Make a list of several topics that can be used for a one-minute impromptu speech. The topics should be GERUND PHRASES. Exchange topics with another group. After your group has its topics, each member in turn should give a one-minute speech to the rest of the group. One group member should keep time. After all the speeches have been given, choose one speech from your group to be presented to the rest of the class.

Examples of topics: eating at fast-food restaurants, traveling to a foreign country, taking care of your health.

☐ **EXERCISE 29 — WRITTEN:** What do you do for fun and recreation in your spare time? Write about one or two spare-time activities that you enjoy. What do you do? Where? When? Why? Mention some interesting experiences. Try to get your readers interested in doing the same things in their free time. Do you enjoy exploring caves? Is playing tennis one of your passions? Have you ever gone skydiving? Maybe collecting ceramic horses is one of your hobbies. Have you ever gone waterskiing? Do you enjoy simple pleasures such as walking in a park? Do you go jogging for recreation? Maybe watching sports on television is your way of relaxing. It is important for all of us to have spare-time activities that we enjoy. What are yours?

10-13 MORE PHRASAL VERBS (SEPARABLE)*

ask out	*ask someone to go on a date*
call back	*return a telephone call*
call off	*cancel*
call up	*make a telephone call*
give back	*return something to someone*
hang up	*(1) hang on a hanger or a hook; (2) end a telephone call*
pay back	*return money to someone*
put away	*put something in its usual or proper place*
put back	*return something to its original place*
put out	*extinguish (stop) a fire, a cigarette, a cigar*
shut off	*stop a machine or light, turn off*
try on	*put on clothing to see if it fits*
turn down	*decrease the volume*
turn up	*increase the volume*

*See 9-8 and 9-9 for more information about phrasal verbs.

□ **EXERCISE 30:** Complete the sentences with pronouns and particles.

1. A: Could you lend me a couple of bucks?

   B: Sure.

   A: Thanks. I'll pay _____*you back*_____ tomorrow.

2. A: The radio is too loud. Could you please turn _____?

   B: Sure.

3. A: I can't hear the TV. Could you please turn _____?

   B: I'd be glad to.

4. A: Have you heard from Jack lately?

   B: Yes. He called _____ last night.★

5. A: Someone's at the door. Can I call _____ in a few

   minutes?

   B: Sure.

6. A: Where's my coat?

   B: I hung _____.

7. A: Is the oven on?

   B: No. I shut _____.

_____

★There is no difference in meaning between *He called me last night* and *He called me up last night*.

8. A: May I borrow your small calculator tonight?

   B: Sure.

   A: I'll give _____ to you tomorrow.

   B: Okay.

9. A: You can't smoke that cigarette in the auditorium. You'd better put

   _____ before we go in.

   B: Okay.

10. A: Do you have any plans for Saturday night?

    B: Yes. I have a date. Jim Olsen asked _____.

11. A: Did you take my eraser off of my desk?

    B: Yes, but I put _____ on your desk when I was

    finished.

    A: Oh? It's not here.

    B: Look under your notebook.

    A: Ah. There it is. Thanks.

12. A: Your toys are all over the floor, kids. Before you go to bed, be sure to

    put _____.

    B: Okay, Daddy.

13. A: Did you go to Kathy's party last night?

    B: She didn't have a party. She called _____.

14. A: This is a nice-looking coat. Why don't you try _____?

    B: How much does it cost?

CHAPTER *11*

Passive Sentences

11-1 ACTIVE SENTENCES AND PASSIVE SENTENCES

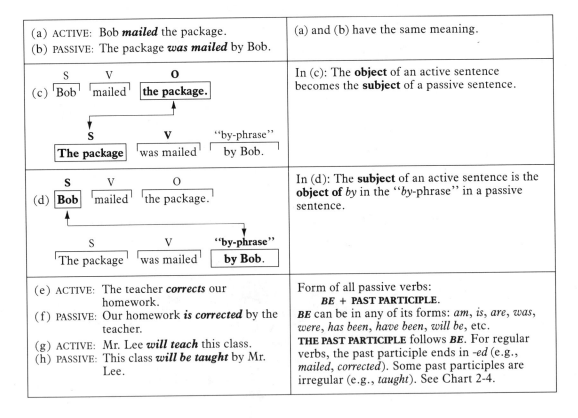

(a) ACTIVE: Bob *mailed* the package. (b) PASSIVE: The package *was mailed* by Bob.	(a) and (b) have the same meaning.
(c) S V O Bob mailed **the package.** S V "by-phrase" **The package** was mailed by Bob.	In (c): The **object** of an active sentence becomes the **subject** of a passive sentence.
(d) S V O **Bob** mailed the package. S V "by-phrase" The package was mailed **by Bob**.	In (d): The **subject** of an active sentence is the **object of** *by* in the "*by*-phrase" in a passive sentence.
(e) ACTIVE: The teacher *corrects* our homework. (f) PASSIVE: Our homework *is corrected* by the teacher. (g) ACTIVE: Mr. Lee *will teach* this class. (h) PASSIVE: This class *will be taught* by Mr. Lee.	Form of all passive verbs: *BE* + PAST PARTICIPLE. *BE* can be in any of its forms: *am, is, are, was, were, has been, have been, will be,* etc. THE PAST PARTICIPLE follows *BE*. For regular verbs, the past participle ends in *-ed* (e.g., *mailed, corrected*). Some past participles are irregular (e.g., *taught*). See Chart 2-4.

11-2 TENSE FORMS OF PASSIVE VERBS

Notice that all the passive verbs are formed with **BE** + **PAST PARTICIPLE**.				
TENSE	**ACTIVE**		**PASSIVE**	
SIMPLE PRESENT	The news	*surprises* me.	I	***am*** *surprised* by the news.
	The news	*surprises* Sam.	Sam	***is*** *surprised* by the news.
	The news	*surprises* us.	We	***are*** *surprised* by the news.
SIMPLE PAST	The news	*surprised* me.	I	***was*** *surprised* by the news.
	The news	*surprised* us.	We	***were*** *surprised* by the news.
PRESENT PERFECT	Bob	*has mailed* the letter.	The letter	***has been*** *mailed* by Bob.
	Bob	*has mailed* the letters.	The letters	***have been*** *mailed* by Bob.
FUTURE	Bob	*will mail* the letter.	The letter	***will be*** *mailed* by Bob.
	Bob *is going to mail* the letter.		The letter ***is going to be*** *mailed*	by Bob.

☐ **EXERCISE 1:** Change the active verbs to passive verbs. Write the subject of the passive sentence.

1. SIMPLE PRESENT

   a. The teacher *helps* **me**. _____*I*_____ ____*am helped*____ by the teacher.

   b. The teacher *helps* **Jane**. _____ _____ by the teacher.

   c. The teacher *helps* **us**. _____ _____ by the teacher.

2. SIMPLE PAST

   a. The teacher *helped* **me**. _____ _____ by the teacher.

   b. The teacher *helped* **them**. _____ _____ by the teacher.

3. PRESENT PERFECT

   a. The teacher *has helped* **Joe**. _____ _____ by the teacher.

   b. The teacher *has helped* **us**. _____ _____ by the teacher.

4. FUTURE

   a. The teacher *will help* **me**. _____ _____ by the teacher.

   b. The teacher *is going to help* **me**. _____ _____ by the teacher.

   c. The teacher *will help* **Tim**. _____ _____ by the teacher.

   d. The teacher *is going to help* **Tim**. _____ _____ by the teacher.

□ **EXERCISE 2:** Change the verbs to the passive. Do not change the tense.

		BE	+	PAST PARTICIPLE	
1. Bob *mailed* the package.	The package	**was**		**mailed**	by Bob.
2. Mr. Catt *delivers* our mail.	Our mail	_____		_____	by Mr. Catt.
3. The children *have eaten* the cake.	The cake	_____		_____	by the children.
4. Linda *wrote* that letter.	That letter	_____		_____	by Linda.
5. The jeweler *is going to fix* my watch.	My watch	_____		_____	by the jeweler.
6. Ms. Bond *will teach* our class.	Our class	_____		_____	by Ms. Bond.
7. That company *employs* many people.	Many people	_____		_____	by that company.
8. That company *has hired* Sue.	Sue	_____		_____	by that company.
9. The secretary *is going to fax* the letters.	The letters	_____		_____	by the secretary.
10. A college student *bought* my old car.	My old car	_____		_____	by a college student.
11. Mr. Adams *will do* the work.	The work	_____		_____	by Mr. Adams.
12. Mr. Fox *washed* the windows.	The windows	_____		_____	by Mr. Fox.

□ **EXERCISE 3:** Change the sentences from active to passive.

1. Ms. Hopkins invited me to dinner.

_____*I was invited to dinner by Ms. Hopkins.*_____

2. Thomas Edison invented the phonograph.

_____

3. Water surrounds an island.

_____

4. A maid will clean our hotel room.

   _____

5. A plumber is going to fix the leaky faucet.

   _____

6. A doctor has examined the sick child.

   _____

7. The police arrested James Swan.

   _____

8. A large number of people speak Spanish.

   _____

9. The secretary is going to answer the letter.

   _____

10. The teacher's explanation confused Carlos.

    _____

    _____

11. My mistake embarrassed me.

    _____

    _____

12. Helicopters fascinate children.

    _____

    _____

13. Shakespeare wrote *Hamlet*.*

    _____

14. This news will amaze you.

    _____

---

*Notice that *Hamlet*, the title of a play, is printed in italics. In handwritten or typed sentences, the title of a book or a play is underlined.

    Printed: Tolstoy wrote *War and Peace*.
    Handwritten: *Tolstoy wrote War and Peace.*
    Typed: Tolstoy wrote War and Peace.

□ **EXERCISE 4:** Change the active sentences to passive sentences that have the same meaning and tense.

	ACTIVE	PASSIVE	
1. a.	The news surprised John.	*John was surprised*	by the news.
b.	The news didn't surprise me.	*I wasn't surprised*	by the news.
c.	Did the news surprise you?	*Were you surprised*	by the news?
2. a.	The news surprises Erin.	_____	by the news.
b.	The news doesn't surprise us.	_____	by the news.
c.	Does the news surprise you?	_____	by the news?
3. a.	The news will shock Steve.	_____	by the news.
b.	The news won't shock Jean.	_____	by the news.
c.	Will the news shock Pat?	_____	by the news?
4. a.	Liz wrote that petition.	_____	by Liz.
b.	Don didn't write it.	_____	by Don.
c.	Did Ryan write it?	_____	by Ryan?

PETITION

We, the undersigned, believe that the house at 3205 Tree Street is an historic building. We believe that it should not be destroyed in order to build a fast-food restaurant at that location.

Robert C. Miller   *Wm. H. Brock*

Elizabeth J. Wilson   *Ms. Catherine Ann Jackson*

James Walsh   *An Binh Nguyen*

Alicia Alvarez

---

5. a.	Bob has signed the petition.	_____	by Bob.
b.	Paul hasn't signed it.	_____	by Paul.
c.	Has Jim signed it yet?	_____	by Jim yet?
6. a.	Sue is going to sign it.	_____	by Sue.
b.	John isn't going to sign it.	_____	by John.
c.	Is Carol going to sign it?	_____	by Carol?

□ **EXERCISE 5:** Change the sentences from active to passive.

1. A thief stole Ann's purse.

     Ann's purse was stolen by a thief.

2. Did a cat kill the bird?

3. My cat didn't kill the bird.

4. A squirrel didn't bite the jogger.

5. A dog bit the jogger.

6. Do a large number of people speak English?

7. Did Johnny break the window?

8. Is the janitor going to fix the window?

9. More than one hundred people have signed the petition.

10. Did Shakespeare write *A Midsummer Night's Dream?*

_____

11. Ernest Hemingway didn't write *A Midsummer Night's Dream.*

_____

12. Will a maid clean our hotel room?

_____

13. Does the hotel provide clean towels?

_____

14. Sometimes my inability to understand spoken English frustrates me.

_____

11-3 TRANSITIVE AND INTRANSITIVE VERBS

(a) **TRANSITIVE VERBS**
    ACTIVE: Bob *mailed* the letter.
    PASSIVE: The letter *was mailed* by Bob.
 	
(b) **INTRANSITIVE VERBS**
    ACTIVE: An accident *happened.*
    PASSIVE: *(not possible)*
 	
(c) INCORRECT: An accident was happened.
	Only transitive verbs can be used in the passive. A transitive verb is a verb that is followed by an object. Examples:
	    S V O
	    Bob mailed the letter.
	    Mr. Lee signed the check.
	    A cat killed the bird.

	An intransitive verb is a verb that is not followed by an object. Example:
	    S V
	    An accident happened.
	    John came to our house.
	    I slept well last night.
	
	An intransitive verb CANNOT be used in the passive.

□ **EXERCISE 6:** Change the sentences to the passive if possible. Write the symbol ''∅'' if a sentence cannot be changed to the passive.

1. Jack walked to school yesterday. ____∅_____

2. We stayed in a hotel. _____

3. Susie broke the window. _____

4. The leaves fell to the ground. _____

5. I slept at my friend's house last night. _____

6. The second baseman caught the ball. _____

7. Ann's cat died last week. _____

8. That book belongs to me. _____

9. The airplane arrived twenty minutes late. _____

10. The teacher announced a quiz. _____

11. I agree with George. _____

12. Do you agree with me? _____

13. Dick went to the doctor's office. _____

14. An accident happened at the corner of Third and Main. _____

15. An accident occurred at the corner of Third and Main. _____

16. Many people saw the accident. _____

11-4 USING THE "BY-PHRASE"

(a) This sweater *was made* **by my aunt.**	The "*by*-phrase" is used in passive sentences when it is important to know who performs an action. In (a): *by my aunt* is important information.
(b) That sweater *was made* in Korea. (*by someone*) (c) Spanish *is spoken* in Colombia. (*by people*) (d) That house *was built* in 1940. (*by someone*) (e) Rice *is grown* in many countries. (*by people*)	Uusually there is no "*by*-phrase" in a passive sentence. The passive is used when it is not known or not important to know exactly who performs an action. In (b): The exact person (or people) who made the sweater is not known and is not important to know, so there is no "*by*-phrase" in the passive sentence.

☐ **EXERCISE 7:** Change the sentence from active to passive. Include the "*by*-phrase" only if necessary.

1. Bob Smith built that house.

   That house was built by Bob Smith.

2. Someone built this house in 1904.

   This house was built in 1904.   (*by someone = unnecessary*)

3. People grow rice in India.

   _____

4. People speak Spanish in Venezuela.

   _____

5. Do people speak Spanish in Peru?

_____

6. Alexander Graham Bell invented the telephone.

_____

7. When did someone invent the wheel?

_____

8. People sell hammers at a hardware store.

_____

9. People use hammers to pound nails.

_____

10. The president has canceled the meeting.

_____

11. Someone has canceled the soccer game.

_____

12. Someone will list my name in the new telephone directory.

_____

13. Charles Darwin wrote *The Origin of Species.*

_____

14. Someone published *The Origin of Species* in 1859.

_____

15. Someone serves beer and wine at that restaurant.

_____

"DEEP ASLEEP... DEEP ASLEEP..
YOU FEEL VERY SLEEPY... DEEP..."

16. Has anyone ever hypnotized you?

_____

17. Something confused me in class yesterday.

_____

18. Something embarrassed me yesterday.

_____

19. Someone has changed the name of this street from Bay Avenue to Martin Luther King Way.

_____

20. Someone filmed many of the Tarzan movies in the rain forest in Puerto Rico.

_____
_____
_____

"CAMERA! ACTION!"

☐ **EXERCISE 8—ORAL:** Change the sentences from active to passive. Include the "*by*-phrase" only if it contains important information.

      Example: Someone has invited us to a party.
      Response: We have been invited to a party.

      Example: No one has invited John to the party.
      Response: John hasn't been invited to the party.

1. Someone established the Red Cross in 1864.
2. When did someone establish this school?
3. Someone collects the garbage on Thursdays.

4. No one will collect the garbage tomorrow.
5. People spell "writing" with one "t."
6. People don't spell "writing" with two "t's."
7. People spell "written" with two "t's."
8. Someone is going to build a new hospital next year.
9. When did someone build the Suez Canal?
10. Olga wrote that composition.
11. The University of Minnesota has accepted me.
12. People don't teach calculus in elementary school.
13. People held the 1988 Summer Olympics in Seoul, Korea.
14. No one delivers the mail on holidays.
15. Will someone deliver the mail tomorrow?
16. Someone made my tape recorder in Japan.
17. Where did someone make your tape recorder?
18. My grandfather made that table.
19. No one has ever hypnotized me.
20. Did my directions confuse you?

☐ **EXERCISE 9:** Complete the sentences with the correct form of the verb (active or passive) in parentheses.

1. Yesterday our teacher (*arrive*) _____**arrived**_____ five minutes late.

2. The morning paper (*read*) _____ by over 200,000 people every day.

3. Last night my favorite TV program (*interrupt*) _____ _____ by a special news bulletin.

4. That's not my coat. It (*belong*) _____ to Louise.

5. Our mail (*deliver*) _____ before noon every day.

6. The "b" in "comb" (*pronounce, not*) _____. It is silent.

7. A bad accident (*happen*) _____ on Highway 95 last night.

8. When I (*arrive*) _____ at the airport yesterday, I (*meet*) _____ by my cousin and a couple of her friends.

9. Yesterday I (*hear*) _____ about Margaret's divorce. I (*surprise*) _____ by the news. Janice (*shock*) _____.

10. A new house (*build*) _____ next to ours next year.

11. Roberto (*write*) _____ this composition last week. That one (*write*) _____ by Abdullah.

12. Radium (*discover*) _____ by Marie and Pierre Curie in 1898.

13. At the soccer game yesterday, the winning goal (*kick*) _____ by Luigi. Over 100,000 people (*attend*) _____ the soccer game.

14. A: Do you understand the explanation in the book?

    B: No, I don't. I (*confuse*) _____ by it.

15. A: Where are you going to go to school next year?

    B: I (*accept*) _____ by Shoreline Community College.

16. A: I think football is too violent.

    B: I (*agree*) _____ with you. I (*prefer*) _____ baseball.

17. A: When (*your bike, steal*) _____?

    B: Two days ago.

18. A: (*you, pay*) _____ your electric bill yet?

    B: No, I haven't, but I'd better pay it today. If I don't, my electricity (*shut off*) _____ by the power company.

19. A: Did you hear about the accident?

    B: No. What (*happen*) _____?

    A: A bicyclist (*hit*) _____ by a taxi in front of the dorm.

    B: (*the bicyclist, injure*) _____?

    A: Yes. Someone (*call*) _____ an ambulance. The bicyclist (*take*) _____ to City Hospital and (*treat*) _____ in the emergency ward for cuts and bruises.

    B: What (*happen*) _____ to the taxi driver?

    A: He (*arrest*) _____ for reckless driving.

    B: He's lucky that the bicyclist (*kill, not*) _____.

20. The Eiffel Tower (*be*) _____ in Paris, France. It (*visit*) _____ by millions of people every year. It (*design*) _____ by Alexandre Eiffel (1832–1923). It (*erect*) _____ in 1889 for the Paris exposition. Since that time, it (*be*) _____ the most famous landmark in Paris. Today it (*recognize*) _____ by people throughout the world.

11-5 THE PASSIVE FORMS OF THE PRESENT AND PAST PROGRESSIVE

ACTIVE	PASSIVE	Passive form of the present progressive:
The secretary *is copying* some letters. Someone *is building* a new hospital.	(a) Some letters **are being copied** by the secretary. (b) A new hospital **is being built**.	am is } + **being** + PAST PARTICIPLE are
The secretary *was copying* some letters. Someone *was building* a new hospital.	(c) Some letters **were being copied** by the secretary. (d) A new hospital **was being built**.	Passive form of the past progressive: was } + **being** + PAST PARTICIPLE were

☐ **EXERCISE 10:** Change the sentences from active to passive. Include the "*by*-phrase" only if it contains important information.

1. Someone is building a new house on Elm Street.

   _____

2. The Smith Construction Company is building that house.

   _____

3. Yoko is reading this sentence.

   _____

4. We can't use our classroom today because someone is painting it.

 We can't use our classroom today because _____

5. We couldn't use our classroom yesterday because someone was painting it.

 We couldn't use our classroom yesterday because _____

6. We can't use the language lab today because someone is fixing the equipment.

 We can't use the language lab today because _____

7. We couldn't use the language lab yesterday because someone was fixing the equipment.

 We couldn't use the language lab yesterday because _____

8. Someone is repairing my shoes.

 _____

9. Someone was repairing my shoes.

 _____

10. Someone is organizing a student trip to the art museum.

 _____

11-6 PASSIVE MODAL AUXILIARIES

ACTIVE MODAL AUXILIARIES	PASSIVE MODAL AUXILIARIES (MODAL + **BE** + PAST PARTICIPLE)	Modal auxiliaries are often used in the passive.
Bob *will mail* it. Bob *can mail* it. Bob *should mail* it. Bob *ought to mail* it. Bob *must mail* it. Bob *has to mail* it. Bob *may mail* it. Bob *might mail* it.	It *will be mailed* by Bob. It *can be mailed* by Bob. It *should be mailed* by Bob. It *ought to be mailed* by Bob. It *must be mailed* by Bob. It *has to be mailed* by Bob. It *may be mailed* by Bob. It *might be mailed* by Bob.	FORM: modal + **BE** + past participle See Chapter 5 for information about the meanings and uses of modal auxiliaries.

☐ **EXERCISE 11:** Change the sentences from active to passive. Include the "*by*-phrase" only if it contains important information.

 1. Someone might cancel class. _____ ***Class might be canceled.*** _____

 2. A doctor can prescribe medicine. _____

3. People should plant tomatoes in the spring. _____

4. Mr. Hook must sign this report. _____

5. Someone may build a new post office on First Street.

_____

6. People may not sell beer to minors. _____

7. People can reach me at 555–3815. _____

8. People have to place stamps in the upper right-hand corner of an

envelope.

_____

9. Someone ought to paint that fence. _____

10. People cannot control the weather. _____

11. Someone had to fix our car before we left for Chicago.

_____

12. All of the students must do the assignment.

_____

11-7 SUMMARY: PASSIVE VERB FORMS

REMINDER: All passive verbs are formed with **BE** + **PAST PARTICIPLE**.

ACTIVE			PASSIVE		
Dr. Gray	*helps*	Tom.	Tom	*is helped*	by Dr. Gray.
Dr. Gray	*is helping*	Tom.	Tom	*is being helped*	by Dr. Gray.
Dr. Gray	*has helped*	Tom.	Tom	*has been helped*	by Dr. Gray.
Dr. Gray	*helped*	Tom.	Tom	*was helped*	by Dr. Gray.
Dr. Gray	*was helping*	Tom.	Tom	*was being helped*	by Dr. Gray.
Dr. Gray	*had helped*	Tom.	Tom	*had been helped*	by Dr. Gray.
Dr. Gray	*is going to help*	Tom.	Tom	*is going to be helped*	by Dr. Gray.
Dr. Gray	*will help*	Tom.	Tom	*will be helped*	by Dr. Gray.
Dr. Gray	*can help*	Tom.	Tom	*can be helped*	by Dr. Gray.
Dr. Gray	*should help*	Tom.	Tom	*should be helped*	by Dr. Gray.
Dr. Gray	*ought to help*	Tom.	Tom	*ought to be helped*	by Dr. Gray.
Dr. Gray	*must help*	Tom.	Tom	*must be helped*	by Dr. Gray.
Dr. Gray	*has to help*	Tom.	Tom	*has to be helped*	by Dr. Gray.
Dr. Gray	*may help*	Tom.	Tom	*may be helped*	by Dr. Gray.
Dr. Gray	*might help*	Tom.	Tom	*might be helped*	by Dr. Gray.

□ EXERCISE 12—ORAL (BOOKS CLOSED): Practice using passive forms.

Example: Someone will paint this room.
Response: This room will be painted.

I. *Someone . . . this room.*
1. should paint
2. ought to paint
3. must paint
4. will paint
5. is going to paint
6. may paint
7. is painting
8. was painting
9. has painted
10. painted

II. *Someone . . .*
11. must solve this problem.
12. is preparing dinner.
13. has to pay this bill.
14. should eat this food.
15. will mail the package.
16. may raise the price of gas.
17. has made a mistake.
18. ought to wash the windows.

III. 19. No one has washed the dishes yet.
20. Someone should wash them soon.
21. No one has sent that package yet.
22. Someone should send it soon.
23. No one has solved that problem yet.
24. Someone must solve it soon.
25. No one invited me to the party.
26. Did someone invite you to the party?
27. Someone built the Suez Canal in the nineteenth century.
28. No one built the Suez Canal in the twentieth century.
29. When did someone build the Panama Canal?
30. Did someone build the Panama Canal in the twentieth century?

□ EXERCISE 13: Complete the sentences with the correct form of the verbs (active or passive) in parentheses.

1. This book (*have to return*) _____ to the library today.

2. The other books (*return*) _____ yesterday.

3. That book (*should return*) _____ tomorrow.

4. These letters (*be going to mail*) _____ tomorrow.

5. That letter (*ought to send*) _____ immediately.

6. This letter (*must send*) _____ today.

7. Those letter (*arrive*) _____ yesterday.

8. I don't have my car today. It's in the garage. It (*repair*) _____ _____ right now.

9. Kate didn't have her car last week because it was in the garage. While it (*repair*) _____, she took the bus to work.

10. The mechanic (*repair*) _____ Tina's car last week.

11. Glass (*make*) _____ from sand.

12. You (*should carry, not*) _____ large sums of money with you.

13. Large sums of money (*ought to keep*) _____ in a bank, don't you think?

14. At our high school, the students' grades (*send*) _____ to their parents four times each year.

15. I'm sorry, but the computer job is no longer available. A new computer programmer (*hire, already*) _____.

16. Household cleaning agents (*must use*) _____ with care. For example, mixing chlorine bleach with ammonia (*can produce*) _____ toxic gases.

17. What products (*manufacture*) _____ in your country?

18. Aluminum* is a valuable metal that (*can use*) _____ again and again. Because this metal (*can recycle*) _____ _____, aluminum cans (*should throw away, not*) _____.

19. Endangered wildlife (*must protect*) _____ from extinction.

20. People with the moral courage to fight against injustices (*can find*) _____ in every corner of the world.

_____

Aluminum in American English = *aluminium* in British English.

☐ **EXERCISE 14:** Complete the sentences with any appropriate tense, active or passive, of the verbs in parentheses.

1. In prehistoric times, huge herds of horses (*live*) _____
   throughout the Americas. But then, for some unknown reason, they
   (*disappear*) _____ completely from North and
   South America. Even though the early horses (*die*) _____
   out in the Americas, they (*survive*) _____ in Asia.

2. Long ago, horses (*domesticate*)* _____ by
   central Asian nomads. At first, horses (*use*) _____
   in war and in hunting, and oxen (*use*) _____ for
   farming. Later, horses also (*become*) _____ farm
   animals.

3. Horses (*reintroduce*) _____ into the
   Americas by Spaniards in the early fifteenth century. Spanish explorers
   (*come*) _____ in ships to the New World with their horses
   on board.

4. When the explorers (*return*) _____ to Spain, they
   (*leave*) _____ some of their horses behind. These
   (*develop*) _____ into wild herds. Native American
   tribes in the western plains (*begin*) _____ to use horses
   around 1600. Wild horses (*capture*) _____ and
   (*tame*) _____ for use in war and in hunting.

5. In the 1800s, there were several million wild horses in North America.
   By the 1970s, that number had become less than 20,000. The wild
   horses (*hunt*) _____ and (*kill*) _____
   principally for use as pet food. Today in the United States, wild horses
   (*protect*) _____ by law. They (*can kill, not*)
   _____ for sport or profit. What is your opinion?
   (*Should protect, wild horses*) _____ by law?

_____
*People domesticate (tame) animals.

11-8 USING PAST PARTICIPLES AS ADJECTIVES (STATIVE PASSIVE)

BE + ADJECTIVE (a) Paul **is** **young**. (b) Paul **is** **tall**. (c) Paul **is** **hungry**. **BE + PAST PARTICIPLE** (d) Paul **is** **married**. (e) Paul **is** **tired**. (f) Paul **is** **frightened**.	**Be** can be followed by an adjective. The adjective describes or gives information about the subject of the sentence. **Be** can be followed by a past participle (the passive form). The past participle is often like an adjective. The past participle describes or gives information about the subject of the sentence. Past participles are used as adjectives in many common, everyday expressions.
(g) Paul *is married* **to** Susan. (h) Paul *was excited* **about** the game. (i) Paul *will be prepared* **for** the exam.	Often the past participles in these expressions are followed by particular prepositions + an object. For example: • **married** is followed by **to** (+ an object). • **excited** is followed by **about** (+ an object). • **prepared** is followed by **for** (+ an object).

SOME COMMON EXPRESSIONS WITH *BE* + PAST PARTICIPLE

1. *be acquainted (with)*	13. *be excited (about)*	25. *be opposed (to)*
2. *be bored (with, by)*	14. *be exhausted (from)*	26. *be pleased (with)*
3. *be broken*	15. *be finished (with)*	27. *be prepared (for)*
4. *be closed*	16. *be frightened (of, by)*	28. *be qualified (for)*
5. *be composed of*	17. *be gone (from)*	29. *be related (to)*
6. *be crowded (with)*	18. *be hurt*	30. *be satisfied (with)*
7. *be devoted (to)*	19. *be interested (in)*	31. *be scared (of, by)*
8. *be disappointed (in, with)*	20. *be involved (in)*	32. *be shut*
9. *be divorced (from)*	21. *be located in, south of, etc.*	33. *be spoiled*
10. *be done (with)*	22. *be lost*	34. *be terrified (of, by)*
11. *be drunk (on)*	23. *be made of*	35. *be tired (of, from)*★
12. *be engaged (to)*	24. *be married (to)*	36. *be worried (about)*

★I'm **tired *of*** the cold weather. = *I've had enough cold weather. I want the weather to get warm.*
I'm **tired *from*** working hard all day. = *I'm exhausted because I worked hard all day.*

☐ **EXERCISE 15:** Complete the sentences with the expressions in the list. Use the SIMPLE PRESENT TENSE.

be acquainted	*be exhausted*	*be related*
be broken	*be located*	*be satisfied*
be composed	*be lost*	*be scared*
be crowded	*be made*	*be spoiled*
be disappointed	*be qualified*	✔*be worried*

1. Dennis isn't doing well in school this semester. He _____ **is worried** _____

about his grades.

2. My shirt _____ of cotton.

3. I live in a one-room apartment with four other people. Our apartment

   _____.

4. Vietnam _____ in Southeast Asia.

5. I'm going to go straight to bed tonight. It's been a hard day. I

   _____.

6. I _____ to Jessica Adams. She's my cousin.

7. Excuse me, sir, but I think I _____. Could you

   please tell me how to get to the bus station from here?

8. My tape recorder doesn't work. It _____.

9. We leave a light on in our son's bedroom at night because he

   _____ of the dark.

10. Alice thinks her boss should pay her more money. She _____

    not _____ with her present salary.

11. The children _____. I had promised to take them

    to the beach today, but now we can't go because it's raining.

12. _____ you _____ with Mrs. Novinsky?

    Have you ever met her?

13. According to the job description, an applicant must have a Master's

    degree and at least five years of teaching experience. Unfortunately, I

    _____ not _____ for that job.

14. This milk doesn't taste right. I think it _____. I'm

    not going to drink it.

15. Water _____ of hydrogen and oxygen.

□ **EXERCISE 16:** Complete the sentences with appropriate prepositions.

1. The day before Christmas, the stores are crowded ___**with**___ last-
   minute shoppers.

2. Are you qualified _____ that job?

3. Mr. Heath loves his family very much. He is devoted _____ them.

4. Our dog runs under the bed during storms. He's terrified _____
   thunder.

5. My sister is married _____ a law student.

6. Are you prepared _____ the test?

7. I'll be finished _____ my work in another minute or two.

8. Jason is excited _____ going to Hollywood.

9. Ms. Brown is opposed _____ the new tax plan.

10. Jane isn't satisfied _____ her present apartment. She's looking for a new one.

11. I failed the test because I didn't study. I'm disappointed _____ myself.

12. Janet doesn't take good care of herself. I'm worried _____ her health.

13. I'm tired _____ this rainy weather. I hope the sun shines tomorrow.

14. In terms of evolution, a hippopotamus is related _____ a horse.

15. The students are involved _____ many extracurricular activities.

16. Are you acquainted _____ this author? I think her books are excellent.

17. When will you be done _____ your work?

18. I'm starving! Right now I'm interested _____ only one thing: food.

19. The children want some new toys. They're bored _____ their old ones.

20. Sam is engaged _____ his childhood sweetheart.

21. Our daughter is scared _____ dogs.

22. You've done a good job. You should be very pleased _____ yourself.

□ **EXERCISE 17—ORAL (BOOKS CLOSED):** Supply appropriate prepositions + "*someone*" or "*something.*"

> *Example:* I'm worried . . . .
> *Response:* about someone/something.

1. I'm interested . . . .   4. I'm related . . . .
2. I'm married . . . .   5. I'm disappointed . . . .
3. I'm scared . . . .   6. I'm qualified . . . .

7. I'm satisfied	13. I'm engaged . . . .
8. I'm prepared	14. I'm worried . . . .
9. I'm acquainted	15. I'm tired . . . .
10. I'm opposed	16. I'm finished . . . .
11. I'm frightened	17. I'm done . . . .
12. I'm excited	18. I'm involved . . . .

Repeat the exercise. Use only the past participles as cues and make your own sentences.

    Example: worried

    Response: I'm worried about my brother./The teacher is worried about my grades./We are worried about the next test./etc.

☐ **EXERCISE 18:** Complete the sentences with the words in parentheses. Use the PASSIVE form, SIMPLE PRESENT or SIMPLE PAST. Include PREPOSITIONS where necessary.

1. (*close*)   When we got to the post office, it _____ ***was closed*** _____.

2. (*make*)   My earrings _____ ***are made of*** _____ gold.

3. (*divorce*)   Sally and Tom were married for six years, but now they

         _____.

4. (*relate*)   Your name is Tom Hood. _____ you _____

         Mary Hood?

5. (*spoil*)   This fruit _____. I think I'd better throw it out.

6. (*exhaust*)   Last night I _____, so I went straight to bed.

7. (*involve*)   Last week I _____ a three-car accident.

8. (*locate*)   The University of Washington _____

         Seattle.

9. (*drink*)   Ted _____. He's making a fool

         of himself.

10. (*interest*)   I _____ learning more about that subject.

11. (*devote*)   Linda loves her job. She _____ her work.

12. (*lose*)   What's the matter, little boy? _____ you _____?

13. (*terrify*)   Once when we were swimming at the beach, we saw a

         shark. All of us _____.

14. (*acquaint*)   _____ you _____ Sue's roommate?

15. (*qualify*)   I didn't get the job. The interviewer said that I

_____ not _____ it.

16. (*disappoint*)   My son brought home a report card with all D's and F's.

I can't understand it. I _____ him.

17. (*do*)   At last, I _____ my homework. Now I

can go to bed.

18. (*crowd*)   There are too many students in our class. The classroom

_____.

19. (*shut*)   It's starting to rain. _____ all of the windows

_____?

20. (*go*)   Where's my wallet? It _____! Did you

take it?

11-9   PARTICIPIAL ADJECTIVES: -*ED* vs. -*ING*

Indian art interests me.
(a) I am ***interested*** in Indian art.
    INCORRECT: I am interesting in Indian art.
(b) Indian art is ***interesting***.
    INCORRECT: Indian art is interested.
 	
The news surprised Kate.
(c) Kate was ***surprised***.
(d) The news was ***surprising***.
	The past participle (-*ed*)★ and the present participle (-*ing*) can be used as adjectives.
	In (a): The past participle (*interested*) describes how a person feels.
	In (b): The present participle (*interesting*) describes the ***cause*** of the feeling. The cause of the interest is Indian art.
	In (c): "surprised" describes how Kate felt. The past participle carries a passive meaning: *Kate was surprised by the news*.
	In (d): "the news" was the cause of the surprise.

★The past participle of regular verbs ends in -*ed*. Some verbs have irregular forms. See Chart 2-4.

☐ **EXERCISE 19:** Complete the sentences with the -*ed* or -*ing* form of verbs in italics.

1. Greg's classes *interest* him.

   a. Greg's classes are _____ ***interesting*** _____.

   b. Greg is an _____ ***interested*** _____ student.

2. Jane's classes *bore* her.

   a. Jane's classes are _____.

   b. Jane is a _____ student.

3. Mike heard some bad news. The bad news *depressed* him.

    a. Mike is very sad. In other words, he is _____.

    b. The news made Mike feel sad. The news was _____.

4. The exploration of space *interests* me.

    a. I'm _____ in the exploration of space.

    b. The exploration of space is _____ to me.

5. Nancy's rude behavior *embarrassed* her parents.

    a. Nancy's rude behavior was _____.

    b. Nancy's parents were _____.

6. The nation's leader stole money. The scandal *shocked* the nation.

    a. It was a _____ scandal.

    b. The _____ nation soon replaced the leader.

7. I like to study sea life. The subject of marine biology *fascinates* me.

    a. I'm _____ by marine biology.

    b. Marine biology is a _____ subject.

8. Emily is going to Australia. The idea of going on this trip *excites* her.

    a. Emily is _____ about going on this trip.

    b. She thinks it is going to be an _____ trip.

☐ **EXERCISE 20:** Circle the correct form (*-ing* or *-ed*) of the words in parentheses.

    1. Don't bother to read that book. It's (*boring,* *bored*).

    2. The students are (*interesting, interested*) in learning more about the subject.

    3. Ms. Green doesn't explain things well. The students are (*confusing, confused*).

    4. Have you heard the latest news? It's really (*exciting, excited*).

    5. I don't understand these directions. I'm (*confusing, confused*).

    6. I read an (*interesting, interested*) article in the newspaper this morning.

    7. I heard some (*surprising, surprised*) news on the radio.

    8. I'm (*boring, bored*). Let's do something. How about going to a movie?

    9. Mr. Sawyer bores me. I think he is a (*boring, bored*) person.

    10. Mr. Ball fascinates me. I think he is a (*fascinating, fascinated*) person.

11. Most young children are (*fascinating, fascinated*) by animals.

12. Young children think that animals are (*fascinating, fascinated*).

13. I was very (*embarrassing, embarrassed*) yesterday when I spilled my drink on the dinner table.

14. That was an (*embarrassing, embarrassed*) experience.

15. I read a (*shocking, shocked*) report yesterday on the number of children who die from starvation in the world every day. I was really (*shocking, shocked*).

16. The children went to a circus. For them, the circus was (*exciting, excited*). The (*exciting, excited*) children jumped up and down.

11-10 *GET* + ADJECTIVE; *GET* + PAST PARTICIPLE

GET + ADJECTIVE (a) I *am getting hungry*. Let's eat. (b) Eric *got nervous* before the job interview.	*Get* can be followed by an adjective. *Get* gives the idea of change—the idea of becoming, beginning to be, growing to be. In (a): *I'm getting hungry = I wasn't hungry before, but now I'm beginning to be hungry.*
GET + PAST PARTICIPLE (c) I*'m getting tired*. Let's stop working. (d) Steve and Rita *got married* last month.	Sometimes *get* is followed by a past participle. The past participle after *get* is like an adjective; it describes the subject of the sentence.

GET + ADJECTIVE			**GET + PAST PARTICIPLE**		
get angry	get dry	get quiet	get acquainted	get drunk	get involved
get bald	get fat	get rich	get arrested	get engaged	get killed
get big	get full	get serious	get bored	get excited	get lost
get busy	get hot	get sick	get confused	get finished	get married
get close	get hungry	get sleepy	get crowded	get frightened	get scared
get cold	get interested	get thirsty	get divorced	get hurt	get sunburned
get dark	get late	get well	get done	get interested	get tired
get dirty	get nervous	get wet	get dressed	get invited	get worried
get dizzy	get old				

☐ **EXERCISE 21:** Complete the sentences. Use each word in the list only one time.

angry	confused	hot	married
arrested	dizzy	hungry	rich
bald	dressed	hurt	sick
bored	drunk	late	sleepy
✔cold	full	lost	tired

1. In winter, the weather gets _____**cold**_____.

2. In summer, the weather gets _____.

3. This food is delicious, but I can't eat any more. I'm getting

   _____.

4. I overslept this morning. When I finally woke up, I jumped out of bed,

   got _____, picked up my books, and ran to class.

5. Mom and Dad are going to celebrate their 50th wedding anniversary

   next month. They got _____ fifty years ago.

6. When Jane gave us directions to her house, I got _____.

   So I asked her to explain again how to get there.

7. I didn't understand Jane's directions very well, so on the way to her

   house last night I got _____. I couldn't find her house.

8. Calm down! Take it easy! You shouldn't get _____. It's not good for your blood pressure.

9. Mr. Anderson is losing some of his hair. He's getting _____.

10. I didn't like the movie last night. It wasn't interesting. I got _____ and wanted to leave early.

11. When's dinner? I'm getting _____.

12. We should leave for the concert soon. It's getting _____. We should leave in the next five minutes if we want to be on time.

13. I want to make a lot of money. Do you know a good way to get _____ quick?

14. Jake got _____ for stealing a car yesterday. He is in jail now.

15. Was it a bad accident? Did anyone get _____?

16. When I turned around and around in a circle, I got _____.

17. I don't feel very good. I think I'm getting _____. Maybe I should see a doctor.

18. My friends got _____ at the party Saturday night, so I drove them home in my car. They were in no condition to drive.

19. I think I'll go to bed. I'm getting _____.

20. Let's stop working and take a break. I'm getting _____.

□ **EXERCISE 22:** Complete the sentences with an appropriate form of *get*.

1. Shake a leg! Step on it! _____*Get*_____ busy. There's no time to waste.

2. Tom and Sue _____*got*_____ married last month.

3. Let's stop working for a while. I _____*am getting*_____ tired.

4. I don't want _____*to get*_____ old, but I guess it happens to everybody.

5. I _____ interested in biology when I was in high school, so I decided to major in it in college.

6. My father started _____ bald when he was in his twenties. I'm in my twenties, and I'm starting _____ bald. It must be in the genes.

7. Brrr. It _____ cold in here. Maybe we should turn on the furnace.

8. When I was in the hospital, I got a card from my aunt and uncle. It said, "_____ well soon."

9. When I went downtown yesterday, I _____ lost. I didn't remember to take my map of the city with me.

10. A: Why did you leave the party early?
    B: I _____ bored.

11. A: I _____ hungry. Let's eat soon.
    B: Okay.

12. A: What happened?
    B: I don't know. Suddenly I _____ dizzy, but I'm okay now.

13. A: Do you want to go for a walk?
    B: Well, I don't know. It _____ dark outside right now. Let's wait and go for a walk tomorrow.

14. I always _____ nervous when I have a give a speech.

15. A: Where's Bud? He was supposed to be home two hours ago. He always calls when he's late. I _____ worried. Maybe we should call the police.

    B: Relax. He'll be home soon.

16. A: Hurry up and _____ dressed. We have to leave in ten minutes.

    B: I'm almost ready.

17. A: I'm going on a diet.

    B: Oh?

    A: See? This shirt is too tight. I _____ fat.

18. A: Janice and I are thinking about _____ married in June.

    B: That's a nice month for a wedding.

☐ **EXERCISE 23—ERROR ANALYSIS:** Find and correct the errors in the following sentences.

> *Example:*   I am agree with him.
> *Correction:*   I agree with him.

1. An accident was happened at the corner yesterday.

2. This is belong to me.

3. I am very surprise by the news.

4. I'm interesting in that subject.

5. He is marry with my cousin.

6. Thailand is locate in Southeast Asia.

7. Mary's dog was died last week.

8. Were you surprise when you saw him?

9. When I went downtown, I get lost.

10. Last night I very tire.

11. The bus was arrived ten minutes late.

12. When are you going to get marry?

13. I am agree with you.

14. We are not agree with him.

11-11 USING *BE USED/ACCUSTOMED TO* AND *GET USED/ACCUSTOMED TO*

(a) I *am used to* hot weather. (b) I *am accustomed to* hot weather. (c) I *am used to living* in a hot climate. (d) I *am accustomed to living* in a hot climate.	(a) and (b) have the same meaning: "Living in a hot climate is usual and normal for me. I'm familiar with what it is like to live in a hot climate. Hot weather isn't strange or different to me." Notice in (c) and (d): *to* (a preposition) is followed by the *-ing* form of a verb (a gerund).★
(e) I just moved from Florida to Alaska. I have never lived in a cold climate before, but I *am getting used to (accustomed to)* the cold weather here.	In (e): *I'm getting used to/accustomed to* = something is beginning to seem usual and normal to me.

★COMPARE: To express the habitual past (see 2-9), the infinitive form follows *used*: *I used to live* in Chicago, but now I live in New York. However, *be used to* is followed by a gerund: *I am used to living* in a big city.
NOTE: In both *used to* (habitual past) and *be used to*, the "d" is not pronounced in "used."

☐ **EXERCISE 24:** Complete the sentences with *be used to*, affirmative or negative.

1. Juan is from Mexico. He ____**is used to**____ hot weather. He ____**isn't used to**____ cold weather.

2. Alice was born and raised in Chicago. She _____ living in a big city.

3. My hometown is New York City, but this year I'm going to school in a town with a population of 10,000. I _____ living in a small town. I _____ living in a big city.

4. We do a lot of exercises in class. We _____ doing exercises.

Complete the sentences with ***be accustomed to***, *affirmative or negative.*
NOTICE: ***accustomed*** *is spelled with two "c's" and one "m."*

5. Spiro is from Greece. He _____ eating Greek food, but he _____ eating American food.

6. I always get up around 6:00 A.M. I _____ getting up early. I _____ sleeping late.

7. Our teacher always gives us a lot of homework. We _____

   _____ having a lot of homework every day.

8. We rarely take multiple choice tests. We _____

   taking that kind of test.

☐ **EXERCISE 25—ORAL (BOOKS CLOSED):** Talk about yourself. Use *be
used/accustomed to.*

> *Example:* cold weather
> *Response:* I am (OR: I am not) used/accustomed to cold weather.

1. hot weather	7. getting up early
2. cold weather	8. sleeping late
3. living in a warm climate	9. eating a big breakfast
4. living in a cold climate	10. drinking coffee in the morning
5. living in a big city	11. (American) food
6. living in a small town	12. being on my own*

☐ **EXERCISE 26—ORAL (BOOKS CLOSED):** Answer the questions.

> *Example:* What time are you accustomed to getting up?
> *Response:* I'm accustomed to getting up (at 7:30).

1. What time are you accustomed to getting up?
2. What time are you used to going to bed?
3. Are you accustomed to living in (*name of this city*)?
4. Are you accustomed to living in a big city?
5. Are you used to speaking English every day?
6. Who lives with a roommate? Are you accustomed to that?
7. Who lives alone? Are you accustomed to that?
8. What are you accustomed to eating for breakfast?
9. Our weather right now is hot/cold/humid/cold and wet/etc. Are you used to this kind of weather?
10. How are you used to getting to school every day?
11. Where are you accustomed to eating lunch?
12. What time are you accustomed to eating dinner?
13. What kind of food are you accustomed to eating?
14. Who lives in a dorm? Are you used to the noise in a dorm?
15. Are you used to speaking English everyday, or does it seem strange to you?

To be on one's own is an idiom. It means to be away from one's family and responsible for oneself.

☐ **EXERCISE 27:** You are living in a new place (country, city, apartment, dorm, etc.) and going to a new school. What adjustments have you had to make? Write about them by completing the sentences with your own words.

1. I'm getting used to _____

2. I'm also getting accustomed to _____

3. I have gotten accustomed to _____

4. I haven't gotten used to _____

5. I can't get used to _____

6. Do you think I will ever get accustomed to _____

11-12 USING *BE SUPPOSED TO*

(a) Mike *is supposed to call* me tomorrow. (IDEA: I expect Mike to call me tomorrow.) (b) We *are supposed to write* a composition. (IDEA: The teacher expects us to write a composition). (c) It *is supposed to rain* today. (IDEA: People expect it to rain today.) (d) Alice *was supposed to be* home at ten. (IDEA: Someone expected Alice to be home at ten.)	*Be supposed to* is used to talk about an activity or event that is expected to occur. In (a): The idea of *is supposed to* is that Mike is expected (by me) to call. I asked him to call me. He promised to call me. I expect him to call me.
	NOTE: The present form of *be* is used for both future expectations and present expectations.

☐ **EXERCISE 28—ORAL:** Make sentences with a similar meaning by using *be supposed to.*

1. The teacher expects us to be on time for class.
   → *We are supposed to be on time for class.*
2. People expect the weather to be cold tomorrow.
3. People expect the plane to arrive at 6:00.
4. I expect Tom to call me.
5. My boss expects me to work late tonight.
6. I expect the mail to arrive at noon.
7. Someone expected me to return this book to the library yesterday, but I didn't.
8. Our professor expects us to read Chapter 9 before class tomorrow.
9. Someone expected me to go to a party last night, but I stayed home.
10. The teacher expects us to do exercise 10 for homework.
11. The weather bureau has predicted rain for tomorrow. According to the weather bureau, it . . . .

12. The directions on the pill bottle say, "Take one pill every six hours."
According to the directions on the bottle, I . . . .

13. My mother expects me to dust the furniture and (to) vacuum the carpet.

☐ EXERCISE 29—ORAL: Read the dialogues and then answer the questions. Use *be supposed to.*

1. TOM'S BOSS: Mail this package.
   TOM: Yes, sir.
   What is Tom supposed to do?
   →*He is supposed to mail a package.*

2. MARY: Call me at nine.
   ANN: Okay.
   What is Ann supposed to do?

3. MS. MARTINEZ: Please make your bed before you go to school.
   JOHNNY: Okay, Mom.
   What is Johnny supposed to do?

4. MR. TAKADA: Put your dirty clothes in the laundry basket.
   SUSIE: Okay, Dad
   What is Susie supposed to do?

5. MRS. WILSON: Bobby, pick up your toys and put them away.
   BOBBY: Okay, Mom.
   MRS. WILSON: Annie, please hang up your coat.
   ANNIE: Okay, Mom.
   What are the children supposed to do?

6. DR. KETTLE: You should take one pill every eight hours.
   PATIENT: All right, Dr. Kettle. Anything else?
   DR. KETTLE: Drink plenty of fluids.
   What is the patient supposed to do?

7. PROF. LARSON: Read Chapter 10 and answer the questions at the end
   of the chapter.
   STUDENTS: (no response)
   What are the students supposed to do?

8. PROF. THOMPSON: Read the directions carefully, use a No. 2 pencil,
   and raise your hand if you have any questions.
   STUDENTS: (no response)
   What are the students supposed to do?

☐ EXERCISE 30—WRITTEN: Describe how a particular holiday is celebrated in your
country. What is done in the morning, the afternoon, the evening? What are
some of the things that people typically do on this holiday? NOTE: Many of
your sentences will be active, but some of them should be passive.

CHAPTER *12*
Adjective Clauses

12-1 ADJECTIVE CLAUSES: INTRODUCTION

ADJECTIVES	ADJECTIVE CLAUSES*
An **adjective** modifies a noun. "*Modify*" means to change a little. An adjective gives a little different meaning to a noun. It describes or gives information about a noun. (See Chart 4-4).	An **adjective clause** modifies a noun. It describes or gives information about a noun.
An adjective usually comes in front of a noun.	An adjective clause follows a noun.
(a) I met a *adjective* **kind** + *noun* man. (b) I met a *adjective* **famous** + *noun* man.	(c) I met a *noun* man + *adjective clause* **who is kind to everybody**. (d) I met a *noun* man + *adjective clause* **who is a famous poet**. (e) I met a *noun* man + *adjective clause* **who lives in Chicago**.

*Grammar terminology:

A **clause** is a structure that has a subject and a verb.

There are two kinds of clauses: independent and dependent. An **independent clause** is a main clause. It can stand alone as a sentence. A **dependent clause** must be connected to an independent clause. A dependent clause cannot stand alone as a sentence. An adjective clause is a dependent clause.

    I met a man = *an independent clause*

    who is kind to everybody = *a dependent clause*

12-2 USING *WHO* AND *WHOM* IN ADJECTIVE CLAUSES

(a) The man is friendly.	S V **He** lives next to me. ↕ **who** ↓ S V **who** lives next to me	In (a): **He** is a subject pronoun. **He** refers to "the man." To make an adjective clause, we can change **he** to **who**. **Who** is a subject pronoun. **Who** refers to "the man."
(b) The man **who lives next to me** is friendly.		In (b): An adjective clause immediately follows the noun it modifies. INCORRECT: *The man is friendly who lives next to me.*
(c) The man was friendly.	S V **O** I met **him**. ┌────── **whom** **O** S V **whom** I met	In (c): **Him** is an object pronoun. **Him** refers to the "the man." To make an adjective clause, we can change **him** to **whom**. **Whom** is an object pronoun. **Whom** refers to "the man."* **Whom** comes at the beginning of an adjective clause.
(d) The man **whom I met** was friendly.		In (d): An adjective clause immediately follows the noun it modifies. INCORRECT: *The man was friendly whom I met.*

*In informal English, **who** is often used as an object pronoun instead of **whom**:
　　FORMAL: *The man **whom** I met was friendly.*
　　INFORMAL: *The man **who** I met was friendly.*

☐ **EXERCISE 1:** Combine the two sentences into one sentence. Make "b." an adjective clause. Use *who* or *whom*.

　　1. a. Do you know the people?　　b. They live in the white house.

　　　　→ *Do you know the people who live in the white house?*

　　2. a. The woman gave me some information.　　b. I called her.

　　　　→ *The woman whom I called gave me some information.*

　　3. a. The police officer was friendly.　　b. He gave me directions.

　　4. a. The waitress was friendly.　　b. She served us dinner.

　　5. a. I don't know the man.　　b. He is talking to Rita.

　　6. a. The people were very nice.　　b. I met them at the party last night.

　　7. a. The woman thanked me.　　b. I helped her.

　　8. a. Do you like the mechanic?　　b. He fixed your car.

　　9. a. Mr. Polanski is a mechanic.　　b. You can trust this mechanic.

　　10. a. The people have three cars.　　b. They live next to me.

11. a. I talked to the woman.   b. She was sitting next to me.

12. a. I talked to the people.   b. They were sitting next to me.

13. a. The woman was walking her dog.   b. I saw her.

14. a. The people were playing football.   b. I saw them at the park.

☐ **EXERCISE 2:** Complete the sentences in Column A with the adjective clauses in Column B. Consult your dictionary if necessary.

Example: A Bostonian is someone who lives in Boston.

COLUMN A

1. A Bostonian is someone . . . .

2. A pilot is a person . . . .

3. A procrastinator is someone . . . .

4. A botanist is a scientist . . . .

5. An insomniac is somebody . . . .

6. A revolutionary is someone . . . .

7. A misanthrope is a person . . . .

8. A meteorologist is a person . . . .

9. A jack-of-all-trades is someone . . . .

10. An expert can be defined as a person . . . .

COLUMN B

a. who has trouble sleeping.

b. who seeks to overthrow the government.

c. who flies an airplane.

d. who studies weather phenomena.

✔e. who lives in Boston.

f. who hates people.

g. who always puts off doing things.

h. who has special knowledge in one area.

i. who has many skills.

j. who studies plants.

☐ **EXERCISE 3:** Complete the sentences with your own words. Consult your dictionary if necessary.

1. A baker is a person who _____

2. A mechanic is someone who _____

3. A bartender is a person who _____

4. A philatelist is someone who _____

5. A spendthrift is somebody who _____

6. An astronomer is a scientist who _____

7. A carpenter is a person who _____

8. A miser is someone who _____

12-3   USING *WHO*, *WHOM*, AND *THAT* IN ADJECTIVE CLAUSES

(a) The man is friendly. **S** V *He* lives next to me. ↓ *who* *that* **S** V (b) The man *who lives next to me* is friendly. (c) The man *that lives next to me* is friendly.	In addition to *who*, we can use *that* as the subject of an adjective clause. (b) and (c) have the same meaning.
	A subject pronoun cannot be omitted: INCORRECT: *The man lives next to me is friendly.* CORRECT: *The man who/that lives next to me is friendly.*
(d) The man was friendly. S V **O** I met *him*. ↓ *whom* *that* **O** S V (e) The man *whom I met* was friendly. (f) The man *that I met* was friendly. (g) The man *Ø I met* was friendly.	In addition to *whom*, we can use *that* as the object in an adjective clause. (e) and (f) have the same meaning.
	An object pronoun can be omitted from an adjective clause. (e), (f), and (g) have the same meaning. In (g): The symbol "Ø" means "nothing goes here."

☐ **EXERCISE 4:** Change *that* to *who* or *who(m)*.★ Also, omit *that* if possible.

1. The woman that I met last night was interesting.
   → *The woman who(m) I met last night was interesting.*
   → *The woman Ø I met last night was interesting.*

2. The man that answered the phone was polite.

3. The people that Ann is visiting live on Elm Street.

4. Do you like the boy that is talking to Jennifer?

5. The students that came to class late missed the quiz.

6. I didn't know any of the people that Bill invited to his party.

7. The woman that I saw in the park was feeding the pigeons.

8. The woman that was feeding the pigeons had a sackful of bread crumbs.

9. I like the barber that usually cuts my hair.

10. The person that I admire most is my grandmother.

★The parentheses around the "m" in *who(m)* indicate that sometimes (in everyday informal usage) *who* is used as an object pronoun instead of *whom*.

12-4   USING *WHICH* AND *THAT* IN ADJECTIVE CLAUSES

(a) The river is polluted. $\boxed{\begin{array}{cc} \text{S} & \text{V} \\ \textit{\textbf{It}} & \text{flows through town.} \\ \downarrow & \\ \textit{which} & \\ \textit{that} & \end{array}}$	***Who*** and ***whom*** refer to people. ***Which*** refers to things. ***That*** can refer to either people or things.
	In (a): To make an adjective clause, we can change *it* to ***which*** or ***that***. *It*, ***which***, and ***that*** all refer to a thing (the river). (b) and (c) have the same meaning.
S V (b) The river ***which*** *flows through town* is polluted. (c) The river ***that*** *flows through town* is polluted.	
	When ***which*** and ***that*** are used as the subject of an adjective clause, they CANNOT be omitted.
(d) The books were expensive. I bought $\boxed{\begin{array}{c} \text{O} \\ \textit{\textbf{them}}. \\ \downarrow \\ \textit{which} \\ \textit{that} \end{array}}$	***Which*** or ***that*** can be used as an object in an adjective clause, as in (e) and (f).
	An object pronoun can be omitted from an adjective clause, as in (g). (e), (f) and (g) have the same meaning.
O S V (e) The books ***which*** *I bought* were expensive. (f) The books ***that*** *I bought* were expensive. (g) The books Ø *I bought* were expensive.	

☐ **EXERCISE 5:** Combine the two sentences into one sentence. Make "b." an adjective clause. Give all the possible forms.

1. a. The pill made me sleepy.   b. I took it.
   → *The pill which I took made me sleepy.*
   → *The pill that I took made me sleepy.*
   → *The pill Ø I took made me sleepy.*

2. a. The soup was too salty.   b. I had it for lunch.

3. a. I have a class.   b. It begins at 8:00 A.M.

4. a. I know a man.   b. He doesn't have to work for a living.

5. a. My daughter asked me a question.   b. I couldn't answer it.

6. a. All of the people can come.   b. I asked them to my party.

7. a. I lost the scarf.   b. I borrowed it from my roommate.

8. a. A lion is an animal.   b. This animal lives in Africa.

9. a. A globe is a ball.   b. This ball has a map of the world on it.

10. a. Where can I catch the bus?   b. It goes downtown.

11. a. The bus is always crowded.   b. I take it to school every morning.

12. a. The woman predicted my future.   b. She read my palm.

13. a. I have some valuable antiques.   b. I found them in my

grandmother's attic.

14. a. The notes helped me a lot.   b. I borrowed them from you.

☐ **EXERCISE 6:** Complete the sentences in Column A with the adjective clauses in Column B.

Example: A quart is a liquid measure that equals two pints.

COLUMN A

1. A quart is a liquid measure . . . .
2. A puzzle is a problem . . . .
3. Cake is a dessert . . . .
4. A passport is a special paper . . . .
5. A hammer is a tool . . . .
6. A barometer is an instrument . . . .
7. A coin is a piece of metal . . . .
8. A pyramid is a structure . . . .

COLUMN B

a. that is difficult to solve.

b. that measures air pressure.

✓ c. that equals two pints.

d. that is used to pound nails.

e. that is square at the bottom and has four sides that come together at the top in a point.

f. that is used as money.

g. that permits a citizen to travel in other countries.

h. that is made of flour, eggs, milk, and sugar.

12-5 SINGULAR AND PLURAL VERBS IN ADJECTIVE CLAUSES

(a) I know **the man** *who **is** sitting over there.*	In (a): The verb in the adjective clause (**is**) is singular because **who** refers to a singular noun, "man."
(b) I know **the people** *who **are** sitting over there.*	In (b): The verb in the adjective clause (**are**) is plural because **who** refers to a plural noun, "people."

☐ **EXERCISE 7:** Circle the correct word in parentheses.

1. The students who (*is, are*) in my class come from many countries.

2. I met some people who (*knows, know*) my brother.

3. The student who (*is, are*) talking to the teacher is from Peru.

4. I talked to the men who (*was, were*) sitting near me.

5. Do you know the people that (*lives, live*) in that house?

6. Biographies are books which (*tells, tell*) the stories of people's lives.

7. A book that (*tells, tell*) the story of a person's life is called a biography.

8. The woman that (*was, were*) sitting in front of me at the movie was wearing a big hat.

9. The people who (*was, were*) standing in line to get into the theater were cold and wet.

10. Water is a chemical compound that (*consists, consist*) of oxygen and hydrogen.

11. There are two students in my class who (*speaks, speak*) Portuguese.

12. Cedar waxwings are gray-brown birds that (*lives, live*) in most parts of North America. If you see a crested bird that (*is, are*) a little larger than a sparrow and (*has, have*) a band of yellow across the end of its tail, it may be a cedar waxwing.

13. The heart of education is in a culture's literature. People who (*reads, read*) gain not only knowledge but also pleasure. A person who (*does, do*) not read is no better off than a person who cannot read.

12-6 USING PREPOSITIONS IN ADJECTIVE CLAUSES

<table>
<tr>
<td>
(a) The man was helpful.   I talked ***to him***.
 (PREP Obj.)

(b) The man   ***whom*** I talked ***to***   was helpful.
 (Obj.   PREP)
(c) The man   ***that*** I talked ***to***   was helpful.
(d) The man   Ø   I talked ***to***   was helpful.

(e) The man   ***to whom*** I talked   was helpful.
 (PREP Obj.)
</td>
<td>
Whom, ***which***, and ***that*** can be used as the object of a preposition in an adjective clause.

REMINDER: An object pronoun can be omitted from an adjective clause, as in (d) and (i).
</td>
</tr>
<tr>
<td rowspan="2">
(f) The chair is hard.   I am sitting ***in it***.
 (PREP Obj.)

(g) The chair   ***which*** I am sitting ***in***   is hard.
 (Obj.   PREP)
(h) The chair   ***that*** I am sitting ***in***   is hard.
(i) The chair   Ø   I am sitting ***in***   is hard.

(j) The chair   ***in which*** I am sitting   is hard.
 (PREP Obj.)
</td>
<td>
In very formal English, a preposition often comes at the beginning of an adjective clause, as in (e) and (j). The preposition is followed by either ***whom*** or ***which*** (not ***that***) and the pronoun CANNOT be omitted.
</td>
</tr>
<tr>
<td>
(b), (c), (d), and (e) have the same meaning.

(g), (h), (i), and (j) have the same meaning.
</td>
</tr>
</table>

☐ **EXERCISE 8:** Combine the two sentences in each pair. Use "b." as an adjective clause. Give all the possible forms of the adjective clauses.

1. a. The movie was interesting.

   b. We went to it.

   → *The movie which we went to was interesting.*

   → *The movie that we went to was interesting.*

   → *The movie Ø we went to was interesting.*

   → *The movie to which we went was interesting.*

2. a. The woman pays me a fair salary.

   b. I work for her.

3. a. The man is over there.

   b. I told you about him.

4. a. I want to tell you about the party.

   b. I went to it last night.

5. a. The person is sitting at that desk.

   b. You should talk to her about your problem.

6. a. Alicia likes the family.

   b. She is living with them.

7. a. The picture is beautiful.

   b. Tom is looking at it.

8. a. I enjoyed the music.

   b. We listened to it after dinner.

☐ **EXERCISE 9—ORAL:** Combine the sentences, using the second sentence as an adjective clause. Practice omitting the object pronoun (*whom, which, that*).

> *Example:* The hill was steep. I climbed it.
> *Response:* The hill I climbed was steep.

1. I met the people. You told me about them.

2. The bananas were too ripe. My husband bought them.

3. The market has fresh vegetables. I usually go to it.

4. I couldn't understand the woman. I talked to her on the phone.

5. The scrambled eggs were cold. I had them for breakfast at the cafeteria.

6. The office is on Main Street. Amy works in it.

7. I had a good time on the trip. I took it to Glacier National Park.

8. The blouse is made of silk. Mary is wearing it.

9. The doctor prescribed some medicine for my sore throat. I went to him yesterday.

10. The cream was spoiled. I put it in my coffee.

11. The fast-forward button on the tape recorder doesn't work. I bought it last month.

12. Here is the brochure. You asked me about it.

13. The man is tall, dark, and handsome. My sister goes out with him.

14. The university is in New York. I want to go to it.

15. The plane leaves at 7:08 P.M. I'm taking it to Denver.

16. I'm going to call about the want ad. I saw it in last night's paper.

12-7 USING *WHOSE* IN ADJECTIVE CLAUSES

(a) The man called the police. **His car** ↓ **whose car** was stolen.	**Whose*** shows possession. In (a): We can change **his car** to **whose car** to make an adjective clause.
(b) The man **whose car was stolen** called the police.	In (b): *whose car was stolen* = an adjective clause.
(c) I know a girl. **Her brother** ↓ **whose brother** is a movie star.	In (c): We can change *her brother* to *whose brother* to make an adjective clause.
(d) I know a girl **whose brother** *is a movie star.*	
(e) The people were friendly. We bought **their house.** ↓ **whose house**	In (e): We can change *their house* to *whose house* to make an adjective clause.
(f) The people **whose house** *we bought* were friendly.	

*Whose and *who's* have the same pronunciation but NOT the same meaning.
Who's = *who is*: *Who's (who is) your teacher?*

☐ **EXERCISE 10:** Combine the two sentences into one sentence. Make "b." an adjective
clause. Use *whose*. Situation: You and your friend are at a party. You are
telling your friend about the people at the party.

1. a. There is the man.   b. His car was stolen.
   → *There is the man whose car was stolen.*

2. a. There is the woman.   b. Her cat died.

3. a. Over there is the man.   b. I'm dating his daughter.

4. a. Over there is the woman.   b. You met her husband yesterday.

5. a. There is the professor.   b. I'm taking her course.

6. a. That is the man.   b. His son is an astronaut.

7. a. That is the girl.   b. I borrowed her camera.

8. a. There is the boy.   b. His mother is a famous musician.

9. a. They are the people.   b. We visited their house last month.

10. a. That is the couple.   b. Their apartment was burglarized.

☐ **EXERCISE 11—ORAL:** Combine the sentences. Use *whose*.

> *Example:* The man called the police. His car was stolen.
> *Response:* The man whose car was stolen called the police.

1. The woman was sad. Her cat died.

2. The man is friendly. I'm dating his daughter.

3. The woman is my teacher. You met her husband.

4. The professor gives hard tests. I'm taking her course.

5. The man is very proud. His daughter is an astronaut.

6. The girl is a good friend of mine. I borrowed her camera.

7. The boy wants to be a violinist. His mother is a famous musician.

8. The people were very nice. We visited their house.

9. The couple bought new locks. Their apartment was burglarized.

10. I have a friend. Her brother is a police officer.

11. I have a neighbor. His dog barks all day long.

12. I like the people. We went to their house.

13. I thanked the woman. I borrowed her dictionary.

14. The woman shouted "Stop, thief!" Her purse was stolen.

15. The man is famous. His picture is in the newspaper.

☐ **EXERCISE 12:** Complete the following sentences with *who, whom, which, whose,* or *that*. Discuss all the possible completions. Discuss the possibility of omitting the pronoun.

1. People _____*who* OR: *that*_____ live in New York City are called New Yorkers.

2. Tina likes the present _____*which* OR: *that* OR: Ø___ I gave her for her birthday.

3. George Washington is the president _____ picture is on a one-dollar bill.

4. I like the people with _____ I work.

5. Have you seen the movie _____ is playing at the Fox Theater?

6. A stenographer is a person _____ can write shorthand.

7. Do you know the woman _____ Michael is engaged to?

8. I have a friend _____ father is a famous artist.

9. The camera _____ I bought has a zoom lens.

10. Students _____ have part-time jobs have to budget their time very carefully.

11. The person to _____ you should send your application is the Director of Admissions.

12. That's Tom Jenkins. He's the boy _____ parents live in Switzerland.

13. A thermometer is an instrument _____ measures the temperature.

14. A high-strung person is someone _____ is always nervous.

15. The man _____ I told you about is standing over there.

16. Monkeys will eat eggs, grass, fruit, birds, snakes, insects, nuts, flowers, leaves, and frogs. Monkeys will eat almost anything _____ they can find.

☐ **EXERCISE 13—ORAL (BOOKS CLOSED):** Add adjective clauses to the main sentence.

    I. MAIN SENTENCE: The man was nice. (*written on the board*)

        Example: I met him yesterday.
        Response: The man (whom/that) I met yesterday was nice.

    1. You introduced me to him.
    2. He helped me yesterday.

3. I spoke to him on the phone.
4. I called him.
5. He answered the phone.
6. I had dinner with him last week.
7. He opened the door for me.
8. I told you about him.
9. (. . .) went to a movie with him last night.
10. He gave me directions to the post office.
11. (. . .) roomed with him.
12. He visited our class yesterday.
13. We visited his house.
14. He helped us at the hardware store.
15. I borrowed his pen.
16. I met him at the party last night.

II. MAIN SENTENCE: Do you know the woman? (*written on the board*)

    Example: She is standing over there.
    Response: Do you know the woman who/that is standing over there?

1. (. . .) is talking to her.
2. Her car was stolen.
3. (. . .) is going to marry her.
4. (. . .) is talking about her.
5. She is waving at us.
6. Her apartment was burglarized.
7. She works in that office.
8. She is sitting over there.
9. My brother is engaged to her.
10. Her son was arrested by the police.

III. MAIN SENTENCE: The movie was good. (*written on the board*)

    Example: I saw it yesterday.
    Response: The movie (which/that) I saw yesterday was good.

1. We went to it.
2. I watched it on TV last night.
3. (. . .) told me about it.
4. It was playing at (*name of a local theater*).
5. (. . .) saw it.
6. It starred (*name of an actor/actress*).

□ **EXERCISE 14—ERROR ANALYSIS:** All of the following sentences contain mistakes. Can you find the mistakes and correct them?

1. The book which I bought it at the bookstore was very expensive.

2. The woman was nice that I met yesterday.

3. The people which live next to me are friendly.

4. I met a woman who her husband is a famous lawyer.

5. Do you know the people who lives in that house?

6. The professor teaches Chemistry 101 is very good.

7. I wrote a thank-you note to the people who I visited their house on Thanksgiving Day.

8. The people who I met them at the party last night were interesting.

9. I enjoyed the music which we listened to it.

10. The man was very angry whose bicycle was stolen.

□ **EXERCISE 15:** Underline the adjective clause and complete the sentence with your own words.

1. One of the things I like best _____ *is* ★ *hot and spicy food* _____

2. One of the places I want to visit someday _____

3. One of the people I admire most _____

4. Some of the cities I would like to visit _____ *are*★ _____

5. Some of the places I hope to visit someday _____

   _____

6. One of the cities I would like to visit while I'm in this country _____

   _____

7. One of the programs my roommate likes to watch on TV _____

   _____

8. One of the subjects I would like to know more about _____

   _____

★*One of the* + *plural noun* (+ *adjective clause*) + **singular** *verb*.
Some of the + *plural noun* (+ *adjective clause*) + **plural** *verb*.

9. Some of the things I like most in life _____

_____

10. One of the best books I've ever read _____

11. One of the hardest classes I've ever taken _____

12. One of the most fascinating people I've ever met _____

_____

☐ **EXERCISE 16—WRITTEN:** Complete the sentences with your own words. (Use your own paper.)

1. My friend knows a man who . . . .
2. I have a friend whose . . . .
3. I returned the book that . . . .
4. The person who . . . .
5. The people I . . . .
6. The movie we . . . .
7. The people whose . . . .
8. Do you know the woman who . . . ?
9. The book I . . . .
10. The person to whom . . . .
11. One of the places I . . . .
12. Some of the things I . . . .

☐ **EXERCISE 17—WRITTEN:** Imagine that you are in a room full of people. You know everyone who is there. I (your reader) know no one. Tell me who these people are. Write your description of these people. Practice using adjective clauses.

Begin your composition with: *I'm glad you came. Let me tell you about the people who are here. The woman who . . . .*

12-8 MORE PHRASAL VERBS (SEPARABLE)*

cross out	*draw a line through*
do over	*do again*
fill in	*complete a sentence by writing in a blank*
fill out	*write information in a form (e.g., an application form)*
fill up	*fill completely with gas, water, coffee, etc.*
find out	*discover information*
give up	*quit doing something or quit trying*
leave out	*omit*
start over	*start again*
tear down	*destroy a building*
tear off	*detach, tear along a dotted or perforated line*
tear out of	*remove a piece of paper from a book or notebook*
tear up	*tear into small pieces*

*See 9-8 and 9-9 for more information about phrasal verbs.

☐ **EXERCISE 18:** Complete the phrasal verbs.

1. Maria Alvarez's name is supposed to be on this list, but it isn't. Someone probably left it _____ by mistake.

2. I can't solve this math problem. I give _____.

3. I'm not satisfied with my composition. I think I'll do it _____.

4. Dick had trouble figuring out what to say in his letter to his girlfriend. He started the letter _____ three times.

5. A: Good news! I've been accepted at the University of Tennessee.

   B: Great. When did you find _____?

   A: I got a letter in the mail today.

6. A: My roommate moved last week. Before he left, he filled out a change-of-address card at the post office, but I'm still getting some of his mail. What should I do?

   B: Cross _____ the old address on a letter and write in his new one. Also write "please forward" on the letter. You don't have to use another stamp.

7. How much does it cost to fill _____ your gas tank?

8. We're doing an exercise. We're filling _____ blanks with prepositions.

9. When I went to Dr. Green's office for the first time, I had to fill _____ a long form about my health history.

10. I made a mistake on the check I was writing, so I tore it _____ and wrote another check.

11. An old building was in the way of the new highway through the city, so they tore the old building _____.

12. John tore a piece of paper _____ _____ his spiral notebook.

13. When I pay my MasterCard bill, I have to tear _____ the top portion of the bill along the perforated line and send it back with my check.

12-9 MORE PHRASAL VERBS (NONSEPARABLE)*

(a) Last night some friends **dropped in**.	In (a): **drop in** is not followed by an object.
(b) Let's **drop in on** *Alice* this afternoon. Let's **drop in on** *her* this afternoon.	In (b): **drop in on** is followed by an object.
	Some phrasal verbs are three-word verbs when they are followed by an object. These verbs are nonseparable.

drop in (on).	*visit without calling first or without an invitation*
drop out (of).	*stop attending (school)*
fool around (with).	*have fun while wasting time*
get along (with)	*have a good relationship with*
get back (from)	*return from (a trip)*
get through (with).	*finish*
grow up (in).	*become an adult*
look out (for)	*be careful*
run out (of).	*finish the supply of (something)*
watch out (for).	*be careful*

*See 9-8 and 9-9 for more information about phrasal verbs.

☐ **EXERCISE 19**: Complete the phrasal verbs.

1. Look ____*out*____! There's a car coming!

2. Look ___*out*___ ___*for*___ that car!

3. Where did you grow _____?

4. I grew _____ _____ Springfield.

5. I couldn't finish the examination. I ran _____ _____ time.

6. A: What did you do yesterday?

   B: Nothing much. I just fooled _____.

7. A: Hi, Chris! What's up? I haven't seen you in a long time. Where have you been?

   B: I went to California last week to visit my brother.

   A: Oh? When did you get _____ _____ California?

   B: Just yesterday.

8. A: Where's Jack? He hasn't been in class for at least two weeks.

   B: He dropped _____ _____ school.

9. A: Watch _____ _____ that truck!

   B: What truck?

10. A: What time do you expect to get _____ _____ your homework?

    B: In about an hour, as soon as I finish reading this chapter.

11. A: I haven't seen the Grants for a long time. Let's drop _____ _____ them this evening.

    B: We'd better call first. They may not like unexpected company.

12. A: I want to change my room in the dorm.

    B: Why?

    A: I don't get _____ _____ my roommate.

CHAPTER *13*

Comparisons

☐ **EXERCISE 1—ORAL:** Use the given words to make comparisons.

    1. short/long lines (Compare the lengths of the lines.)

        line A _____

        line B _____

        line C _____

        line D _____

        line E _____

        → *Line C is shorter than lines A and B.*

        → *B is the longest line of all.*

        → *C isn't as long as A.*

        → *(continue to make comparisons)*

    2. happy/sad look on his face

       DAVID   MIKE   RICK   JIM

    3. large/small country (in total land area)

       Brazil: 3,286,488 sq. mi. (8,511,965 sq km)

       Egypt: 385,229 sq. mi. (997,739 sq km)

       Spain: 194,897 sq. mi. (504,782 sq km)

       Canada: 3,553,303 sq. mi. (9,203,054 sq km)

4. easy/difficult question

    FIRST QUESTION: What's 2 plus 2?
    SECOND QUESTION: What's the square root of 937 divided by 16?
    THIRD QUESTION: What's 3 times 127?
    FOURTH QUESTION: What's 2 plus 3?

5. good/bad handwriting

    EXAMPLE A: *The meeting starts at eight!*
    EXAMPLE B: *The meeting starts at eight!*
    EXAMPLE C: *The meeting starts at eight!*

13-1 MAKING COMPARISONS WITH *AS . . . AS*

(a) Tina is 21 years old. Sam is also 21.
    Tina is **as old as** Sam (is).
 	
(b) Mike came **as quickly as** he could.
	As . . . as is used to say that the two parts of a comparison are equal or the same in some way.
	    In (a): *as + adjective + as*
	    In (b): *as + adverb + as*

(c) Ted is 20. Tina is 21. Ted is **not as old as** Tina. (d) Ted is**n't quite as old as** Tina. (e) Amy is 5. She is**n't nearly as old as** Tina.	Negative form: **not as . . . as.*** **Quite** and **nearly** are often used with the negative: In (d): **not quite as . . . as** = a small difference. In (e): **not nearly as . . . as** = a big difference.
(f) Sam is **just as old as** Tina. (g) Ted is **nearly/almost as old as** Tina.	Common modifiers of **as . . . as** are **just** (meaning "exactly") and **nearly/almost**.

*Also possible: **not so . . . as:** *Ted is **not so old as** Tina.*

TINA
age 21

SAM
age 21

TED
age 20

AMY
age 5

☐ EXERCISE 2—ORAL: Make comparisons using **as . . . as**.

1. Rita is very busy. Jason is very busy.
    →Rita is . . . *(just) as busy as Jason (is)*.
2. Rita is not very busy at all. Jason is very, very busy.
    → Rita isn't . . . *(nearly) as busy as Jason (is)*.

3. I was very tired. Susan was very tired. → I was ....
4. Adam wasn't tired at all. Susan was very tired. → Adam wasn't ....
5. My apartment has two rooms. Po's apartment has two rooms. (use *big*)
6. My apartment has two rooms. Ali's apartment has three rooms. (use *big*)
7. My apartment has two rooms. Anna's apartment has six rooms. (use *big*)
8. Compare the fullness of the glasses. (use *full*)

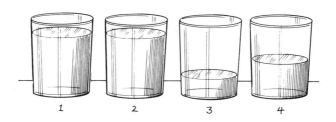

☐ **EXERCISE 3:** Using the given words, complete the sentences with **as . . . as**. Use a negative verb if appropriate.

1. *a housefly/an ant*   **An ant isn't (quite) as** big as **a housefly** .

2. *honey/sugar*   **Honey is (just) as** sweet as **sugar.** .

3. *health/money* _____ important as _____.

4. *adults/children* _____ patient as _____.

5. *a lake/a sea* _____ big as _____.

6. *a lion/a tiger* _____ dangerous and wild as _____.

7. *a galaxy/a solar system* _____ large as _____.

8. *the Atlantic Ocean/the Pacific Ocean** _____ deep as

_____.

9. *monkeys/people* _____ agile in climbing trees as

_____.

10. *reading a novel/listening to music*   In my opinion, _____

_____ relaxing as _____.

11. *a mother/a father*   I think that _____ important

in raising children as _____.

---

*Maximum depths: Atlantic = approx. 30,000 feet/9000 meters.
    Pacific = approx. 36,000 feet/11,000 meters.

□ **EXERCISE 4:** Complete the sentences by using *as . . . as.*

1. I need you right away! Please come . . . **as soon as possible.**

2. We can't go any farther. This is . . . **as far as we can go.**

3. I can't work any faster. I'm working . . . .

4. An orange is sweeter than a lemon. In other words, an orange is not . . . .

5. A stream is usually much narrower than a river. In other words, ...

6. I had expected the test to be difficult, and it was. In other words, the test was just . . . .

7. It's important to use your English every day. You should practice speaking English . . . .

8. You're only old if you feel old. You are . . . young . . . .

9. You might think it's easy to do, but it's not quite . . . .

10. It takes an hour to drive to the airport. It takes an hour to fly to Chicago. In other words, it takes . . . .

□ **EXERCISE 5:** *As . . . as* is used in many traditional phrases. These phrases are generally spoken rather than written. See how many of these phrases you're familiar with by completing the sentences with the given words.

✔ *a bear*	*the hills*	*a pin*
a beet	*a kite*	*a rock*
a bird	*a mule*	*a wet hen*
a bull/an ox		

1. When will dinner be ready? I'm as hungry as _____ **a bear** _____!

2. Did Bill really lift that heavy box all by himself? He must be as strong as _____.

3. It was a lovely summer day. School was out, and there was nothing in particular that I had to do. I felt as free as _____.

4. Jeremy won't change his mind. He's as stubborn as _____.

5. Was she angry? You'd better believe it! She was as mad as _____.

6. Of course I've heard that joke before! It's as old as _____.

7. Nicole felt very embarrassed. She turned as red as _____.

8. I tend to be a little messy, but my roommate is as neat as _____.

9. When Erica received the good news, she felt as high as _____.

10. How can anyone expect me to sleep in this bed? It's as hard as _____.

13-2 COMPARATIVE AND SUPERLATIVE

(a) "A" is *older than* "B." (b) "A" and "B" are *older than* "C" and "D." (c) Ed is *more generous than* his brother.	The comparative compares "this/these" to "that/those." Form: *-er* or *more*. (See Chart 13-3.) NOTICE: A comparative is followed by *than*.
(d) "A", "B", "C", and "D" are sisters. "A" is *the oldest* of all four sisters. (e) A woman in Turkey claims to be *the oldest person* in the world. (f) Ed is *the most generous person* in his family.	The superlative compares one part of a whole group to all the rest of the group. Form: *-est* or *most*. (See Chart 13-3 for forms.) NOTICE: A superlative begins with *the*.

☐ EXERCISE 6—ERROR ANALYSIS: All of the following sentences contain errors. Find and correct the mistakes.

1. Alaska is large than Texas.

    → *Alaska is larger than Texas.*

2. Alaska is largest state in the United States.

3. Texas is the larger from France in land area.

4. Old shoes are usually more comfortable that new shoes.

5. My running shoes are the more comfortable shoes I own.

6. My running shoes are more comfortable as my boots.

7. Mr. Molina writes the most clearly than Ms. York.

8. English is the most widely used language from the world.

9. I have one sister and one brother. My sister is younger in the family.

10. Mark's knife was as sharper from a razor blade.

11. I like Chinese food more better than French food.

13-3 COMPARATIVE AND SUPERLATIVE FORMS OF ADJECTIVES AND ADVERBS

		COMPARATIVE	SUPERLATIVE	
ONE-SYLLABLE ADJECTIVES	old wise	older wiser	the oldest the wisest	For most one-syllable adjectives, **-er** and **-est** are added.
TWO-SYLLABLE ADJECTIVES	famous pleasant	more famous more pleasant	the most famous the most pleasant	For most two-syllable adjectives, **more** and **most** are used.
	busy pretty	busier prettier	the busiest the prettiest	**-Er/-est** are used with two-syllable adjectives that end in -y. The -y is changed to -i.
	clever gentle friendly	cleverer more clever gentler more gentle friendlier more friendly	the cleverest the most clever the gentlest the most gentle the friendliest the most friendly	Some two-syllable adjectives use **-er/-est** or **more/most**: able, angry, clever, common, cruel, friendly, gentle, handsome, narrow, pleasant, polite, quiet, simple, sour.
ADJECTIVES WITH THREE OR MORE SYLLABLES	important fascinating	more important more fascinating	the most important the most fascinating	**More** and **most** are used with long adjectives.
IRREGULAR ADJECTIVES	good bad	better worse	the best the worst	**Good** and **bad** have irregular comparative and superlative forms.
-LY ADVERBS	carefully slowly	more carefully more slowly	the most carefully the most slowly	**More** and **most** are used with adverbs that end in **-ly**.*
ONE-SYLLABLE ADVERBS	fast hard	faster harder	the fastest the hardest	The **-er** and **-est** forms are used with one-syllable adverbs.
IRREGULAR ADVERBS	well badly far	better worse farther/further**	the best the worst the farthest/furthest	

*Exception: **early** is both an adjective and an adverb. Forms: *earlier, earliest.*

Both **farther and **further** are used to compare physical distances: *I walked farther/further than my friend did.* **Further** (but not **farther**) can also mean "additional": *I need further information.*

☐ **EXERCISE 7:** Give the COMPARATIVE and SUPERLATIVE forms of the following adjectives and adverbs.

1. high → *higher, the highest*
2. careful
3. slow
4. slowly
5. active
6. funny
7. wet*
8. sweet*
9. late*
10. thin
11. clean
12. serious
13. good
14. bad
15. clear
16. clearly
17. happy
18. confusing
19. courageous
20. common
21. friendly
22. red
23. wild
24. dangerous

☐ **EXERCISE 8—ORAL:** Choose five to ten movable objects (in this room or in the possession of anyone in this room) and put them in a central place. Compare the items using the given words. Use both the COMPARATIVE (*-er/more*) and the SUPERLATIVE (*-est/most*).

Example: big/small
STUDENT A: Omar's pen is bigger than Anya's ring.
STUDENT B: Sergio's calculator is smaller than Kim's briefcase.
STUDENT C: The biggest thing on the table is the briefcase.
STUDENT D: Etc.

1. big/small
2. soft/hard
3. rough/smooth
4. light/heavy
5. cheap/expensive
6. new/old
7. important/unimportant
8. common/unusual

---

*Spelling notes:
- When a one-syllable adjective ends in **one vowel + a consonant**, double the consonant and add *-er/-est*. Example: *hot, hotter, hottest.*
- When an adjective ends in **two vowels + a consonant**, do NOT double the consonant: *cool, cooler, coolest.*
- When an adjective ends in *-e*, do NOT double the consonant: *wide, wider, widest.*

13-4 USING COMPARATIVES

(a) I'm older *than **my brother*** (*is*). (b) I'm older *than **he** is*. (c) I'm older *than **him***. (*informal*)	In formal English, a subject pronoun (e.g., *he*) follows ***than***, as in (b). In everday, informal spoken English, an object pronoun (e.g., *him*) often follows ***than***, as in (c).
(d) He works harder *than **I do***. (e) I arrived earlier *than **they** did*.	Frequently an auxiliary verb follows the subject after ***than***. In (d): *than I do = than I work*.
(f) Tom is ***much*/*a lot*/*far** older* than I am. INCORRECT: Tom is very older than I am. (g) Ann drives ***much*/*a lot*/*far** more carefully* than she used to. (h) Ben is ***a little*** (***bit***) *older* than me.	***Very*** often modifies adjectives and adverbs: e.g., *Tom is very old. He drives very carefully.* However, ***very*** is NOT used to modify comparative adjectives and adverbs. Instead, they are often modified by ***much***, ***a lot***, or ***far***, as in (f) and (g). Another common modifier is ***a little*/*a little bit***, as in (h).
(i) A pen is ***less** expensive **than*** a book. (j) A pen is ***not as** expensive **as*** a book. (k) A pen is *not as large as* a book. INCORRECT: A pen is less large than a book.	The opposite of *-er*/*more* is expressed by ***less*** or ***not as . . . as***. (i) and (j) have the same meaning. ***Less*** (***not as . . . as***) is used with adjectives and adverbs of **more than one syllable**. Only ***not as . . . as*** (NOT ***less***) is used with one-syllable adjectives or adverbs, as in (k).

☐ **EXERCISE 9:** Complete the following. Use pronouns in the completions.

1. My sister is only six. She's much younger than   ___***I am***___

    OR: (*informally*) ___***me***___ .

2. Peggy is thirteen, and she feels sad. She thinks most of the other girls in school are far more popular than _____.

3. The children can't lift that heavy box, but Mr. Ford can. He's stronger than _____.

4. Jim isn't a very good typist. I can type much faster than _____.

5. I was on time. Jack was late. I got there earlier than _____.

6. Ted is out of shape. I can run a lot faster and farther than _____.

☐ **EXERCISE 10—ORAL:** Add *very, much, a lot,* or *far* to the following sentences.

1. It's hot today. → *It's **very** hot today.*
2. It's hotter today than yesterday. → *It's **much/a lot/far** hotter today . . . .*
3. Learning a second language is difficult.
4. Learning a second language is more difficult than learning chemistry formulas.
5. An airplane is fast.
6. Taking an airplane is faster than hitchhiking.
7. You can live more inexpensively in student housing than in a rented apartment.
8. You can live inexpensively in student housing.

☐ **EXERCISE 11—ORAL:** All of the following sentences contain *not as . . . as.* If possible, change them to sentences with the same meaning using *less.*

1. I don't live as close to my brother as I do to my sister.
   → *(no change using **less**)*
2. I don't visit my brother as often as I visit my sister.
   → *I visit my brother less often than I visit my sister.*
3. George isn't as nice as his brother.
4. George isn't as generous as his brother.
5. I'm not as eager to go to the circus as the children are.
6. A notebook isn't as expensive as a textbook.
7. Wood isn't as hard as metal.
8. Some people think that life in a city isn't as peaceful as life in a small town.
9. The moon isn't nearly as far from the earth as the sun is.
10. I don't travel to Europe on business as frequently as I used to.

☐ **EXERCISE 12:** Complete the following with comparatives by using *more/-er* or *less,* as appropriate. Use the words in parentheses plus your own words.

1. This test wasn't hard. It was a lot (*difficult*) _____ **less difficult than the last test.** _____
2. Dr. Lee's tests are far (*difficult*) _____ **more difficult than Dr. Barton's tests.** _____
3. A piano is a lot (*heavy*) _____
4. To me, science is much (*interesting*) _____
5. Saltwater is (*dense*) _____
6. People are far (*intelligent*) _____
7. Fish are considerably (*intelligent*) _____
8. She rarely comes to see us. She visits us much (*frequently*) _____

9. When you're hot and tired, nothing is (*refreshing*) _____

10. In my life, I have always tried to help those who are (*fortunate*) _____

☐ **EXERCISE 13—ORAL (BOOKS CLOSED):** Answer the question. Begin your response with "Not really, but at least . . . ."

"Not really, but at least . . .'' (*Written on the board.*)

Example: Is the mayor of this city famous?
Response: Not really, but at least s/he is more famous than I am.

1. Is the weather warm/cold today?
2. Is a mouse big?
3. Is this room large?
4. Is your desk comfortable?
5. Is an elephant intelligent?
6. Was the last exercise easy?
7. Is the floor clean?

8. Is a pen expensive?
9. Is this book heavy?
10. Are you relaxed right now?
11. Is blue a bright color?
12. Is (*name of a city*) close to (*name of this city*)?

13-5 USING *MORE* WITH NOUNS

(a) Would you like some ***more coffee***? (b) Not everyone is here. I expect ***more people*** to come later.	In (a): "coffee" is a noun. When ***more*** is used with nouns, it often has the meaning of *additional*. It is not necessary to use ***than***.
(c) There are ***more people*** in China ***than*** there are in the United States.	***More*** is also used with nouns to make complete comparisons by using ***than***.
(d) Do you have enough coffee, or would you like some ***more***?	When the meaning is clear, the noun may be omitted and ***more*** used by itself.

☐ **EXERCISE 14:** Use *-er* or *more* and the words in the list to complete the following. Discuss whether the words are nouns, adjectives, or adverbs and review how comparatives are formed with each of these parts of speech. When do you use *-er* and when you do you use *more*?

✔bright	happiness	people	responsibly
✔brightly	happy	quick	salt
doctors	information	responsibilities	✔traffic
happily	mistakes	responsible	

1. A city has _____ **more traffic** _____ than a small town.

2. Sunlight is much _____ **brighter** _____ than moonlight.

3. Did you know that a laser burns billions of times ___*more brightly*___ than the light at the sun's surface?

4. There is _____ about geography in an encyclopedia than (there is) in a dictionary.

5. I used to be sad, but now I'm a lot _____ about my life (than I used to be).

6. Unhappy roommates or spouses can live together _____ _____ if they learn to respect each other's differences.

7. She's had a miserable life. I hope she finds _____ in the future.

8. I made _____ on the last test than (I did) on the first one, so I got a worse grade.

9. My daughter Annie is trustworthy and mature. She behaves much _____ than my nephew Louie.

10. A twelve-year-old has _____ at home and in school than a nine-year-old.

11. My son is _____ about doing his homework than his older sister is.

12. A rabbit is _____ than a turtle.

13. This soup doesn't taste quite right. I think it needs just a little _____.

14. Health care in rural areas is poor. We need _____ to treat people in rural areas.

15. At present, approximately two-fifths of the world's population can speak English. English is taught to _____ in the world than any other language is or ever has been.

13-6 REPEATING A COMPARATIVE

(a) Because he was afraid, he walked *faster and faster*. (b) Life in the modern world is becoming *more and more complex*.	Repeating a comparative gives the idea that something becomes progressively greater, i.e., it increases in intensity, quality, or quantity.

□ **EXERCISE 15:** Using the words in the following list or your own words, complete the sentences. Repeat the comparative.

angry	*enthusiastic*	*long*
big	*good*	*loud*
discouraged	*hot*	

1. Her English is improving. It is getting _____ **better and better** _____ .

2. They just had their sixth child. Their family is getting _____
_____ .

3. The line of people waiting to get into the theater got _____
_____ .

4. As the soccer game progressed, the crowd became _____
_____ .

5. The weather is getting _____ with each passing day.

6. I've been looking for a job for a month and still haven't been able to find one. I'm getting _____ .

7. As the ambulance came closer to us, the siren became _____
_____ .

8. She sat there quietly, but during all that time she was getting _____
_____ . Finally she exploded.

13-7 USING DOUBLE COMPARATIVES

(a) **The harder** you study, **the more** you will learn. (b) **The older** he got, **the quieter** he became. (c) **The more** she studied, **the more** she learned. (d) **The warmer** the weather (is), **the better** I like it.	A double comparative has two parts; both parts begin with *the*, as in the examples. The second part of the comparison is the **result** of the first part. In (a): If you study harder, the result will be that you will learn more.

(e) A: Should we ask Jenny and Jim to the party too?
     B: Why not? **The more, the merrier.**
 (f) A: When should we leave?
     B: **The sooner, the better.**
	The more, the merrier and **the sooner, the better** are two common expressions.
	 In (e): It is good to have more people at the party.
	 In (f): It is good if we leave as soon as we can.

☐ **EXERCISE 16:** Combine the ideas in the parentheses into a DOUBLE COMPARATIVE. You need to decide which of the two given ideas should come first in the comparison to make a logical statement.

1. (*I became bored. He talked.*)
   I met a man at a party last night. I tried to be interested in what he was saying, but the . . . *more he talked, the more bored I became.*

2. (*I waited long. I got angry.*)
   My friend told me that she would pick me up at the corner at seven o'clock. By seven-thirty, she still hadn't come. The . . . .

3. (*You understand more. You are old.*)
   There are many advantages to being young, but the . . . .

4. (*She drove fast. I became nervous.*)
   Erica offered to take me to the airport, and I was grateful. But we got a late start, so on the way she stepped on the accelerator. I got more than a little uncomfortable. The . . . .

5. (*He thought about his family. He became homesick.*)
   Pierre tried to concentrate on his studying, but his mind would drift to his family and his home. The . . . .

6. (*We ran fast to reach the house. The sky grew dark.*)
   A storm was threatening. The . . . .

7. (*I became confused. I thought about it.*)
   At first I thought I'd understood what she'd said, but then the . . . .

8. (*The air is polluted. The chances of developing respiratory diseases are great.*)
   Pollution poses many dangers. For example, the . . . .

13-8 USING SUPERLATIVES

(a) Tokyo is one of *the largest cities in the world*.	Typical completions when a superlative is used: In (a): superlative + *in* a place (*the world, this class, my family, the corporation,* etc.)
(b) David is *the most generous person I have ever known*.	In (b): superlative + adjective clause. In (c): superlative + *of all*.
(c) I have three books. These two are quite good, but this one is the *best* (book) *of all*.	
(d) I took four final exams. The final in accounting was *the least difficult* of all.	*The least* has the opposite meaning of *the most*.

☐ **EXERCISE 17:** Use the appropriate SUPERLATIVE form (***most*** or ***-est***) for the word in parentheses and complete the sentences with your own words.

1. Physics is (*difficult*) __the most difficult__ course __I have ever taken__.

2. My grandparents are (*wise*) _____ people _____.

3. My hometown is (*friendly*) _____ place _____.

4. What is (*embarrassing*) _____ experience _____?

5. Who is (*important*) _____ political figure _____?

6. What is (*high*) _____ mountain _____?

7. Margaret is one of (*lazy*) _____ people _____.

Use ***least*** in the following:

8. Ed is not lazy, but he is certainly one of (*ambitious*) _____ people _____.

9. I always look for (*expensive*) _____ items _____.

10. What is (*useful*) _____ or (*important*) _____ thing _____?

☐ **EXERCISE 18:** Use SUPERLATIVES of the given words and your own words to complete the sentences.

1. *bad* __"Sea Monsters"__ is the _____worst_____ movie __I've ever seen__.

2. *popular* The _____ sport in _____ is _____.

3. *large* The _____ city in _____ is _____.

4. *good* _____ is the _____ restaurant in _____.

5. *good* One of the _____ places to eat in _____ is _____.

6. *famous* _____ is one of the _____

   people in _____.

7. *hot* There are several hot months, but _____ is

   usually the _____ of all.

8. *valuable* The _____ thing I have is _____.

9. *important* The three _____ things in life are _____

   _____.

10. *serious* The _____ problems in _____

   today are _____.

☐ **EXERCISE 19—ORAL:** Compare the items in each list using the given words. Use *as
...as*, the COMPARATIVE (*-er/more*), and the SUPERLATIVE (*-est/most*).

> *Example:* roads in this city: *wide/narrow/busy/dangerous*
>
> *Responses:* First Avenue is *wider* than Market Street.
> Second Avenue is *nearly as wide as* First Avenue.
> First Avenue is *narrower* than Interstate Highway 70.
> Highway 70 is *the widest* of all the roads in this city.
> It is also *the busiest.*
> Usually First Avenue is *busier* than Market Street.
> *The most dangerous* street in the city is Olive Boulevard.
> Etc.

1. a lemon, a grapefruit, and an orange:
   sweet/sour/large/small
2. this book, that book, and that book:
   thin/fat/interesting/useful/good/bad
3. a kitten, a cheetah, and a lion:
   weak/powerful/wild/gentle/fast
4. air, water, and wood:
   heavy/light/important to human life
5. boxing, soccer, and golf:
   dangerous/safe/exciting/boring
6. three movies you have seen:
   good/bad/exciting/sad
7. the food (at places in this city where you have eaten):
   delicious/appetizing/inexpensive/good/bad
8. sounds or noises:
   loud/soft/pleasant/annoying
9. geographical regions:
   mountainous/flat/dry/humid/populated/unpopulated

13-9 USING *THE SAME, SIMILAR, DIFFERENT, LIKE, ALIKE*

(a) John and Mary have **the same books**. (b) John and Mary have **similar books**. (c) John and Mary have **different books**. (d) Their books are **the same**. (e) Their books are **similar**. (f) Their books are **different**.	**The same**, **similar**, and **different** are used as adjectives. Notice: **the** always precedes **same**.

(g) This book is **the same as** that one.
 (h) This book is **similar to** that one.
 (i) This book is **different from** that one.
	Notice: **the same** is followed by **as**;
	        similar is followed by **to**;
	        different is followed by **from**.*

(j) She is **the same age as** my mother. My shoes are **the same size as** yours.	A noun may come between **the same** and **as**, as in (j).

(k) My pen **is like** your pen.
 (l) My pen and your pen **are alike**.
	Notice in (k) and (l):
	    noun + **be like** + *noun*
	    noun and *noun* + **be alike**

(m) She **looks like** her sister.
     It **looks like** rain.
     It **sounds like** thunder.
     This material **feels like** silk.
     That **smells like** gas.
     This chemical **tastes like** salt.
     Stop **acting like** a fool.
     He **seems like** a nice fellow.
	In addition to following **be**, **like** also follows certain verbs, primarily those dealing with the senses. Notice the examples in (m).

(n) The twins **look alike**.
     We **think alike**.
     Most four-year-olds **act alike**.
     My sister and I **talk alike**.
     The little boys **are dressed alike**.
	Alike may follow a few verbs other than **be**. Notice the examples in (n).

*In informal speech, native speakers might use **than** instead of **from** after **different**. **From** is considered correct in formal English, unless the comparison is completed by a clause: *I have a different attitude now than I used to have.*

☐ **EXERCISE 20:** Use *the same (as), similar (to), different (from), like,* and *alike* in the following. There may be more than one possible response in some of the sentences. Use whatever response sounds best to you.

1. Jennifer and Jack both come from Rapid City. In other words, they come from _____*the same*_____ town.

2. This city is _____*the same as/similar to/like*_____ my hometown. Both are quiet and conservative.

3. You and I don't agree. Your ideas are _____ mine.

4. Eric never wears _____ clothes two days in a row.

5. Ants are fascinating. An ant colony is _____ a well-disciplined army.

6. In terms of shape, cabbage looks _____ lettuce. But cabbage and lettuce don't taste _____.

7. A male mosquito is not _____ size _____ a female mosquito. The female is larger.

8. I'm used to strong coffee. I think the coffee most North Americans drink tastes _____ dishwater!

9. The pronunciation of "caught" is _____ the pronunciation of "cot."

10. "Meet" and "meat" are homonyms; i.e., they have _____ pronunciation.

11. My dictionary is _____ yours.

12. Trying to get through school without studying is _____ trying to go swimming without getting wet.

13. "Flower" has _____ pronunciation _____ "flour."

14. A crocodile and an alligator are _____ in appearance.

15. If it looks _____ a duck, quacks _____ a duck, and walks _____ a duck, it is a duck. (*a humorous saying*)

Do you have sayings in your language that are similar to or the same as the following English proverbs?

1. Don't count your chickens before they hatch.
2. The early bird gets the worm.
3. Too many cooks spoil the broth.
4. A bird in the hand is worth two in the bush.
5. A stitch in time saves nine.
6. When in Rome, do as the Romans do.
7. Birds of a feather flock together.
8. A rolling stone gathers no moss.

□ **EXERCISE 22—ORAL:** Before you come to class, prepare statements of comparison and contrast on the following topics. Be inventive, original, and specific. Prepare at least three statements on each topic to share with the rest of the class.

Topics:

1. Language
2. Food
3. Seasons of the year
4. Children/adults
5. Sports

□ **EXERCISE 23—WRITTEN:** Following are topics for writing.

Compare and contrast:

1. Being single and being married.
2. Cities you have lived in or have visited.
3. Different schools you have attended.
4. Your way of life before and after you became a parent.
5. Yourself now to yourself ten years ago.
6. Your country now to your country 100 years ago.
7. Life today to life 100 years from now.

CHAPTER *14*
Noun Clauses

14-1 NOUN CLAUSES: INTRODUCTION

(a) S V O I know **his address**. *(noun phrase)*	Verbs are often followed by objects. The object is usually a noun phrase,★ as in (a): **his address** is a noun phrase; **his address** is the object of the verb *know*. Some verbs can be followed by noun clauses.★ In (b): **where he lives** is a noun clause; **where he lives** is the object of the verb *know*.
(b) S V O I know **where he lives**. *(noun clause)*	
(c) S V O S V I know **where he lives**.	A noun clause has its own subject and verb. In (c): **he** is the subject of the noun clause; **lives** is the verb of the noun clause.
(d) I know **where he lives**. *(noun clause)*	A noun clause can begin with a question word. (See 14-2.)
(e) I don't know **if he is married**. *(noun clause)*	A noun clause can begin with *if* or **whether**. (See 14-4.)
(f) I know **that the world is round**. *(noun clause)*	A noun clause can begin with *that*. (See 14-5.)

★Grammar terminology:
    A **phrase** is a group of related words. It does not contain a subject and a verb.
    A **clause** is a group of related words. It contains a subject and a verb.
  A noun clause is a dependent clause and cannot stand alone as a sentence. It must be connected to an independent clause (a main clause).

14-2 NOUN CLAUSES THAT BEGIN WITH A QUESTION WORD

The following question words can be used to introduce a noun clause: **when, where, why, how, who, whom, what, which, whose**.

INFORMATION QUESTIONS	NOUN CLAUSES	Notice in the examples:
Where **does he live**?	(a) I don't know *where **he lives***.	Question word order is NOT used in a noun clause.
When **did they leave**?	(b) Do you know *when **they left***?	INCORRECT:
What **did she say**?	(c) Please tell me *what **she said***.	*I know where does he live.*
Why **is Tom** absent?	(d) I wonder *why **Tom is** absent*.	CORRECT:
		I know where he lives.

☐ **EXERCISE 1:** Complete the sentences by changing the questions to noun clauses.

1. *Where did Paul go?* I don't know _____*where Paul went.*_____

2. *How old is Kate?* I don't know _____

3. *Why did Tim leave?* I don't know _____

4. *When did Tim leave?* I don't know _____

5. *Where did he go?* I don't know _____

6. *Where is he?* I don't know _____

7. *Where does he live?* I don't remember _____

8. *What did he say?* I didn't hear _____

9. *Where is the post office?* Could you please tell me _____

10. *What time is it?* Could you please tell me _____

11. *How much does this book cost?* Could you please tell me _____

12. *What does this word mean?* Could you please tell me _____

13. *What country is Anna from?* Do you know _____

14. *Why was Kathy absent yesterday?* Do you know _____

15. *How far is it to Chicago?* I wonder _____

16. *When does the semester end?* Can you tell me _____

17. *What is Sue talking about?* I don't understand _____

18. *When did David arrive?* I don't know _____

19. *When is he going to leave?* Do you know _____

20. *Where can I buy a good radio?* Do you know _____

☐ **EXERCISE 2:** Complete the sentences by changing the questions to noun clauses.

1. *Who(m) did you see at the party?* Tell me **who(m) you saw at the party.**

2. *Who came to the party?* Tell me **who came to the party.**★

3. *Who(m) did Helen talk to?* Do you know _____

4. *Who lives in that apartment?* Do you know _____

5. *What happened?* Tell me _____

6. *What did he say?* Tell me _____

7. *What kind of car does Pat have?* I can't remember _____

8. *How old are their children?* I can't ever remember _____

9. *Why did you say that?* I don't understand _____

10. *Where can I catch the bus?* Could you please tell me _____

11. *Who broke the window?* Do you know _____

12. *Who did Sara invite?* I don't know _____

13. *How long has Ted been living here?* Do you know _____

14. *What time is flight 677 supposed to arrive?*

    Can you tell me _____

15. *Why is Yoko angry?* Do you know _____

14-3 NOUN CLAUSES WITH *WHO, WHAT, WHOSE* + *BE*

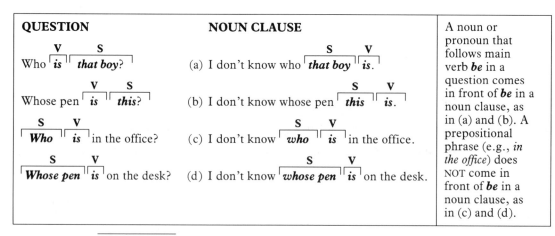

QUESTION	NOUN CLAUSE	
V S Who ⌐is⌐ ⌐that boy?⌐	(a) I don't know who ⌐**that boy**⌐ ⌐**is**⌐. S V	A noun or pronoun that follows main verb *be* in a question comes in front of *be* in a noun clause, as in (a) and (b). A prepositional phrase (e.g., *in the office*) does NOT come in front of *be* in a noun clause, as in (c) and (d).
V S Whose pen ⌐is⌐ ⌐this?⌐	(b) I don't know whose pen ⌐**this**⌐ ⌐**is**⌐. S V	
S V ⌐Who⌐ ⌐is⌐ in the office?	(c) I don't know ⌐**who**⌐ ⌐**is**⌐ in the office. S V	
S V ⌐Whose pen⌐ ⌐is⌐ on the desk?	(d) I don't know ⌐**whose pen**⌐ ⌐**is**⌐ on the desk. S V	

_____
★Usual question word order is not used when the question word (e.g., *who* or *what*) is the subject of a question. (See Charts 6-2 and 6-3.) In this case, the word order in the noun clause is the same as the word order in the question.

□ **EXERCISE 3:** Complete the sentences by changing the questions to noun clauses.

1. *Who is she?* I don't know _____

2. *Who are they?* I don't know _____

3. *What is that?* Do you know _____

4. *What are those?* Can you tell me _____

5. *Whose book is that?* I don't know _____

6. *Whose books are those?* Do you know _____

7. *What is a wrench?* Do you know _____

8. *Who is that woman?* I wonder _____

9. *Whose house is that?* I wonder _____

10. *What is a clause?* Don't you know _____

11. *What is in that drawer?* I don't know _____

12. *Who is in that room?* I don't know _____

13. *Whose car is in the driveway?* Do you know _____

14. *Whose car is that?* Do you know _____

15. *What is on TV tonight?* I wonder _____

16. *What is a carrot?* Do you know _____

17. *Whose glasses are those?* Could you tell me _____

18. *Who am I?* He doesn't know _____

19. *What's at the end of the rainbow?* The little girl wants to know _____

_____

☐ **EXERCISE 4—ORAL (BOOKS CLOSED):** Change the questions to noun clauses. Begin your response with *"I don't know . . . ."*

> *Example:* Where does (. . .) live?
> *Response:* I don't know where (. . .) lives.

1. Where did (. . .) go yesterday?
2. What did (. . .) buy yesterday?
3. Why is (. . .) absent?
4. Where is (. . .)?
5. How old is (. . .)?
6. Where does (. . .) live?
7. Where does (. . .) eat lunch?
8. What is (. . .)'s last name?
9. Why does (. . .) go downtown every day?
10. What time does (. . .) usually get up?
11. Why did (. . .) go downtown yesterday?
12. When did (. . .) get home last night?
13. What time did (. . .) go to bed last night?
14. What time is it?
15. What time does (. . .) eat dinner?
16. How long has (. . .) been living here?
17. Who broke that window?
18. Who did (. . .) call last night?
19. What happened in (Brazil) yesterday?
20. What did (. . .) eat for breakfast?
21. Who wrote (*War and Peace*)?
22. Who did (. . .) see yesterday?
23. What caused the earthquake in (Iran)?
24. What causes earthquakes?
25. Who is that girl?
26. Who are those people?
27. Whose (backpack) is that?
28. Whose (gloves) are those?
29. What kind of tree is that?
30. What kind of car does (. . .) have?

☐ **EXERCISE 5—ORAL (BOOKS CLOSED):** STUDENT A: Change the noun clause to a question. STUDENT B: Answer the question.

> *Example:* Ask (. . .) where (. . .) lives.
> TEACHER TO A: Toshi, ask Ingrid where Mustafa lives.
> STUDENT A: Ingrid, where does Mustafa live?
> STUDENT B: I don't know where Mustafa lives. OR: Mustafa lives in Reed Hall.

1. Ask (. . .) where (. . .) ate breakfast this morning.
2. Ask (. . .) what (. . .)'s favorite color is.
3. Ask (. . .) when (. . .) got up this morning.
4. Ask (. . .) why (. . .) isn't sitting in his/her usual seat today.
5. Ask (. . .) how (. . .) got to class today.
6. Ask (. . .) who (. . .) lives with.
7. Offer (. . .) this (*candy bar*) and that (*candy bar*). Ask him/her which one he/she wants.
8. Ask (. . .) what time it is.
9. Ask (. . .) what kind of watch (. . .) has.

10. Ask (. . .) why (. . .) didn't come to class yesterday.
11. Ask (. . .) who (. . .)'s best friend is.
12. Ask (. . .) where (. . .) went after class yesterday.

□ **EXERCISE 6—ORAL (BOOKS CLOSED):** Change the questions to noun clauses. Begin your response with "*Could you please tell me . . . .*"

Example: Where does (. . .) live?
Response: Could you please tell me where (. . .) lives?

1. What time is it?
2. Where is the post office?
3. Where is the library?
4. Where is the rest room?
5. How much does this pen cost?
6. How much does this book cost?
7. How much do these shoes cost?
8. What does this word mean?
9. What does "complex" mean?
10. What does "steam" mean?
11. Where is the nearest hospital?
12. Why were you late for class?
13. Where can I buy a garden hose?
14. What is a garden hose?
15. Whose pen is this?
16. Whose papers are those?

□ **EXERCISE 7—ORAL (BOOKS CLOSED):** Practice using noun clauses while reviewing irregular verbs. Begin your response with "*I don't know . . . .*"

Example: What did (. . .) find?
Response: I don't know what he/she found.

1. Where did (. . .) sit yesterday?
2. What did (. . .) wear yesterday?
3. When did (. . .) wake up?
4. What did (. . .) buy?
5. Where did (. . .) lose his/her umbrella?
6. How did (. . .) tear his shirt/her blouse?
7. Who did (. . .) speak to yesterday?
8. How long did (. . .) sleep last night?
9. What did (. . .) make for dinner last night?
10. What did (. . .) give (. . .) for his/her birthday?
11. Why did (. . .) fly to New York?
12. What did (. . .) steal?
13. How much money did (. . .) lend (. . .)?
14. Why did (. . .) fall down?
15. Which book did (. . .) choose?
16. When did (. . .) quit smoking?
17. What did (. . .) see?
18. Why did (. . .) shake his/her head?
19. Why did (. . .) bring his/her radio to class?
20. Why did (. . .) take your dictionary?
21. Why did (. . .) draw a picture?
22. Who did (. . .) write a letter to?
23. How did (. . .) meet his wife/her husband?

24. Why did (. . .) bite his/her lip?

25. When did this (*term, session, semester*) begin?

26. How did (. . .) break his/her arm?

27. How did (. . .) catch a cold?

28. When did (. . .) get married?

29. When did (. . .) do his/her homework?

30. Where did (. . .) grow up?

14-4 NOUN CLAUSES WHICH BEGIN WITH *IF* OR *WHETHER*★

YES/NO QUESTION	NOUN CLAUSE	When a yes/no question is changed to a noun clause, *if* is usually used to introduce the clause.
Is Eric at home?	(a) $\overline{\text{S}}$ $\overline{\text{V}}$ $\overline{\text{O}}$ I ⌐don't know⌐ *if Eric is at home.*	
Does the bus stop here?	(b) Do you know *if the bus stops here?*	
Did Alice go to Chicago?	(c) I wonder *if Alice went to Chicago.*	

(d) I don't know *if Eric is at home **or not**.*	When *if* introduces a noun clause, the expression *or not* frequently comes at the end of the clause, as in (d).
(e) I don't know ***whether*** Eric is at home. (f) I don't know ***whether*** Eric is at home *or not*. (g) I don't know ***whether or not*** Eric is at home.	In (e): ***whether*** has the same meaning as *if*. In (f): *or not* can come at the end of the noun clause. In (g): *or not* can come immediately after ***whether***. (NOTE: *or not* cannot come immediately after *if*.)

★See Chart 15-5 for the use of *if* and ***whether*** with ***ask*** in reported speech.

☐ **EXERCISE 8—ORAL:** Complete the sentences by changing the yes/no questions to noun clauses. Introduce the noun clause with *if* or ***whether***. Practice using *or not*.

1. *Is Mary at the library?* I don't know . . . .
   → . . . *if Mary is at the library.*
   . . . *if Mary is at the library or not.*
   . . . *whether Mary is at the library.*
   . . . *whether Mary is at the library or not.*
   . . . *whether or not Mary is at the library.*

2. *Does Bob live in an apartment?* I don't know . . . .

3. *Did Joe go downtown?* I don't know . . . .

4. *Will Ann be in class tomorrow?* I wonder . . . .

5. *Is Tom at home?* Do you know . . . .

□ **EXERCISE 9:** Change the questions to noun clauses.

1. *Did Steve go to the bank?* I don't know ____*if (whether) Steve went*____
   ____*to the bank.*____

2. *Where did Steve go?* I don't know ____*where Steve went.*____

3. *Is Karen at home?* Do you know _____

4. *Where is Karen?* Do you know _____

5. *How is Pat feeling today?* I wonder _____

6. *Is Pat feeling better today?* I wonder _____

7. *Does the bus stop here?* Do you know _____

8. *Where does the bus stop?* I wonder _____

9. *Why is Elena absent today?*

   The teacher wants to know _____

10. *Is Elena going to be absent again tomorrow?*

    I wonder _____

11. *Where did Janet go last night?* Do you know _____

12. *Should I buy that book?* I wonder _____

13. *Which book should I buy?* I wonder _____

14. *Can Jerry speak French?* I don't know _____

15. *How much does that book cost?* Do you know _____

16. *Is there life on other planets?* No one knows _____

17. *Are we going to have a test tomorrow?*

    Let's ask the teacher _____

18. *Is there a Santa Claus?*

    The little boy wants to know _____

19. *Who is that man?* I'm going to ask Nicole _____

20. *Is that man a teacher?* I'm going to ask Nicole _____

□ **EXERCISE 10—ORAL (BOOKS CLOSED):** Make sentences with noun clauses. Begin your response with "*I wonder . . . .*"

Example: Did (. . .) go to the bank?
Response: I wonder if (. . .) went to the bank.

Example: Where did (. . .) go?
Response: I wonder where (. . .) went.

1. Why is (. . .) absent today?
2. Where is (. . .)?
3. Is (. . .) sick?
4. Will it (snow) tomorrow?
5. Will the weather be nice tomorrow?
6. Is (. . .) going to be in class tomorrow?
7. How long has (. . .) been living here?
8. Did (. . .) go to the library last night?
9. How much does (a Rolls Royce) cost?
10. Where did (. . .) go last night?
11. Who lives in that house?
12. Who is that woman?
13. Is that woman a teacher?
14. Whose (book) is that?
15. Whose (gloves) are those?
16. Whose (pen) is that?
17. Whose (papers) are those?
18. Did (. . .) study last night?
19. Does (. . .) have a car?
20. How far is it to (St. Louis)?

□ **EXERCISE 11:** Change the questions to noun clauses.

1. *Will it rain tomorrow?* I wonder _____ ***if it will rain tomorrow.*** _____

2. *What is an amphibian?*

   Do you know _____

3. *Is a frog an amphibian?*

   Can you tell me _____

4. *What's on TV tonight?*

   I wonder _____

5. *What is the speed of sound?*

   Do you know _____

6. *Does sound travel faster than light?*

   Do you know _____

7. *Are dogs color blind?*

   Do you know _____

8. *Why is the sky blue?*

   Annie wants to know _____

9. *Does that store accept credit cards?*

   Do you know _____

10. *Do insects have ears?*

    The little girl wants to know _____

11. *When will the next earthquake occur in California?*

    No one knows _____

12. *Will there be another earthquake in California this year?*

    No one knows _____

13. *Do animals have the same emotions as human beings?*

    The little boy wants to know _____

14. *How do dolphins communicate with each other?*

    Do scientists know _____

15. *Can people communicate with dolphins?*

    I want to find out _____

16. *Have beings from outer space ever visited the earth?*

    I wonder _____

□ **EXERCISE 12—ORAL (BOOKS CLOSED):** Make sentences with noun clauses.

STUDENT A: Ask a question beginning with "*Do you know . . . ?*"
STUDENT B: Answer "*no.*" Give a short answer and then a full answer.

Example: Does (. . .) live in the dorm?
STUDENT A: Do you know if (. . .) lives in the dorm?
STUDENT B: No, I don't. I don't know whether or not (. . .) lives in the dorm.

Example: Where does (. . .) live?
STUDENT A: Do you know where (. . .) lives?
STUDENT B: No, I don't. I don't know where (. . .) lives.

1. Does (. . .) have (a car)?
2. Who is (that woman)?
3. Can (. . .) sing?
4. What does "gossip" mean?
5. What time does the mail come?
6. Is the mail here yet?
7. Does (. . .) have a job?
8. Is (. . .) married?
9. Why is (. . .) absent today?
10. Is (the library) open on Sundays?
11. What time does (the bookstore) close?
12. Does (. . .) speak (*language*)?
13. What kind of (car) does (. . .) have?
14. Is (. . .) planning to take another English course?
15. Is there a pay phone in this building?

□ **EXERCISE 13—ORAL:** Answer the questions using the given words.

QUESTION 1: What do you know?
    a. *where*
      → STUDENT A: I know *where* Madagascar is located.
         STUDENT B: I know *where* (. . .)'s dictionary is.
         STUDENT C: I know *where* my parents got married.
         STUDENT D: I know *where* the Blueberry Cafe is.
         STUDENT E: etc.
    b. *what*
    c. *why*
    d. *who*

QUESTION 2:   What do you NOT know?
  a. *where*
       → STUDENT A: I don't know *where* Madagascar is located.
         STUDENT B: etc.
  b. *if*
  c. *why*
  d. *who*

QUESTION 3:   What do you want to know?
  a. *if*
  b. *when*
  c. *what*
  d. *who*

QUESTION 4: What do you wonder?
  a. *why*
  b. *if*
  c. *what*
  d. *who*
  e. *how*
  f. *whether*

14-5   NOUN CLAUSES WHICH BEGIN WITH *THAT*

(a) I think *that Mr. Jones is a good teacher.* (S V O)	A noun clause can be introduced by the word *that*. In (a): *that Mr. Jones is a good teacher* is a noun clause. It is the object of the verb *think*. "*That*-clauses" are frequently used as the objects of verbs which express mental activity. (See the list below.)
(b) I hope *that you can come to the game.* (c) Mary realizes *that she should study harder.* (d) I dreamed *that I was on the top of a mountain.*	
(e) I think *that Mr. Jones is a good teacher.* (f) I think Ø *Mr. Jones is a good teacher.*	The word *that* is often omitted, especially in speaking. (e) and (f) have the same meaning.

COMMON VERBS FOLLOWED BY "*THAT*-CLAUSES"★

assume that	*guess that*	*learn that*	*realize that*
believe that	*hear that*	*notice that*	*suppose that*
discover that	*hope that*	*predict that*	*suspect that*
dream that	*know that*	*prove that*	*think that*

★The verbs in the above list are those that are emphasized in the exercises. Some other common verbs that can be followed by "*that*-clauses" are:

agree that	*fear that*	*imagine that*	*read that*	*reveal that*
conclude that	*feel that*	*indicate that*	*recall that*	*show that*
decide that	*figure out that*	*observe that*	*recognize that*	*teach that*
demonstrate that	*find out that*	*presume that*	*regret that*	*understand that*
doubt that	*forget that*	*pretend that*	*remember that*	

☐ **EXERCISE 14:** Complete the sentences with the clauses in the list or with your own words. Use *that* to introduce the clause, or omit *that* if you wish.

> *All people are equal.*
> *Flying in an airplane is safer than riding in a car.*
> *He always twirls his mustache when he's nervous.*
> *High school students in the United States don't study as hard as the students in my country do.*
> *A huge monster was chasing me.*
> *I should study tonight.*
> *I will get married someday.*
> ✔ *I will have a peanut butter sandwich.*
> *John "Cat Man" Smith stole Mrs. Adams's jewelry.*
> *More than half of the people in the world go hungry every day.*
> *People are pretty much the same everywhere.*
> *Plastic trash kills thousands of marine animals every year.*

1. I'm hungry. I guess ___**(that) I will have a peanut butter sandwich.**___

2. I have a test tomorrow. I suppose _____,
   but I'd rather go to a movie.

3. Why are you afraid to fly in an airplane? Read this report. It proves
   _____

4. Right now I'm single. I can't predict my future exactly, but I assume
   _____

5. Last night I had a bad dream. In fact, it was a nightmare. I dreamed
   _____

6. The police are investigating the burglary. They don't have much
   evidence, but they suspect _____

7. My cousin feels that people in the United States are unfriendly, but I
   disagree with him. I've discovered _____

8. I've learned many things about life in the United States since I came
   here. For example, I've learned _____

9. I always know when Paul is nervous. Have you ever noticed
   _____

10. I believe that it is wrong to judge another person on the basis of race,
    religion, or sex. I believe _____

11. World hunger is a serious problem. Do you realize _____

_____

12. Don't throw that plastic bag into the sea! Don't you know _____

_____

☐ **EXERCISE 15—WRITTEN:** Complete the following sentences with your own words. Omit the word *that* if you wish. (Use your own paper.)

1. I believe that	9. Have you ever noticed that . . . ?
2. I assume that	10. I suspect that . . . .
3. Do you realize that . . . ?	11. I hope that . . . .
4. I can prove that	12. Do you think that . . . ?
5. I predict that	13. I've discovered that . . . .
6. I've heard that	14. Did you know that . . . ?
7. I guess that	15. Last night I dreamed that . . . .
8. I suppose that	

14-6 SUBSTITUTING *SO* FOR A "*THAT*-CLAUSE" IN CONVERSATIONAL RESPONSES

(a) A: Is Pedro from Mexico? B: **I think *so*.** (*I think **that Pedro is from Mexico.***) (b) A: Does Judy live in Dallas? B: **I believe *so*.** (*I believe **that Judy lives in Dallas.***) (c) A: Did you pass the test? B: **I hope *so*.** (*I hope **that I passed the test.***)	***Think*, *believe*,** and ***hope*** are frequently followed by ***so*** in conversational English in response to a yes/no question. They are alternatives to answering *yes*, *no*, or *I don't know.*★
	So replaces a "*that*-clause." In (a): ***so*** = *that Pedro is from Mexico.*
(d) A: Is Ali at home? B: **I don't think *so*.** (*I don't think **that Ali is at home.***) (e) A: Is Jack married? B: **I don't believe *so*.** (*I don't believe **that Jack is married.***)	Negative usage of ***think so*** and ***believe so***: *I don't think so.* *I don't believe so.*
(f) A: Did you fail the test? B: **I hope *not*.** (*I hope **that I didn't fail the test.***)	Negative usage of ***hope*** in conversational responses: *I hope not.*

★In addition to expressions with ***think, believe,*** and ***hope,*** the following expressions are commonly used in conversational responses: *I guess so, I guess not, I suppose so, I suppose not, I'm afraid so, I'm afraid not.*

□ EXERCISE 16—ORAL: Give the full idea of SPEAKER B's answers to A's questions by using a "*that*-clause."

    1. A: Is Karen going to be home tonight?

        B: I think so. → *I think that Karen is going to be home tonight.*

    2. A: Is the library open on Sunday evenings?

        B: I believe so.

    3. A: Does Ann speak Spanish?

        B: I don't think so.

    4. A: Are we going to have a test in grammar tomorrow?

        B: I don't believe so.

    5. A: Will Tina be at the conference in March?

        B: I hope so.

    6. A: Will your flight be canceled because of the bad weather in Denver?

        B: I hope not.

□ EXERCISE 17—ORAL (BOOKS CLOSED): Answer the questions by using ***think so*** or ***believe so*** if you are not sure, or ***yes*** or ***no*** if you are sure.

    Example: Does this book have more than (400) pages?
    Response: I think/believe so. OR: I don't think/don't believe so. OR: Yes, it does. OR: No, it doesn't.

    1. Does (. . .) have a car?
    2. Are we going to have a test tomorrow?
    3. Is there a fire extinguisher in this building?
    4. Is Chicago farther north than New York City?
    5. Does the word "patient" have more than one meaning?
    6. Does the word "dozen" have more than one meaning?
    7. Is your left foot bigger than your right foot?
    8. Do gorillas eat meat?
    9. Do spiders have eyes?
   10. Don't look at your watch. Is it (10:45) yet?
   11. Is the nearest post office on (Pine Street)?
   12. Is next (Tuesday) the (24th)?
   13. Are cats colorblind?
   14. Can I buy a window fan at (*name of a local store*)?

15. Can you jog (five miles) without stopping?
16. Do any English words begin with the letter "x"?
17. In terms of evolution, is a pig related to a horse?
18. Is a tomato a vegetable?
19. Have I asked you more than 20 questions in this exercise?
20. Do you know what a noun clause is?
21. Is (. . .) planning to get married soon?
22. Does (. . .) usually use chopsticks when s/he eats at home?

14-7 OTHER USES OF "*THAT*-CLAUSES"

(a) I'm **sure that** the bus stops here. (b) I'm **glad that** you're feeling better today. (c) I'm **sorry that** I missed class yesterday. (d) I **was disappointed that** the peace conference failed.	"*That*-clauses" can follow certain expressions with **be** + *adjective* or **be** + *past participle.* The word "*that*" can be omitted with no change in meaning: *I'm sure Ø the bus stops here.*

(e) **It is true that** the world is round.
 (f) **It is a fact that** the world is round.
	Two very common expressions followed by "*that*-clauses" are:
	     it is true (that)
	     it is a fact (that)

COMMON EXPRESSIONS FOLLOWED BY "*THAT*-CLAUSES"★

be afraid that	*be disappointed that*	*be sorry that*	*It is true that . . .*
be aware that	*be glad that*	*be sure that*	*It is a fact that . . .*
be certain that	*be happy that*	*be surprised that*	
be convinced that	*be pleased that*	*be worried that*	

★The above list contains expressions emphasized in the exercises. Some other common expressions with **be** that are frequently followed by "*that*-clauses" are:

be amazed that	*be delighted that*	*be impressed that*	*be sad that*
be angry that	*be fortunate that*	*be lucky that*	*be shocked that*
be ashamed that	*be furious that*	*be positive that*	*be terrified that*
be astounded that	*be horrified that*	*be proud that*	*be thrilled that*

☐ **EXERCISE 18—ORAL:** Complete the sentences. Use any appropriate verb form in the "*that*-clause." (Notice the various verb forms used in the example.) Omit *that* if you wish.

    Example: I'm glad that . . . .

    Responses: I'm glad that
{
the weather is nice today.
I passed the test.
Sam is going to finish school.
I've already finished my homework.
I can speak English.
}

1. I'm pleased that . . . .
2. I'm sure that . . . .
3. I'm surprised that . . . .
4. Are you certain that . . . ?
5. I'm very happy that . . . .
6. I'm sorry that . . . .
7. I'm not sorry that . . . .

8. I'm afraid that . . . . *
9. Are you aware that . . . ?
10. I'm disappointed that . . . .
11. I'm convinced that . . . .
12. It is true that . . . .
13. It is a fact that . . . .
14. It's not true that . . . .

☐ **EXERCISE 19—WRITTEN:** Complete the following with your own words. Use noun clauses. (Use your own paper.)

1. I feel that . . . .
2. I regret that . . . .
3. I wonder if . . . .
4. You are lucky that . . . .
5. I'm delighted that . . . .
6. Do you know where . . . ?
7. I doubt that . . . .
8. I can't remember what . . . .
9. It is a fact that . . . .

10. The little boy is ashamed that . . . .
11. I'm amazed that . . . .
12. Do you know whether . . . ?
13. I want to know why . . . .
14. My friend and I agree that . . . .
15. I'm worried that . . . .
16. Are you certain that . . . ?
17. I don't know when . . . .
18. I don't know if . . . .

☐ **EXERCISE 20—ORAL (BOOKS CLOSED)** Review separable phrasal verbs by completing the sentences with pronouns and prepositions.

Example: I wanted to be sure to remember (. . .)'s phone number, so I wrote . . . .

Response: it down.

1. I can't hear the tape. Could you please turn . . . ?
2. I have an application form for (*name of a school*). I have to fill . . . .
3. I dropped my book. Could you please pick . . . ?
4. This is a hard problem. I can't figure . . . .
5. I bought these shoes a few days ago. Before I bought them, I tried . . . .
6. Where's your homework? Did you hand . . . ?

---

*Sometimes **be afraid** expresses fear:
    I don't want to go near that dog. I'm afraid that it will bite me.
Sometimes **be afraid** expresses polite regret:
    I'm afraid you have the wrong number. = I'm sorry, but I think you have the wrong number.
    I'm afraid I can't come to your party. = I'm sorry, but I can't come to your party.

7. (...) asked (...) to go to a movie with him. He asked....
8. We postponed the picnic. We put....
9. I misspelled a word on my composition, so I crossed....
10. I didn't know the meaning of a word, so I looked....
11. We don't need that light. Would you please turn...?
12. My coat was too warm to wear inside, so I took....
13. That music is too loud. Could you please turn...?
14. These papers are for the class. Could you please hand...?
15. (...) was going to have a party, but s/he canceled it. S/he called....
16. I was thirsty, but my glass was empty. So I filled....
17. My coat is in the closet. I hung....
18. The story I told wasn't true. I made....
19. When I wrote a check, I made a mistake. So I tore....
20. I was cold. So I reached for my sweater and put....
21. (...) fell asleep in class, so I woke....
22. I was finished with the tools, so I put....
23. I don't need these papers, so I'm going to throw....
24. Let's listen to the radio. Would you please turn...?

CHAPTER *15*

Quoted Speech and Reported Speech

15-1 QUOTED SPEECH

Sometimes we want to quote a speaker's words—to write a speaker's exact words. Exact quotations are used in many kinds of writing, such as newspaper articles, stories and novels, and academic papers. When we quote a speaker's words, we use quotation marks.

SPEAKER: SPEAKER'S EXACT WORDS	QUOTING THE SPEAKER'S WORDS
Jane: *Cats are fun to watch.*	(a) Jane said, **"C**ats are fun to watch.**"**
Mike: *Yes, I agree. They're graceful and playful. Do you own a cat?*	(b) Mike said, **"Y**es, I agree. They're graceful and playful. Do you own a cat**?"**

HOW TO WRITE QUOTATIONS:

1. Put a comma after *said*.★ ⟶ Jane said,
2. Put quotation marks. ⟶ Jane said, "
3. Capitalize the first word of the quotation. ⟶ Jane said, "**C**
4. Write the quotation. Put a final period. ⟶ Jane said, "Cats are fun to watch.
5. Put quotation marks *after* the period. ⟶ Jane said, "Cats are fun to watch."

6. When there are two (or more) sentences in a quotation, put the quotation marks at the beginning and end of the whole quote. Do not put quotation marks around each sentence.	Mike said, **"**Yes, I agree. They're graceful and playful. Do you own a cat?**"**
7. As with a period, put the quotation marks after a question mark at the end of a quote.	INCORRECT: Mike said, "Yes, I agree." "They're graceful and playful." "Do you own a cat"?

8. Be sure to put quotation marks above the line, not on the line.

INCORRECT: *Ann said, ,, My book is on the table.,,*

CORRECT: *Ann said, " My book is on the table."*

★Other common verbs besides *say* that introduce quotations: *admit, announce, answer, ask, complain, explain, inquire, report, reply, shout, state, write.*

☐ **EXERCISE 1:** Write sentences in which you quote the speaker's exact words. Use *said*. Punctuate carefully.

    1. ANN: My sister is a student.

<u>   **Ann said, ''My sister is a student.''**   </u>

    2. JENNIFER: We're hungry.

    3. JENNIFER: We're hungry. Are you hungry, too?

    4. JENNIFER: We're hungry. Are you hungry, too? Let's eat something.

    5. HAMLET: To be or not to be: that is the question.

    6. JOHN F. KENNEDY: Ask not what your country can do for you. Ask what you can do for your country.

    7. THE FOX: I'm going to eat you.*

        THE RABBIT: You have to catch me first!

———————

*In folk tales, animals are frequently given the ability to speak.

☐ **EXERCISE 2—ORAL/WRITTEN (BOOKS CLOSED):** Practice writing quoted speech.

1. Write exactly what I say. Identify that I said it. Punctuate carefully.
   a. (Say one short sentence—e.g., *The weather is nice today.*)
   b. (Say two short sentences—e.g., *The weather is nice today. It's warm.*)
   c. (Say two short sentences and one question—e.g., *The weather is nice today. It's warm. Do you like warm weather?*)

2. Write exactly what your classmates say.
   a. (. . .), please say one short sentence.
   b. (. . .), please ask one short question.
   c. (. . .), please say one short sentence and ask one short question.

3. (. . .) and I are going to have a short conversation. Everyone should write exactly what we say.

4. Pair up with another student. Have a brief conversation. Then write your conversation using quoted speech.

☐ **EXERCISE 3—WRITTEN:** Write a composition. Choose one of the following topics.

Topic 1: Write a folk tale from your country in which animals speak. Use quotation marks.

Topic 2: Write a children's story that you learned when you were young. When the characters in your story speak, use quotation marks.

Topic 3: Make up a children's story or any kind of story. When the characters in your story speak, use quotation marks.

Topic 4: Write a joke in which at least two people are talking to each other. Use quotation marks when the people are speaking.

Topic 5: Make up an interview you would like to have with a famous person. Use your imagination. Write the imaginary interview using quotation marks.

15-2 QUOTED SPEECH vs. REPORTED SPEECH★

QUOTED SPEECH:	*Quoted speech* refers to reproducing another person's exact words. Quotation marks are used.
REPORTED SPEECH:	*Reported speech* refers to reproducing the idea of another person's words. Not all of the exact words are used: verb forms and pronouns may change. Quotation marks are not used.

QUOTED SPEECH	**REPORTED SPEECH**	Notice in the examples:
(a) Ann said, **"I am hungry."**	(b) Ann said **that she was hungry.**	The verb forms and pronouns change from quoted speech to reported speech.
(c) Tom said, **"I need my pen."**	(d) Tom said **that he needed his pen**.	

★*Quoted speech* is also called *direct speech*. *Reported speech* is also called *indirect speech*.

15-3 VERB FORM USAGE IN REPORTED SPEECH: FORMAL SEQUENCE OF TENSES

FORMAL:	If the main verb of the sentence is in the past (e.g., *said*), the verb in the noun clause is usually also in a past form.* Notice the verb form changes in the examples below.

QUOTED SPEECH	REPORTED SPEECH
(a) He said, "I *work* hard." ———→	He said (that) he *worked* hard.
(b) He said, "I *am working* hard." ———→	He said (that) he *was working* hard.
(c) He said, "I *have worked* hard." ———→	He said (that) he *had worked* hard.
(d) He said, "I *worked* hard." ———→	He said (that) he *had worked* hard.
(e) He said, "I *am going to work* hard." ———→	He said (that) he *was going to work* hard.
(f) He said, "I *will work* hard." ———→	He said (that) he *would work* hard.
(g) He said, "I *can work* hard." ———→	He said (that) he *could work* hard.
(h) He said, "I *may work* hard." ———→	He said (that) he *might work* hard.
(i) He said, "I *have to work* hard." ———→	He said (that) he *had to work* hard.
(j) He said, "I *must work* hard." ———→	He said (that) he *had to work* hard.
(k) He said, "I *should work* hard." ———→	He said (that) he *should work* hard. (*no change*)
(l) He said, "I *ought to work* hard." ———→	He said (that) he *ought to work* hard. (*no change*)

INFORMAL:	Sometimes, especially in speaking, the verb in the noun clause is not changed if the speaker is reporting something *immediately* or *soon after* it was said.

(m) Immediate reporting:	A: What did Ann just say? I didn't hear her.
	B: She *said* (that) she *is* hungry.
(n) Later reporting:	A: What did Ann say when she got home last night?
	B: She *said* (that) she *was* hungry.

*If the main verb of the sentence is in the present (e.g., *says*), no change is made in the verb tense or modal in the noun clause.

He says, "I *work* hard." ———→ He says (that) he *works* hard.
He says, "I'*m working* hard." ———→ He says (that) he'*s working* hard.
He says, "I *worked* hard." ———→ He says (that) he *worked* hard.
He says, "I *will work* hard." ———→ He says (that) he *will work* hard.

☐ **EXERCISE 4:** Change the quoted speech to reported speech. Change the verb in quoted speech to a past form in reported speech as appropriate.

1. Jim said, "I am sleepy." _____*Jim said (that) he was sleepy.*_____

2. Sally said, "I don't like chocolate." _____

3. Mary said, "I am planning to take a trip." _____

4. Tom said, "I have already eaten lunch." _____

5. Kate said, "I called my doctor." _____

6. Mr. Rice said, "I'm going to go to Chicago." _____

7. Eric said, "I will come to the meeting." _____

8. Jean said, "I can't afford to buy a new car." _____

9. Jessica said, "I may go to the library." _____

10. Ted said, "I have to finish my work." _____

11. Ms. Young said, "I must talk to Professor Reed." _____

12. Alice said, "I should visit my aunt and uncle." _____

15-4 USING *SAY* vs. *TELL*

(a) Ann *said that* she was hungry.	*Say* is followed immediately by a noun clause.
(b) Ann ***told me*** *that* she was hungry. (c) Ann ***told us*** *that* she was hungry. (d) Ann ***told John*** *that* she was hungry. (e) Ann ***told someone*** *that* she was hungry.	*Tell* is NOT followed immediately by a noun clause. *Tell* is followed immediately by a (pro)noun object (e.g., *me, us, John, someone*) and then by a noun clause. INCORRECT: Ann told that she was hungry.

☐ **EXERCISE 5—ORAL:** Practice using *told (someone)* in reported speech.

Example: I need to talk to you.
STUDENT A: (*With book open, choose a sentence at random and whisper to B.*)
I need to talk to you.
STUDENT B: (*With book closed, report to the group.*)
(Ali) **told me** that he needed to talk to me.*

I will call you tomorrow.	I walked to school this morning.
I know your cousin.	I have to take another English course.
I have met your roommate.	I think you speak English very well.
I'm getting hungry.	You should see (*title of a movie*).
I'm not married.	I'll meet you after class for a cup of coffee.
I like your (*shirt/blouse*).	I'm going to take a vacation in (*Hawaii*).
I won't be in class tomorrow.	Your pronunciation is very good.
I can't read your handwriting.	I've already seen (*title of a movie*).
I don't like (*a kind of food*).	I may be absent from class tomorrow.

---

*In immediate reporting, it is not necessary to change the noun clause verb to a past form. You may wish to practice both forms:

Immediate reporting, informal: *(Ali) told me that he **needs** to talk to me.*

Formal sequence of tenses: *(Ali) told me that he **needed** to talk to me.*

NOTE: In spoken English and in informal written English, sometimes native speakers change noun clause verbs to past forms and sometimes they don't.

☐ **EXERCISE 6—ORAL (BOOKS CLOSED):** Practice reporting a writer's words.

STUDENT A: Write one sentence on a piece of paper. Begin your sentence with "I." Sign your name. Hand your paper to STUDENT B.

STUDENT B: Report what STUDENT A has written. Use the verb ***wrote*** instead of ***said.***

Example: (Pablo) writes something on a piece of paper.
Written: **I'm going to have lunch at MacDonald's.**
Reported: (Pablo) wrote that he was (OR: is) going to have lunch at MacDonald's.

15-5 USING *ASK IF*

Ask, NOT *say* or *tell*, is used to report yes/no questions.

YES/NO QUESTION	NOUN CLAUSE
Sam said to me, *"Are you hungry?"*	(a) Sam ***asked*** me ***if*** *I was hungry.*
Sam said to Jane, *"Are you hungry?"*	(b) Sam ***asked*** Jane ***if*** *she was hungry.*

(c) INCORRECT: Sam asked me that I was hungry.	*If*, NOT *that*, is used after *ask* to introduce a noun clause.
(d) Sam *asked* me ***if*** I was hungry. (e) Sam *asked* me ***whether*** I was hungry.	***Whether*** has the same meaning as *if*. (See Chart 14-4 for the use of ***or not***.)
(f) Sam ***asked if*** I was hungry.	The (pro)noun object (e.g., *me*) may be omitted after *ask*.
(g) Sam ***wanted to know if*** I was hungry. (h) Sam ***wondered if*** I was hungry. (i) Sam ***inquired whether*** or not I was hungry.	In addition to ***ask***, yes/no questions can be reported by using ***want to know***, ***wonder***, and ***inquire***.

☐ **EXERCISE 7—ORAL:** Practice using ***asked if***.

STUDENT A: Say the words in the book to STUDENT B.

STUDENT B: Don't look at your book. Report STUDENT A's question. Use ***asked***.

Example: Are you married?

STUDENT A: Are you married?

STUDENT B: (Ali) asked me if I am married. OR: (Ali) asked me if I was married.*

---

*Immediate reporting, informal: *(Ali) asked me if **I'm** married.*
Formal sequence of tenses: *(Ali) asked me if **I was** married.*

1. Do you know my cousin?
2. Are you hungry?
3. Can you speak (French)?
4. Did you enjoy your vacation?
5. Are you going to take another English course?
6. Will you be at home tonight?
7. Have you ever been in (Mexico)?
8. Can you hear me?
9. Are you listening to me?
10. Do you need any help?
11. Did you finish your homework?
12. Do you think it's going to rain?
13. Are you going to go downtown tomorrow?
14. Do you know how to cook?
15. Do you know whether or not (. . .) is married?
16. Can you come to my party?
17. Do you have a car?
18. Have you ever been in (Russia)?
19. Did you move into a new apartment?
20. Are you going to call me tonight?

☐ **EXERCISE 8—ORAL:** Practice using noun clauses after *asked.* ★

STUDENT A: Say the words in the book to STUDENT B.
STUDENT B: Don't look at your book. Report STUDENT A's question. Use
asked.

Example: Where do you live?
STUDENT A: Where do you live?
STUDENT B: (Maria) asked me where I live. OR: (Maria) asked me where I
lived.

1. Where is your apartment?
2. Is your apartment far from here?
3. What do you need?
4. Do you need a pen?
5. When does the semester end?
6. Does the semester end in (December)?
7. Why is (. . .) absent?
8. Is (. . .) absent?
9. How often do you go downtown?
10. Do you go downtown every week?

---

*See 14-2 for the use of question words in noun clauses.

□ **EXERCISE 9:** Complete the sentences by changing the quoted speech to reported speech. Practice using the formal sequence of tenses.

1. Bob said, "Where do you live?"

   Bob asked me _____ *where I lived.* _____

2. He said, "Do you live in the dorm?"

   He asked me _____

3. I said, "I have my own apartment."

   I told him _____

4. He said, "I'm looking for a new apartment."

   He said _____

5. He said, "I don't like living in the dorm."

   He told me _____

6. I said, "Do you want to move in with me?"

   I asked him _____

7. He said, "Where is your apartment?"

   He asked me _____

8. I said, "I live on Seventh Avenue."

   I told him _____

9. He said, "I can't move until the end of the semester."

   He said _____

10. He said, "I will cancel my dorm contract at the end of the semester."

    He told me _____

11. He said, "Is that okay?"

    He asked me _____

12. I said, "I'm looking forward to having you as a roommate."

    I told him _____

□ **EXERCISE 10:** Change the reported speech to quotations. Use quotation marks.

1. Eric asked me if I had ever gone skydiving.

   Eric said ___, *"Have you ever gone skydiving?"* _____

2. Chris wanted to know if I would be at the meeting.

   Chris said _____

3. Kate wondered whether I was going to quit my job.

   Kate said _____

4. Anna asked her friend where his car was.

   Anna said _____

5. Brian asked me what I had done after class yesterday.

   Brian said _____

6. Luigi asked me if I knew Italian.

   Luigi said _____

7. Debra wanted to know if I could guess what she had in her pocket.

   Debra asked _____

8. My boss wanted to know why I wasn't working at my desk and why I
   was wasting the company's time.

   My boss angrily asked me _____

☐ **EXERCISE 11:** Complete the sentences by changing the sentences in quotation marks to noun clauses. Practice using the formal sequence of tenses.

1. *"Where do you live?"* Tom asked me . . . ***where I lived.***

2. *"Do you live in the dorm?"* He asked me . . . ***if I lived in the dorm.***

3. *"I stole the money."* The thief admitted . . . ***that he had stolen the money.***

4. *"Where is Jane?"* Ed asked me . . . .

5. *"I'm going to quit school and get a job."* Jessica announced . . . .

6. *"Did you mail the letter?"* Tim asked me . . . .

7. *"What are you thinking about?"* Karen asked me . . . .

8. *"I have to go to the drug store."* Steve said . . . .

9. *"I can't pick you up at the airport."* Alice told me . . . .

10. *"I will take a taxi."* I told her . . . .

11. *"You should speak English as much as possible."* My teacher told me . . . .

12. *"Do you like spaghetti?"* Don asked me . . . .

13. *"Have you already eaten dinner?"* Sue asked me . . . .

14. *"Did you finish your work?"* Jackie asked me . . . .

15. *"What time do you want to leave for the airport?"* Harry asked me ....

16. *"I made a mistake."* Carol admitted ....

17. *"The final exam will be on the 15th."* The teacher announced ....

18. *"An earthquake occurred in Peru."* The newspaper reported ....

☐ **EXERCISE 12—WRITTEN:** Complete the following. Use the formal sequence of tenses.

1. ... asked me if ....
2. ... asked me where ....
3. ... told me that ....
4. ... said that ....
5. ... asked me when ....
6. ... told my friend that ....
7. ... asked my friend if ....
8. ... asked my friend why ....

☐ **EXERCISE 13:** Read the dialogues and complete the sentences. Use the formal sequence of tenses.

1. A: *Oh no! I forgot my briefcase! What am I going to do?*
   B: *I don't know.*

   → When Bill got on the bus, he realized that he ___ *had forgotten* ___

   his briefcase.

2. A: *Where's your bicycle, Jimmy?*
   B: *I sold it to a friend of mine.*
   A: *You what?*

   → Yesterday I asked my fourteen-year-old son where his bicycle

   _____. He told me that he _____ it to

   a friend of his. I was flabbergasted.

3. A: *Look at this!*
   B: *What?*
   A: *My test paper. I got an "F." I'm sorry I didn't study harder.*

   → When George got his test paper back, he was sorry that he

   _____ harder.

4. A: *The bus is supposed to be here in three minutes. Hurry up! I'm afraid we'll
      miss it.*
   B: *I'm ready. Let's go.*

   → I told my friend to hurry because I was afraid that we _____

   _____ the bus.

5. A: *Can you swim?*
   B: *Yes.*
   A: *Thank heavens.*

   → When the canoe tipped over, I was glad that my friend _____

   _____ .

6. A: *Do you want to go downtown?*
   B: *I can't. I have to study.*

   → When I asked Kathy if she _____ to go downtown,

   she said that she _____ because she _____

   _____ .

7. A: *Ow! My finger really hurts! I'm sure I broke it.*
   B: *Let me see.*

   → When Nancy fell down, she was sure that she _____

   her finger.

8. A: *Where's Jack? I'm surprised he isn't here.*
   B: *He went to Chicago to visit his sister.*

   → When I got to the party, I asked my friend where Jack _____ .

   I was surprised that he _____ there. My friend told

   me that Jack _____ to Chicago to visit his sister.

9. A: *Will you be home in time for dinner?*
   B: *I'll be home around 5:30.*

   → My wife asked me if I _____ home in time for dinner.

   I told her that I _____ home around 5:30.

10. A: *Have you ever been in Mexico?*
    B: *Yes, I have. Several times.*

    → I asked George if he _____ ever _____ in Mexico. He said

    that he _____ there several times.

15-6 USING VERB + INFINITIVE TO REPORT SPEECH

QUOTED SPEECH	REPORTED SPEECH
(a) Joe said, "Please come to my party."	
(b) Joe said, "Can you come to my party?"	(d) Joe *invited me to come to his party*.
(c) Joe said, "Would you like to come to my party?"	

	S + V + O + INFINITIVE PHRASE	Some verbs are followed immediately by a (pro)noun object and then an infinitive phrase. These verbs (see the list below) are often used to report speech.
(e)	Joe *invited me to come* to his party.	
(f)	I *told Ann to study* harder.	

REPORTING SPEECH: VERB + (PRO)NOUN OBJECT + INFINITIVE*

advise someone to	*invite someone to*	*remind someone to*
ask someone to	*order someone to*	*tell someone to*
encourage someone to	*permit someone to*	*warn someone to*

*Other common verbs followed by a (pro)noun object and an infinitive:

allow	*convince*	*instruct*
beg	*direct*	*persuade*
challenge	*expect*	*urge*

□ **EXERCISE 14:** Complete each sentence with an infinitive phrase which, combined with the main verb (*invited, advised,* etc.), reports the idea of the speaker's words.

1. Joe said, "Please come to my party."

   Joe invited me _____*to come to his party.*_____

2. My teacher said, "I think you should take another English course."

   My teacher advised me _____*to take another English course.*_____

3. Mrs. Jacobson said, "You may use the phone."

   Mrs. Jacobson permitted me _____

4. The doctor said, "Take a deep breath."

   The doctor told the patient _____

5. My mother said, "Make an appointment with the dentist."

   My mother reminded me _____

6. My friend said, "I think you should take a long vacation."

   My friend encouraged me _____

7. The Smiths said, "Would you like to come to our house for dinner?"

   The Smiths invited us _____

8. My friend said, "You should see a doctor about the pain in your knee."

My friend advised me _____

9. The judge said, "You must pay a fine of fifty dollars."

The judge ordered Mr. Silverman _____

10. Bill said, "Don't touch that hot pot."

Bill warned me _____ ***not to touch that hot pot.*** _____

11. Sue said, "Don't buy a used car."

Sue advised me _____

12. Mr. Gray said, "Don't play in the street."

Mr. Gray warned the children _____

☐ **EXERCISE 15:** Following are some dialogues. Report *the first speaker's words.* Use the verb in parentheses and an infinitive phrase.

1.   JOE: Would you like to go to a movie with me?
     MARY: Yes.

     (*invite*) _____ ***Joe invited Mary to go to a movie with him.*** _____

2. DR. MILLER: You should get more exercise.
         STEVE: I'll try.

     (*advise*) _____

3. MS. HOLT: Could you please open the door for me?
        TOM: I'd be happy to.

     (*ask*) _____

4. NANCY: Call me around nine.
      ME: Okay.

     (*tell*) _____

5.   MR. WARD: You may have a cookie and a glass of milk.
     THE CHILDREN: Thanks, Dad.

     (*permit*) _____

6. PROF. LARSON: You should take a physics course.
            ME: Oh?

     (*encourage*) _____

---

*To make an infinitive negative, put ***not*** in front of it.

7. THE POLICE OFFICER: Put your hands on top of your head!

   THE THIEF: Who? Me? I didn't do anything!

   (order) _____

   _____

8. JACK: Don't worry about me.

   HIS MOTHER: I won't.

   (tell) _____

   _____

9. SUE: Don't forget to call me.

   ME: I won't.

   (remind)★ _____

10. ALICE: Don't forget to lock the door.

    HER ROOMMATE: Okay.

    (remind) _____

11. MRS. PETERSON: Please don't slam the door.

    HER DAUGHTER: Okay, Mom.

    (ask) _____

12. PROF. ROTH: Don't look directly at the sun during a solar eclipse.

    US: Okay.

    (warn) _____

★Two possible sentences: *Sue reminded me to call her.*
Sue reminded me not to forget to call her.

All of the following sentences contain mistakes in grammar. Can you find the mistakes and correct them?

1. She asked me that I wanted to go to the music festival.

2. Tom said me that he was hungry.

3. Bob asked me where do you live.

4. Ann told that she had enjoyed the party.

5. Kathy asked me open the window.

6. My friend told to me that she understood my problem.

7. My mother asked me when am I coming home?

8. Do you know where is the nearest gas station?

9. David invited me for eating dinner with him.

10. I asked Tom that when will your plane arrive?

11. I told Bobby don't pull the cat's tail.

12. Ann said, Are you tired?

15-7 SOME TROUBLESOME VERBS: *ADVISE, SUGGEST,* AND *RECOMMEND*

(a) Ed *advised me* **to call** a doctor. (b) Ed *advised* **calling** a doctor.	(a) and (b) have the same meaning. In (a): When **advise** is followed by a (pro)noun object, an infinitive is used. In (b): When there is no (pro)noun object after **advise**, a gerund is used.
(c) Ed *suggested* **calling** a doctor. (d) Ed *recommended* **calling** a doctor.	**Suggest** and **recommend** can also be followed immediately by a gerund.

(e) CORRECT: Ed **suggested that I should call** a doctor.
  INCORRECT: Ed suggested me to call a doctor.
 (f) CORRECT: Ed **recommended that I should call** a doctor.
  INCORRECT: Ed recommended me to call a doctor.
	Suggest and **recommend** cannot be followed by a (pro)noun object and an infinitive, but they can be followed by a "*that*-clause" in which **should** is used.*

*The use of **should** in the noun clause is not necessary. However, if **should** is not used, the verb in the noun clause is always in the simple form after *suggest* and *recommend:*

Ed **suggested**/**recommended** that ⎰ *I call* a doctor. (not *called*)
⎱ *we call* a doctor. (not *called*)
⎰ *Ann call* a doctor. (not *calls* or *called*)
⎱ *he call* a doctor. (not *calls* or *called*)

□ **EXERCISE 17:** Complete the sentences. Give the idea of the speaker's words.

1. The doctor said to me, "You should lose weight."
   a. The doctor advised me ___*to lose weight.*___
   b. The doctor advised ___*losing weight.*___
   c. The doctor suggested _____
   d. The doctor recommended _____
   e. The doctor suggested that _____
   f. The doctor recommended that _____

2. My teacher said, "You should study harder."
   a. My teacher suggested that _____
   b. My teacher advised me _____
   c. My teacher advised _____
   d. My teacher recommended _____

3. Mr. Madison said, "Why don't you buy a motorcycle?"
   Mr. Madison suggested _____

4. Don said, "I think you should see a doctor about that problem."
   Don recommended _____

5. Mary said, "Let's go to a movie."
   Mary suggested _____

6. Sharon said, "I think you should go to Iowa State University."
   Sharon advised _____

□ **EXERCISE 18:** Work in pairs. Each pair should create a short dialogue (five to ten sentences) based on one of the given situations. Each pair will then present their dialogue to the class. After the dialogue, the class will report what was said.

Sample situation: Have a conversation about going somewhere in this city.

   Sample dialogue:
   ANN: Would you like to go to the zoo tomorrow?
   BOB: I can't. I have to study.
   ANN: That's too bad. Are you sure you can't go? It will take only a few hours.
   BOB: Well, maybe I can study in the morning and then go to the zoo in the afternoon.

ANN: Great! What time do you want to go?

BOB: Let's go around two o'clock.

Sample report:

Ann asked Bob if he wanted to go to the zoo tomorrow. Bob said that he could not go because he had to study. Ann finally persuaded him to go. She said that it would take only a few hours. Bob decided that he could study in the morning and go to the zoo in the afternoon. Ann asked Bob what time he wanted to go. He suggested going around two o'clock.

(Notice in the sample report: The writer gives the idea of the speakers' words without necessarily using the speakers' exact words.)

1. Have a conversation in which one of you invites the other one to a party.

2. One of you is a teenager and the other one is a parent. The teenager is having problems at school and is seeking advice and encouragement.

3. The two of you are a married couple. One of you is reminding the other one about the things s/he should or has to do today.

4. Have a conversation in which one of you persuades the other one to begin a health program by taking up a new kind of exercise (jogging, walking, tennis, etc.). Beginning of the dialogue:

   A: I need to get some physical exercise.

   B: Why don't you take up . . . ?

   A: No, I don't want to do that.

5. One of you is fourteen years old and the other is the parent. The fourteen-year-old wants to say out late tonight. What will the parent say?

6. One of you is a store detective and the other is a shoplifter. The store detective has just seen the shoplifter take something.

7. One of you is a stubborn, old-fashioned, uneducated person who thinks the world is flat. The other one tries to convince the stubborn one that the world is round.

CHAPTER *16*

Using Wish; Using If

16-1 EXPRESSING WISHES ABOUT THE PRESENT/FUTURE

THE TRUE SITUATION	EXPRESSING A WISH ABOUT THAT SITUATION	
I *don't know* how to dance.	(a) I *wish* (that) I ***knew*** how to dance.	People often make wishes when they want reality to be different, to be exactly the opposite of (contrary to) the true situation.
I *don't have* a bicycle.	(b) I *wish* I ***had*** a bicycle.	A noun clause* usually follows ***wish***. Special verb forms are used in the noun clause. When a speaker expresses a wish about a *present* situation, s/he uses a *past* verb form.
Ron *has to work* tonight.	(c) Ron *wishes* he ***didn't have to work*** tonight.	
I *can't speak* Chinese.	(d) I *wish* I ***could speak*** Chinese.	
I'm *not* home in bed. Ann *isn't* home in bed. It's cold today. We *aren't* in Hawaii.	(e) I *wish* ***I were*** home in bed. (f) Ann *wishes* ***she were*** home in bed. (g) I *wish* ***it weren't*** cold today. (h) We *wish* ***we were*** in Hawaii.	Notice in (e), (f), (g), and (h): ***were*** is used for all subjects: *I wish* $\begin{Bmatrix} I \\ you \\ he \\ she \\ it \\ we \\ they \end{Bmatrix}$ *were* . . . .

*For more information about noun clauses which begin with ***that,*** see Chapter 14.

□ **EXERCISE 1:** Use the given information to complete the sentences.

THE TRUE SITUATION	EXPRESSING A WISH
1. I don't have a car.	I wish ____**(that) I had a car.**____
2. Alice doesn't have a car.	Alice wishes ____**(that) she had a car.**____
3. I have a cold.	I wish _____
4. I don't have a tape recorder.	I wish _____
5. I don't know how to swim.	I wish _____
6. Bill doesn't have a good job.	Bill wishes _____
7. I live in the dorm.	I wish _____
8. I don't live in an apartment.	I wish _____
9. I can't speak French.	I wish _____
10. Sue can't find a good job.	Sue wishes _____
11. My friend can't come.	I wish _____
12. I'm not at home right now.	I wish _____
13. James isn't here.	I wish _____
14. It isn't Saturday.	I wish _____
15. My friends aren't here.	I wish _____
16. I have to study for a test.	I wish _____
17. I have to write a composition.	I wish _____

□ **EXERCISE 2—ORAL (BOOKS CLOSED):** Make sentences beginning with "*I wish* . . . ."

Example: You don't have a bicycle.
Response: I wish (that) I had a bicycle.

1. You don't have a car.
2. You don't have a color TV.
3. You can't whistle.
4. You have a headache.
5. (. . .) isn't here today.
6. It isn't (Sunday).
7. You have to study tonight.
8. You have to go to the dentist.
9. You can't speak (*language*).
10. You can't go to (*place*).
11. You don't have a window fan.
12. You're sleepy.
13. You don't know how to dance.
14. You don't know how to play chess.
15. It's (hot/cold) today.
16. You don't have enough money to buy (a car).
17. You have to work tonight.
18. You can't go to (the zoo) today.
19. You're not rich and famous.
20. You're not in (*country*) right now.

☐ **EXERCISE 3:** Study the examples and then complete the sentences with auxiliary verbs.

1. I don't have a car, but I wish I _____*did*_____.
2. I have to study tonight, but I wish I _____*didn't*_____.
3. I can't speak Italian, but I wish I _____*could*_____.
4. I'm not tall, but I wish I _____*were*_____.
5. Alan is tall, but he wishes he _____*weren't*_____.
6. I don't know Mary Morningstar, but I wish I _____.
7. I have to take a history course, but I wish I _____.
8. I can't dance very well, but I wish I _____.
9. I'm not a good cook, but I wish I _____.
10. Linda isn't a good writer, but she wishes she _____.
11. Jack has to go to the laundromat, but he wishes he _____.
12. Carol doesn't live in the same city as her boyfriend, but she wishes she

    _____.

13. It's too cold to go swimming today, but I wish it _____.
14. Sally can't afford to go to Hawaii, but she wishes she _____.
15. I have to clean my apartment, but I wish I _____.
16. I don't remember that man's name, but I wish I _____.

☐ **EXERCISE 4:** Complete the following conversations. Use auxiliary verbs in the completions.

1. A: Can you go to the lecture tonight?

   B: No, _____*I can't*_____, but I wish _____*I could*_____.

2. A: Are you a good musician?

   B: No, _____, but I wish _____.

3. A: Do you smoke?

   B: Yes, _____, but I wish _____.

4. A: Does your son know how to play a musical instrument?

   B: No, _____, but I wish _____.

5. A: Can you play a musical instrument?

   B: No, _____, but I wish _____.

6. A: Do you have to take the bus to work?

B: Yes, _____, but I wish _____.

7. A: Is Maria in your class?

B: No, _____, but she wishes _____.

8. A: Do you understand what Professor Martin is talking about?

B: No, _____, but I wish _____.

9. A: Do you know the people who live in the apartment next to yours?

B: No, _____, but I wish _____.

10. A: Is your roommate neat?

B: No, _____, but I wish _____.

11. A: Are the students always on time for class?

B: No, _____, but the teacher wishes _____.

12. A: Do you have enough time to drink a cup of coffee between classes?

B: No, _____, but I wish _____.

13. A: Can you come over to my house for dinner tomorrow night?

B: I'm sorry, but we _____. We wish _____.

14. A: Is there a grocery store near your apartment?

B: No, _____, but I wish _____.

15. A: Is there an art museum in this town?

B: No, _____, but I wish _____.

16-2 EXPRESSING WISHES ABOUT THE PAST

The PAST PERFECT* is used after **wish** when people make wishes about a past situation.

THE TRUE SITUATION	MAKING A WISH ABOUT THE PAST
I *didn't study* for the test. Jim *didn't finish* his work. I *went* to the meeting.	(a) *I wish* (that) I **had studied** for the test. (b) *Jim wishes* he **had finished** his work. (c) *I wish* I **hadn't gone** to the meeting.

*See Chart 7-10 for the forms of the past perfect.

☐ **EXERCISE 5:** Use the given information to make sentences with *wish*.

THE TRUE SITUATION	MAKING A WISH
1. Bobby didn't tell me the truth.	I wish *(that) Bobby had told me the truth.*
2. I didn't call my friend last night.	I wish _____
3. I didn't cash a check yesterday.	I wish _____
4. Tom spent all of his money yesterday.	Tom wishes _____
5. I didn't go to class yesterday.	I wish _____
6. Anna didn't finish high school.	Anna wishes _____
7. Jerry wasn't at the meeting last week.	I wish _____
8. Jerry isn't here today.	I wish _____
9. Emily doesn't understand my problem.	I wish _____
10. Emily didn't help me.	I wish _____

☐ **EXERCISE 6:** Complete the sentences with the correct form of the words in parentheses.

1. It took me three days to get to Chicago by bus. I wish I (*fly*) _____ _____ there instead of taking the bus.

2. I miss my family. I wish they (*be*) _____ here now.

3. The kitchen is a mess this morning. I wish I (*wash*) _____ the dishes last night.

4. I'd like to wear my black suit to the meeting today, but it's wrinkled and dirty. I wish I (*take*) _____ it to the cleaner's last week.

5. I have to walk up three flights of stairs to get to my apartment. I wish my apartment building (*have*) _____ an elevator.

6. I wish I (*know*) _____ more English.

7. Sue bought a used car a couple of months ago. It's given her nothing but trouble. She wishes she (*buy, not*) _____ it.

8. I'm tired today. I wish I (*stay up, not*) _____ late last night.

9. I'd like to go camping this weekend. I wish the weather (*be, not*) _____ so cold.

10. I wish I (*can remember*) _____ where I put the

pliers. I can't find them anywhere.

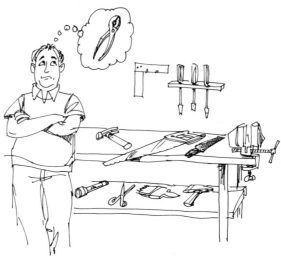

11. You told me to save a little money out of each of my paychecks, but I

didn't. I wish I (*take*) _____ your advice.

12. My brother goes to school in another city. He came here last Friday to

spend a few days with me. I've enjoyed having him here. I wish he

(*have to, not*) _____ leave today. I wish he (*can*

spend) _____ a few more days here.

□ **EXERCISE 7:** Complete the sentences with auxiliary verbs.

1. Bobby didn't tell me the truth, but I wish he _____**had**_____.

2. I don't know Carol Jones, but I wish I _____**did**_____.

3. I can't move into a new apartment, but I wish I _____.

4. I didn't finish my homework last night, but I wish I _____.

5. Sally didn't come to the party last night, but I wish she _____.

6. I don't have enough money to buy that coat, but I wish I _____.

7. I'm too tired to go for a walk, but I wish I _____.

8. I didn't study any English before I came here, but I wish I _____.

9. Dick doesn't live close to school, but he wishes he _____.

10. Jane can't speak Arabic, but she wishes she _____.

☐ **EXERCISE 8:** Complete the following conversations. Use auxiliary verbs in the completions.

1. A: Did you go to the party last night?

   B: Yes, _____*I did*_____, but I wish _____*I hadn't*_____. It was boring.

2. A: Did you eat breakfast this morning?

   B: No, _____, but I wish _____. I'm hungry. My stomach is growling.

3. A: Do you exercise regularly?

   B: No, _____, but I wish _____. I always feel better when I exercise regularly.

4. A: Did you study for the test?

   B: No, _____, but I wish _____. I got an "F" on it.

5. A: Are you a good artist?

   B: No, _____, but I wish _____. I'd like to be able to draw.

6. A: Did you go to the movie last night?

   B: Yes, _____, but I wish _____. It was a waste of time and money.

7. A: Do you have to eat at the student cafeteria?

   B: Yes, _____, but I wish _____. The food is lousy.

8. A: Can you speak Chinese?

   B: No, _____, but I wish _____.

9. A: Is it hard to learn a second language?

   B: Yes, _____, but I wish _____.

☐ **EXERCISE 9—ORAL (BOOKS CLOSED):** Answer *no*. Use *wish*.

   Example: Can you speak Arabic?
   Response: No, I can't, but I wish I could.

1. Did you study last night?
2. Did you go to bed early last night?
3. Do you have a car?
4. Are you (*a movie star*)?
5. Can you speak (*language*)?
6. Did you eat breakfast?

7. Is (. . .) here today?
8. Do you know how to dance?
9. Did (. . .) call you last night?
10. Can you play (*a musical instrument*)?
11. Are you full of energy today?
12. Do you live in an apartment?
13. Is the weather nice today?
14. Did (. . .) help you with your homework?
15. Is your family here?
16. Do you have to go to class tomorrow?
17. Can you buy (a Rolls Royce)?
18. Do you know how to type?

☐ **EXERCISE 10—ORAL:** Make wishes based on the given situations. Try to think of as many possible wishes as you can for each situation.

Example: You're hungry. What do you wish?
Responses: I wish I'd eaten breakfast.
I wish I had a candy bar.
I wish I could go to (*name of a place*) and get a hamburger.
I wish I weren't in class right now.
I wish I didn't have to go to another class after this one.
I wish the classroom were a restaurant and I had a steak in front of me instead of my grammar book.
Etc.

1. You're tired.
2. You're broke.
3. The weather is . . . today.
4. You live in (*kind of residence*).
5. You don't have many talents.
6. This is a nice classroom, but . . . .
7. You're very busy. You have a lot of things to do today.
8. Things about yourself and your life that you would like to change.
9. There are many problems in today's world.

☐ **EXERCISE 11—ORAL (BOOKS CLOSED):** Mention something that is not perfect in your life and then make a wish.

Example: Not everything in your life is perfect. Tell me something that makes you unhappy about your life.
Response: My classes begin at 8 o'clock in the morning.
Teacher: What do you wish?
Response: I wish my classes didn't begin at eight.
I wish my classes began at ten.
I wish I didn't have to get up so early.

*(To the teacher: You may wish to expand the exercise to include an introduction to conditional sentences with **if**.)*

Teacher: What would you do if your classes didn't begin at eight?
Response: If my classes didn't begin at eight, I would sleep until the middle of the morning.

16-3   USING *IF*: CONTRARY-TO-FACT IN THE PRESENT/FUTURE

If is often used to talk about situations that are contrary to fact, i.e., situations that are the opposite of the true situation.	

TRUE SITUATION: (a) I *don't have* enough money.
MAKING A WISH: (b) I wish I *had* enough money.
USING *IF*: (c) If I *had* enough money, I *would buy* a car.
    (d) If I *had* enough money, I *could buy* a car.

TRUE SITUATION: (e) The weather *isn't* nice today.
MAKING A WISH: (f) I wish the weather *were* nice today.
USING *IF*: (g) If the weather *were* nice today, I *would go* to the park.
    (h) If the weather *were* nice today, I *could go* to the park.

Contrary-to-fact sentences with an "*if*-clause" and a "result clause" are called *conditional sentences*. Special verb forms are used. The SIMPLE PAST TENSE is used to discuss a present or future situation in an "*if*-clause." *Would* or *could* is used in the result clause.

IF-CLAUSE: simple past tense   RESULT CLAUSE: *would/could* + simple form

if-clause result clause (i) ⌐If I *had* enough money,¬ ⌐I *would buy* a car.¬	In (i) and (j), the speakers are talking about present/future situations, but they use the simple past in the "*if*-clause."★
result clause *if*-clause (j) ⌐I *would go* to the park¬ ⌐if the weather *were* nice.¬	

(k) If I had enough money, I *would* buy a car.
    (The speaker wants to buy a car.)
(l) If I had enough money, I *could* buy a car.
    (The speaker is expressing a possibility.)
	Would expresses intended or desired results.
	Could expresses possible options.
	Could = would be able to.

(m) If the *weather were* nice, I'd go to the park. (n) If *Kate were* here, she would help us. (o) If *I were* you, I wouldn't accept that job.	Notice in (m), (n), and (o): *were* (instead of *was*) is usually used for singular subjects in a contrary-to-fact "*if*-clause."

★An "*if*-clause" is a kind of adverb clause. See Chart 9-6.

☐ **EXERCISE 12:** Complete the sentences with words in parentheses.

1. TRUE SITUATION: I don't have enough time.

   a. I wish I (*have*) _____ enough time.

   b. If I (*have*) _____ enough time, I (*go*) _____
   to the park.

2. TRUE SITUATION: I don't have enough money.

   a. I wish I (*have*) _____ enough money.

   b. If I (*have*) _____ enough money, I (*fly*) _____
   home this weekend.

3. TRUE SITUATION: It's cold today.

   a. I wish it (*be, not*) _____ cold today.

   b. If it (*be, not*) _____ cold today, I (*go*) _____
   swimming.

4. TRUE SITUATION: I don't know how to swim.

   a. I wish I (*know*) _____ how to swim.

   b. If I (*know*) _____ how to swim, I (*go*) _____
   to the beach with you.

5. TRUE SITUATION: I don't understand that sentence.

   a. I wish I (*understand*) _____ that sentence.

   b. If I (*understand*) _____ that sentence, I (*explain*)
   _____ it to you.

6. TRUE SITUATION: I have to go to class today.

   a. I wish I (*have to go, not*) _____ to class
   today.

   b. If I (*have to go, not*) _____ to class today, I
   (*go*) _____ shopping, or I (*visit*) _____
   _____ my friends.

7. TRUE SITUATION: It isn't Saturday.

   a. I wish it (*be*) _____ Saturday.

   b. If it (*be*) _____ Saturday, I (*go*) _____
   to the beach.

8. TRUE SITUATION: I'm not rich.

    a. I wish I (*be*) _____ rich.

    b. If I (*be*) _____ rich, I (*live*) _____ on

      a farm and (*raise*) _____ horses.

☐ **EXERCISE 13:** Complete the sentences with the words in parentheses.

  1. Jim doesn't study hard. If he (*study*) _____ **studied** _____ harder,

    he (*get*) _____ **would get** _____ better grades.

  2. The weather isn't nice. I (*take*) _____ a walk if the

    weather (*be*) _____ nice.

  3. My wife and I want to buy a house, but houses are too expensive. We

    (*buy*) _____ a house if we (*have*) _____

    enough money for a down payment.

  4. If money (*grow*) _____ on trees, all of us (*be*) _____ rich.

  5. Life (*be*) _____ boring if everyone (*have*) _____

    _____ the same opinions about everything.

  6. If I (*be*) _____ you, I (*tell*) _____ Brian

    the truth.

  7. Airplane tickets are expensive. If they (*be*) _____ cheap, I

    (*fly*) _____ to Singapore for the weekend.

  8. I wish I (*have*) _____ a camera. I (*take*) _____

    a picture of the sunset tonight if I (*have*) _____ a camera.

  9. The student cafeteria is relatively inexpensive, but the food isn't very

    good. I (*eat*) _____ there all the time if the food

    (*be*) _____ better.

10. Sometimes our teacher gives surprise quizzes. If I (*teach*) _____

    this English class, I (*give, not*) _____ surprise

    quizzes.

11. I wish I (*have*) _____ a car. If I (*have*) _____ a car, I

    (*drive*) _____ to school.

12. I'm very tired tonight. If I (*be, not*) _____ tired, I (*go*)

    _____ to the movie with you.

☐ **EXERCISE 14—ORAL (BOOKS CLOSED):** *What would you do if you were . . . ?* Practice using verb forms in contrary-to-fact sentences with *if*.

Example: (What would you do if you were) a house painter?
Response: If I were a house painter, I would (paint houses, paint your house, etc.).

Example: a cat
Response: If I were a cat, I would (chase mice, jump into your lap, etc.).

1. a bird	11. sleepy	21. a magician
2. a mountain climber	12. at home	22. an astronaut
3. an artist	13. (. . .)	23. ninety years old
4. a secretary	14. (*name of a famous person*)	24. at/in (*a particular place*)
5. a dog	15. a professional athlete	25. a genius
6. a good cook	16. a surgeon	26. a billionaire
7. a teacher	17. a photographer	27. the captain of a ship
8. a police officer	18. a mouse	28. ambitious
9. a parent	19. (*name of a world leader*)	
10. hungry	20. the leader of your country	

16-4   USING *IF*: TRUE vs. CONTRARY-TO-FACT IN THE PRESENT/FUTURE

TRUE SITUATION:
 	
(a) If you **need** some money, I $\left\{ \begin{array}{c} will \\ can \end{array} \right\}$ **lend** you some.
    (*simple present*)
 	
CONTRARY-TO-FACT SITUATION:
 	
(b) If you **needed** some money, I $\left\{ \begin{array}{c} would \\ could \end{array} \right\}$ **lend** you some.
    (*simple past*)
	In (a): Perhaps you need some money. If that is true, I will (or can) lend you some.
	
	Reminder: Do not use **will** in an ''*if*-clause.'' (See Chart 3-5.)
	
	In (b): In truth, you don't need any money. But if the opposite were true, I would (or could) lend you some.

VERB FORM USAGE SUMMARY (PRESENT/FUTURE)

SITUATION:	*IF*-CLAUSE:	RESULT CLAUSE:
TRUE	**simple present**	$\left\{ \begin{array}{c} will \\ can \end{array} \right\}$ + **simple form**
CONTRARY-TO-FACT	**simple past**	$\left\{ \begin{array}{c} would \\ could \end{array} \right\}$ + **simple form**

Complete the sentences with the words in parentheses. Some of the sentences express true situations, and some of the sentences express contrary-to-fact situations.

1. Maybe I will have enough time tonight. If I (have) _____*have*_____ enough time, I (write) _____***will write***_____ a letter to my cousin.

2. I won't have enough time tonight. But if I (have) _____*had*_____ enough time, I (write) _____***would write***_____ a letter to my cousin.

3. Maybe I will have enough money. If I (have) _____ enough money, I (buy) _____ a ticket to the rock concert.

4. Unfortunately, I don't have enough money. But if I (have) _____ enough money, I (buy) _____ a ticket to the rock concert.

5. Maybe I will buy a car. If I (buy) _____ a car, I (drive) _____ to Springfield next month to visit my friend.

6. I'm not going to buy a car. But, if I (buy) _____ a car, I (drive) _____ to Springfield next month to visit my friend.

7. The weather is terrible today. But if the weather (be) _____ good, I (go) _____ for a five-mile walk.

8. Maybe the weather will be nice tomorrow. If the weather (be) _____ nice, I (go) _____ for a long walk.

9. I know that you don't want to go to a movie tonight. But if you (want) _____ to go to a movie, I (go) _____ with you.

10. What would you like to do tonight? Do you want to go to a movie? If you (want) _____ to go to a movie, I (go) _____ with you.

☐ EXERCISE 16: Complete the following with your own words.

1. If I have enough money, _____

2. If I had enough money, _____

3. If I have enough time, _____

4. If I had enough time, _____

5. If the weather is nice tomorrow, _____

6. If the weather were nice today, _____

7. If you studied hard, _____

8. If you study hard, _____

9. If my uncle comes to visit me, _____

10. If my uncle were here, _____

11. I would fly to London if _____

12. I will fly to London if _____

13. You would get angry if _____

14. I will get angry if _____

15. I won't be in class tomorrow if _____

16. If I didn't have to go to class tomorrow, _____

16-5 USING *IF*: CONTRARY-TO-FACT IN THE PAST

Conditional sentences that discuss past time have special verb forms:
If-CLAUSE: the past perfect **RESULT CLAUSE:** *would have/could have* + past participle

TRUE SITUATION:	(a) I *didn't have* enough money.
MAKING A WISH:	(b) I wish I *had had* enough money.
USING **IF**:	(c) If I *had had* enough money, I *would have bought* a car.
	(d) If I *had had* enough money, I *could have bought* a car.
TRUE SITUATION:	(e) The weather *wasn't* nice yesterday.
MAKING A WISH:	(f) I wish the weather *had been* nice yesterday.
USING **IF**:	(g) If the weather *had been* nice yesterday, I *would have gone* to the park.
	(h) If the weather *had been* nice yesterday, I *could have gone* to the park.

☐ **EXERCISE 17:** Complete the sentences with the words in parentheses.

1. TRUE SITUATION: I didn't have enough time yesterday.

   a. I wish I (*have*) _____ enough time yesterday.

   b. If I (*have*) _____ enough time yesterday. I (*go*)

   _____ to the park.

2. TRUE SITUATION: I didn't have enough money last night.

    a. I wish I (*have*) _____ enough money last night.

    b. If I (*have*) _____ enough money last night, I (*go*)

    _____ to a show.

3. TRUE SITUATION: Mary didn't come to my party last week.

    a. I wish she (*come*) _____ to my party.

    b. If she (*come*) _____ to my party, she (*meet*) _____

    _____ my fiancé.

4. TRUE SITUATION: It was cold yesterday.

    a. I wish it (*be, not*) _____ cold yesterday.

    b. If it (*be, not*) _____ cold yesterday, I (*go*) _____

    _____ swimming.

5. TRUE SITUATION: Jack didn't study for the test.

    a. Jack wishes he (*study*) _____ for the test.

    b. If he (*study*) _____ for the test, he (*pass*)

    _____ it.

16-6 SUMMARY: VERB FORMS IN SENTENCES WITH *IF* (CONDITIONAL SENTENCES)

SITUATION	*IF*-CLAUSE	RESULT CLAUSE	EXAMPLES
TRUE IN THE PRESENT/FUTURE	simple present	*will* / *can* + simple form	If I *have* enough money, I *will buy* / *can buy* a ticket.
CONTRARY-TO-FACT IN THE PRESENT/FUTURE	simple past	*would* / *could* + simple form	If I *had* enough money, I *would buy* / *could buy* a ticket.
CONTRARY-TO-FACT IN THE PAST	past perfect	*would have* / *could have* + past participle	If I *had had* enough money, I *would have bought* / *could have bought* a ticket.

☐ **EXERCISE 18:** Complete the sentences with the words in parentheses.

1. I didn't feel good yesterday. If I (*feel*) _____ better, I (*come*) _____ to class yesterday.

2. I don't feel good today. If I (*feel*) _____ better, I (*take*) _____ a walk in the park today.

3. I have a cold today, but I will probably feel better tomorrow. If I (*feel*) _____ better tomorrow, I (*go*) _____ to class.

4. I'm sorry that you didn't come to the party. If you (*come*) _____ _____, you (*have*) _____ a good time.

5. I didn't know that Bob was sick. If I (*know*) _____ that he was sick, I (*take*) _____ him some chicken soup.

6. I'm tired. If I (*be, not*) _____ tired, I (*help*) _____ you.

7. Snow is predicted for tomorrow. If it (*snow*) _____ tomorrow, I (*stay*) _____ home.

8. I may have a dollar. Let me look in my wallet. If I (*have*) _____ a dollar, I (*lend*) _____ it to you.

9. I don't have any money. If I (*have*) _____ a dollar, I (*lend*) _____ it to you.

10. I didn't have a dollar yesterday. If I (*have*) _____ a dollar yesterday, I (*lend*) _____ it to you.

11. I didn't know it was your birthday yesterday. I wish you (*tell*) _____ me. I (*get*) _____ you a present if I (*know*) _____ it was your birthday yesterday.

12. Why didn't you tell me when your plane was supposed to arrive? If you (*tell*) _____ me, I (*pick*) _____ you up at the airport.

☐ **EXERCISE 19—ORAL:** Make sentences with *wish* and *if*. Follow the patterns in the examples.

> *Example:* I don't have enough time.
> *Response:* I wish I had enough time. If I had enough time, I (would/could go shopping this afternoon, etc.).

> *Example:* I didn't have enough time.
> *Response:* I wish I had had enough time. If I'd had enough time, I (would have/could have gone shopping yesterday afternoon, etc.).

1. I don't have enough money.
2. I didn't have enough money.
3. I don't have enough time.
4. I didn't have enough time.
5. The weather isn't nice.
6. The weather wasn't nice.
7. I'm in class right now.
8. I came to class yesterday.
9. My friend isn't at home.
10. My friend wasn't at home.
11. I don't know how to play the guitar.
12. I didn't know that my uncle was in the hospital.

☐ **EXERCISE 20—ORAL:** Make sentences with *if*. Follow the patterns in the examples.

> *Example:* If I have enough money, ...
> STUDENT A: If I have enough money, I'll buy (can buy) a car.
> STUDENT B: If I buy a car, I'll drive (can drive) to Florida.
> STUDENT C: If I drive to Florida, I'll go (can go) to Miami.
> STUDENT D: If I go to Miami, I . . . .

> *Example:* If I had enough money, ...
> STUDENT A: If I had enough money, I would buy (could buy) a car.
> STUDENT B: If I bought a car, I would drive (could drive) to Florida.
> STUDENT C: If I drove to Florida, I would go (could go) to Miami.
> STUDENT D: If I went to Miami, I . . . .

> *Example:* If I had had enough money, ...
> STUDENT A: If I had had enough money, I would have bought (could have bought) a car.
> STUDENT B: If I had bought a car, I would have driven (could have driven) to Florida.
> STUDENT C: If I had driven to Florida, I would have gone (could have gone) to Miami.
> STUDENT D: If I had gone to Miami, I . . . .

1. If I have enough money, ...
2. If I had enough money, ...
3. If I had had enough money, ...
4. If I have enough time, ...
5. If I had enough time, ...
6. If I had had enough time, ...
7. If the weather is hot/cold tomorrow, ...
8. If the weather were hot/cold, ...
9. If the weather had been hot/cold yesterday, ...
10. If I had a million dollars, ...

☐ **EXERCISE 21—ORAL (BOOKS CLOSED):** Answer the questions in complete sentences.

1. Where would you be right now if you weren't in class?
2. What would you have done yesterday if you hadn't come to class?
3. What would you do today if you had enough time?
4. What would you have done yesterday if you had had enough time?
5. What would you buy if you had enough money?
6. What would you have bought yesterday if you had had enough money?
7. What would you do if there were a fire in this building?
8. If you had your own private plane, where would you go for dinner tonight?
9. (. . .) is tired today. Give him/her some advice. What would you do if you were (. . .)?
10. (. . .) wants to learn English as quickly as possible. What would you do if you were (. . .)?
11. Could ships sail around the world if the earth were flat?
12. What would happen if there were a nuclear war?
13. What would you do if you were the teacher of this class?
14. Tell me one thing that you did yesterday. What would have happened if you had not (done that)?
15. What would you do tonight if you didn't have to study?
16. What do you wish were different about the world we live in?

☐ **EXERCISE 22—WRITTEN:** Write on the following topic.

In what ways do you wish the world were different? Why do you wish these things? What would be the results?

APPENDIX 1
Preposition Combinations

A *be* absent from
   be accustomed to
      add *(this)* to *(that)*
   be acquainted with
      admire *(someone)* for *(something)*
   be afraid of
      agree with *(someone)* about/on *(something)*
   be angry at/with
      apologize to *(someone)* for *(something)*
      apply to *(a place)* for *(something)*
      approve of
      argue with *(someone)* about *(something)*
      arrive at *(a building, a room)*
      arrive in *(a city, a country)*
      ask *(someone)* about *(something)*
      ask *(someone)* for *(something)*
   be aware of

B *be* bad for
      believe in
      belong to
   be bored with/by
      borrow *(something)* from *(someone)*

C *be* clear to
      compare *(this)* to/with *(that)*
      complain to *(someone)* about *(something)*
   be composed of
      concentrate on
      consist of
   be crazy about
   be crowded with

D depend on/upon *(someone)* for *(something)*
   be dependent on/upon *(someone)* for *(something)*
   be devoted to

be different from
    disagree with *(someone)* about *(something)*
be disappointed in
    discuss *(something)* with *(someone)*
    divide *(this)* into *(that)*
be divorced from
be done with
    dream about/of

E *be* engaged to
    be equal to
      escape from
    be excited about
      excuse *(someone)* for *(something)*
    be exhausted from

F *be* familiar with
      forgive *(someone)* for *(something)*
    be friendly to/with
    be frightened of/by
    be full of

G   get rid of
    be gone from
    be good for
      graduate from

H   happen to
    hear about/of
    hear from
    help *(someone)* with *(something)*
    hide *(something)* from *(someone)*
    hope for
  be hungry for

I   insist on
    be interested in
      introduce *(someone)* to *(someone)*
      invite *(someone)* to *(something)*
    be involved in

K *be* kind to
    know about

L   laugh at
    listen to
    look at
    look for
    look forward to

M *be* mad at
be made of
be married to
matter to
be the matter with
multiply *(this)* by *(that)*

N *be* nice to

O *be* opposed to

P pay for
be patient with
be pleased with
point at
be polite to
be prepared for
protect *(this)* from *(that)*
be proud of

Q *be* qualified for

R *be* ready for
be related to
rely on/upon
be responsible for

S *be* satisfied with
be scared of/by
search for
separate *(this)* from *(that)*
be similar to
be sorry about *(something)*
be sorry for *(someone)*
speak to/with *(someone)* about *(something)*
stare at
subtract *(this)* from *(that)*
be sure of

T take care of
talk to/with *(someone)* about *(something)*
tell *(someone)* about *(something)*
be terrified of/by
thank *(someone)* for *(something)*
be thirsty for
be tired from
be tired of
travel to

W wait for
wait on
be worried about

APPENDIX *2*
Phrasal Verbs

This list contains only those phrasal verbs used in the exercises in the text. The verbs with an asterisk (*) are nonseparable. The others are separable. See Charts 9-8 and 9-9 for a discussion of separable and nonseparable phrasal verbs.

A ask out . . . . *ask someone to go on a date*
C call back . . . . *return a telephone call*
　　 call off . . . . *cancel*
　　 *call on . . . . *ask to speak in class*
　　 call up . . . . *make a telephone call*
　　 cross out . . . . *draw a line through*
D do over . . . . *do again*
·　 *drop in (on) . . . . *visit without calling first or without an invitation*
　　 *drop out (of) . . . . *stop attending school*
F figure out . . . . *find the solution to a problem*
　　 fill in . . . . *complete a sentence by writing in a blank*
　　 fill out . . . . *write information in a form (e.g., an application form)*
　　 fill up . . . . *fill completely with gas, water, coffee, etc.*
　　 find out . . . . *discover information*
　　 *fool around (with) . . . . . *have fun while wasting time*
G *get along (with) . . . . *have a good relationship with*
　　 *get back (from) . . . . *return from a trip*
　　 *get in . . . . *enter a car, a taxi*
　　 *get off . . . . *leave a bus, an airplane, a train, a subway, a bicycle*
　　 *get on . . . . *enter a bus, an airplane, a train, a subway, a bicycle*
　　 *get out (of) . . . . *leave a car, a taxi*
　　 *get over . . . . *recover from an illness*
　　 *get through (with) . . . . . *finish*
　　 give back . . . . *return something to someone*
　　 give up . . . . *quit doing something or quit trying*
　　 *grow up (in) . . . . *become an adult*

H   hand in . . . . *give homework, test papers, etc., to a teacher*

      hand out . . . . *give something to this person, then that person, then another person, etc.*

      hang up . . . . *(1) hang on a hanger or a hook; (2) end a telephone call*

K *keep on . . . . *continue*

L   leave out . . . . *omit*

    *look out (for) . . . . *be careful*

      look up. . . . . *look for information in a reference book*

M make up . . . . *invent*

P   pay back . . . . *return money to someone*

      pick up . . . . *lift*

      put away . . . . *put something in its usual or proper place*

      put back . . . . *return something to its original place*

      put down. . . . . *stop holding or carrying*

      put off . . . . *postpone*

R *run into . . . . *meet by chance*

    *run out (of) . . . . *finish the supply of something*

S   shut off . . . . *stop a machine or light, turn off*

      start over. . . . . *start again*

T   take off . . . . *remove clothes from one's body*

      tear down . . . . *destroy a building*

      tear off. . . . . *detach, tear along a dotted or perforated line*

      tear out (of) . . . . *remove a piece of paper from a book or notebook*

      tear up . . . . *tear into small pieces*

      throw away/out. . . . . *put in the trash, discard*

      try on . . . . *put on clothing to see if it fits*

      turn down. . . . . *decrease the volume*

      turn off . . . . *stop a machine or a light, shut off*

      turn on. . . . . *start a machine or a light*

      turn up. . . . . *increase the volume*

W wake up. . . . . *stop sleeping*

    *watch out (for) . . . . *be careful*

      write down . . . . *write a note on a piece of paper*

APPENDIX **3**

Guide for Correcting Writing Errors

To the student: Each number represents an area of usage. Your teacher will use these numbers when marking your writing to indicate that you have made an error. Refer to this list to find out what kind of error you have made and then make the necessary correction.

①	SINGULAR-PLURAL	① ① He have been here for six month. *He has been here for six months.*
②	WORD FORM	② I saw a beauty picture. *I saw a beautiful picture.*
③	WORD CHOICE	③ She got on the taxi. *She got into the taxi.*
④	VERB TENSE	④ He is here since June. *He has been here since June.*
⑤+	ADD A WORD	⑤+ I want ∧ go to the zoo. *I want to go to the zoo.*
⑤–	OMIT A WORD	⑤– She entered to the university. *She entered the university.*
⑥	WORD ORDER	⑥ I saw five times that movie. *I saw that movie five times.*

A6 □

⑦   INCOMPLETE SENTENCE

⑦
I went to bed. Because I was tired.
I went to bed because I was tired.

⑧   SPELLING

⑧
An accident occured.
An accident occurred.

⑨   PUNCTUATION

⑨
What did he say.
What did he say?

⑩   CAPITALIZATION

⑩
I am studying english.
I am studying English.

⑪   ARTICLE

⑪
I had a accident.
I had an accident.

⑫?   MEANING NOT CLEAR

⑫?
He borrowed some smoke.
(? ? ?)

⑬   RUN-ON SENTENCE★

⑬
My roommate was sleeping, we didn't
   want to wake her up.
My roommate was sleeping. We didn't
   want to wake her up.

★A run-on sentence occurs when two sentences are incorrectly connected: the end of one sentence and the beginning of the next sentence are not properly marked by a period and a capital letter. (See Chart 9-1.)

APPENDIX *4*

Basic Vocabulary List

The following list contains approximately 750 of the most commonly used words in English. *Fundamentals of English Grammar* assumes that students using this book are familiar with most of the words on the list.

The text uses many other words that are not on the list. Students may wish to add new vocabulary to this list.

The list is divided into two groups. Group One contains the most frequently used words. Group Two has other common words that the students will encounter in the text.

The words are listed according to their usual usage: NOUN, VERB, ADJECTIVE, or ADVERB.

BASIC VOCABULARY LIST: GROUP ONE

NOUNS (Group One)

accident	body	country
address	book	cup
afternoon	box	date
age	boy	daughter
air	bread	day
airplane	breakfast	desk
animal	brother	dictionary
apartment	building	dinner
arm	bus	direction
aunt	car	doctor
baby	chair	door
back	child	ear
bank	circle	earth
bed	city	end
beginning	class	evening
bicycle	clothes	eye
bird	coat	face
birthday	color*	family
boat	corner	father

_____

*British English = colour

finger
fire
fish
floor
food
foot
friend
front
fruit
future
garden
glass
girl
hair
half
hand
hat
head
holiday
home
homework
hospital
hotel
hour
house
human being
husband
idea
information
insect
job
juice
land
language
leg
letter
library
life
light
line
lunch
man
meat
mile
minute
mistake
money
month
moon
morning
mother

movie
music
name
night
noon
nose
notebook
number
office
page
parents
park
part
party
past
pen
pencil
people
pepper
person
picture
place
plant
present
price
problem
question
reason
restaurant
rice
river
room
roommate
school
shoe
side
sister
sky
smile
son
sound
street
student
sun
table
teacher
test
thing
time
town
tree

trouble
uncle
university
vacation
vegetable
vocabulary
voice
wall
water
way
weather
week
wife
window
woman
word
work
world
year
zoo

VERBS (Group One)

answer
arrive
ask
be
become
begin
believe
break
bring
build
buy
call
carry
catch
change
close
come
continue
cost
cry
cut
die
do
drink
eat
end
enter
explain

		ADJECTIVES (Group One): Opposites

fall	start	bad	good
feel	stay	beautiful	ugly
fight	stop	big	little
find	study	big	small
finish	take	cheap	expensive
fix	talk	clean	dirty
get	teach	cold	hot
give	tell	cool	warm
go	think	dangerous	safe
grow	touch	dark	light
happen	try	deep	shallow
have	turn	different	same
hear	use	difficult	simple
help	wait	dry	wet
hold	walk	early	late
hope	want	east	west
hurt	wash	empty	full
interest	watch	fast	slow
keep	work	fat	thin
know	write	first	last
laugh	understand	happy	sad
learn	visit	hard	easy
leave		hard	soft
let		healthy	ill
like		healthy	sick
listen		heavy	light
live		high	low
look		intelligent	stupid
lose		large	little
love		large	small
make		long	short
mean		messy	neat
meet		modern	old-fashioned
move		narrow	wide
need		noisy	quiet
open		north	south
pay		old	new
plan		old	young
put		poor	rich
rain		private	public
read		right	left
ride		right	wrong
run		rough	smooth
say		short	tall
see		sour	sweet
sell		strong	weak
send			
sit			
sleep			
speak			
stand			

ADVERBS (Group One)

again
ago
also
always
early
ever
fast
finally
generally
hard
here
immediately
late
maybe
never
now
occasionally
often
once

BASIC VOCABULARY LIST: GROUP TWO

NOUNS (Group Two)

amount	game
army	gas(oline)**
art	gold
bag	government
ball	grass
beach	group
bill	hall
blood	health
bottom	heart
bridge	heat
business	hill
cat	history
ceiling	hole
center*	horse
century	hundred
chance	ice
clock	individual
cloud	industry
coffee	island
college	key
computer	kitchen
concert	knife
condition	lake
conversation	law
course	list
crowd	luck
definition	magazine
difference	mail
distance	market
dog	math(ematics)
dress	meaning
earthquake	member
egg	middle
enemy	midnight
example	milk
experience	million
fact	mind
fall/autumn	mountain
fear	mouth
field	nation
flower	nature
forest	neck
form	neighbor
furniture	newspaper

---

*British English = centre
**British English = petrol

noise
object
ocean
office
opinion
pain
paint
pair
pants
peace
period
picnic
pleasure
pocket
position
power
pronunciation
purpose
radio
result
ring
rule
salt
sandwich
science
sea
season
seat
shape
shirt
shoulder
situation
size
skin
snow
song
space
spelling
spring
stamp
star
store
subject
success
sugar
storm
suit
summer

tape recorder
tea
telephone
television
theater*
thousand
top
toy
train
trip
trouble
umbrella
universe
valley
value
war
wind
wing
winter
wood

VERBS (Group Two)

accept
act
add
agree
allow
appear
attempt
attend
beat
blow
borrow
burn
cause
choose
collect
complete
consider
contain
control
cook
cross
count
cover
dance
decide

disappear
discover
divide
doubt
draw
dream
dress
drive
drop
enjoy
exist
expect
fail
fill
fit
flow
fly
forget
guess
hang
hate
hit
hurry
improve
include
introduce
invite
join
kill
kiss
lead
lend
lift
marry
notice
obtain
offer
order
own
pass
permit
pick
point
pour
practice
prepare
promise
prove

*British English = theatre (This spelling is also frequently used in American English.)

provide
pull
push
reach
realize
receive
recognize
refuse
remember
repeat
reply
report
require
return
rise
save
search
seem
separate
serve
share
shout
show
sign
sing
smell
spell
spend
spread
succeed
suggest
supply
surprise
surround
taste
tear
thank
tie
travel
wave
wear
win
wish
wonder
worry

ADJECTIVES (Group Two)

absent
angry
bald
bright
busy
calm
dead
delicious
delightful
dizzy
essential
famous
flat
foolish
foreign
free
fresh
funny
glad
great
handsome
humid
hungry
lazy
mad
native
nervous
nice
pretty
proud
rapid
ripe
round
serious
sharp
sorry
special
strange
terrific
tough
unique
various
whole
wild
wise
wonderful

ADJECTIVE OPPOSITES

accurate	inaccurate
certain	uncertain
clear	unclear
comfortable	uncomfortable
common	uncommon
complete	incomplete
convenient	inconvenient
dependent	independent
direct	indirect
fair	unfair
familiar	unfamiliar
happy	unhappy
healthy	unhealthy
important	unimportant
interesting	uninteresting
kind	unkind
lawful	unlawful
legal	illegal
logical	illogical
necessary	unnecessary
normal	abnormal
pleasant	unpleasant
polite	impolite
possible	impossible
proper	improper
rational	irrational
real	unreal
regular	irregular
responsible	irresponsible
sure	unsure
true	untrue
usual	unusual
visible	invisible

ADVERBS (Group Two)

actually
afterward(s)
almost
already
anymore
anywhere
apparently
carefully
certainly
completely
constantly
downtown
easily
enough
entirely
especially
everywhere
extremely
fortunately
just
later
next
obviously
perhaps
quietly
rarely
regularly
seldom
seriously
somewhere
still
surely
together
too
well
yet

APPENDIX 5

Differences between American English and British English

DIFFERENCES IN VOCABULARY

Speakers of American English and speakers of British English have no trouble understanding each other. The differences are small and do not interfere with communication. Some differences in the usage of common vocabulary are listed below.

American English	British English
attorney, lawyer	barrister, solicitor
bathrobe	dressing gown
can (of beans)	tin (of beans)
cookie	biscuit
corn	maize
diaper	nappy
driver's license	driving license
drug store	chemist's
elevator	lift
eraser	rubber
flashlight	torch
gas, gasoline	petrol
hood of a car	bonnet of a car
living room	sitting room, drawing room
raise in salary	rise in salary
rest room	public toilet, WC (water closet)
schedule	timetable
sidewalk	pavement, footpath
sink	basin
soccer	football
stove	cooker
truck	lorry, van
trunk of a car	boot of a car
be on vacation	be on holiday

DIFFERENCES IN SPELLING

American English and British English have a few differences in spelling. The list below shows the spelling differences in some common words.

American English spelling	British English spelling
theater, center, liter	theatre, centre, litre
color, honor, labor, odor	colour, honour, labour, odour
jewelry, traveler, woolen	jewellry, traveller, woollen
skillful, fulfill	skilful, fulfil
check	cheque (bank note)
curb	kerb
forever	for ever/forever
jail	gaol
program	programme
specialty	speciality
story	storey (of a building)
tire	tyre (of a car)
realize, analyze, apologize	realise, analyse, apologise
defense, offense, license	defence, offence, licence (n.)
burned	burnt (*or* burned)
dreamed	dreamt (*or* dreamed)
smelled	smelt (*or* smelled)
spelled	spelt (*or* spelled)
spoiled	spoilt (*or* spoiled)

Index

A/an, 193, 206–207 *(Look on pages 193 and* *pages 206 through 207.)*	The numbers following the words listed in the index refer to page numbers in the main text.
Adjectives: vocabulary list, A10 *(Look in the back part of this* *book on the tenth page of* *the Appendixes.)*	Numbers in the index that are preceded by the letter ''A'' (e.g., A10) refer to pages in the Appendixes, which are found in the last part of the text. The main text ends on page 398, and the Appendixes immediately follow. Page 398 is followed by page A1.
Consonants, 8*fn.* *(Look at the footnote on* *page 8.)*	The letters ''*fn.*'' mean ''footnote.'' Footnotes are at the bottom of a page or the bottom of a chart.

A

A/an, 193, 206–207
A vs. **an**, 210*fn.*
Accustomed to, 305
Active verbs, 276
Adjective clauses, 309–323
Adjectives, defined, 72, 309
    following *be*, 72, 294
    comparative and superlative, 331–332
    following *get*, 301
    nouns used as, 73
    participial (*-ing/-ed*), 298
    possessive (*my, our*), 79
    vocabulary list, A10, A13
Adverb clauses, 234
    with *because*, 234
    with *even though/although*, 237

    if-clauses, 53, 389–395
    time clauses, 37, 53, 171
Adverbs:
    comparative and superlative, 332
    frequency, 6, 181
    midsentence, 181
    vocabulary list, A11, A14
Advise, **suggest**, **recommend**, 378
A few/a little, 193
After, 37, 53, 71
Alike, 342
Already, 181, 184
Although, 237
Always, etc. (midsentence adverbs), 181
And, 58, 222, 228
    with *so, too, neither, either*, 230
Another, 84, 88

Any, 217
Anymore, 184
Apostrophe, 77
Articles, 206–207
As . . . as comparisons, 328
   not as . . . as vs. *less*, 334
Ask if, 369
As soon as, 53
At as time preposition, 45
Auxiliary verbs:
   after *and* and *but*, 228, 230
   modal, 94
   in questions, 128
   in short responses to yes/no questions, 124
   in tag questions, 156
   after *wish*, 383–384

B

Be, 3
Be about to, 65
Be afraid, 362*fn.*
Be + adjective, 72, 294
   followed by *that*-clause, 361
Because, 234
Before, 37, 53, 71
Be going to, 47
   vs. *will*, 51
Be + past participle (*be interested in*), 294
   (SEE ALSO Passive)
   followed by noun clause, 361
Be supposed to, 307
Better:
   and *best*, 332
   had better, 94
   like better, 119
Be used to/accustomed to, 305
British English, 45*fn.*, 170*fn.*, 173*fn.*
   spelling vs. American English, A16
   vocabulary vs. American English, A15
But, 224, 228
By:
   followed by –*ing* (*by doing*), 262
   with passive (*by*-phrase), 276, 283
   with reflexive pronoun (*by myself*), 81
   vs. *with*, 262

C

Can, 94
   ability, 95
   permission, 98
   polite question, 100
Capitalization, 91, 222*fn.*
Clauses, defined, 37, 309*fn.* (SEE ALSO
     Adjective clauses, Adverb clauses,
     If-clauses, Noun clauses, Time clauses)
Commas:
   with adverb clauses, 37, 55*fn.*, 234
   in connecting ideas with *and*, 222
   vs. period, 222
   in quoted speech, 364
Comparatives, 331–338
   with adjectives and adverbs, 332
   double (*the more . . . , the more*), 338
   with nouns, 336
   repeated (*more and more*), 337
Comparisons, 327–345
   as . . . as, 328
   comparatives, 331–338
   same, similar, different, like, alike, 342
   superlatives, 331–332, 339
Conditional sentences, 389–395
   contrary-to-fact, past, 394
   contrary-to-fact, present/future, 389
   true, present/future, 53
   verb form summary, 395
Conjunctions (*and, but, or, so*), 222–228
Consonants, 8*fn.*
Continuous verbs (SEE Progressive verbs)
Contractions of verbs:
   be, 3*fn.*
   had, 105
   have, 161
   with *not*, 3*fn.*, 19, 32, 49, 161
   with nouns, 49
   with question words, 134
   will, 49
   would, 119
Could, 94
   in conditional sentences, 389–393
   past ability, 95
   in polite questions, 100
   possibility, present/future, 100

Count/noncount nouns, 193–207
  noncount nouns, 193–195, 198, 202

D

Dependent clause, defined, 309*fn.* (SEE ALSO
  Adjective clauses, Adverb clauses, Noun
  clauses)
Different from, 342
Direct speech (SEE Quoted Speech)
Does, *do*, *did*:
  in negative, 3, 19
  in questions, 3, 19, 128
  in short answers, 12, 19
Do, as main verb in *what*-questions, 135

E

–Ed, 18, 21
  past participle, 21
    as adjective, 294, 298
  spelling, 29
Either, 230
Enough, 270
-Er/more and *-est/most*, 331
Etc., 240*fn.*
Even though, 237
Expressions of quantity, 193, 216

F

Farther/further, 332*fn.*
A few, 193
For (purpose), 267
For and *since* (time), 171, 176
For (*someone*) to do (*something*), with *it*, 266
Frequency adverbs, 6, 181
A friend of + possessive, 80
Future time, 47–65
  be going to and *will*, 47, 49, 51
  in *if*-clauses, 53
  immediate (*be about to*), 65
  using present tenses to express, 61–63
  in time clauses, 53

G

Gerunds, 246
  following prepositions, 260
  as subjects, 264
  verbs followed by, 247, 253

Get + adjective/past participle, 301
Get used to/accustomed to, 305
Go + *ing* (*go shopping*), 250

H

Habitual past, 42
Had:
  contracted with pronouns, 105
  in past perfect, 189
Had better, 94, 105
Hanged vs. *hung*, 169*fn.*
Have, auxiliary in present perfect, 161
  progressive vs. nonprogressive, 9*fn.*
  in questions, main verb, 126*fn.*
Have got to, 94, 108
Have to, 94, 108
  do not have to, 109
  form in questions, 129*fn.*
Helping verbs (SEE Auxiliary verbs,
  Negatives, Questions, and individual
  items)
How, 144, 152
  how about, 154
  how far, 146
  how long, 148
  how many/much, 199
  how often, 145

I

If-clauses, 53
  contrary-to-fact, 389–395
  expressing future time in, 53, 389, 392
  punctuation of, 55*fn.*
If/whether in noun clauses, 352, 369
Immediate future (*be about to*), 65
Imperative sentences, 114
In as time preposition, 45
Independent clause, defined, 309*fn.*
Indirect speech (SEE Reported speech)
Infinitives, 246, 251
  with *it*, 147, 264–266
  with modals, 94
  purpose (*in order to*), 267
  to report speech, 375
  with *too* and *enough*, 270
  uncompleted, 259
  verbs followed by, 251–252

Information questions, 128
-Ing:
  gerund, 246
  present participle, 21
    as adjective, 298
    in tenses, 3, 32, 176–177
  spelling, 29
In order to, 267
Intend, *plan*, *hope*, 64
Interested vs. *interesting*, 298
Irregular noun plurals, 68–69, 77
Irregular verbs, list, 22
It + infinitive, 264–266
Its vs. *it's*, 79*fn.*
It takes (length of time), 147

L

Less . . . than, 334
Let's, 116
Lied vs. *lay*, *lain*, 31*fn.*
Like, *alike*, 342
Like . . . better, 119
A little, 193

M

Main clause, 37, 234
Many/much, 193
Mass noun, 194*fn.*
May, 94, 98
  permission, 98
  polite question, 100
  possibility, 98
Maybe vs. *may be*, 98
Measure, units of (*a cup of*, *a piece of*), 204
Midsentence adverbs, 181
Might, 94, 98
Modal auxiliaries, 94–113 (SEE ALSO
    individual items)
  in passive, 289
More/-er . . . than, 331–334
The most/-est, 331–332, 339
Must, 94
  logical conclusion, 112
  necessity, 108
Must not, 109, 112

N

Negatives, with helping verbs:
  past progressive (*was/were not*), 32
  present perfect (*has/have not*), 161
  present progressive (*am/is/are not*), 3
  simple past (*did not*), 19
  simple present (*does/do not*), 3
  will + *not* (*won't*), 49
Neither, 230
Noncount nouns, 193–195, 198, 202
  units of measure with, 204
Nonprogressive verbs, 9
Not (SEE Negatives)
Noun clauses, 346–369
  with *if/whether*, 352, 369
  with question words, 347
  reported speech, sequence of tenses, 367
  with *that*, 357, 361
  after *wish*, 381, 384
Nouns:
  used as adjectives, 73
  count/noncount, 193–207
  plural forms, 68–69
  possessive, 77
  as subjects and objects, 70
  vocabulary list, A8–A9, A11–A12

O

Object pronouns, personal, 46
  in adjective clauses, 310–313
  nonspecific (*some*, *any*, *one*), 217
Objects:
  of a preposition, 71
  of a verb, 70
On as time preposition, 45
One, as nonspecific object pronoun, 217
One of + plural noun, 322*fn.*
Or, 224
Other, 84–88
Ought to, 94, 105

P

Parallel structure with *and*, *but*, *or*, 222–224
  with verbs, 58
Participial adjectives (*interested* vs.
    interesting), 298
Particles, in phrasal verbs, 241

Partitives (SEE Units of measure)
Passive, 276–308
  use of *by*-phrase, 276, 283
  with *get*, 301
  modal auxiliaries, 289
  stative, 294
  summary of forms, 290
Past habit, 42
Past participles, 18, 21, 22, 160, 276–277, 294, 298, 301
Past perfect, 189, 384, 394–395
Past progressive, 32
Past time, 18–44, 160–189 (SEE ALSO Tenses)
Period, 222
Personal pronouns, 46
Phrasal verbs, list, A4–A5
  nonseparable, 244, 325
  separable, 241, 273, 323
Phrase, defined, 346*fn.*
Plural nouns, 68–69 (SEE ALSO Singular and plural)
Polite questions, using modals, 100–102, 119
Possessive
  in adjective clauses (*whose*), 318
  nouns, 77
  pronouns and adjectives (*mine* and *my*), 79
Prefer, 119
Prepositional phrases, 71
Prepositions, list, 71
  combinations with verbs and adjectives, A1–A3
  followed by gerunds, 260
  objects of, 71
  use as particle in phrasal verbs (*put off, put on*) 241
  of place, 16, 72
  placement in adjective clauses, 316
  placement in information questions, 133*fn.*
  in stative passive (*be married to*), 294
  of time (*in, on, at*), 45
Present participles, 21
  as adjective (*interesting*), 298
  vs. gerund, 246*fn.*
Present perfect, 160–189
Present time, 3–16 (SEE ALSO Tenses)
Principal parts of a verb, 21
Probably, 50, 181

Progressive verbs, 21
  vs. nonprogressive (*I am thinking* vs. *I think*), 9
  in passive (*is being done*), 288
  past (*was doing*), 32
  present (*is doing*), 3, 61
  present perfect (*has been doing*), 176–177
Pronouns
  in adjective clauses (*who, which*), 310–318
  contractions with, 3*fn.*, 49
  expressions of quantity (*many, some*) used as, 216
  nonspecific objects (*some, any, one*), 217
  personal (*I, them*), 46
  possessive (*mine, theirs*), 79
  reflexive (*myself, themselves*), 81
Punctuation:
  apostrophe, 77 (SEE ALSO Contractions)
  comma:
    in adverb clauses, 37, 55*fn.*, 234
    vs. a period, 222
    in quoted speech, 364
    in a series with *and*, 222
  period, 222
  quotation marks, 364
Purpose (*in order to, for*), 267

Q

Quantity, expressions of, 216
Question forms:
  past progressive (*were you doing?*), 32
  present perfect (*have you done?*), 161
  present progressive (*are you doing?*), 3
  simple past (*did you do?*), 19
  simple present (*do you do?*), 3
  with *will* (*will you do?*), 49
Questions:
  information, 128, 347
  polite, 100–102, 119
  tag, 156
  yes/no, 124, 128, 352
Question words, 128, 347 (SEE ALSO Noun clauses and individual items)
Quotation marks, 364
Quoted speech, 364–366

R

Recommend/suggest, 378
Reflexive pronouns, 81
Relative clauses (SEE Adjective clauses)
Reported speech, 366–375
Run-on sentences, A7*fn.*

S

-S/-es:
   with plural nouns, 68, 193
   with simple present verbs, 3
   spelling, 8
Same, similar, different, like, alike, 342
Say vs. *tell*, 368
Sequence of tenses, noun clauses, 367
Shall, 47
Short answers to questions, 124
Should, 94, 105, 378
Simple form of a verb, 21, 94, 246
Simple past, 18–19, 21, 32, 164
Simple present, 3, 12, 53, 63
Since and *for*, 162, 171, 176
Singular and plural:
   nouns, 70, 193
   nouns used as adjectives, 73
   personal pronouns, 76
   possessive nouns, 77
   present tense verbs, 8
   verbs in adjective clauses, 315
So, conjunction, 266
So, substitute for *that*-clause (*I think so*), 359
So/too/neither/either, 230
Some, 193, 206–207, 217
Spelling:
   American vs. British, A16
   -ed, 29
   -er/-est, 333*fn.*
   -ing, 29
   -s/-es, 8, 68
Stative passive, 294
Stative verbs (nonprogressive verbs), 9
Still, 184
Stop (*stop doing it* vs. *stop to do it*), 247*fn.*
Subject pronouns, personal, 76
   in adjective clauses, 310
Subjects, verbs, objects, 70, 282
Suggest, 378

Superlatives, 331–332, 339
Supposed to, 307

T

Tag questions, 156
Take, with *it* to express length of time, 147
Tell vs. *say, ask*, 368
Tenses:
   past perfect, 189, 384, 394–395
   past progressive, 32
   present perfect, 161–164, 171
   present perfect progressive, 176–177
   present progressive, 3
      future meaning, 61
   simple future, 47
   simple past, 18–19, 21, 32, 164
   simple present, 3, 12
      future meaning, 53, 63
Than, 119
   in comparatives, 331, 334
That:
   in adjective clauses, 312–316
   in noun clauses, 357
The, 206–207
Their, they're, there, 80*fn.*
Think, progressive vs. nonprogressive, 9*fn.*
Time clauses, form, 37
   future, 53
   past, 37
   with *since*, 171
To + simple form (infinitive), 246, 251, 259
   (*in order*) *to*, 267
Too, 270
   and . . . too, 230
Transitive/intransitive verbs, 282
Two-word verbs, 241*fn.* (SEE Phrasal verbs)

U

Uncompleted infinitives, 259
Units of measure (*a cup of, a piece of*), 204
Used to (past habit), 42
(*Be*) *used to*, 305

V

Verbs, vs. subjects and objects, 70, 282
   vocabulary list, A9–A10, A12–A13

(SEE ALSO Auxiliaries, Modal auxiliaries, Passive, Phrasal verbs, Tenses, and individual items)

Vowels, 8*fn.*

W

Was, *were*, 19*fn.*, 32
What, 132
  what about, 154
  what + a form of *do*, 135
  what kind of, 137
  what time vs. *when*, 129*fn.*
  in noun clauses, 347–348
When:
  in questions, 128, 129*fn.*
  in time clauses, 32, 37, 53
Where, 128, 347
Whether, 352, 369
Which:
  in adjective clauses, 313–316
  in noun clauses, 347–348
  in questions, 139
While, 32, 37
Who/who(m):
  in adjective clauses, 310–312
  in noun clauses, 348
  in questions, 128, 132
  who's vs. *whose*, 141, 318*fn.*
Whose:
  in adjective clauses, 318
  in noun clauses, 348
  in questions, 141
Why, 128, 347
Why don't, 116
Will, 94
  vs. *be going to*, 51
  forms, 49
  future, 47
  in polite questions, 102
  with *probably*, 50
Wish, 381–388
With vs. *by*, 262
Would, 94
  in conditional sentences, 389–393
  contractions and pronouns, 119
  in polite questions, 102
  in reported speech, 367

Would rather, 119

Y

Yes/no questions, 124, 128, 352
Yet, 184